The CERI Series in Comparative Politics and International Studies

Series editors: CHRISTOPHE JAFFRELOT AND CHRISTIAN LEQUESNE

This series consists of translations of noteworthy publications in the social sciences emanating from the foremost French research centre in international studies, the Paris-based Centre d'Etudes et de Recherches Internationales (CERI), part of Sciences Po and associated with the CNRS (Centre National de la Recherche Scientifique)

The focus of the series is the transformation of politics and society by transnational and domestic factors – globalisation, migration, and the post-bipolar balance of power on the one hand, and ethnicity and religion on the other. States are more permeable to external influence than ever before and this phenomenon is accelerating processes of social and political change the world over. In seeking to understand and interpret these transformations, this series gives priority to social trends from below as much as the interventions of state and non-state actors.

Founded in 1952, CERI has forty full-time fellows drawn from different disciplines conducting research on comparative political analysis, international relations, regionalism, transnational flows, political sociology, political economy and on individual states.

JAPAN: THE BURDEN OF SUCCESS

JEAN-MARIE BOUISSOU

Japan

The Burden of Success

LYNNE
RIENNER
PUBLISHERS

BOULDER

in association with the
Centre d'Etudes et de Recherches Internationales, Paris

Published in the United States of America in 2002 by
Lynne Rienner Publishers, Inc.
1800 30th Street, Boulder, Colorado 80301
www.rienner.com

Library of Congress Cataloging-in-Publication Data

Bouissou, Jean-Marie.
    [Japon depuis 1945. English]
    Japan, the burden of success / Jean-Marie Bouissou.
        p. cm.
    Includes bibliographical references and index.
    ISBN 1-58826-041-0 (alk. paper) --ISBN 1-58826-017-8 (pbk. : alk. paper)
    1. Japan--History--1945- I. Title.

DS889 .B6613 2002
952.04--dc21

                                                                2002017818

Printed in India

The paper used in this publication meets the requirements
of the American National Standard for Permanence of
Paper for Printed Library Materials Z39.48-1984.

ACKNOWLEDGEMENTS

During my fifteen-year stay in Japan, from 1975 to 1990, so many people helped me first to survive, then to enjoy, then to understand that country that I am bound to be unjust to many. I would like to mention first the late Hajime Ogawa, who used to be my student and my friend, and was immensely useful to my studies since he worked at the National Diet Library and turned it into a treasure chest of documents for me. His premature death means that I can never repay the *giri*[1] I owe him. My utmost gratitude also goes to Jean-Luc Domenach, an eminent sinologist but also a good connoisseur of Japan, who airlifted me back to Paris in 1990, arranged my *amakudari*[2] at the Fondation Nationale des Sciences Politiques, and provided both relentless stimulus and far-sighted guidance for my work.

The Japan Foundation's continuous support has proved to be an invaluable asset for me, as for so many researchers and academics all around the world. And the institutional support of the Centre d'Etudes et de Recherches Internationales, to which I belong, was rock-solid.

Among the many Japanese academics I came to know, I thank especially Professor Yoshiharu Tsuboi (now of Waseda University), for his sometimes critical but always friendly advice and logistical support for every of my field-studies. Professor Eiko Nakamura, from Fukuoka Seinan University, treated me like a spoiled child to be disciplined – which I was – but tirelessly introduced me to everybody I begged her to. I am also heavily indebted to Professor Hideo Otake of Kyoto National University, Muneyuki Shindo of Rikkyo University, Masaharu Nakamura of Sophia University, Hirotaka Watanabe from Tokyo University of Foreign Studies, the late Sakio Takayanagi from Chûô, and Susumu Takahashi, Ikuo Kabashima and Junko Katô – the three of them from Tôdai.

---

[1] *Giri*: the moral debt owed to one's parents, teachers, employer and benefactors.
[2] *Amakudari*: 'the descent from Heaven' (the profitable retirement of Japanese civil servants in private sector jobs).

v

On the French side, Loïc Hennekine and André Ross, both former ambassadors to Japan, know how grateful I am to them and why. Gérard Coste, former French Cultural Counsellor in Tokyo, who later helped to engineer the birth of the ASEM as Ambassador to Singapore, made my stay in Japan possible from 1984 to 1990.

From the British side, Professor Richard Higgott and Glenn Hook made me discover something that I never suspected before enjoying both intellectual interaction and the life with them – that *l'honnête homme* can also be an Englishman. This discovery was decisive for convincing me that my work might eventually be suitable for use abroad. In this connection I am also very grateful to my translator, Jonathan Derrick, who had to grapple with my rather too literary style.

Last but not least, I am immensely grateful to Elisabeth for her love and forbearance during the tense period of writing the first edition of this book, and to Masami for the second one.

Paris, January 2002   J.-M. B.

CONTENTS

FIGURES

xiv

PREFACE

'Japanology' is alive and well in France, though many know nothing of it, and has been so especially since the founding of the Ecole Française d'Extrême-Orient and the Institut National des Langues et Civilisations Orientales in the 19th century. Academics such as Vladimir Elisseief and Bernard Frank – to mention only the founding fathers – have been recognised as among the best in the world in their respective fields. Their heirs have since maintained a very high standard of academic research in Japanese history, civilisation, literature, language, philosophy, the history of ideas and science, and religion. Unfortunately, owing to the lack of sustained and meaningful relationships between France and Japan since the Second World War in the economic, political and even cultural fields, only a handful of researchers have turned to contemporary Japan. It was left to journalists – among them Robert Guillain and Philippe Pons of *Le Monde*, who did better than the others through their mastery of language, their academic background and their thirty-plus years' assignments in Japan, and parts of whose works have been translated into English. Economists also ventured into the Japanese field, most noticeably the former Socialist Minister of Finance Christian Sautter. But as a rule, French academics cherished the comfort of their own parochial tribe and rarely ventured into the global world of Japanology, which they resented as ruled exclusively by the Americans and British, whose methods and topics many of them did not share. Only recently have works about Japan by French researchers been translated into English – most noticeably books by the sociologist Muriel Jolivet. This one is a modest addition, which comes after several of my papers appeared in English.

Like every Japanologist, I have been regularly engaged in field studies, whose findings have been published in French, but also in *The Pacific Review* (autumn 2000) and in a chapter of B. Grafman and B. Woodall, eds, *Elections and Campaigning in Japan, Korea and Taiwan*, University of Michigan Press, 1999. I also dutifully did my theoretical homework in political science applied to the

Japanese case. Most of this work has been for a French audience only – among others a collective book about conflict management in Japan as a modest attempt to build upon the path-breaking works of Ellis and Krauss; an analysis of the LDP's fall from power, centred on the dysfunction of intra-party mechanisms for conflict management; research into the patterns of voter choice during the transitional period 1990–96; and a collective comparative study about political change after the end of the Cold War in two so-called *Uncommon Democracies*, bringing together researchers from Italy, France and Japan. One piece of work from this theoretical vein – replete, if not complete, with calculations, statistics, graphs and conceptual apparatus – appeared in *Electoral Studies* (December 2001), owing to the help of Prof. Michael Laver of Dublin, the most convivial political theoretician I ever met.

I must confess being a pure product of the peculiar French system of the *grandes écoles*, since in 1969 I entered a prestigious one – if one call 'prestigious' an institution unknown to 99 per cent of the intelligentsia outside France. As a product of this very peculiar intellectual breeding ground, at the age of 18 I was able to read ancient Greek and Latin and I had more than rudiments in philosophy, history, geography, literature and social sciences. The passing of time progressively erased or rendered obsolete these sparse pieces of knowledge, until I was no more able to read Greek nor explain any Hegelian concept. But I remained stubbornly imbued with the old-fashioned French ideal of *'l'honnête homme'*: the intellectual who hates prejudice, who tries to combine facts and ideas from many fields, who is deeply suspicious about any narrowly focused approach and convinced that no unequivocal and definite explanation can be given for anything involving human beings, since human actions cannot be reduced to statistics and graphs.

To give only one example, the policy of bursting the Japanese speculative land price bubble in 1990 may be convincingly linked to the grandiose restructuring of the world order after the end of the Cold War (which permitted the USA to apply unbridled pressure upon Japan for the removal of the so-called 'structural impediments' to imports, among which land prices figured prominently), but also to the down-to-earth worries of petty but very powerful Japanese Ministry of Finance bureaucrats who feared that they would not be able to buy comfortable lodgings for themselves after retirement. It can also be linked to the much-vaunted 'peasant soul' of Japan, which gives land something of a sacred character and makes public opinion especially hostile to the idea of land being fodder for speculation; and also to the peculiar structure of the Japanese media which leads them to follow and flatter public opinion and, in that peculiar case, led them to denounce the inflated land prices while they ignored the equally bursting equity market. Beside these geopolitical, spiritual and sociological factors, the Japanese land policy of 1990 can also be convincingly explained, certainly, by pure economic logic. To focus upon only one explanation may prove intellectually convenient and academically rewarding; but by doing so, one fails to capture the whole picture and misses the main point: how it happened that a policy which seemed rational for every actor involved proved be the starting point of an uncontrolled chain of events that led Japan into a decade-long economic depression. No unequivocal explanation will suffice. Henceforth, I think that the best way to turn such an episode into useful food for thought is to describe the chain of events (the decision-making process of land policy) as precisely as possible, while supplying the reader with the sparse elements to combine into a puzzle-like explanation – mixing geostrategy with abstract economics, deeply rooted cultural elements and petty individual worries for well-being. That's simply the complex way life is.

This approach may be denounced as confusing; it would be so, if the book had not been organised as carefully as possible to present the pieces of the puzzle in an orderly manner. It also may be denounced as a cover for the laziness of a would-be 'researcher' who conveniently entered a large amount of second-hand information into his computer, then remixed it without enduring the pain of any analytical work. If so, I'm proud to be as 'lazy' as the French *Encyclopédistes* of the past, and even as some renowned Japanologists of the present, including Edwin O. Reischauer, whose superb work – although beyond all comparison with mine – is based upon the same approach: facts and orderly narration, orderly narration and facts.

My book may also be rightly characterised – and possibly denounced – as passionless, for it certainly is. I'm neither a Japan-lover nor a Japan-hater, as far as academic work is concerned. Hate and love, admiration and rejection, have nothing to do with

serious academic work, especially when a subject arouses such
passions as the Western world's relationship with Japan. Many
books – in France as elsewhere – made a killing with either uncrit-
ical praise for or strident denunciation of anything Japanese. As
time went by, most of these bestsellers proved to have nothing to
do with the real Japan, and now they seem like obsolete products
of either naïveté or prejudice. My approach rests upon Steven
Reed's way of *Making Common Sense of Japan*: search for facts, postulate that there is nothing 'inscrutable', 'abnormal' or even irremediably specific about Japan, and look for chains of causality
similar to those that shaped the history of other countries, including Western ones. The end-product will seem boring to those
who look for polemics – but there is plenty of other reading
matter for them to indulge their preferred prejudice.

My work may also be derided as 'chasing too many rabbits and
catching none' – since it encompasses political life, economic and
social development, culture including movies and literature, and
foreign policy. Obviously, very few people can rightfully claim to
be specialists in all these fields altogether, and the reader will easily
notice that I am more at ease with politics than with some other
aspects. Nevertheless, with the help of my French and Japanese
friends, and a large amount of reading, I hope that I was able to
produce a valuable overview of what happened in Japan since
1945 in those various fields – something which will be helpful for
the common sense reader. I also hope that I have made clear the
relationships between politics, economics, foreign policy and culture in Japan during the past fifty years, for all these fields are
closely inter-related – something that narrowly focused academic
works often do not take into account.

This is not to say that I am either ignorant of or indifferent to
the academic debates about Japan. Theoretical questions like
Japan: who Governs?, the patterns of Japanese democracy (unipolar
or multipolar? responding to the universal *Political Marketplace*
logic or to the stimuli of a peculiar value system?) or the characteristics of decision-making process are not foreign to me. For the
sole benefit of a French audience, I took part in these debates,
especially the one about who controls the decision-making, siding
with the few who argue that the politicians do whenever a matter
is of electoral concern. But this book is simply not intended for
that purpose. Anybody waiting for a definite conclusion about the

very nature of Japanese democracy, or the patterns of Japanese relationships with the outside world, will be disappointed: among the (too?) many rabbits I chased, there was no theoretical game. Nevertheless, this book is not 'neutral' and 'down to the facts' to the point of being emasculated. I never disguise my assumption that Japan is not a dreamland of harmony and social peace, but a 'normal' country whose history is full of bloodshed, treason, social unrest and injustice done to the feeble and the poor by the powerful. I don't believe in anything like a superbly efficient *Japan Inc.* or an omniscient and all-powerful élite, and I describe Japanese development as an adjustment process by trial and error, shaped through social tensions and conflicts of interests, rather than a clever grand plot by Japanese leaders to become the Masters of the World. Japan succeeded, but not without many people having to carry the burden. Also, as it modernised and developed successfully, new problems constantly arose from this very process to burden Japan – as witnessed by the profound crisis of the 1990s. Hence the title ...

All in all, my hope is that this book will be useful in three ways. First, I hope to provide students and common-sense readers with a broad overview of Japanese history from the Second World War to the new century, packed with neatly arranged facts – in the tradition of the *jardin à la française* – and sustained by the proper apparatus of index, glossary and classified bibliography. Secondly, I hope to make a convincing case for a multi-pronged approach to reality – one which does not sink into confusion or superficiality, but hopefully will help the specialists of various fields to put their analysis into perspective. Thirdly, I hope to mitigate the ideological prejudices that have permeated too many books about Japan. Since Japanese studies often have hidden political or ideological agendas which preclude a common sense approach, and since the *jardin à la française* is not a familiar structure in the global academic world, this work might be criticised as overpacked for the average student, superficial for specialists, and boring for those who loved *The Coming War with Japan*. But, as the French say, *On ne peut contenter tout le monde et son père.*

JAPANESE NAMES AND WORDS

For the convenience of readers, names of persons are, contrary to normal Japanese practice, placed in the Western order: the forename before the family name.

Circumflex accents on Japanese words denote long syllables. They have been deliberately omitted on the most commonly used names: thus 'Tôkyô' is written 'Tokyo' as in Western writing generally.

For correct reading of Japanese words in roman script, 'u' is pronounced 'oo' as in 'food', and 'r' is pronounced 'l'.

English-language titles given for books and films originally in Japanese are in some cases the ones used for English versions, in other cases the author's and translator's own words.

1

JAPAN IN 1945: HISTORICAL BACKGROUND

JAPAN, STATE AND NATION: A 'NORMAL' HISTORY

The strength of Japanese national feeling and the original identity on which it is based are important characteristics of the Japanese people. They have enabled the Japanese to overcome major traumatic events caused by the forced opening to the outside world in 1853 and the defeat in 1945, and to become the only non-white nation to take up the challenge of modernisation with complete success. They are a major element in the dynamics that place Japan firmly among the major economic powers today – the present economic crisis notwithstanding. What might be called the 'national energy' in Japan is deeply rooted in history – a history that remains very present in Japan in 2001.

For a long time this history has been manipulated and put to good use by the powers that be. It has been systematically distorted in order to make it appear longer and much more harmonious than it has really been, when in fact it has been bloodstained by wars, uprisings and murders as much as the history of any other country.

Fallacies, conspiracies, bloodshed and treason

The unification of the Japanese archipelago was achieved in several stages. Around the end of the first century of our era a model of civilisation based on swamp rice cultivation, imported from Korea, was established as far as the north of the main island Honshû. In the fifth century rulers of still unclear origin – according to one theory, horsemen who moved from China to Korea, then to the south-western Japanese island of Kyûshû – went eastward from Kyûshû; they asserted their authority over local clans and established a state in the Yamato plain (the modern-day Kyoto

1

region) which controlled Honshû up to the Kantô area (the modern-day Tokyo region). From the seventh century onward, immigration from the Asian mainland came to a halt, and since then the population has not had any significant admixture from the outside. It took until the end of the twelfth century for the Yamato state to reduce the northern tribes – known as *emishi* but otherwise shrouded in mystery – to submission and assert its control up to the north of Honshû. The northern island of Hokkaido, populated by Caucasian people known as the Ainu, remained something like the American Far West until the nineteenth century. Thus the date when the natural limits of the archipelago came to coincide with the frontier of the Japanese state and the 'territory' of the Japanese 'race' (which was in fact originally a mixed bag) was not so early as many Japanese and foreigners seem to think.

Nevertheless, the rhetoric about the imperial dynasty 'uninterrupted for more than two thousand years' (from the mythical emperor Jimmu, 660–585 BCE), is still alive and well among Japanese nationalists, who boast of Japan having 'the oldest dynasty in the world'. According to the mythical narrative put together in the eighth century, the imperial line is descended from the sun-goddess Amaterasu, worshipped at the Ise sanctuary, and the symbols of its power are 'the three sacred treasures' – a bronze mirror, an iron sabre and a jewel in the form of a claw. The same myth, temple and three objects are still at the heart of the traditions of the imperial family whose line of descent is supposed to have been maintained until today. This alleged continuity of the ruling family is an essential element of national identity – despite the fact that history does not support it and several 'sacred' emperors have been assassinated in the course of history.

The Yamato court was in regular contact with China. From 600 to 894 Japanese 'embassies' regularly visited the Chinese imperial court and brought back books, plants, scholars, and every available technology. Crown Prince Shôtoku (574–622), who came to power following a coup in 587 by the 'reform faction' of the court – and the assassination of the emperor – set off a systematic attempt by the Yamato regime to duplicate the Chinese structure of government in setting up a highly bureaucratic state. Two capitals were built, on the model of the Chinese T'ang dynasty capital: Nara (710) and then Heian, modern Kyoto (794). The foundation myths were set out systematically in two official chronicles: the *Record of Ancient Matters (Kojiki,* 712) and the *Chronicles of Japan (Nihon shoki,* 720). Today this mythology still figures in school curricula, and the image of Prince Shôtoku, the initiator of the reforms, has for long adorned the 10,000-yen note. Not so many present-day Japanese are aware that after his death, the offspring of the national hero were to be completely weeded out by bloody court intrigues. The centralised state was too complex for that time and soon fell into decay. At Heian real power was usurped by the Fujiwara family. On becoming adults the emperors, one after another, were forced to retire into Buddhist monasteries, giving up the throne to their still infant sons. The infant emperors were placed under the guardianship of Fujiwara regents and married to girls from the Fujiwara clan, only to be forced in turn into retirement when they grew up. This separation of the emperor's nominal power from real power lasted ten centuries; during that period the sovereign, forgotten deep inside his palace in Kyoto, was sometimes reduced to selling his own calligraphic works to survive. But the imperial line, protected by its very insignificance, remained in being as the final refuge of legitimacy and the symbol of Japan's continuity through the worst vicissitudes of its history. The Fujiwara were to lose the reality of power in their turn, but they retained the pathetic function of powerless regents for obscure emperors – only to rise again at the Meiji Restoration and give contemporary Japan some of its prime ministers, including Prince Fumimaro Konoe (1937–9 and 1940–1) and his grandson Morihiro Hosokawa (August 1993-April 1994).

From the tenth century Japan sank into anarchy as the feudal clans ruthlessly fought for power. The Minamoto, lords of Kantô (in the modern Tokyo region), emerged victorious at first. They established the centre of real power at Kamakura in 1185 and took the title of *shôgun* ('generalissimo'), leaving the emperor in Kyoto and the nominal regency with the Fujiwara. In 1219 the Minamoto, while still *shôgun* in name, were reduced to ineffectiveness by the Hôjô clan, which used the same strategy that permitted the Fujiwara to become the rulers-behind-the-throne in Heian. After repelling attempted Mongol invasions in 1274 and 1281 with the aid of providential typhoons ('the wind of the gods', *kamikaze*) the Kamakura regime was overthrown by the Ashikaga

The 47 regions (ken) of Japan

1.	Hokkaidô	24.	Mie
2.	Aomori	25.	Shiga
3.	Akita	26.	Kyoto
4.	Iwate	27.	Ôsaka
5.	Yamagata	28.	Hyôgo
6.	Miyagi	29.	Nara
7.	Fukushima	30.	Wakayama
8.	Gumma	31.	Tottori
9.	Tochigi	32.	Shimane
10.	Ibaraki	33.	Okayama
11.	Saitama	34.	Hiroshima
12.	Chiba	35.	Yamaguchi
13.	Tokyo	36.	Kagawa
14.	Kanagawa	37.	Ehime
15.	Niigata	38.	Tokushima
16.	Toyama	39.	Kôchi
17.	Ishikawa	40.	Fukuoka
18.	Fukui	41.	Saga
19.	Nagano	42.	Nagasaki
20.	Yamanashi	43.	Ôita
21.	Shizuoka	44.	Kumamoto
22.	Gifu	45.	Miyazaki
23.	Aichi	46.	Kagoshima
		47.	Okinawa

● 1 to 5 million inhabitants

◉ 500,000 to 1 million inhabitants

○ 200,000 to 500,000 inhabitants

100 kms

Fig. 1.1.   JAPAN, SHOWING CAPITALS AND MAJOR CITIES

MYTHS OF JAPAN'S ORIGIN

In the beginning the earth floated shapeless like oil, or jelly-fish, on the sea. In the heavens the male principle and the female principle gave birth to six generations of gods before Izanagi and his sister Izanami descended to solidify the earth. Standing on the Heavenly Bridge (*Hamanohashidate*), they plunged a sword or a spear into the sea. From the splashes the first island of Japan was born. The brother and sister joined together and brought forth new gods. They sent their daughter Amaterasu (Heaven Shining Deity) up to the heavens and their son Suzanoo, the storm god, down to the underworld. Then Izanami died giving birth to the Fire God. For a time, Izanagi kept giving birth to more deities by himself, then he vanishes from the text.

The fierce Suzanoo kept provoking and insulting his sister Amaterasu, going so far as throwing a flayed horse at her; the outraged sun goddess then withdrew in a rage into the Rock-Cave of Heaven (*ame no iwato*). Darkness invaded the earth. Then the goddess Uzume undressed and danced a rollicking grotesque dance, which aroused the gods' noisy hilarity. Out of curiosity Amaterasu peeped out of the entrance of her refuge. A mirror had been laid there, and when she saw her reflection, she was so surprised that a muscular god succeeded in grabbing her out of the cave. The three sacred treasures of the imperial family are linked to this episode. They are, according to belief, the mirror used to entice the sun goddess out of her cave, the sabre that Suzanoo handed over to her afterwards as a sign of submission, and a jewel (the *magatama*) which the gods gave as a present to soothe her.

Suzanoo was banished to the archipelago of Japan (to Korea, according to one version), but he left a large, unruly offspring. Having reached an agreement with the hero Onamochi, the strongest son of Suzanoo, Amaterasu then sent her grandson there; he landed in Kyûshû, bringing the three sacred treasures with him. His offspring in the sixth generation was to be Jimmu-tennô, the legendary founder of the 'Empire of the Rising Sun'. The emperor Jimmu is said to have reigned from 660 to 585 BCE and to have left Kyûshû, cradle of the first civilisations, to set up the state in the plain of Yamato.

Studying the myths was banned by the Americans, but reintroduced in schools from 1951 on. Teachers were then called upon to subject them to 'a proper scientific examination'. But in 1958 new directives laid down that they should be presented 'in a spirit of love of the native soil' to 'forge the national character'. In 1968 teachers were ordered to emphasise 'the superior cultural heritage ... of the ancients'. In the 1980s the Ministry of Education censored school books which showed the *Kojiki* and *Nihon shoki* in their historical context as myths compiled to legitimise the imperial power.

Source: adapted from Vadime and Danielle Elisseef, *La civilisation japonaise*, Paris: Arthaud, 1974, pp. 14–17.

in 1333. The centre of power was moved back to Kyoto, but the Ashikaga shôgun never succeeded in getting real control. After 1467 struggles among feudal lords plunged Japan into endemic wars; savage peasant uprisings erupted and urban communes took their defence into their own hands. Egalitarian and milleniarist leagues called *ikkô ikki*, inspired by Buddhist sects and organised by petty village warriors (*jizamurai*), took over control of whole regions in central Honshû from the second half of the fourteenth century to the end of the fifteenth. This era of bloodshed and anarchy is known as *Gekokujô* – 'The world turned upside down'.

In 1543 the Portuguese landed in Kyûshû near Nagasaki. They brought the Bible and effective firearms. Among the many feudal lords who opened their doors to the missionaries in order to get the muskets, Oda Nobunaga (1534–82), lord of Nagoya, was the first to gather large corps of musketeers on the battlefield – an innovative tactic that enabled him to cut the armoured cavalry and samurai infantry of his rivals into pieces. He reduced the feudal lords of central Japan to submission and wiped out the remnants of *ikkô ikki* leagues there, butchering more than 60,000 peasants in the process and burning alive hundreds of Buddhist monks in their monasteries. After Oda was cornered by treacherous vassals and committed suicide, his lieutenant Hideyoshi – a 'self-made warrior' of obscure origin – crushed the rebellion, then completed the unification of the country (1587–92) and established his government at Osaka. After his death in 1592 his leading ally, Ieyasu Tokugawa, lord of Edô (the modern Tokyo), crushed a new attempt by feudal lords to break free, proclaimed himself the shôgun, and brought the centre of power back to the Kantô area, there to remain. He preseved national unity by weeding out Hideyoshi's offspring, to remain sole master of Japan.

To uproot anarchy and stabilise the country, the Tokugawa then isolated the country and systematically tried to fit Japanese society into a straitjacket of hierarchical mentalities and structures watched over by a meddlesome authority. But the anarchic violence of the Middle Ages, in which fierce popular revolts recurred only to be crushed in a sea of blood, warlords bitterly fought against each other and vassals treacherously stabbed their lords in the back is a part of Japan's historical and cultural heritage – as in so many countries – much more than the vaunted 'harmony'.

The way to 'harmony': submissive ideologies

Shintoism ('the way of the gods') is Japan's indigenous religion. It is derived from primitive nature worship of peasant communities and the clan totem cults of the Yamato era. A form of nature worship, it worships innumerable local deities (*kami*) in the form of trees, caves, animals and rare stones. It is almost completely devoid of moral precepts; for Shintoism, there is nothing like sin, only impurity – mostly from accidental contact with death or blood. Shintoism lays down in great detail rites to purify oneself and mobilise the beneficent energy of the *kami* (which are mostly neutral or ambivalent from the point of view of Good vs Bad) for one's best advantage. It emphasises respect for the ancestors and considers man as a mere link in the infinite chain of generations, rather than as an individual bearing a unique destiny. It is inextricably mixed up with the practices of agrarian society: fertility festivals at harvest time, rites to appease the dead or purify the house at the new year.

During the eighth century, the Yamato court ordered the systematic arrangement of the confused mix of local rites and legends in the *Nihon Shoki* (720), where the word *shintô* ('the way of the gods') appears for the first time. At the same time, the mythical narrative of the divine origin of the imperial line was incorporated alongside the popular myths, thus transforming Shintoism into a state religion and rooting the legitimacy of the rulers deeply in the most ancient popular beliefs. These deep roots, both popular and political, explain how a very archaic religion, reserved for the exclusive use of one race, managed to survive up to the twenty-first century. For it is not so much a religion as an element in the national heritage, a receptacle for the oldest popular culture, a web of social customs – and an instrument of power.

Buddhism was imported from China in the sixth century via ambassadors from Korea. Unlike Shintoism, the new religion offered answers to mankind's basic questions – 'What are we doing here?', 'What will happen after death?' That is why it rapidly succeeded among the nobility at the Yamato court. Buddhism was the driving force behind the coup by the 'reformist faction' in 587. Soon the abbots were mixed up in politics; the monasteries became such a powerful force that the court left Nara in 794 and established itself in Heian in order to escape the threat from thousands of militarily trained monks mustered in temples surrounding the capital.

In the Kamakura era (1185–1333) Buddhism underwent profound changes and took root among the common people. Originally it was a pessimistic religion preaching contempt for the things of this world and asceticism that would allow the believer to break the cycle of reincarnations to attain *nirvâna,* the dissolution of his being within the cosmos. Japanese sects progressively abandoned the too sophisticated idea of reincarnation and turned *nirvâna* into a classical paradise – a 'land flowing with milk and honey' – which the believer could reach rather easily through the intercession of the innumerable deities in the Buddhist pantheon, without bothering too much about asceticism or morality. In the thirteenth century the True Pure Land sect (Jôdo shinshû) reduced the formalities for attaining *nirvâna* to absolute reliance upon the mechanical repetition of the name of the Buddha Amida 'The compassionate' – thus permitting the most ignorant or weak-minded people (its founder chose the nickname of 'Stupid Shavepate') to enter its paradise. Jôdo shinshû allowed priests to marry and entrusted lay people with the management of temples. The Buddhist sects accumulated wealth and military power that gave them a major role in the civil conflicts. Oda Nobunaga needed ten years to subdue the heavily fortified temple of the True Pure Land sect at Osaka.

Among the modifications that occurred in Buddhism over time was a nationalist version preached by the monk Nichiren, founder of the Lotus sect (1222–82). Nichiren is said to have been the man who 'invented' the flag of the Rising Sun (Hinomaru). He proclaimed that Japan was 'the land of the gods', the centre of the universe, and preached that a religious state based on his doctrine should be established there. Seven centuries later this idea inspired the creation of the 'Clean Government Party' (Kômeitô) by the Buddhist sect Sôkagakkai; it received 8–10 per cent of votes at elections from 1967 and then took part in several coalition governments after 1999.

At village level Shintoism and Buddhism merged quietly with each other. The Buddhist deities were 'Japanised' as a special sort of *kami*, specialising particularly in anything related to death and the after-life, which it was advisable to venerate also. The Shintô sanctuary and the new temple were often side by side and the same worshippers turned to the one or the other according to circumstances. This practice has continued and, according to the Cultural Affairs Agency's statistics, in 1997 Japan had 95,117,730 Buddhists and 104,533,179 Shintoists – out of only 127 million inhabitants. Thus Japanese popular Buddhism was stripped of all the ascetic and mystical aspects that have elsewhere made it a sterilising religion or, sometimes, a rebellious one.

In reaction to this over-simplification of Buddhism by popular preachers, the samurai warrior caste developed its own élite, highly sophisticated and demanding version: Zen. Zen emphasised physical and mental asceticism both as a way for attaining illumination (*satori*: a reminder of the original idea of *nirvâna*) and as a practical means of spiritual and physical training for the hardship of war. Since Zen calls for heroic self-discipline and rejects all rationalism, it is inseparable from Bushidô, the samurai code of conduct and honour whose first informal version ('the Way of the Bow and the Horse') appeared in the Kamakura era. Whereas feudal relationships in the West were of a contractual type, and therefore conditional and reciprocal, in Japan they were based on a moral imperative (*giri*) which gave them an absolute value. At least they came to be so in theory during the Tokugawa era, when Bushidô was systematically promoted as a means to ensure the obedience of the samurai class. The samurai's duty towards his lord (*daimyô*) left no place for free will. It was was not subject to any condition of rationality, duration or reciprocity; it included death without a second thought, even if it was useless or arbitrarily ordered by an unworthy master. The master owed his men paternal protection, but if he failed in this, his samurai were not released from their duty, just as children cannot break free from their debt deriving from nature to their parents. And when the samurai were trapped by conflicting allegiance to their lord and to the shôgun, the only way out was death – as in the famous case of the 'Forty-Seven Rônin' (masterless samurai).

Confucianism also contributed greatly to the curbing of the spirit of revolt. That vision of social and political hierarchies on the lines of family relationships was the essential principle of the doctrine of the Chinese philosopher Kongzi or Confucius (551–479 BCE), who inspired the first outline of a constitution that Japan has known, Prince Shôtoku's Seventeen Articles (604). Confucius based the order of human societies on the subordination of each person to his natural superior – children to parents, the wife to her husband, subjects to the government – and on the virtue of governments receiving authority from heaven. But while the Chinese doctrine laid down that unworthy governments lost their 'Mandate from Heaven' and could be rightly overthrown by rebellious subjects, its Japanese adaptation deleted the subjects' right to revolt and made their absolute obedience the essential principle of the harmony of things.

In 1441 thousands of peasants in revolt broke into Kyoto and rampaged for weeks in the city. But instead of overthrowing and eventually beheading the emperor – as the English and French did – they only asked him for an 'edict of virtuous government' which supposedly would bring back the Golden Age. Under the Tokugawa regime, the official statistics counted 6,889 peasant revolts, but most of them were were no more than riots around the lord's castle. The rioting throng only wanted to force the lord to listen to village spokesmen. Those spokesmen knew they would be executed afterwards, according to the 'natural order' of the world, but their sacrifice proved their sincerity and showed that the situation desperately needed corrective measures, which on many occasions the authorities eventually took. Just as Bushidô made the samurai feel that the only way out in extreme circumstances was death, so did the Confucianist hierarchical system make the common people feel the same way. In 1970 the suicide of Yukio Mishima at the army headquarters in Tokyo followed a similar impulse; the famous writer had no plan for a coup d'état, but threw his life into the balance to denounce with all his strength the decline in traditional values, so as to provoke an

upsurge in national virtue. Like Tokugawa peasants, he had no
other aim than to make himself heard by the authorities – not to
overthrow them. Despite Bushidô and Confucianism, Japan's history has been
rich in uprisings and treason. But the idea that rebellion is an act
contrary to nature which leads nowhere except to loss of life for
the rebels became ingrained in the collective mentality. The
bloody crushing of the peasant revolts at the end of the sixteenth
century greatly helped produce this state of mind, as did two and a
half centuries of indoctrination and repression throughout the
Tokugawa era.

Closed country and 'straitjacket' society: the Tokugawa era (1603–1867)

From 1603 to 1853 the Tokugawa preserved the country's stability through a sophisticated and ubiquitous system of social and
political controls, at the cost of isolation and – relative – immobil-
ity, all of which had a profound impact on the nation: one that
lasted until well after the Second World War.

The Tokugawa police state could be envied even by the totalitarian regimes of the twentieth century. The country was still
divided into fiefs, but the daimyôs were closely watched; their
armed forces were strictly limited and their castles dismantled
except one per fief. While retaining large powers in their domains,
they were forced to stay in Edô for half the year and leave family
members as hostages there when they travelled back home. Clans
which had resisted the Tokugawa or joined them late, especially
those of Kyûshû and Shikoku, were deprived of any right to participate in state affairs. The samurai warriors were cut off from the
land and gathered in cities around the lords' castles. Each one now
received an annual stipend in rice, fixed in accordance with his
hereditary rank. Since peace now prevailed all around the country
they were employed mostly in the feudal or shogunate administration; they studied for such work in domain schools that
sprouted up. They formed a class of salaried warrior-administra-
tors, competent and dedicated, but they retained from military
tradition a brutal arrogance expressed by the principle *kan son min
pi* ('bureaucracy honoured, people despised'). Except for the samurai, the population was disarmed; soldiers searched the hamlets

all around the country for concealed weapons. Villages and urban districts alike were divided into groups of ten households, called *tonigarumi*, which had to watch and report on each other under the threat of collective punishment. The Buddhist clergy was enslaved to the government: to flush out the Christians, every family had to register in a temple. All the same the government left each village to manage its own affairs as long as order was assured and tax collection went smoothly. Each of the 70,000 plus rural hamlets thus formed an isolated, closely knit community, administered by the assembly of family heads in a semi-democratic way – although the richest and oldest usually had the last word and monopolised the office of village chief. To stabilise rural society, the Tokugawa outlawed alienation of land – thus effectively keeping a nation of smallholders chained to the soil.

Society was stratified according to an archaic model which placed merchants behind samurai, peasants and craftsmen, and just ahead of the outcasts (*eta*) who were condemned to dirty tasks – especially the ones related to the death of living beings (butchers, shoemakers). For every caste the shogunate laid down in great detail behaviour, dress, food and sumptuary spending – e.g. 'rites' in the Confucian parlance. Thus every Japanese was assigned by birth a fixed place in the hierarchy, from which one could normally never escape, with detailed rules of conduct attached. Strong emphasis was placed on reverence due to one's superiors, and every petition for redress by subjects had to be sent through the hierarchical order, under pain of death. The effects of this attempt to create a rigid society went as far as stagnation of the population, which seems to have remained around 30 million between 1720 and the start of the Meiji era (although some researchers suspect dissimulation to escape taxation). The Tokugawa society was indeed the prototype of the Japanese *kanri shakai* ('straitjacket society'), which the psychiatrist Masao Miyamoto denounced in a best-selling book in the 1990s.

Foreign contacts were brutally interrupted. Until the sixteenth century Japan had active relations with foreign countries. It had been fed by migrations, and by ideological, artistic and technical contributions from China and Korea, from rice cultivation to Buddhism, from ideograms to the art of bronze casting. It had also moved out into the outside world itself. From the thirteenth to the fifteenth century, while Japan was torn apart by civil wars, the merchant guilds, the large monasteries, the daimyôs and the shôgun built fleets of ships as large as Christopher Columbus' famous caravels for trade and piracy. As the state did not strike any currency, all cash needed for the economy had to be imported in exchange for pearls, gold, artefacts and swords – for which Japanese craftsmen were renowned all over Asia. Japanese merchant-adventurers were active in all the seas of eastern Asia and ventured as far as Siam (Thailand) and the Malacca Straits in the west and present-day New Guinea in the east.

At the beginning of the sixteenth century they encountered the Europeans around the Malacca Straits. In 1543 the Portuguese landed in Kyûshû. The firearms which they brought were treasures in the eyes of the warring daimyôs, and they opened their fiefs to Christian missionaries as a means to get muskets. By about 1600 there were nearly 300,000 converts to Christianity, mostly in the Nagasaki region. But after Ieyasu Tokugawa succeeded in reuniting the country, he was keen to cut the daimyôs off from any source of modern weaponry. He was also alarmed by the beginnings of European colonisation in Asia and by the seeds of rebellion sowed by Christian doctrine. He expelled all Westerners and brutally suppressed Christianity. From 1636 all contacts with foreign countries and all reading of non-Japanese works were punished by death. Building ocean-going ships was prohibited. An order was given – if not always strictly enforced – to execute any lost seaman who happened to reach Japan. Only a small colony of Dutch traders, confined on an artificial island and limited to sending a few boats a year, was tolerated in the port of Nagasaki, together with a handful of boats from China and Korea.

Seeds of change behind closed doors

The Tokugawa stabilised the country; there was no more challenge to the government. But the peace itself made it possible for forces of change to get to work.

The cash economy developed around the big cities, Osaka and Edô; the latter had over a million inhabitants because the daimyôs' obligation to live there attracted all kinds of craftsmen, merchants, male and female servants, prostitutes and adventurers. Lords and samurais traded in their rice levies, for which commodity exchanges in those two cities determined daily prices. Big traders and financiers like the Mitsuis of Osaka, bankers to the lords and the shôgun, acquired power out of all proportion to their theoretically humble status. There developed a rich middle-class culture to which Japan owes the art of woodblock printing and the *kabuki* theatre. A class of rural entrepreneurs emerged in the villages – *sake* distillers, rice dealers and money lenders. To get around the ban on land purchase they turned their debtors into their effective tenants, while leaving them owners of the fields in theory only. The rural notables who thus emerged owing to the peaceful Tokugawa regime were to play a major role in modern political life, and many prime ministers came from this social class, up to and including Sosuke Unô in 1989.

A sturdy hereditary administrative élite was formed from the former warrior caste. It was to provide the star players in the government, the world of business and the intelligentsia in the Meiji era. The country was kept effectively under control by the shogunate bureaucracy. In the fiefs, especially those of the south-west, the lords' administration carried out planned economic policies comparable to Colbert's in seventeenth-century France – setting up manufacturing industries, creating monopolies and controlling exports out of the domain of a fief. The autonomy left to villages, combined with the collective responsibility imposed on them, ensured that the administration had a very good hold; its basic grades were provided by the traditional representatives of each community. Thus an administrative structure was installed, capable of running the country even if the political authority were found wanting.

Even under the policy of isolation, Japan was never 'cut off' from the world. In return for the right to trade, the Dutch had to make a detailed yearly report to the shogunate about world affairs. After 1720 reading of foreign technical works was allowed again. 'Dutch studies' (*rangaku*) developed. By about 1850 Japan had a significant number of specialists trained in Western technical knowledge and medicine, and able to read Western languages. Far away from the shôgun's eyes, the large fiefs in Kyûshû carried on active smuggling; their ships met Westerners in the Ryûkyû islands, and a few promising young samurai even ventured abroad for studying. All around Japan, education spread as far as the countryside, through elementary schools linked with temples. By about 1850 45 per cent of men and 10 per cent of women could

read and write, more than in France at the same period. So, behind
the façade of the 'straitjacket society', conditions emerged that
would make possible the adaptation to the modern world which
Japan, alone among the countries of Asia, achieved from the end
of the nineteenth century.

In the realm of ideas, there was enhancement of the national
ideology which was to be a great help to the Japanese response
when Westerners arrived. To keep a tight grip on society, the
regime revived Bushidô and Confucianism. Since the samurai
were numerous (about 6 per cent of the population), militarily
trained and in key positions, they were potentially dangerous. The
'Way of the Warrior' was codified in writing for their use and subjected to extensive exegesis. The samurai's submission to his lord
and the shôgun was taken so far that he was no longer free even to
commit suicide without an order, on pain of collective punishment of his descendants. One commentator in 1716 summed up
the spirit of total sacrifice expected of the samurai by the phrase,
'The way of the warrior is to die'. Paradoxically, while military
feudalism was losing its very raison d'être, its ideology was inculcated in an extreme form to those who were to provide the framework for a modernised Japan.

In the domain schools rigid Confucianism was the basis of
teaching. But to some extent it 'modernised' on its own; a middle-
class version, 'The Study of the Heart' (*Shingaku*), was developed
around 1730 by Baigan Ishida (1685–1744), a chief clerk in a merchant house in Kyoto. Ishida stressed social consciousness and the
virtues of thrift and hard work to produce a Japanese version of
the merchant-class morality that contributed to the success of
Protestant Europe. This morality remained echoed in the culture
of many Japanese entrepreneurs until it was shattered by the
excesses of the 'bubble economy' (1985–90) and the ensuing
inroads of the American model of capitalism.

Isolation and reaction against foreign ideas led to the development of 'national studies' (*kokugaku*) which emphasised the special superiority of the Japanese nation. The *Kojiki* and *Nihon shoki*
were dug up, translated into 'modern' Japanese, printed and subjected to lengthy commentaries. Shintoism, which had been collapsing, was honoured again as a tree with Confucianism and
Buddhism as its branches. Work was started on a mammoth 'History of Great Japan' by the Mitô fief school. This whole trend of

glorifying the 'national soul' (*kokutai*) and the 'Japanese heart' (*Yamato-gokoro*) was to contribute greatly to the national upsurge in the Meiji era. Even today it fuels Japan's collective mentality and national energy, as is shown by the never ending success of books dealing with Japanese identity (*nihonjinron*), and by the recent upsurge in a neo-nationalist school of thought which looks into Japan's past to find cures for the crisis the country has faced since 1990, an example being the 'Meiji boom' – a movement to study how the Meiji regime confronted the challenge of a new international environment, in order to learn from it.

Revival of respect for the Emperor was a result of the 'national studies' which rediscovered him at the centre of the foundation myths. Ieyasu is said to have once thought of making him a simple high priest at the Ise shrine, but his successors provided him with a decent civil list: 10,000 measures of rice in 1601, ten times more in 1700. In the eighteenth century there were occasions, as the shogunate government was getting weaker, when Edô made reports to the court at Kyoto and received advice from it; this gave substance to a theory of delegation of power that would be the basis of the Meiji Restoration.

Restoration, renovation or revolution? The Meiji era (1868–1912)

The American fleet under Commodore Perry which forced its way into Edô bay in July 1853 did not take the Japanese élite by surprise. Since the end of the eighteenth century foreign ships had regularly appeared along the Japanese coasts and clashes had occasionally occurred with Japanese outposts. The shogunate had closely monitored the advance of the Europeans in Asia, culminating in the Opium Wars of 1839–42. Thus a debate had already been started on ways to save Japan from the fate of enslaved China. Some recommended purely and simply 'driving out the barbarians' (*joi*); others thought that a temporary opening was unavoidable in order to import foreign technical know-how to build 'a rich country and a strong army' (*fukoku-kyôhei*) and then expel the foreigners. While debate raged, the shogunate had to sign the so-called 'unequal treaties' with the Westerners. Five ports were opened to foreign trade, customs duties were almost abolished and extraterritorial privileges were granted to foreigners. All over Asia those concessions led to the crumbling of indigenous economies and imposition of Western tutelage. In a not-so-subtle attempt to share responsibility the shogunate asked for the daimyôs' advice and the Emperor's approval. Immediately the large fiefs headed by the south-western Satsuma and Chôsu claimed a right to participate in the government. The ensuing conflict between Edô and the lords was subsumed by an activist movement among lesser samurai for the immediate expulsion of foreigners. Those self-proclaimed 'men of virtue' (*shishi*) opposed the wait-and-see attitude of their lords and the court and Edô. They embarked on terrorism; such a strategy was to bloom again in the 1930s and terrorism is still continued today among the Japanese far right groups, whose most recent victims were a journalist of the centre-left *Asahi Shimbun* in 1987 and the Mayor of Nagasaki in 1990.

With the power of the shogunate crumbling, the conflicting parties turned towards the emperor for legitimacy. Under the cover of 'restoring the reign of the emperor' each party tried to take control of the court, and highly contradictory imperial edicts followed one another, depending on whether Kyoto was being occupied by shogunate troops, rebellious daimyôs or *shishi* activists. After brief clashes between the Powers' fleet and the Satsuma and Chôsu forces in 1863–4, the strategy of driving the foreigners out was shown to be inapplicable. The *shishi* movement was contained by the daimyôs and the Shôgun. The strategy of opening up and copying was left as the only way forward. The rebel fiefs and Edô joined in a race to modernise. They called on foreigners to trade and supply arms and industrial equipment. In Edô and the fiefs alike a new generation of young samurai, often linked to the 'men of virtue' and knowledgeable about Western technology, took control of the administration. In Kyoto the old court nobility came back onto the political stage through the intrigues surrounding the emperor. Together they formed the backbone of the Meiji era governments. In contrast, no popular movement developed, except an outbreak of cheerful disorder of milleniarist inspiration in the Kansai era in 1867 – the so-called *Eijanaika* movement.

In 1865–6 the failure of an offensive against Chôsu sounded the death knell for the shogunate. On 3 January 1866 a coalition of five daimyôs entered Kyoto and secured from the new Emperor Mutsuhito (then aged 15) the dismissal of the Shôgun. The

Tokugawa put up only sporadic resistance, until the beginning of 1869.

THE FIRST JAPANESE MIRACLE (1868–1931)

Japan needed only twenty-five years to bring the Westerners to give up the unequal treaties and achieve a reversal of roles by attacking in turn Formosa (1874), Korea (1876), then confronting China militarily (1895) before inflicting a world-shaking defeat on Russia in 1905. In that period it carried out modernisation with unprecedented speed, while still preserving its cohesion and culture and the essentials of the traditional élites' power. At the same time, under the impact of the same foreign aggression neighbouring China descended into chaos. That first 'miracle' provided the basis for the whole development process that made today's Japan the second world power. The factors making this possible were many and complex.

Why did Japan escape the fate of China?

Japan occupied a confined area, densely occupied by about thirty million inhabitants with a high degree of ethnic cohesiveness. Although national feeling was at best shaky among the populace because of the divisive strategy of the Tokugawa regime, it cemented the samurai class. The shogunate had placed the whole archipelago under the wing of a strong, centralised and fairly efficient bureaucracy. Thus it was difficult for the powers to divide Japan against itself – unlike many other, less cohesive Asian nations.

The samurai élite was numerous enough to supervise and control the population closely. Combining military and administrative cultures, it reacted to the new situation with both vigour (*joi*) and pragmatism (*fukoku-kyôhei*). Its code of honour – despite being mostly an artificial creation by the shogunate – gave it strong cohesion. No split appeared in the ruling class which could have allowed a popular movement to emerge. The leaders of the shogunate bureaucracy and even the army were pardoned and absorbed into the Meiji administration. Even the *shishi* terrorist movement, imbued with feudal sentiments of loyalty, did not seek to overthrow the leaders, but if possible to persuade them to change policies.

The survival of the imperial line, obscure as it was, proved an invaluable asset. The memory of age-long experience of a central-ised state and technical borrowing from abroad was naturally linked with the idea of imperial restoration. This made it possible to pass off modernisation under the cover of a return to the Golden Age of the eighth century. Significantly – though only for a short period – the government positions and titles established in 1868 were those of the Heian era. The duality of power between the shôgun and the emperor was a decisive element. The Tokugawa played the role of a safety-fuse and protected the emperor whose legitimacy, being in a sense 'intact' because it had been out of use for a thousand years, was a point of reference for all parties in a dispute. So a pivot of national unity remained. Without the emperor any power emerging from civil conflicts would have had no other principle but force – which would have led to an era of civil wars, as in China.

The seeds of change sown during the lasting period of peace ensured by the Tokugawa made it possible to assimilate imported techniques rapidly. For example, the Japanese textile industry quickly succeeded in manufacturing silk thread of a sufficiently high quality for export to Europe where silkworms were destroyed by disease in the 1860s, while China was not able to take advantage of that market opportunity.

Japan's marginal position and small size also helped, because it was never to be an important stake for the powers, whose interest was concentrated on China. Westerners' economic and political pressure was thus limited. Instead of subjugating Japan, from the end of the century they manoeuvred to win its support in their Asian rivalries. It was because Britain was seeking Japan's alliance against Russian ambitions in northern China that it was the first country to renounce its privileges (1894) – giving a signal to all the others – and helped it to build a modern naval force, and then con-cluded a formal alliance with Tokyo in 1902, which raised the country to the dignity of a partner.

But Japan also had considerable handicaps, starting with the almost complete lack of raw materials needed for large-scale modern industry and an exiguous, mountainous territory. It was because of its own genius that it was able to exploit the situation to the maximum.

Pragmatic way to economic growth

In this period Japan offered to the world a first glimpse of its economic prowess. In 1868 82 per cent of its population were peasants tilling the soil with almost the same tools as centuries before, and it had no sort of modern industry at all. By 1940 it was capable of keeping up for four years what was then a 'high-tech' war by land, sea and air against the greatest power in the world. Throughout that period it demonstrated its skill at adapting to circumstances, drawing maximum advantage from the First World War and pulling itself out of the 1929 Slump in three years. Lastly, despite sweeping social changes and completely new rules for the political game, the élites emerging from the Restoration managed to retain power. Growth, adaptability, stability – these three elements met again as foundations for the second 'miracle', the one which made Japan a great country again after the collapse in 1945. But it is between 1868 and 1940 that the Japanese 'modernisation machine' can be observed in action for the first time.

This 'machine' operated through a typical advance and adjustment process. After the abolition of the feudal regime and the first efforts to create a modern infrastructure, severe deflation was necessary because of the state's financial situation, from 1883 to 1887. This favoured the emergence of industrial conglomerates or Zaibatsus. The economy bounced back thanks to the victorious wars against China (1895) and Russia (1905), while the abolition of the unequal treaties permitted Japan to regain control of its Customs administration. The First World War was a decisive stimulus. Japan penetrated Asian markets left unsupplied by the belligerents. Its balance of payments, chronically in deficit, recorded a net credit of 3 billion yen in four years. But there was a rude awakening when the Westerners came back. After 1923 the economy went through a long period of readjustment and concentration, aggravated by policy errors and collapsing prices of rice and silk on the world market. The ensuing social tensions were a major cause of the rise in power of the army. From the conquest of Manchuria (1931) onwards the military placed the political power under their tutelage. They imposed greater protection of the peasants and small and medium enterprises, and reflation which was contrary to the orthodoxy of the time but engineered a spectacular recovery.

Japan's dynamic rested on population growth and the domestic market. From 1873 to 1940 the population rose from 32.5 million to 73.1 million, providing abundant manpower and an ever-expanding consumer market. In 1935 Japan only accounted for 3.6 per cent of world trade. While state contracts played a decisive role for some heavy industries, private consumption, stimulated by population growth, progress in agriculture and new sources of income from wages, provided the main engine for economic growth. Even when Japan got rid of foreign tutelage over its Customs, tariffs remained modest for consumer goods – averaging no more than 9 per cent *ad valorem* in 1919. However, local products were not flushed out of the market like India's textiles, because the population kept its age-old habits where clothing, housing and diet were concerned. Western industry did not provide suitable products and left the field open for millions of small retail craftsmen, who absorbed excess manpower. The shops and crafts sector created twice as many jobs as manufacturing industry between 1914 and 1930, and remained for a century a valuable cushion against unemployment, at least until the crisis of the 1990s.

Investment in education amounted to a hefty third of Meiji state expenditure. The system of compulsory education surpassed that of most Western countries in terms of rationalisation and centralisation. From the beginning, the ideology of the 'imperial system' was everywhere to be found in the classrooms, but the large number of vocational colleges showed that there was also a systematic concern to train the skilled manpower needed by the economy, a very progressive concern alien to the much-vaunted French education system at that time.

The roles of the state and private initiative varied over time. In the first period the state took over the model manufacturing industries set up by the daimyôs and built others: naval dockyards and shipyards, but also cement works, breweries, sugar manufactures, etc. It spread technical know-how, purchased foreign machinery, recruited hundreds of Western experts, and built communications infrastructure. But these investments, and the buying out of feudal privileges, swelled the state's debt. After 1880 most factories were privatised. The state did not withdraw from production completely – in 1901 it set up Yawata Iron and Steel, which accounted for most Japanese production in that sector – but it employed less than one worker out of ten. Privatisation encouraged the emergence of the four great Zaibatsus that were to dominate economic life until 1945: Mitsui, Mitsubishi, Sumitomo and Yasuda. Their founders were in some cases descended from old merchant dynasties (Mitsui, Sumitomo); others rose from the samurai ranks like Yatarô Iwasaki (1835–85), the founder of Mitsubishi. During the early days of the Restoration, they established a special relationship with the future leaders of the Meiji government by financing the movement; for his part, Iwasaki provided the ships for attacking Taiwan in 1975. As a reward, they got the lion's share of privatisation at bargain prices. They cultivated this special relationship with the government and administrative élite as their most precious asset. Thus was forged a 'feeling of kinship' (*miuchi isshiki*) which ensured their cooperation with the state for purposes of investment in strategic industries and formation of cartels for sensitive sectors. The Zaibatsus were the most important instrument for flexible guiding of the economy.

The rise of the Zaibatsus did not lead to creation of monopolies, in contrast to the experience of American capitalism. Each one was driven by a fierce spirit of competition and strove to be wherever the others were. In most branches the market was divided into 15–20 per cent shares for each of the Zaibatsus, while medium-sized enterprises retained a share. However, the Zaibatsus were a formidable power. They developed extensive horizontal and vertical integration. They traded through their own commercial firms and financed themselves through their own banks, which absorbed a quarter of national savings. Since they did without the Stock Exchange, control remained firmly in the hands of the founding families. As they strengthened, they tended to pursue their own profits without consideration for the national interest. After 1920 they began aggressively entering such activities as production and marketing of silk and rice, or sake distilling, which had been until then reserved to small-scale enterprises, thus threatening the whole balance of the rural economy. In 1931–2, after the return to the gold standard, they rushed to export the country's gold reserves in a few months of frenzied speculation. Their relations with politicians and bureaucrats were notoriously corrupt and scandals erupted one after another. So they were to become the target of social discontent and military extremists. The assassination in 1931 of the Chairman of Mitsui, Baron Dan Takuma, was an important step in the army's march to power.

The state's economic policy was empirical and its methods varied according to sector. National independence was its first concern, and strategic industries were developed with full strength under state control. It was the state corporation Yawata that enabled Japan to meet three quarters of its needs in steel after 1929. Sea transport, vital for any island nation, was heavily subsidised and shipping lines were operated by semi-state companies. In 1868 Japan had no ocean-going ships; as early as 1913, it handled the greater part of its trade itself. The state also intervened to stop what it considered 'excessive competition' harmful to the national interest: it ordered the sugar industry to integrate to end a feud between refiners of imported sugar and the owners of plantations on Formosa (1911), and divided the oil market between Japanese firms (35 per cent) and American ones (65 per cent) to ensure stable supplies. In contrast the textile industry, which accounted for the biggest share of exports, developed freely on the initiative of rural entrepreneurs. The government only checked the quality of thread, to ensure that it satisfied the demands of mechanical weaving. There was some concentration, but around 1930 Japan still had thousands of small textile workshops and tens of thousands of domestic looms, some of which still survive today.

A huge small-enterprise sector developed through adaptation of traditional crafts. It supplied the domestic market but also produced for export. For example, the gunsmiths of Osaka went over to production of bicycles, and the Kobe match manufacturers to producing rubber shoes, as sub-contractors to a Dunlop plant; the Nagoya pottery industry, reorganised into twenty large-scale assembly-line plants and four thousand sub-contractors, was exporting a third of its production around 1930. The state helped by subsidising producers' cooperatives which also laid down quality standards and inspected the finished products. After 1925 they became corporations under administrative guidance and their authority was extended over manufacturers who were not members. Such quasi-official cooperative organisations (*kumiai*) were also set up to organise fishermen and to help the peasants in time of crisis.

Thus took shape many of the characteristics of the Japanese economy until the present day. At the top, several highly diversified conglomerates (today, seven *keiretsu*) derived their strength a 'special relationship' with government and bureaucracy, which in turn made it possible for the élite to 'guide' the economy. Conglomerates combined in a dual structure with a mass of dynamic and versatile small and medium-scale enterprises, and a crafts sector serving very specific consumption habits, from tatami mats to soya paste (*tôfu*). In 1998 small and medium-scale industries with under 300 workers still employed 74 per cent of all manufacturing industry's manpower and accounted for 52.2 per cent of its sales. There remains also a state industrial policy whose prime goals are fostering national independence, regulating potentially disruptive competition and promoting technical efficiency. Lastly, there remains a concern to protect the 'small guy', a concern which has sometimes been qualified by circumstances, but underlay many post-war measures – though it is now openly confronted by the liberal economic logic of globalisation.

Political modernisation: democracy vs. the 'imperial system'

Democratic ideals were foreign to the leaders of the Restoration, having few roots in Japanese culture. But institutional arrangements copied from Western democracies were necessary for those countries to consider Japan as an equal and give up the unequal treaties. In addition, domestic opposition emerged from the 1880s under the name of the 'Movement for the People's Rights' (Jiyu Minken Undô). The movement's leaders were not diehard democrats, but samurai excluded from the Meiji government; nevertheless they understood that their best argument against those who had expelled them from power was to call for freedom of speech and representative assemblies. From 1868 onwards the Emperor promised to summon consultative assemblies. But ten years elapsed before the government commissioned experts to study the future Fundamental Law, and ten more before the Meiji Constitution was promulgated on 11 February 1889. The first legislative elections were held the following year (25 July 1890). They began a pragmatic process of change towards democratisation, which was to make it possible for Japan to pass in only 35 years to a system very close, in appearance, to the European constitutional monarchies.

The elections were held under a property qualification franchise which limited the electorate to a mere 1.1 per cent of the whole population. Government candidates were opposed by those of 'people's parties' (*mintô*) developed from the Jiyû minken undô: the Liberal Party and the Progressive Party. They represented the desire of prominent rural people and entrepreneurs for a role in public affairs, but their founders, Taisuke Itagaki and Shigenobu Ôkuma, were hardly democrats at heart. Against them the hard core of the Meiji élite around the Emperor formed the *genrô*, a group of about fifteen people who had governed on their own for the past twenty years. They relied for support on the administration which they had recruited at their discretion, and on the new nobility whom they had appointed to the House of Peers.

The Meiji Constitution, copied from the Prussian model, left all real power in the hands of the sacred Emperor. The Diet could not depose the government that he appointed; its only weapon was passive resistance. However, it was difficult to govern without a minimum of agreement between it and the palace. From 1890 to 1930 a series of clashes and progressive adjustments between the two centres of power resulted in *de facto* democratisation.

In 1890 the *mintô* won the elections. The government dissolved the legislature in 1892, but the *mintô* won again. The *genrô* tried corruption to control the Diet, but the result was shaky, at best. A compromise was inevitable. In 1895–6 Itagaki and Ôkuma joined the cabinet, and in 1898 the government was entrusted to the politicians. Ôkuma was appointed Prime Minister, but his cabinet broke up after five months. The *genrô* then tried to govern by force, but failed. A new compromise followed; in 1900 many politicians from the Liberal Party allowed themselves to be lured by Hirobumi Itô, leader of the palace's moderate wing, into a new party, the Association of Friends of Constitutional Government (Seiyûkai), whose ranks were also swollen with bureaucrats. The strength of this alliance between palace, administration and career politicians permitted the Seiyûkai to keep a majority in the Lower House for the next twelve years.

In 1912, on the death of Emperor Meiji, the *genrô* hard-liners led by General Katsura lured politicians from the former Progressive Party into an alliance with small palace-sponsored political groups that gave birth to the Constitutional Association, which later became Kenseikai (1916) and then Minseitô (1927). Democratisation gathered pace, encouraged by the weakness of new Emperor Taishô. In 1918 a commoner, Takashi Hara, became head of the government for the first time. Regular alternate spells of power for the two parties became the norm. In 1925 universal male suffrage was established. Japan had needed only 35 years to pass from an absolute monarchy to a stage which the British political system had taken six centuries to reach.

However, the democracy transplant was fragile. The politicians failed to establish their legitimacy in the eyes of public opinion. Since 1890 electoral corruption had been widely practised, and universal suffrage did not alter this at all. Candidates bought bloc votes of hamlets and urban districts through local notables or professional vote-gathering 'bosses', and took the place of feudal protectors for local communities. This patronage system guaranteed regular re-election to politicians, but it did not foster support for democratic ideals. Candidates needed abundant funds and were vulnerable to corruption. Around 1920 the Seiyukai was commonly identified as Mitsui's party and the Minseitô as Mitsubishi's party.

As against democracy, an abstract and imported ideal, the palace oligarchy and the administration developed an ideology closer to national tradition: that of the family-state (*ichizoku kokka*) gathered around the emperor, whose sacred ancestry made Japan the land of the gods (*shinkoku*). The emperor was the father of the people, the Japanese were his children and owed him absolute obedience and an unlimited debt of gratitude (*kô-on*). It was that ideology which was inculcated to the whole nation through the school system, during military service and through the network of Shintô temples – Shintô being declared the state religion. That this old ideology has not completely disappeared even today is clearly demonstrated by Yoshirô Mori (born 1937, Prime Minister from April 2000 to March 2001), who stunned Japanese by reminding them publicly that 'Japan is the land of the gods with the Emperor at the centre', and called on uncommitted voters to 'stay at home and sleep' on the eve of the Lower House elections of 25 June 2000. Thus the balance between democracy and the imperial sovereignty system was very fragile. It was to be destroyed under the impact of tension provoked by modernisation within the nation and external constraints arising from an expansionist policy.

The perils of modernisation: the land of rising class struggles

In Japan, as elsewhere, industrialisation led to the emergence of a harshly exploited proletariat and class polarisation. Until the First World War all collective action by workers was outlawed. The first Socialist groups were banned as soon as they were formed; even so those groups – mixed bags of Marxist, Anarchist-inclined and Christian Socialist intellectuals – prepared the ground for the future. In its opposition to the war against Russia the Plebeians' Society started a pacifist tradition which the Japanese left continues to this day. But that first generation was decimated (twelve death sentences were carried out in 1911). The workers' world experienced outbreaks of violence, especially in the mines, but trade unionism existed only in the form of barely tolerated mutual aid organisations.

The peasants' lot had always been hard, but until 1873 they were protected from the worst by the ban on alienation of fields. The Restoration removed that ban and started a process of dispossession of the small peasants. Agricultural productivity grew rapidly, but in 1940 half of the peasants no longer owned their own land. Against this mass of peasants, weighed down by rents that could amount to 50 per cent of their crops, there were some hundreds of thousands of big landowners who held half the land. In the countryside also, class polarisation of society rapidly set in.

The First World War and the Russian Revolution crystallised discontent. In 1918 riots provoked by the high price of rice shook the urban centres, and were combined with modern-type strikes. There were hundreds of dead. In the wake of this episode the first trade union federations were formed. In 1920 strike movements involved nearly 300,000 workers. The Japan Communist Party was formed secretly in 1922. Rural protest erupted with the formation of the Japan Peasants' League (Nichinô), as violence was fuelled by the crisis in rice and silk prices. In 1924 the police recorded two thousand violent incidents. The peasant movement came together with the Socialists to give birth to the Farmer-Labour Party (Nômin-Rôdôtô) in 1925. The government reacted with a mixture of repression and concessions. Universal suffrage was granted in 1925 and the first legal 'proletarian parties' were able to participate in the 1928 parliamentary elections, winning eight seats. But they suffered police repression, and the Public Order Law was strengthened as far as prescribing the death penalty for any 'conspiracy against the political system of Japan'. Minimal regulation of labour conditions was imposed, but five bills aimed at recognition of trade union rights were rejected between 1921 and 1931.

The employers took action on their side, especially as firms suffered from a chronic shortage of qualified manpower. Around 1930 the system of employment for life with rudimentary social provisions appeared in the major enterprises. This system was not rooted in anything like a 'cultural tradition', nor in a desire for 'harmonious' social relations; its sole aim was the very pragmatic one of retaining the most qualified workers, who were frequently changing employers in search of better pay. For other, less valuable employers conditions remained so severe that young peasant girls employed in the textile industry had to be locked into their dormitories to stop them escaping during their contracts. This distinction between a minority aristocracy of skilled workers and an insecure, harshly treated labour force recurred in post-war Japan.

The Socialist movement continued nonetheless to make progress. Under the impetus of the Depression, the proletarian parties came to win 17 seats in the Diet. Trade union membership – albeit still illegal – rose to 421,000 in 1936, about 8 per cent of the workforce. The foreign doctrine believing in violent division of the nation into classes and the overthrow of hierarchical order seemed like an intolerable danger to supporters of the traditional system.

Learning the power game: the first phase of Japan's
colonial expansion
Until the Second World War all industrialising powers sought to conquer captive markets, sources of cheap raw materials, and

strategic positions along world trade routes. Japan was forced to do so more than any other country, since it lacked the raw materials indispensable for the first industrial revolution, except for an insufficient quantity of coal. To obtain them it had to export. In addition, after 1925, as its population grew explosively, it had to import food too. It was thus totally dependent on maritime trade routes for survival. Eventually these constraints were to push Japan into it into an aggressive policy which led it to repeated clashes with Western powers.

The first drive (1874–95) enabled Japan to annex Taiwan and Okinawa, then to turn towards the Korean peninsula. After Japan gained the upper hand there against China, its armies advanced to the border of Manchuria, an area rich in minerals and good land. There the powers, led by Russia, put a stop to its advance: Japan had to relinquish part of its gains, which went to the Westerners (Treaty of Shimonoseki, April 1895). Only after securing the British alliance was Japan able to take revenge against Russia in 1905. Once again Tokyo was unable to gain everything it had hoped for, when peace was concluded at the Treaty of Portsmouth; but the victory placed Manchuria under its influence, then enabled it to annex Korea officially in 1910. The First World War gave Japan the opportunity to enforce upon China the so-called 'Twenty-One Demands' that gave it preponderant influence there. But the Powers came back as soon as the War was over. For the third time, Japan had to give up the essential part of what it had gained. Finally, Tokyo agreed to limit its navy to three-fifths of the strength permitted to each of the British and US navies, and to maintenance of the status quo in Asia, precluding any further move by any power for ten years (Washington Conference, August 1921-February 1922).

The military reacted violently to these concessions – Prime Minister Takashi Hara was assassinated during the conference. Nevertheless, Japan paused until 1930. It was preoccupied with its domestic problems: the aftermath of the disastrous Tokyo earthquake (1923), the looming economic crisis in rural areas and the ensuing social unrest. The politicians, now more powerful than ever before owing to the weak-mindedness of the Emperor Taishô (who had to be placed under the regency of his son, Crown Prince Hirohito, in 1921), were against foreign adventures; and so were the Zaibatsus. They tried to clip the wings of the army; between 1919 and 1926 the military budget was cut by a full half. But social agitation, the poverty and rising tension in the countryside, and the Slump of 1929 undermined the civilian élites' power. The army was then able to promote expansionist policies as a solution to the economic crisis and social unrest, and to ensure at the same time a leading role for itself.

JAPAN UNDER MILITARY CONTROL (1931–45)

The Army's march to power

The Japanese army around 1930 was hardly monolithic. The officer corps was naturally the repository of Bushidô and the Imperial ideology, imbued with the ideal of the superiority of the Japanese race and worried at the sight of foreign values, baseball and eccentric behaviour by young *môga* ('modern girls') being spread. But most officers came from the peasantry and were very sensitive to the poverty in the countryside and the inroads made by the Zaibatsus into the rural economy. The samurai spirit was thus mixed with agrarian sensitivity and populist anti-capitalism also found in the origins of European Fascism and Naziism. The young ideologues of the 'Imperial Way Faction', imbued with the ideology of Japanese racial superiority, advocated resolute moves to throw the Powers out of Asia. They revived the terrorist methods of the 'men of virtue' of the 1850s and 60s against the moderate senior officers of the 'Control Faction', which remained close to the palace and the civilian élites. As a whole, the army opposed the parties, the Zaibatsus and the administration, but it joined hands with a faction of young, nationalistic technocrats in the Ministry of Industry who resented the growing independence of the Zaibatsus and advocated reining them in. They agreed with the military in their desire to establish tight control over the Zaibatsus. Their leader was Nobusuke Kishi, who was later to be Deputy Minister and then Minister of War Industries and Economic Mobilisation from 1939 to 1944, then a war criminal, then Prime Minister (1957–60) and one of the Liberal Democrat Party's kingmakers until his death in 1987.

To make matters worse, the land, sea and air forces cordially hated each other. The Army was convinced that the unparalleled endurance and moral strength of the common Japanese people would permit the infantry to overcome any enemy. But the technicians of the other two services, fully aware of the technological edge the Westerners still had, were much more cautious. The army's push for power began in the 1920s with some isolated assassinations such as that of Prime Minister Hara in 1921. The general offensive began in 1930, when the moderate Prime Minister Ôsachi Hamaguchi consented (at the London Conference of April 1930) to extend the arms limitation and regional status quo agreed at the Washington Conference eight years before. The military arranged the murder of two prime ministers in a row (Hamaguchi in November 1930, then Tsuyoshi Inukai in May 1932), a finance minister and the Chairman of Mitsui, who dared to oppose the issuing of Defence Bonds. The politicians quickly ducked their heads down and let the palace pick cabinets that were mostly extra-parliamentary, with military ministers having a right of veto. Straight away colonial expansion resumed. The army occupied Manchuria in July 1931, attacked Shanghai in February 1932, and entered northern China. Condemned by the League of Nations, Japan left it in March 1933 and repudiated the naval arms limitation.

On 26 February 1936 the 'Imperial Way Faction' tried to wipe out the moderates. Emperor Hirohito led the counter-attack personally, ordering the mutineers to lay down their arms. The ensuing repression (2,000 officers were cashiered) consolidated the army. The politicians withdrew from the game completely, none of them sat in the cabinet any more. The rising tension in Europe made it possible for Japan to break out of its isolation by joining Germany and Italy in the Anti-Comintern Pact. The Western democracies had their hands full facing the growing threat of the totalitarian powers. The Japanese military thus had a free hand for the general assault on China from 7 July 1937. Several years before the World War, Japan embarked on its own war – total war.

Moulding Fascism into 'Japanese-ness'

The Japanese military was never able completely to reduce the civilian élites to subjection. It had the Lower House of the Diet dissolved in 1937, but most of the incumbents were reelected, including those from the proletarian parties. It was not until 1940 that all the parties were made to merge in an 'Imperial Rule Assistance Association'; this, however, was not at all comparable to the single parties in Fascist Italy, Nazi Germany or the Communist Soviet Union. The political élite remained securely rooted in its constituencies controlled by patronage and waited silently for better days under the umbrella of the Association. In 1942, 70 per cent of the incumbent Diet members deputies were reelected again. There were no longer any parliamentarians in the cabinet, but the Diet remained a centre of passive resistance. It backed the administration which was defending its autonomy against the military. The army wanted to organise the country down to the grassroots level for the war effort by relying directly on the support of civil society – young people's and reservists' associations, guilds, neighbourhood groups – so as to give local power to a new populist élite. But the bureaucracy thwarted this attempt and succeeded in imposing its own control, and that of the traditional notables, over the bodies responsible for mobilising the nation.

To counter the Zaibatsus, the military sought to favour new industrial groups such as Nippon Sangyô (Nissan) and Hitachi. But there was no way to bypass the Zaibatsus. They financed four-fifths of the investment in the colonies. Mitsubishi Heavy Industries alone, which produced the famous Zero fighter, supplied on its own a full quarter of all orders for military equipment. The army sought to take over direct control of the economy. It achieved nationalisation of the steel industry in setting up Nippon Steel (1934), but the Zaibatsus thwarted a further attempt against the electricity companies. When the war effort required complete cartelisation, they succeeded in having their representatives heading the cartels, and used them to absorb their smaller competitors. Contrary to what the military wanted, the war strengthened the Zaibatsus' power; Mitsubishi Heavy Industries' capital multiplied twenty times between 1937 and 1945, and more than half of the banks disappeared, to the benefit of the four big ones.

The civilian élites organised themselves to wait. In 1942 a 'Peace Faction' was organised by some of the Emperor's counsellors and senior civil servants, including Shigeru Yoshida who was to be Prime Minister in 1946–7 and from 1948 to 1954. Above all, the Emperor, surrounded by his private counsellors, remained the repository of legitimacy in the last resort. He retained the power to alter the course of events, and used it on 26 February 1936. Admittedly, this implied a risk to his life, which might help to explain why Hirohito did not dare to intervene openly until 9

August 1945 (some historians go further and argue that he played an active role in support of the military during the years of aggression and war; the debate is still raging). But the presence at the heart of the totalitarian system of the Emperor as an almost untapped reserve of absolute power was an original characteristic of Japanese imperialism compared with both Germany and Italy; it greatly helped find a way out of the war before the country was invaded and Tokyo possibly turned into a battlefield like Berlin.

Thus the army was far from being all-powerful, even though its Commander in Chief, General Hideki Tôjô, monopolised the posts of Prime Minister and Minister of War, the Interior and Foreign Affairs after 1941. A system of relative balance prevailed among the various élites; they were opposed to each other but interdependent, and the Emperor retained the possibility of imposing sovereign arbitration at any moment.

The weak resistance of society also explains the relatively moderate nature of Japanese totalitarianism. Democratic ideals were not yet sufficiently rooted in the nation to make a barrier against totalitarianism. The traditional parties, Seiyukai and Minseitô, were undermined by a long history of corruption and compromises, and the proletarian parties were ravaged by theoretical quarrels, splits and police harassment. In addition some of the Socialists went over to the military, carried away by their populism. So there was no need for savage repression and extermination of opponents as in Germany. Tight surveillance by the ubiquitous secret police (*Kempeitai*) and the Thought Police (*Tokkô*), interspersed with round-ups and disappearances of militants, sufficed to drive the Socialist movement underground. Trade unions and proletarian parties disbanded themselves officially and joined the Imperial Rule Assistance Association.

Japanese totalitarianism did not produce a formalised doctrine on the lines of *Mein Kampf*. The textbook 'Fundamental Principles of the National Soul' *(Kokutai no hongi)* made its ideology clear for the benefit of millions of schoolchildren as a series of refusals: refusal of individualism and egoism, of Westernisation, of unbridled capitalism. Against these evils was set a mixed bag of traditional values. First came love for the Emperor-father, and the will to give one's life for him in order to become a deified spirit (*kami*); then Confucian values of knowing one's place and obeying parents and authorities, the samurai tradition of honour, heroism and the spirit of sacrifice, and the core values of the 'peasant soul of Japan' – endurance, hard work and frugality. New prominence was given to the myth of a pure, unmixed indigenous race (*tan'itsu minzoku*) supposedly 'born with the archipelago', and an 'organic nation' – as opposed to the 'artificial' Western nations – whose superiority rested on divine origin and a perfectly united family-state ('a hundred million people, one single thought'). Underlying the whole ideology was solid xenophobia, poorly concealed beneath a Confucian discourse that magnified Japan's role as the benevolent but strict father for the whole family of Asian nations.

Education and military service, where the imperial cult went to extreme lengths, were the essential channels for the spread of this ideology. In every village it was upheld by the Shintô temples and by the powerful reservists' organisations. But no organisation had any hold over society comparable to that of the single parties of Fascist and Communist Europe. What came nearest to that was the network of 1,120,000 neighbourhood groups (*tonarigumi*), which reproduced the collective surveillance system of the Tokugawa era. Joining those groups was obligatory. They were intended to support the administration by organising rationing and civil defence, but also to arouse patriotic energy and keep an eye on the lukewarm and dissenters.

It is difficult to measure the extent to which people supported militarism. But in the 1942 Lower House elections, even though they coincided with a series of resounding military victories, the candidates of the Imperial Rule Assistance Association won only 64 per cent of the votes. That shows that considerable reticence continued among the public, and that it could not be controlled completely.

Was Japan blind? How 'normal' expansionism went off course

Examining in retrospect the adventure on which Japan embarked from 1931 onwards, three facts stand out, and they explain its ultimate defeat.

First, there was no well defined aim. The occupation of Manchuria followed fairly clear economic and strategic reasoning: to take control of abundant mineral resources, to open a colony of settlement for impoverished Japanese peasants, and to create a barrier against Russian Communism. But the attack on Shanghai in February 1932 was launched above all at the instigation of the Navy, jealous of the land forces' successes in Manchuria. At that time Tokyo still seemed to be adhering to classic gunboat diplomacy – to strike selectively so as to negotiate local advantages. Its objective was to convince Chiang Kai-shek, the then Chinese ruler, to recognise Japan's protectorate over Manchuria and to concede further advantages in northern China in order to strengthen its hand (1932–4). But when Chiang Kai-shek refused to give in further, Japan let itself be drawn into forward thrusts, in reaction to Chinese moves rather than in accordance with planned objectives. Japanese forces ventured far away from Manchuria to occupy bit by bit large parts of the Chinese coastal region, where a Chinese puppet government was established. As if that were not enough, at the same time it launched two attacks against Siberia, which led to costly defeats at the hands of the Red Army (1938–9). But Chiang firmly entrenched his forces deep in the Yangtse basin, and kept resisting with the help of Western powers which sent supplies from their colonies in South-East Asia. The Japanese high command came to think that the only way to end the China war was to take control of South-East Asia to cut off these supply lines. Tokyo prepared to move south by signing a non-aggression pact with the Soviet Union (March 1941), but it was still weighing its options when the USA threatened to strangle Japan's economy through an embargo on scrap-iron and oil. Japan opted for a two-pronged attack – the naval air raid on 7 December 1941 on Pearl Harbor, and an all-out onslaught against Western colonies in South-East Asia.

Secondly, the Japanese were misguided by their contempt for the enemy. To overcome the giant China, the Japanese high command relied on the collapse of its morale. Against the United States the air arm and the Navy promised only 18 months of victories – after which they would lose control over the Pacific. But the Japanese leaders convinced themselves that a cosmopolitan democracy corrupted by its wealth would not find the energy to overcome its first defeats. Japanese strategy was based on a gross underestimate of the adversary's moral worth – the same mistake that was to be fatal to Hitler. But even in the 1980s one could still hear senior Japanese office holders, including Prime Minister Nakasone (1982–7), attributing what then seemed like the USA's economic decline to 'cosmopolitanism'. In fact neither China nor the USA gave up the fight. The Japanese forces had their first set-backs only six months after Pearl Harbor (Midway in June 1942, Guadalcanal in September). Those six months had been enough for Japan to establish control over a vast Asiatic empire including Indochina, Thailand, Burma, Malaysia, the Dutch East Indies (Indonesia) and the Philippines. But it failed to mobilise those countries' resources to face the American counter-offensive.

And thirdly, Japan's inability to play the anti-colonialist card successfully to rally the support of the Asian peoples reduced its chances to nothing. The 'Greater East Asia Co-Prosperity Sphere' was never more than an empty slogan. The reality was the mur-derous rampages of soldiers taking revenge for the brutal disci-pline to which they were subjected themselves (maybe up to 300,000 Chinese massacred in the so called 'Rape of Nanking'), the deportation of two million Korean workers to Japan's mines and factories, the forcible sending of tens of thousands of young women as 'comfort women' to military brothels, the plunder of the occupied countries and brutal contempt for the indigenous people. When on the point of being driven out the Japanese did proclaim independence all over the place, and their passage was the trigger for the region's liberation struggles. But they left behind them the memory of an occupation even more brutal than that of the Westerners, and the wounds have not yet completely healed even today. Even as recently as March 2001, South Korean students attacked Japanese tourists in the streets of Seoul after a Tokyo High Court dismissed the case of former 'comfort women' seeking redress from the Japanese government.

Japan could not win on its own resources alone. At the end of 1943 the Americans passed over to the counter-offensive. After they captured Saipan in July 1944, their bombers were able to pound the whole archipelago systematically. The Tôjô govern-ment resigned, but the Emperor did not intervene to tip the scales in favour of the peace faction. In April 1945 the Americans landed on Okinawa. In eleven weeks of fierce fighting involving the mas-sive use of suicide planes (*kamikaze*), they lost 49,000 men. More than 260,000 Japanese perished, including 150,000 civilians whom the military pushed ruthlessly into committing suicide 'to save honour'. The Emperor then chose a man in his confidence – Admiral Kantarô Suzuki – as Prime Minister, but he continued to

---

THE IMPERIAL PROCLAMATION OF 15 AUGUST 1945

In this declaration Hirohito did not use the words 'defeat' or 'surrender'. He reaffirmed that Japan had gone to war 'to ensure the existence of the Empire and the stability of eastern Asia, without any intention of violating … the sovereignty of any people'. He was agreeing to put an end to the war willingly – he proclaimed – out of compassion for humanity, because of the enemy's exceptional cruelty:

'After reflecting deeply on the general trends in the world, We have ordered the government to notify the United States, Britain, China and the Soviet Union that We accept their joint declaration.

'Ensuring the peace of the Empire's subjects and sharing with all countries of the world the pleasure of co-prosperity: that is the rule which Our illustrious ancestors passed on to Us … Today, however, the military situation is scarcely able to take a favourable turn, and the general trends of the world are no longer in our favour. The enemy has begun to use a new, extremely cruel weapon. The devastation is becoming incalculable. Continuing the war would lead to the destruction of the nation, but also that of human civilisation. How could We then protect Our subjects, who are for Us like new-born children, and ask for pardon from the divine souls of Our imperial ancestors?

' … It is Our wish to open a new era of great peace … by suffering the intolerable and enduring the unendurable … That the whole country, like one single family, should have firm faith in the indestructible character of the Land of the Gods … Let us swear to carry very high the flower of our special national soul, with a resolution not to lag behind the progress of the world. Our subjects, be the embodiment of Our will!'

---

equivocate, allowing four hundred members of the peace faction to be imprisoned. When Germany had already surrendered, the Japanese cabinet still tried to obtain a promise from the Allies that they would not touch the imperial system, would not occupy Japan, and would allow the Japanese to try war criminals themselves. But on 26 July, in the Potsdam Declaration, the Allied powers demanded unconditional surrender and promised occupation, stern punishment, the imposition of war reparations, dismantling of the arms industries, and reduction of Japan to the territory it had occupied in 1905.

On 6 August an atomic bomb was dropped on Hiroshima. Two days later the USSR denounced the Non-Aggression Pact signed in 1941 and attacked the Japanese in Manchuria and the Kurile Islands. On 9 August a second nuclear bomb was dropped on Nagasaki. During the night, in the course of a dramatic meeting of the principal ministers, Hirohito at last forced the military to agree to a cessation of hostilities. Even then, more futile attempts were made to try to obtain guarantees as to the Emperor's fate before Japan surrendered unconditionally on 14 August. On 15 August an imperial proclamation broadcast nationwide through the public address system announced the decision to the nation. Two weeks later General Douglas MacArthur landed at Atsugi airport at the head of a division, to lead the occupation. He found a new government in place, headed by Prince Higashikuni, Hirohito's uncle by marriage, and Prince Fumimaro Konoe, leader of the peace faction. On 2 September the act of surrender was officially signed aboard the battleship *Missouri* in Tokyo Bay.

2

THE OCCUPATION: UNFINISHED DEMOCRATISATION

MacArthur landed in a devastated country. Two million soldiers and nearly 700,000 civilians had died. The big cities, whose wooden houses had provided ideal material for incendiary bombs, were almost wiped out; only Kyoto had been spared, because of its artistic treasures. Half the population of the big cities had fled to the countryside. Industry was paralysed. Incapable of feeding itself, its trade cut off, Japan was dying of starvation. More than six million demobilised soldiers and settlers driven out of Manchuria and Korea landed in a few months at Japan's ports.

The man who took charge of the country had an aura of prestige won by his fierce resistance to the Japanese on the fortified island of Corregidor in Manila Bay in 1941–2, then by his command of the counter-offensive in the Pacific. He had the full confidence of the American government, which gave him a very free hand until 1948. In theory the occupation was directed from Washington by the Far East Commission of which the eleven countries victorious over Japan were members (the USA, the USSR, China, Britain, Australia, New Zealand, France, the Netherlands, Canada, India and the Philippines). In Tokyo the Allied Council – representing the USA, the USSR, China and the Commonwealth – was supposed to assist MacArthur. But in reality he did as he liked, because the USA had a veto in the Commission and could decide on all urgent measures unilaterally. He was backed by hundreds of specialists of the Supreme Command of Allied Powers (SCAP) and by an occupation force which was reduced to only 150,000 men as early as the end of 1945.

The Americans had prepared the occupation methodically. They had defined a policy aimed at punishing Japan, depriving it of the economic and military means to re-offend, and to inculcate in it the democratic values common to Western democracies. But they were to come up against two restraints. In order to 'bring the boys home' as quickly as possible, they opted for a light occupation and did not wish to administer the country themselves. Outside Tokyo their presence was limited to a few groups whose mission was to keep an eye on the Japanese civil servants, who remained in charge everywhere. After the first shock had passed those civil servants were to organise passive resistance of which the control officials were hardly aware, for they did not know the country and its language, despite the effort made to train them.

Most important, international constraints were soon to prevail over the initial intentions. From 1947 the Cold War set in. In January 1949 Mao Zedong entered Beijing; the Vietminh made relentless progress in French Indochina; the Korean War broke out in June 1950. In the face of this Communist onslaught which threatened the whole of Asia, Washington thought only of consolidating Japan, even if that meant abandoning punitive measures, sacrificing democratic principles and re-employing veterans of the anti-Communist struggle trained by the militarists.

PUNISHMENT PLANS CUT SHORT

Purges: unfinished work

The purges, as originally conceived, were supposed to be very extensive. They applied automatically to all officers of the army and police, all the colonial administrators, the leaders of the ultra-nationalist societies, and executives of Japanese businesses in the colonies. They were excluded from public and elective office, but also from private teaching, the press, and numerous specifically designated companies. The investigation was then extended to seek out all those who 'by word, writing or action showed themselves to be active supporters of militant nationalism'. The entire press of the years from 1930 to 1940 was perused. Millions of suspects had to fill in detailed questionnaires. The senior officials of the neighbourhood associations, dissolved in March 1947, were all interrogated. But the international situation was already changing; 90 per cent of the suspects, at that secondary level, were never subjected to any punitive action. About 1,500 senior executives of 245 major enterprises, found guilty of collusion with the army, were purged. But because they could be re-employed by firms spared by the SCAP, their companies systematically 'relocated'

BASIC INITIAL POST-SURRENDER DIRECTIVE

'The ultimate objectives of the United States in regard to Japan, to which policies in the initial period must conform, are:

(a) To insure that Japan will not again become a menace to the United States or to the peace and security of the world.

(b) To bring about the eventual establishment of a peaceful and responsible government which will respect the rights of other states and will support the objectives of the United States as reflected in the ideals and principles of the Charter of the United Nations. The United States desires that this government should conform as closely as may be to principles of democratic self-government, but it is not the responsibility of the Allied Powers to impose upon Japan any form of government not supported by the freely expressed will of the people.

These objectives will be achieved by the following principal means:

(a) Japan's sovereignty will be limited to the islands of Honshu, Hokkaido, Kyushu, Shikoku, and such minor outlying islands as may be determined, in accordance with the Cairo Declaration and other agreements to which the United States is, or may be, a party.

(b) Japan will be completely disarmed and demilitarized. The authority of the militarists and the influence of militarism will be totally eliminated from her political, economic and social life. Institutions expressive of the spirit of militarism and aggression will be vigorously suppressed.

(c) The Japanese people shall be encouraged to develop a desire for individual liberties and respect for fundamental human rights, particularly the freedoms of religion, assembly, speech, and the press. They shall also be encouraged to form democratic and representative organizations.

(d) The Japanese people shall be afforded opportunity to develop for themselves an economy which will permit the peacetime requirements of the population to be met.'

(Cited in J. Livingston, J. Moore and F. Oldfeather (eds), *Postwar Japan, 1945 to the Present*, New York: Pantheon Books, 1973, p. 78.)

them to sub-contracting firms, which in that way came to be more closely linked than before with the mother firm.

Politicians were hit hard. Just before the elections of April 1946 the Progressive Party (the former Minseitô) lost 247 of its 274 candidates, and the Liberal Party (the former Seiyukai) 198 of its most important office holders. The Left was not spared; ten of the 17 outgoing 'proletarian' Diet members were purged. The Liberal leader Ichirô Hatoyama won the elections, but he was purged just before he was to form a government. And in the cabinet then formed by Shigeru Yoshida, four ministers were later ousted in a year by the SCAP. But the administration was spared. 1,809 civil servants were dismissed, most of them for having been leading members of ultranationalist societies; only 356 in the Justice and Interior departments were punished for excessive zeal in repression. Many others were hidden away by their colleagues in low-profile departments; in particular, numerous former members of the Thought Police transferred to Social Affairs and Education, which they were later to turn into a bastion of militant ultra-conservatism, working for the restoration of tradition and national pride.

In all 220,000 people were purged, but the SCAP authorised massive rehabilitation as early as 1949. In 1951 a thousand former army officers resumed service in the National Police Reserve which was set up to face the Communist threat. In 1952 only 8,710 people remained on the black lists. The Treaty of San Francisco did not contain any clause to prevent rehabilitation of those people – and rehabilitation was decreed immediately. In the 1952 elections purged politicians returned in force. Two of them were to govern Japan between 1954 and 1957, Ichirô Hatoyama and Tanzan Ishibashi. And then it was to be Nobusuke Kishi, a Class A war criminal, who reigned as Prime Minister until July 1960.

The war criminals, the Emperor and the Tokyo trial

The Americans prepared a list of war criminals whom they wanted to put on trial. Two hundred and fifty people – including Kishi – were detained at Sugamo prison. 5,700 others were arrested all over Asia, of whom 920 were executed. In the Philippines General Masaharu Honma, responsible for the 'Death March' in which sixteen thousand POWs died (1942), was shot, and General Tomoyuki Yamashita, was hanged for massacres of civilians carried out in Manila. In Tokyo 18 generals, four former prime ministers and six diplomats were selected to appear before eleven judges representing the victorious nations. They were charged with having taking part in 'a conspiracy to wage an aggressive war' which led to various war crimes and crimes against humanity – 55 charges in all. Their trial opened on 3 May 1946 and lasted thirty months.

The question of the Emperor's guilt was deliberately put aside. Washington had refused to make any commitment on his fate during the contacts leading to Japan's surrender, and American public opinion regarded him as a criminal equal to Hitler and Mussolini. In the Far East Commission not only the USSR but also Australia called for abolition of the monarchy and the trial of the monarch. But very soon the SCAP and President Truman decided to preserve him. The Americans had a wondrous surprise when Japan laid down its arms as soon as the Emperor had spoken on 15 August. The people submitted to the occupation with immense goodwill. The fanatical enemies turned into lambs, and that miracle could only be attributed to the Emperor's authority. Maintaining him seemed to guarantee a problem-free occupation, while the SCAP foretold that his removal would provoke disturbances that – according to the most alarmist assessments – a million men would be needed to deal with. In addition Hirohito showed exemplary submission. On 27 September he requested an audience with MacArthur and asked to assume responsibility personally for 'all the political and military decisions taken by [his] people'. On 1 January 1946 he renounced himself, over the radio, 'the erroneous idea that the emperor is divine and the Japanese people superior to others'. He stood by without protest as his vast fortune was confiscated, with barely 10 per cent left for him. At the request of the SCAP he made numerous journeys around the provinces to show that all was well. Last but not least, he approved the new Constitution which stripped him of all power.

Hirohito was indeed too useful. So the official truth was that he had not been informed in advance of the aggressions against Manchuria and China, and that he had never had any choice but to approve policy decided by his government, like a European constitutional monarch. The whole imperial family was whitewashed also; none of the princes who had been at the top of the military hierarchy appeared in the Tokyo trial. In place of Prince Asaka, the Emperor's uncle who had been directly responsible for the Nanking massacres, a commoner, General Iwane Matsui, was hanged. But in fact the incident of 25 February 1936 and the way peace was 'enforced' on 15 August 1945 showed that even the most fanatical extremists could not disobey an express order from the Emperor. Certainly his orders had to be countersigned by his ministers, but they could not refuse him their seal of approval directly, only delay a decision by resigning. The memoirs of high court dignitaries provide ample evidence that Hirohito was very closely involved in the preparation of all the aggressions from 1931 onwards. But political logic prevailed ...

The Tokyo trial was carried out entirely according to the thesis maintained by Washington. The prosecutor, John B. Keenan, controlled all statements of evidence and refused to call any awkward witnesses. The defendants, loyal to the Emperor till the last, accepted the responsibility alleged against them. The judges were sceptical but helpless. On 28 December 1948 Tôjô, five other generals and the former Prime Minister Koki Hirota were hanged. But many war criminals were not tried, like Nobusuke Kishi, who was freed four days before the executions. The others were granted clemency at the end of the Occupation, including sixteen who had been sentenced to life imprisonment at the Tokyo trial. In 1978 the ashes of the men hanged were placed in the great Yasukuni Shintô temple, close to the imperial palace, where millions of soldiers fallen in the service of the emperor are honoured as deified spirits (*kami*), to whom the prime minister comes to pay his respects every year since 1975.

Hirohito's responsibility remains one of the best guarded taboo subjects in Japan. Violent far-right groups still do not hesitate to silence brutally anyone who raises questions about it. After the Emperor's death in January 1989, they sentenced to death, and seriously wounded despite police guards, the conservative mayor of Nagasaki, for having suggested that Hirohito had at least a share of responsibility for the dropping of the atomic bomb on that city.

THE AMERICANS AND THE EMPEROR

Dean Acheson, Political Adviser of the State Department in Japan, to President Truman, 5 November 1945:

'As for the emperor, there would certainly be advantages in having him continue in office until the constitution is revised and launched in order that revision may be expedited through his influence and given sanction under the existing legal framework ... But as between a long period of political confusion and the Imperial institution, the latter is undoubtedly the greater evil, and there seems little question that the Japanese people will never learn and follow the fundamental ways of democracy so long as the Imperial institution exists.'

Acheson to Truman, 4 January 1946:

'The courses for the future which are open to the United States ... depend to a large extent upon how much further effort we are prepared to put forth. If we are prepared to maintain for a period of years a large occupational force, if we are prepared to undertake that the Japanese shall have sufficient food, clothing and shelter and be enabled to put their economy on its feet ... then we can ... try the emperor as a war criminal, and encourage the complete abolition of the emperor system. If we are not so prepared, we may do what we can and continue to proceed cautiously to give the Japanese the framework within which they may work out their own destiny – and then withdraw in due course and let them try it alone, whatever the result may be.

... I have not altered my opinion that the emperor system must disappear if Japan is ever to be really democratic. But ... there is no question that the emperor is most useful. He is obeyed ... He manifests sincerity in wishing to aid in the accomplishment of our general objectives and is seemingly more anxious to be democratic than some of the people around him.'

Source: J. Livingston, J. Moore and F. Oldfeather (eds), *Postwar Japan, 1945 to the Present*, New York: Pantheon, 1973, pp. 13–17.

War reparations and the break-up of the Zaibatsus

Japan had to pay war reparations. The victors had decided on this. But the country was in ruins and the demands presented, in total, far exceeded the value of its production and all its industrial infrastructure. The Far East Commission was at a loss what to do about the matter. Then the SCAP decided to dismantle industrial facilities to give them to creditors in compensation, as in Germany. The list of 1,100 plants comprised notably all the aircraft factories, twenty shipyards, half of the thermal power stations, and the entire steel production capacity above 2.5 million tons. The dismantling was started, while on its side the USSR helped itself directly in Manchuria and sent its 600,000 Japanese prisoners to forced labour on Siberian worksites, where a third of them died.

Meanwhile, the Americans undertook the dismantling of the Zaibatsus in accordance with an economic policy which – as explained in the Basic Post-Surrender Directive – provided for 'the elimination in Japan of those selected industries ... whose chief value to Japan is preparing for war' and called for 'policies ... which permit a wide distribution of ... the ownership of the means of production and trade'. They also accused the Zaibatsus of having profited handsomely from the war – which is beyond dispute: Mitsui, Mitsubishi, Sumitomo and Yasuda controlled in 1945 a quarter of the national capital, compared with 10 per cent in 1936. In October 1945 the SCAP ordered confiscation of the shares in the holdings which controlled those groups and 79 other, smaller ones.

The Zaibatsus promptly put forward their own plan for 'voluntary dissolution': all their shares would be transferred to a Liquidation Commission (headed by the Chairman of Yasuda!) in exchange for treasury bonds, and then sold off 'in such a way as to ensure the greatest possible democratisation of ownership'. All members of the founding families resigned from their posts. The SCAP accepted the principle but imposed stiffer conditions. The bonds exchanged for shares would not be negotiable before a lapse of ten years, to stop the former capitalists buying their shares back. This measure, added to runaway inflation, a 100 per cent tax on war profits and a tax on capital reaching 90 per cent, resulted in a large-scale *de facto* confiscation of the former families' fortunes.

An anti-trust law and a law against excessive concentration of economic power were imposed in 1947. They outlawed holding companies and shareholdings by banks in industrial companies. They set up a supervisory commission, the FTC (Fair Trade Commission). A list of 1,200 enterprises to be split up was drawn up. Initial steps were taken: Nippon Steel was divided into two firms (Yawata and Fuji), and Mitsubishi Heavy Industries into three. Meanwhile hundreds of business which bore the trade marks of the former Zaibatsus became independent after the dissolution of the holding companies; to avoid any surreptitious reconstitution, the SCAP prohibited them from using the former trade marks.

But a lobby was organised in Washington against this 'Socialist' policy. Many American enterprises had invested in Japan before the war. They were owed $400 million by the threatened firms. On 1 December 1947 *Newsweek* denounced, in a sensational article, ' ... the imposition of an economic theory which has ... no counterpart anywhere else in the world [and] far left of anything tolerated in this country.' In February 1948 a mission headed by William Draper, Vice-Chairman of a bank with a $2 million investment in Japan, officially called for a halt to the dismantling of industrial facilities and splitting of big firms. MacArthur complied. The number of firms targeted by the de-concentration programme was reduced to 325, then to 18, finally to nine. Sixty thousand tons of dismantled equipment had already been despatched to countries formerly occupied by Japan, where in many cases it remained unused for lack of qualified people to reassemble it. Washington stopped this programme unilaterally and decreed that the infrastructure built and the property abandoned by the Japanese in Asia at the end of the war were worth $30 billion, and represented the value of reparations, which had thereby been 'paid'.

Gradual reconstitution of the former Zaibatsus was inevitable. In a country ravaged by famine and inflation, private savings were utterly incapable of absorbing the enormous assets in the hands of the Liquidation Commission: 180 million shares, 42 per cent of Japanese capital! The Commission ensured that matters were spun out as long as possible, waiting for a change in the political situation. In 1949 the anti-trust law was revised to allow banks to hold 5 per cent of the capital of industrial enterprises. The former Zaibatsus' banks at once began to buy their shares back, and companies linked together previously restored the ties through crossownership of shares. Most of the shares that they could not buy because of legal restrictions were purchased by institutional investors. There was no democratisation of ownership of the means of production. By about 1950 10 per cent of shareholders again controlled 70 per cent of the capital of the former groups, whose pyramid structures had now become matrix ones, no less solid, built around four banks: Mitsui, Mitsubishi, Sumitomo and Fuji (former Yasuda). The term *keiretsu* (lineage) emerged in 1952 to describe them. The Americans, who had indirectly brought them into being, see them today as a major obstacle to the market economy in Japan, but they have thus far failed to find a way to penetrate those diffused networks where no identifiable centre of decision making is visible.

The SCAP's policy did bring results, however. The founding families never returned to their former role. The traditional employer class was disorganised for years, leaving the field free to self-made men who brought a new generation of firms into being. Soichirô Honda put engines recovered from army stocks on to bicycles; the engineer Konosuke Matsushita invented the pressure cooker for rice by wiring an electric element to a saucepan; both were to be found 15 years later at the head of industrial empires. But most important, the situation enabled civil servants to get economic decision making power into their own hands, especially those of the Ministry of Industry and Foreign Trade (MITI), created in 1949. Paradoxically it was the Occupation that allowed nationalist technocrats of the Kishi faction, allied to the military, to bring the world of business finally under their authority.

DEMOCRATISATION

MacArthur found in place the Assembly elected in 1942 and a government headed by Prince Higashikuni. It was with these political leaders that he was to launch Japan on the road to democracy, thoroughly conservative though they were.

The new constitution: seedbed of future conflicts

According to the initial Directives for the Occupation, Japan was supposed to be provided with a 'peaceful and responsible government' which would 'support the objectives ... reflected in the ideals and principles of the Charter of the United Nations' and 'conform as closely as may be to principles of democratic self-government'. But the prospect of tampering with the 'sacred' Meiji Constitution horrified the Prime Minister, Prince Higashikuni, who

action, private property), the Constitution also guarantees the right to individual respect and the pursuit of happiness (Article 13), the right to choose one's residence and occupation and to travel abroad (Article 22), the 'right to maintain the minimum standards of wholesome and cultured living' (Article 25), 'the right to receive an equal education' (Article 26), and 'the right and the obligation to work' (Article 27).

Separation of the state and all forms of religion was supposed to dismantle official Shintoism, the pillar of the imperial ideology. 'No religious organization shall receive any privileges from the state'; 'No person shall be compelled to take part in any religious act, celebration, rite or practice'; 'The State and its organs shall refrain from religious education or any other religious activity' (Article 20).

Article 9 on the armed forces is one of the most original parts of the Constitution:

> Aspiring sincerely to an international peace based on justice and order, the Japanese people forever renounce war as a sovereign right of the nation and the threat or use of force as means of settling international disputes.

> In order to accomplish the aim of the preceding paragraph, land, sea, and air forces, as well as other war potential, will never be maintained. The right of belligerency of the state will not be recognized.

It seems that it was the Japanese who suggested this clause, which appeared to the SCAP a good way to prove to Washington the sincerity of their conversion to democratic and peace-oriented principles. The Americans were soon to regret it.

In order not to let Japan turn its back to democracy in the future, constitutional amendment was made very difficult. It requires a two-thirds majority in each of the houses of the Diet, and then popular endorsement by referendum.

Approved by the Emperor on 5 March 1946, ratified by the new House of Representatives elected in April and promulgated on 3 November, the Constitution came into force on 3 May 1947, after new elections. But it was to remain until today a subject of polemics and a central issue of political debate. Conservatives charge that the Constitution is a foreign creation, ill adapted to the special features of the Japanese spirit, far too liberal, and an unacceptable symbol of defeat. The left has seen it as the sole guarantee against a return to anti-democratic practices, the bulwark of liberties finally won. After the end of the Occupation the conservatives missed a chance to amend the Constitution during the period when they had the necessary majority (1952–5). But there is still a constitutional study commission within the ruling Liberal Democratic Party, and as late as 1982 Prime Minister Yasuhiro Nakasone was publicly supporting amendment. A Diet commission to study the Constitution in order to suggest amendments was created in 1957. It was dissolved in 1964 without making any proposals, but resurrected in 1999 – and the debate is still going on. In 2000 the debate was still going on. But even if the political parties were to reach a consensus about some amendments, these amendments would still need popular approval by referendum, something abhorrent to most of the Japanese political élite.

Democratising education: the road to overcompetition

The traditional education system, one of the best in the world at the time when it was set up, had become the essential instrument of indoctrination in the imperial fanaticism which the SCAP had to uproot. It comprised six years of compulsory schooling; after that, there was selection at the junior and junior high levels between technical education (agricultural, industrial or business) and classical studies – five years in both cases. Then followed two or three years of specialised training (*semmon gakkô*) for technical education, while on the classical side it was possible to spent two years at higher grammar schools to prepare for three years at university (*daigaku*). Japan had seventy public and private universities, where entrance was by examination. At the top level, in a class apart there were the imperial universities of Tokyo and Kyoto, breeding grounds for the administrative elite, and the private universities of Keio and Waseda, created by liberal thinkers linked to the founders of the 'popular parties', from which a large proportion of the liberal intelligentsia graduated.

The SCAP made the curriculum uniform, in the name of equal opportunity. Compulsory education was extended to nine years. After that, there was now a second three-year level for preparation for higher education. This massive extension of compulsory education led to an acute crisis over facilities; classes had to be held in barracks, in temples, and in the open air. In higher education a uniform four-year period was imposed. In order to preserve their status many *semmon gakkô* and higher grammar schools hastily extended their curricula to obtain recognition as 'universities'. In addition, the SCAP had a public university set up in each of the 46 regions. The number of universities thus rose to more than two hundred, compared with 17 in France in the same period. In 1948 the SCAP also authorised the opening of establishments for shortened (two-year) higher education. Many private grammar schools seized the opportunity and pushed their way into that category of *tanki-daigaku* (short-term universities), where generations of young Japanese women were from then on to spend the time before marriage 'studying' more or less decorative arts. An oversaturated system of higher education was thus created. From the 1960s more than a third of the young people reaching the right age each year were to find a place in it. But many of these 'universities' were at best mediocre. The distinction between a handful of élite establishments and the others led to the emergence of an ultra-competitive system, which still characterises Japanese education as a whole.

Revision of the curriculum was supposed to remove all trace of nationalist and anti-democratic ideology. Military education, martial arts and traditional morality lessons were abolished. Pending the production of new textbooks, schoolchildren blackened the censored passages in their books themselves. Teachers were re-educated by American lecturers who set out the principles of *demokurashii* (democracy). Active pedagogy was given prominence, to develop a critical sense. School pupils were taken into police stations and town halls, where people formerly entered only in a state of trembling, to learn about the functioning of the machinery of state. Teachers welcomed this reform keenly, as it liberated them. They formed a powerful trade union, the Nikkyôso, which was to be one of the principal forces backing the Japan Socialist Party (JSP) and was to wage, until the end of the century, a determined struggle against the constant attempts by the Ministry of Education to put traditional values back at the centre of education.

The SCAP, however, had less success with university teachers, among whom the Marxist tradition had firm roots in their determination to assert their freedom, in a certain analogy between Marxism's deductive logic and that of Confucianism, and in the easy universal explanation Marxism offered of the Western world that was causing so many problems for Japan. With the collapse of the imperial system there was no longer any counterweight to the attraction of an ideology then in a phase of rapid expansion. When the SCAP advised the universities to get rid of their Communist-inclined teaching staff in 1948, the academic world reacted violently. The students' unions set up a national federation, Zengakuren, which was to be at the centre of all the protest movements until the 1970s. The intelligentsia took up a firm far-left position. It was to play a major role alongside the JSP in defending the Constitution, but it cut itself off little by little from the changing social realities, until it had by the 1980s the image of an archaic, ossified caste rapidly losing influence to new opinion makers from the media.

The SCAP took democratisation of the educational system to extremes, in reaction to the draconian control previously exerted by the Ministry of Education. In every region and big city education was entrusted to elected commissions which recruited teachers, chose textbooks and appointed head teachers. The Ministry of Education was now merely a technical adviser providing a list of textbooks to be recommended. There immediately followed violent struggles between the Nikkyôso and conservatives for control over the commissions.

Local government reform: failure of decentralisation

Since the Meiji Restoration the government had placed local authorities under tight control. It had since 1878 allowed election of mayors, municipal councils and regional councils, but appointed governors had the right to dismiss the elected office holders. The all-powerful Ministry of Home Affairs had the municipal authorities under its supervision; to make control easier their number was massively reduced from 71,314 in 1888 to 15,820 in 1890. The SCAP enshrined the principle of local autonomy in the Constitution, as well as the right of municipal and regional authorities to lay down their own rules on almost all matters. The Ministry of Home Affairs itself was abolished altogether in December 1947. An autonomous police force was set up in all local government areas of more than 5,000 inhabitants, under the authority of commissions appointed by the local elected representatives. The national police retained only a minor role – training, and watching over the rural areas.

The SCAP wanted to make local life 'the school of democracy'. Governors were now elected by universal suffrage for four-year terms. Like the education commissions, numerous local administrative commissions were also to be chosen by universal suffrage. According to the Local Autonomy Law, a third of the registered voters was now sufficient to submit a motion of no confidence in the mayor, which makes it obligatory to hold new municipal elections. One-fiftieth sufficed to introduce a resolution before the municipal council or prefecture assembly, which must then discuss and vote on it, or else to call for a central government inspection of the running of local affairs.

But the reform remained incomplete. To ensure real autonomy, municipalities and regions would have had to have their own adequate financial resources. Indeed, in 1949 the Shoup Commission which examined the Japanese fiscal system recommended giving local authorities the greater part of tax income. But the time for reform had passed. The Commission's report was buried and local tax revenue remained limited; it only covered on average one third of expenditure. The central government supplied the rest through tax rebates and subsidies calculated on a very complicated, thus more or less discretionary basis – which gave it a formidable means of pressure and control over the autonomous local government bodies.

REFORMS AND SOCIAL CHANGE

Social problems had greatly contributed to the militarist adventure. It was all the more urgent to find solutions to them because Communism was at the gates of Japan. In Tokyo itself the Soviet representative on the Allied Council, General Derevyenko, assisted by no less than 1,200 'experts', worked to strengthen the Communist Party and exploit the rapidly rising workers and peasants' movement.

Land reform: exceptionally radical

The countryside was then on the brink of explosion. Farmers now represented 42 per cent of the active population, compared with

82 per cent at the start of the Meiji era. But their actual number had hardly diminished: 14 million about 1870, 13.8 million in 1945. In a country whose surface was only about 15 per cent cultivable, the average area available was only one hectare per farm.

Since the Meiji government had lifted the ban on buying and selling of farmland, modernisation had led to gradual dispossession of smallholders. On the one side there were about 2,750,000 families who lost their property and lived on rented land, crushed down by rents which could amount to half the harvest. On the other side there were some hundreds of thousands of absentee landlords. A handful of them (two thousand) owned more than four hundred hectares each and appropriated on their own 20 per cent of the cultivable land. Between those two groups over 2 million smallholders who had no capital to invest seemed destined to be the casualties of further modernisation.

The farmers' movements that had developed after 1920 were broken up by the militarists. In 1934 all cooperatives were regrouped in the Peasants' Association (Nôgyôkai), a body responsible for distribution of fertiliser and equipment, marketing crops and lending at low rates. In every hamlet its bureau was the centre of local authority – and political manipulation.

In 1945 the Peasants' Union (Nichinô) was revived under the leadership of the Socialist Rikizô Hirano and the Communist Hisao Kuroda. Its membership rose from 60,000 in January 1946 to 1.2 million at the beginning of 1947. The success won at that very time by Mao Zedong in the Chinese countryside made the rural problem a priority for the SCAP. In December 1945 an agrarian reform bill plan was presented by Sidehara. Judged insufficient by the SCAP, it was recast and led to the most radical land redistribution ever implemented outside the Communist systems.

The Agrarian Reform Law of October 1946 confiscated all land belonging to absentee landlords. Those who lived in a village but did not farm could keep no more than one hectare each. The big owner-farmers who rented out a portion of their land could keep three hectares to farm themselves, plus one to rent out. All land in excess was bought up by the state, but with galloping inflation the price of a hectare was soon equivalent to no more than that of a few packs of cigarettes on the black market.

In each village a commission elected by universal suffrage decided on the expropriations. They were assisted by 36,000 officials and 250,000 volunteer investigators. The elections produced a fierce struggle between traditional notables and the Peasants' Union. Where the local balance of power was in their favour, landowners managed to save a part of their property; absentees got themselves classified as residents and those who did not farm obliged their farmers to hand fields back to them so as to become 'cultivators'. Woodland and pasture were excluded from the redistribution. Application of the reform was to take more than three years and required the passing of ten laws. In all two million hectares – 36 per cent of all cultivated land – were distributed to 80 per cent of the peasants (4.3 million families) at a price made symbolic by inflation, with the help of thirty years' credit at 3.2 per cent. Japan became a land of smallholders again; in 1950 only 5 per cent of cultivators did not have their own land. Scarcely 10 per cent of fields were still rented, and draconian conditions were laid down for the lessor: rents fixed in cash at a trifling rate brought scarcely a 1 per cent return on capital before tax, and the landlord had no means of getting his land back as long as the farmer cultivated it.

The reform put a halt to the spread of Socialism in rural areas. It knit village communities more closely together by wiping out class distinctions. Many former notables still kept a degree of wealth and influence, because they had many different sources of income – forestry enterprises, sake factories, textile mills. They maintained the patron-client relations between villages and conservative politicians. New leaders had asserted themselves in the commissions and in the new cooperatives created after the dissolution of the Nôgyôkai. But most of them were won over by the conservatives, for example Zenkô Suzuki: elected in 1946 as a Socialist candidate by the fishermen of Iwate in northern Japan, he was re-elected in 1947 on the Liberal Party (conservative) ticket, and later became Prime Minister from 1980 to 1982.

The ruin of the rural left was completed by its own divisions. At its second congress the Socialist minority left the Peasants' Union. Rikizô Hirano was Minister of Agriculture in the Socialist-Democratic coalition government of 1947–48, but he was purged for having concealed his involvement with an ultranationalist magazine before the war; the agrarian wing of the Japanese Socialist Party then fell into decay. On their side the conservatives launched the All-Japan Peasants' Union (Zennichinô) which sought to 'unite all peasants in a spirit of mutual aid without asking each one if he is landlord, owner-culti-vator or farmer'. The cooperatives were regrouped bit by bit in a National Federation (Zenchû) which operated in close contact with the Ministry of Agriculture. They were to keep the country-side firmly in the conservative camp. In 1993 the Liberal Demo-cratic Party (LDP) was still able to sweep two-thirds of the rural seats in the parliamentary elections, and it was spared a humiliat-ing defeat the 1998 Upper House election only because of the unshakeable loyalty of the rural voters. Thus, in a rather paradoxi-cal way, one the most egalitarian agrarian reforms of the twentieth century, one which trampled on property rights, ended by laying the most solid foundation for the conservative government for more than fifty years.

However, the reform halted the modernisation process linked to land concentration. Five million families ended up as owners of one-hectare plots with no capital for modernisation. The civil law code reform that came at the same moment threatened landholdings with division through inheritance. So there was a danger that the social problem narrowly averted could return soon. Finding a solution to this was one of the biggest successes of the conservative government.

Trade union law reform and the outbreak of labour unrest

In the 1920s Japanese workers had shown that they were obsti-nately combative. They, more than the peasants who were con-fined by their community structures, could be the main force for democratisation. For the SCAP, freeing the workers' movement and helping it to become organised was a way of advancing both social justice and democracy.

The trade union law of December 1945 was inspired by Ameri-can legislation, but differed from it in including only a very vague prohibition of house unions and anti-trade union activities, and in leaving open the possibility for the government to outlaw trade unions, at least in theory. The regional tripartite labour relations commissions scarcely had any way to impose their decisions on employers. Those provisions bore the mark of a Japanese bureau-cracy determined to keep a lid on the workers' movement. It was no accident that in 1950 the head of the trade unions bureau in the Ministry of Labour was a former Thought Police officer... Nonetheless, for the first time this law ensured the rights of association and collective bargaining and the right to strike for Japanese workers. Then in 1947 the law on working conditions brought protective regulation, concerning paid holidays, workplace accidents, restrictions on women's work, and other matters – but no minimum wage.

As soon as it was freed from restrictions, the workers' movement expanded rapidly. Two federations were created in August 1946: the Japanese Federation of Labour (Sanbetsu), which was Communist, and the Trade Union Congress (Sodômei) led by the moderate Socialist Suehiro Nishio. The head of the SCAP Labour Division made highly encouraging speeches before both congresses: 'The response of Japanese workers to the opportunities opened to them by SCAP ... has exceeded my most optimistic expectations.' About 13,000 trade unions had been organised by then, with 3.8 million members, 40 per cent under the control of Sanbetsu. At their peak, in early 1949, seven million workers belonged to 34,500 unions – a unionisation rate of more than 45 per cent.

The social situation at the end of the war was terrible. Industry had declined to 30 per cent of its pre-war level; there were 13 million unemployed. The employers halted all investment pending decisions by the SCAP. There was extreme destitution. Deprived of fertiliser, agriculture was now supplying no more than 60 per cent of its pre-war production, and not one grain of rice came from abroad. The government ordered requisitioning, but the farmers hid all that they could; it asked for help from the United States, but Washington considered that it did not have to feed the defeated who were responsible for their own misfortune. At the end of 1945 rice cost 135 times more than the official price on the Tokyo black market. The average ration was below 1,200 calories per day and 20 per cent of the population suffered from tuberculosis. In the early summer of 1946 distribution of rice was halted in many big cities.

The trade unions displayed a keen fighting spirit. They occupied factories and got them working when management failed to do so, while crediting any profits to the employer. Journalists on the major daily *Yomiuri*, coal miners in Hokkaido and railwaymen on some private lines practised this 'production control' (*seisan kanri*). Employers had to face 'mass negotiations' in front of crowds of assembled workers. The agitation became intense in the spring of 1946; a million people marched on May Day. On 14 May women tried to force their way into the imperial palace to protest against the shortage of rice; they returned on the 19th and a delegation made a forcible inspection of the imperial kitchens. Another delegation invaded the residence of Shigeru Yoshida, the Prime Minister designate following the victory of his Liberal Party in the 10 April elections.

The SCAP's turn-about

Relations between the Yoshida government, the SCAP and the workers' movement deteriorated rapidly. From the summer of 1946 'workers' control' and strikes 'contrary to the objectives of the occupation' were outlawed. In the autumn there was a major confrontation between the unions and the management of the three main dailies (*Asahi*, *Mainichi* and *Yomiuri*) who sought to establish house unions with the help of the SCAP, and the worker left suffered its first setback. In September Yoshida secured passage of a labour relations law that forced sensitive sectors (hospitals and coal-mines, for example) to follow an obligatory conciliation procedure during which strike action was to be forbidden. In his new year message for 1947 he denounced 'disloyal and subversive elements holding up reconstruction'. Three weeks later Katsumi Kikunami, the Sanbetsu leader who had led the demonstrations in front of the imperial palace and the Yomiuri strike, was seriously injured by a far-right activist.

The National Coordination Council in which Sanbetsu and Sodômei joined forces called for repeal of the labour relations law and a public apology from Yoshida. A general strike was called for 1 February, but was banned by MacArthur; the Council's General Secretary had to announce the cancellation himself over the radio. The Sanbetsu and Sodômei accused each other of being responsible for the failure, and the Council broke apart.

Political developments aggravated the disagreements in the trade union movement after the April 1947 elections, when the JSP agreed to govern with some conservative parties hostile to Yoshida for 18 months. But it was unable to halt runaway inflation or get the economy moving again. Worse still, it accepted an amendment to the public service law depriving civil servants of the right to strike on pain of dismissal and imprisonment for up to a year, and even of the right to collective bargaining. From then on all labour relations problems, and pay rises, were examined unilaterally by a National Personnel Authority appointed by the government. The law thus amended is still in force today. In accepting it on the orders of the SCAP, the JSP demoralised the trade union movement. It paid dearly for this in the 1949 elections which brought Yoshida back to power, ready to deal a decisive blow to the workers' movement with the blessing of the SCAP, for which the struggle against Communism was now the priority. Repression of trade unionism was at its height. The SCAP imposed a rigorous deflationary policy (the Dodge Plan): 100,000 railwaymen, 220,000 postal workers and nearly 400,000 private salaried employees were laid off in two years. Everywhere trade unionists were the first to go. From the outbreak of the Korean War in June 1950 there were also special measures against Communist militants: 600 journalists and 10,000 civil servants were purged, thousands of suspects were dismissed from firms working for the US Army. The trade unions fought back with the strength of despair. In February and March 1949 Sodômei called for a general strike by coal miners, electricity workers and private transport workers; civil servants had to 'work to rule' to get around the law. But the SCAP broke the movement by forcing a conciliation procedure on the miners, who were the backbone of the movement.

This failure led to reshaping of the federations. They lost a quarter of their members between 1949 and 1951. The SCAP Labour Office was now headed by a delegate of the American anti-Communist trade union organisation, the AFL-CIO. It encouraged 'leagues for democratisation' (*mindô*) which contested with the Communists for control of the Sanbetsu and worked to bring the Sodômei round to moderate, pro-American positions. The Communist federation collapsed from a million members in 1949 to less than 300,000 in 1950. The leagues and a number of small federations regrouped with Sodômei to form a new federation. The General Council of Japanese Trade Unions (Sôhyô) was born in July 1950. But it was soon to disappoint the Americans' hopes. At its second congress in 1952 it refused to join the

International Confederation of Free Trade Unions, and followed the JSP in refusing to approve the San Francisco Treaty and the Security Treaty with the USA, which aligned Japan with the Western camp. The rate of unionisation went up again, and by the end of the Occupation a series of violent conflicts was to show that the workers' movement remained highly combative.

The trade union movement settled down, but it was undermined by serious structural weaknesses. It was now dominated by Sôhyô, to which more than 40 per cent of unionised workers (three million people) belonged. But its right wing broke away in 1951 to form Zenrô, and then a left-wing faction founded Shinsabetsu (New Sambetsu). Sôhyô's strength was concentrated in the civil service, especially among teachers and railwaymen, where there was more than 80 per cent unionisation. But in the private sector the unions fell back on defence of the labour aristocracy with lifetime employment. They abandoned the temporary workers, and the mass of small and medium-scale enterprises, which employed the majority of wage earners, remained completely outside union organisation. Sôhyô had strong points in mining and the steel industry, but elsewhere it was often surpassed by Zenrô. The employers, on their side, came to build systematically house unions bringing together blue- and white-collar workers, under the guidance of staff closely connected with the management. Such unions often joined a fourth, 'neutral' federation, the Chûritsukai.

The trade union movement was now totally excluded from the circle of decision makers. Seven years of violent struggle planted it firmly in a culture of opposition and linked it organically to the left-wing parties: Sôhyô to the JSP, Zenrô (which later became Dômei) to the moderate Socialists who were to form the Democratic Socialist Party in 1960.

Civil law reform: liberation of women

The Civil Code of 1890 was incompatible with a society founded on individual freedom. It considered the family in the widest sense (*ié*), in which several generations lived under the same roof, as the basic unit of society. In practice, the functioning of the *ié* differed from one part of the country to another, with the authoritarian principle more or less strongly asserted according to regional traditions. But legally, all members of such a household, included in the family register (*koseki*), were subjected to the legal authority of the head of the family. That position was usually passed from father to eldest son. The family head's mother, his wife and his brothers and sisters living under the same roof remained under his guardianship. His children could neither marry nor move house without his consent. He could choose their spouses, but also hire them out to a factory or, in the case of girls, to a teahouse of prostitution. His married sons could only escape from him if they were capable of ensuring the subsistence of their own families and setting up their own *ié*. To ensure continuity of households, the entire heritage passed to the family head. If there was no male heir, the law made it easy to adopt a son-in-law who assumed the name and the succession of his father-in-law.

Women's position was one of total inferiority. A woman escaped from her father's authority only to come under that of the husband he had chosen for her. Often she had to undergo a period of probation before her father-in-law made the marriage official; if she was not submissive enough, she was sent back to her family in disgrace. Even when it was made official a marriage could easily be ended 'by mutual consent' – in fact repudiation, which the woman whom it was intended to get rid of, persecuted by the whole household, could not resist for long. Until the death of her mother-in-law a wife, forced into submission, was 'the one who eats the rice cold', after serving the others. Legally she could neither manage her own property nor exercise parental authority. Adultery by the wife was a legitimate ground for divorce, but not adultery by the husband, who could adopt the children of his mistresses as he wished. Prostitution was a grand tradition. In Tokyo the Yoshiwara red-light district had several hundred houses employing thousands of women. Many were peasant girls reduced to a state of semi-slavery under contracts signed by their fathers.

Deprived of political rights, women could not even attend public meetings until 1922. In 1930 they were allowed to join parties, but a bill to give them the right to vote was thrown out by the House of Peers. A feminist movement developed from the foundation in 1927 of the New Woman Society led by Fusae Ichikawa and Shizue Katô. Although hampered by personal and ideological quarrels, it secured the beginnings of recognition of political rights and a law establishing aid for widows and abandoned mothers (1938). But Ichikawa was compromised with the militarists, which led to her being purged from 1947 to 1950 – before staging a political comeback and influencing the careers of some of today's reforming politicians, most notably Naoto Kan (see p. 293).

The Constitution declared the abolition of the *ié* and sexual equality. 'Marriage shall be based only on the mutual consent of both sexes and it shall be maintained through mutual cooperation with the equal rights of husband and wife as a basis' (Article 24). A commission was set up to revise the Civil Code accordingly. On the commission many women opposed the traditional legal experts; the debates were widely echoed among public opinion and in the press. The new Code came into force on 1 January 1948. It abolished the *ié*, establishing equal shares in inheritance and the individual freedom of all adult individuals. A wife now shared parental authority and had rights over her own property. Family courts were established to arbitrate in domestic conflicts. Prostitution was outlawed. The law on working conditions laid down the principle 'equal pay for equal work'. The Eugenics Law of 1948 allowed almost unrestricted abortion.

Women were given the vote, and thirty-nine won parliamentary seats in 1946: 'Flowers on the old red carpet', wrote *Mainichi*. But many of them owed their election to a certain confusion among women voters, who were sometimes convinced that they were legally obliged to vote for a woman, and to the system which allowed every voter to cast two votes, of which the second, 'less serious' one often went to a female candidate, because of the appeal of something new or out of courtesy. Only a few female Diet members were experienced feminists, such as Shizue Katô, who was to lead the struggle against prostitution and for abortion. In the elections of 1947, where the double vote was eliminated, only fifteen women won. Only one was to have a long career – Shizue Yamaguchi, a conservative re-elected twelve times in Tokyo until 1979.

Conventions changed more slowly than the law. In rural areas the rights of first-born sons remained the rule, to avoid division of property; legally, it sufficed only for the younger children to renounce their inheritance by a simple declaration registered at the family court (there were 143,508 such cases in 1949 alone).

Arranged marriage (*miai-kekkon*) and adoption of sons-in-law are still practised today. Traditionalists succeeded in continuing divorce by 'mutual consent' which, in the Japanese social context, was above all at the expense of the wife; if she could be made to sign a document she could be sent away with nothing, because the law had no binding provision for alimony, and the children were most often kept by her former husband's family. Lastly, to ensure continuity in worship of the ancestors, the law allowed the eldest son to inherit exclusively all objects relating to worship (the family altar). At the symbolic level, even today, Japanese people still do not have their individual identity cards; their 'identity' is still linked to registration in the family *koseki* until they marry.

POLITICAL CHANGE

The 1946 elections and the first Yoshida government

Reshaping of the party system began as soon as MacArthur landed at Atsugi. In the autumn of 1945 the traditional parties reorganised under labels of the latest fashion. The Minseitô, which held 274 seats of the 466 in the House elected in 1942, became the Progressive Party (Shimpotô). That was the party most compromised with the militarists, and it was decimated by the purges. Only 27 incumbents were allowed to stand again, and the aged Baron Sidehara led an army of replacement candidates into the elections. The Seiyukai was renamed the Liberal Party (Jiyutô). Being less compromised, it started off as the favourite, and its Chairman Ichirô Hatoyama got ready to occupy the Prime Minister's chair after the elections to be held in April 1946. The Left was then only just emerging from the shadows. After several decades of relentless repression it had no grassroots organisation any more. Communist leaders were only just back from prison or exile. The Japan Socialist Party (JSP) took up the torch passed on by the proletarian parties, but it also inherited their chronic divisions. It was divided between Marxists of the Rônô faction, the moderate Democratic Socialist wing to which its Chairman Tetsu Katayama and the Sodômei leader Suehiro Nishio belonged, and the agrarians under Rikizô Hirano, the Peasants' Union leader. In addition many former proletarian Diet members had compromised themselves with the militarists, and ten out of seventeen were purged.

In a very confused contest, the conservatives won hands down on 10 April 1946. In all 257 parties put forward 2,781 candidates for the 466 seats. Women, and young people from 21 to 25, voted for the first time. Traditional three- or four-member constituencies were replaced by new ten-member ones, where each voter had two votes according to a semi-proportional system. The issues at stake were not clear, since the new Constitution had already been accepted by the Emperor and promulgated by an imperial rescript one month before polling; anyway the SCAP decided everything. The turnout (72 per cent) was therefore noticeably less than before the war (87 per cent on average). The Japanese hardly seemed to hold anything against those who had led them to defeat and disaster: 325 of those elected came directly from the pre-war political élite – either previous Diet members or the sons-in-law, cousins, nephews, wives and private secretaries of purged politicians. The JSP won 17.8 per cent of votes and 92 seats; the Japan Communist Party (JCP) won under 4 per cent and five seats. The big winner was the Liberal Party. Ichirô Hatoyama was therefore getting ready to form a government when he was abruptly purged.

Hatoyama then chose Shigeru Yoshida to take his place. Close to the palace, Yoshida had been Foreign Minister since 1945, and thus the main representative in dealings with the SCAP. He was enthusiastically endorsed by the political class; Sidehara himself recommended him. But it was difficult for him to form his government, since the SCAP crossed out several names, then purged four ministers in the coming months. Yoshida had to face the economic disaster on his own, as the USA refused to help. While production collapsed, the Sidehara government had flooded the country with currency. For months, under the SCAP's nose, it paid vast sums to the big firms on overdue invoices for arms manufacture and as compensation for destroyed facilities. The money supply was swollen beyond measure and prices multiplied ten times between August 1945 and January 1946. The new Minister of Finance, Tanzan Ishibashi, continued this massive injection of public funds. His policy choice was both political and economic; the idea was to save the Japanese productive apparatus which the Americans, so he thought, wanted to dismantle so as to reduce Japan to a country of light industry – this was the time when dismantled factories were being shipped abroad as war reparations

SHIGERU YOSHIDA (1878–1967)

Born in Yokohama, Yoshida was the fifth son of a former samurai of Tôsa who had a political career in the Jiyutô and business activity in Korea under Japanese colonial rule. Born outside marriage, he was adopted by a friend of his father, also a former samurai, who went on to work for the British firm Jardine Matheson. After attending the School for Peers and the Imperial University of Tokyo, he started working for the Foreign Ministry in 1906. He married the daughter of Count Makino, son of a hero of the Meiji Restoration, and one of Hirohito's close advisers from 1920. Thus he gained access to the innermost circle in the palace.

Following his father-in-law, he identified himself with the moderate clan, supporting a foreign policy negotiated with the English-speaking powers. Posted to London in 1908–9, 1920–2 and 1935–8, he cultivated contacts who also included James C. Grew, American ambassador in Tokyo from 1932 to 1941. Reputed to be an Anglophile, he was rejected by the army for appointment as Foreign Minister in the Hirota cabinet in 1936. But in the posts he held in Manchuria, Korea and China (especially between 1920 and 1925) he defended a policy of determined and ruthless expansion of Japanese interests.

He opposed the idea of war against the United States, and was active from 1942 in the 'Peace Faction' organised around certain of Hirohito's advisers, including his father-in-law and Prince Konoe. In April 1945, after publication of a memorandum by Konoe in favour of peace, he was imprisoned for two months. As Minister of Foreign Affairs in the Higashikumi and Sidehara cabinets, it was he who organised the meeting on 27 September 1945 which sealed the 'alliance' between the Emperor and MacArthur. He joined Ichirô Hatoyama's Liberal Party. When Hatoyama was purged soon after his election victory in May 1946, the palace and the conservative élite naturally turned to Yoshida. He became Prime Minister at the age of 67.

Brutal towards the Left and the trade unions, stubborn and skilful towards the Americans, he was to run the country for seven years and two months, with an uncompromising determination to defend the national interest, of which he had a resolutely conservative idea. The return of the purged politicians was to be fatal to him (see pp. 81–4). He fell from power in December 1954. But it was essentially politicians groomed by him – the so-called 'Yoshida school' (*Yoshida gakkô*) – who were to lead Japan until the 1980s.

and the big corporations split up. Ishibashi and the Minister of Industry wanted to overtake the SCAP by getting heavy industry going again whatever the cost. An Economic Stabilisation Office was given full powers to allocate raw materials and fix prices. A Reconstruction Bank distributed subsidies wildly to the three priority industries: coal, steel and chemical fertiliser. State expenditure for 1946, estimated at 56 billion yen, rose to double that figure at the end of the budget year, entirely financed by printing of money. The resulting catastrophic inflation worsened the destitution, the black market and the social unrest. A furious MacArthur purged Ishibashi and, five days after being forced to intervene to stop the general strike called for 1 February 1947, he ordered Yoshida to organise new elections.

The 1947 elections and the Socialist-Conservative coalitions

The new situation was more favourable to the Left. Within a year the trade unions and the Peasants' Union had been organised. The extension of the purges to the local level and the dissolution of the neighbourhood associations disrupted the conservative electoral networks. To oppose the trend Yoshida restored the pre-war electoral system, which made Japan a rather 'uncommon democracy'. Medium-sized districts were allocated three, four or five seats each. These seats were to be filled in a single round by single non-transferable voting. The voter cast his or her vote for only one candidate, and the winner was decided on the 'first past the post' principle. No possibility whatever existed for candidates belonging to the same party to transfer excess votes from one to another. Therefore each candidate was obliged to 'fend for himself' even against those of the same party. This electoral free-for-all favoured well-known personalities and those with the richest *kaban* (war chests); it brought clientelism and corrupt practices – characteristic of Japanese elections since the beginning – into full operation. But it also allowed small parties to enter the field and survive, since it was possible to win the last seat in many constituencies with the support of no more than 10 per cent of the registered voters. With all its merits and demerits, this system was to remain in force until 1994.

On 25 April the JSP won 143 seats compared with 121 for the Liberal Party and 131 for the Democratic Party (the former

Progressive Party) now headed by Itoshi Ashida. The Cooperative Party headed by Takeo Miki, a veteran of pre-war Diets, won 29 seats. The JCP remained insignificant with four. The JSP was in the lead, but it had only won 26.6 per cent of the votes, and the House remained solidly conservative. In the local elections held at the same time the conservatives won 90 per cent of the seats. The Socialists were only able to gain entry into four of the 46 prefecture assemblies, and of the 46 governors elected, 27 were incumbents appointed by the military. In such conditions taking power was a risky gamble for the JSP. But its Chairman Tetsu Katayama, a moderate Christian intellectual and former professor at Tokyo University, decided against the will of his left wing to play to its conclusion the democratic game giving the strongest party the responsibility for forming a government. He proposed a coalition of national unity; Yoshida refused, but Ashida and Miki agreed on condition that the left-wing Socialists were excluded from the cabinet. Katayama formed a cabinet with six Socialists in key positions (Industry, Trade, Agriculture, the Economic Stabilisation Office, Education and Justice) alongside nine conservative ministers.

The Katayama cabinet was brought down in ten months by the economic problems. The wage and price freeze announced with great publicity was a failure, dramatically underlined by the tragic fate of a Tokyo magistrate who allowed himself to die from starvation through trying, out of honesty, to live from his salary alone without resorting to the black market. It was impossible to stop the massive subsidies to industry without causing an explosion of unemployment. Nationalisation of coal, included in the JSP's programme, was rejected by the House which agreed only to a temporary law (repealed in 1950). The money supply ran out of control: 116 billion yen in April 1947, 218 billion a year later. Rigorous deflationary measures were needed, but the party's left wing refused to vote for the budgetary measures required, especially a limit to civil service pay. Already weakened by the defection of the agrarian faction, following the purging of its leader Hirano, Katayama resigned on 10 March 1948 (the fiscal year in Japan begins on 1 April and the budget debate is in February and March).

A second coalition government took over, headed by the conservative Ashida. Once the Cold War had started, Washington decided to aid Japan under the GARIOA (Government Assistance for Reconstruction in Occupied Areas) programme. But it demanded a rigorous economic policy and deflationary measures which implied bringing the trade unions to heel. When the SCAP imposed suppression of almost all trade union rights for government employees (see p. 61), the Socialist ministers' position became untenable. The final blow to Ashida's cabinet was the scandal of Shôwa Denko, a chemicals firm which had paid bribes to the Reconstruction Bank and politicians to obtain credits. This affair, a commonplace one, was denounced by the SCAP which wanted to open the way for a homogeneous and vigorous conservative government. The Director of the Stabilisation Office and the Budget Director at the Finance Ministry, Takeo Fukuda, were arrested. Ashida, abandoned by 36 House members who crossed over to join Yoshida, was implicated in his turn. He resigned on 15 October 1948. Ashida was later charged but not sentenced; as for Takeo Fukuda, who was elected deputy in 1952, the charges against him were eventually dropped and he went on to become Prime Minister (1977–8).

Yoshida's triumphs (1948–52)

The January 1949 elections produced a monolithic majority. Yoshida's Liberal Party won 264 seats. The Democrats were reduced to 69; they disbanded, one section joining the government side while the other joined Takeo Miki's cooperatives to form the Progressive Party. The JSP collapsed, losing 95 seats to win only 48. The JCP benefited from this and won 35 seats through a prudent campaign based on support for the reforms and for democratisation. In January 1950, however, Moscow condemned its Chairman, Sanzô Nosaka, had him removed and forced the party to adopt a strategy of open confrontation with the SCAP. MacArthur and Yoshida replied with 'red purges' which wiped out the Sanbetsu, exclusion from public life of the whole Central Committee of the party, and the banning of its newspaper Akahata (The Red Flag). Police machinations caused the Communists to be held responsible for the suicide of the Chairman of Japan National Railways and two fatal derailments on suburban lines in Tokyo in July 1950. The JCP was reduced to semi-clandestine existence, although it remained legal. Part of its leadership fled to China, and the party held no more congresses until 1958. In the 1952 elections it did not win a single seat, then no more than one or two; its eclipse was to last fifteen years. Now rid of all parliamentary opposition, Yoshida was also given a free hand by the Americans. Washington wanted only to strengthen the Japanese government, and MacArthur had his hands full with running the Korean War (the SCAP covered both Japan and Korea) until he was dismissed in April 1951 for advocating the use of atomic weapons. His successor, General Ridgway, did not have his calibre. Yoshida was authoritarian and sure of himself, and governed without concern for public opinion or the Diet. He groomed a new generation of politicians, most of them coming from the ranks of the bureaucracy: Hayato Ikeda, Eisaku Satô (Nobusuke Kishi's brother), Masayoshi Ohira, Yasuhiro Nakasone. These graduates of the 'Yoshida School' (*Yoshida gakkô*) were to provide Japan with most of its prime ministers up to Nakasone (1982–87).

Yoshida succeeded in reviving the economy. First of all he smashed inflation through the plan imposed by the mission under the banker Joseph M. Dodge (February-March 1949). Subsidies from the Reconstruction Bank were suspended; the state budget was balanced at the cost of grim cuts in the civil service. The economy was opened up to international competition again by the fixing of a unified exchange rate (360 yen to the dollar) and legislation favourable to foreign investment. But the social cost was heavy: more than 700,000 redundancies and the breaking of the most militant trade unions. Tens of thousands of small and medium enterprises went bankrupt. GARIOA aid given by Washington in return amounted to $2 billion, but this was only half the amount given to Germany, a less populous country. Inflation was halted and the black market finally disappeared, but at the beginning of 1950 the economy was in crisis and stocks were accumulating. The Korean War which broke out then provided a huge windfall. From June 1950 to July 1953 it caused nearly two million deaths, but it brought orders worth a billion dollars to Japanese businesses, plus an even larger amount spent in Japan by GIs in transit or on leave. In October 1950 industrial production returned to its pre-war level. In the first year of the war exports doubled, steel production trebled and foreign exchange reserves quadrupled. Unemployment and social tension were brought down. The Korean boom marked the start of Japan's economic resurrection.

At the same time, Japan made its first steps in rearmament. From the onset of the Cold War the Americans bitterly regretted the inclusion of Article 9 in the Constitution. As soon as November 1948 they suggested that the text outlawed 'the use of force as a means of settlement of international disputes' but not to defend the country's territory against an aggressor, and the SCAP proposed the creation of a paramilitary force. In his 1950 New Year message MacArthur declared that Japan had the right of self-defence as recognised by the UN Charter for all states. When John Foster Dulles arrived in Tokyo in June 1950 to negotiate the peace treaty intended to end the Occupation, he pressed the Japanese government to rearm on a massive scale. Yoshida refused. Was it from fear of the Soviet Union, or of an explosion of unrest in Japan? Or from a desire to devote all his resources to reconstruction, leaving the cost of the country's defence to the Americans? He only agreed to the formation of a National Police Reserve of 75,000 men, equipped with tanks and artillery. For the needs of this force a thousand trustworthy officers were restored to favour from the ranks of the purged, under the supervision of General Arisue, former Director of Military Intelligence. This was the embryo of the present Japanese army, called the Self Defence Forces (*Jieitai*). Meanwhile, ex-officers formed secret societies which assumed the mission of combating Communism by infiltrating that new army and restoring traditional values.

THE END OF THE OCCUPATION

The Treaty of San Francisco and the US Security Treaty

In 1947 Washington asked the Far East Commission to study the terms of a peace treaty with Japan. But there were insurmountable differences with the USSR, which demanded very harsh conditions including the stationing of its troops in Japan. In 1949 the USA decided to open bilateral negotiations. They were conducted over fifteen months between Yoshida and the US Secretary of State, John Foster Dulles. The Americans needed a solid Japan accepting their military bases. Yoshida made use of this to secure agreement that the reforms and the condemnation of war criminals should not be made permanent by the treaty, and that any war reparations should be negotiated later between Tokyo and its neighbours. To satisfy him, Washington also rejected France's compensation requests and those from Britain, which wanted to impose very strict economic provisions. The territorial problems were complicated. They concerned the Bônin and Ryûkyû Islands (Okinawa) annexed to Japan in 1879; several islets taken from Korea; the Kurile Islands and southern Sakhalin, disputed with Russia since the nineteenth century; the Spratly and Paracel Islands off the coasts of Indochina; and the former German territories in the Pacific (the Mariana, Caroline and Marshall Islands) which had been assigned to Japan under League of Nations Mandate in 1919.

The San Francisco Peace Treaty was signed on 8 September 1951. Of the 56 countries invited three did not come (India, Burma and Yugoslavia) and three refused to sign (the USSR, Poland and Czechoslovakia). There were two major absentees: Korea, in the midst of war, and China – because Washington refused to invite Beijing while most other countries did not recognise Taiwan. The territorial questions were badly settled. The Bônin islands and Okinawa were placed by the UN under American administration without being legally taken away from Japan. Tokyo renounced claims to Sakhalin and the 'Kurile archipelago', but the text did not specify whether the four southerly islets occupied by the USSR in the last days of the war were a part of it. Japan also renounced claim to three Korean islets, but the two Tokdo islets which it had annexed in 1905 were forgotten. It also gave up the Spratlys and Paracels, but the Treaty did not assign them either to China or to any of the countries bordering the South China Sea, which claimed a part or a whole of those archipelagos. Under the heading of reparations, Japan abandoned all the property that it had left in the occupied countries; for the rest, any matters were to be settled by bilateral negotiations. The Treaty recognised that Japan had 'the natural right to self-defence, individual and collective'. Thus it endorsed the loose interpretation of Article 9 and allowed Tokyo to sign collective security agreements. No sooner said than done! The Japanese-American Security Treaty was signed the same day. A fundamentally unequal treaty, it allowed the USA the use of several bases; Washington could use them, without consulting Tokyo, to intervene all over the Far East, and bring any kind of weapons into them – meaning nuclear weapons. The American army reserved the right to intervene in Japan itself 'in case of disturbances incompatible with its status as a sovereign state' – meaning Communist agitation. Tokyo was to provide necessary land for the bases and contribute to their maintenance. It could not denounce the treaty, nor sign other defence agreements. The United States did not even formally commit itself in return to defending Japan if it were attacked.

In Japan the two treaties set off fierce debate. Nationalists criticised Yoshida for making the country a satellite of the United States. The business world regretted being cut off from the Chinese market and hoped that the government would keep its options open concerning Beijing. The Communists and the majority of the JSP rejected both the principle of a separate peace placing Japan in the Western camp and the American military presence which violated Article 9. They called for Japan to be a neutral country, completely disarmed and protected by its official pacifism and non-alignment. They were followed by all those who feared a return to militarist ways, especially the intelligentsia. A National Peace Conference brought together academics, Buddhists and Christians alongside the JSP and the Sôhyô trade unionists to campaign against the two treaties. But the JSP's right wing, led by Suehiro Nishio, accepted the Peace Treaty while rejecting the Security Treaty; it split off in October 1951, and later, after a temporary reconciliation (1955–9), was to give birth to the Democratic Socialist Party (Minshatô). In spite of the controversy, the Peace Treaty was supported by 80 per cent in opinion polls. But the public was more uneasy about the Security Treaty, of which 30 per cent of Japanese disapproved openly.

Unresolved problems: Korea and China

China and Korea were absent from San Francisco. Washington however tried to normalise relations between Seoul, Taipei and Tokyo, to strengthen the anti-Communist front in Asia; but the Japanese government intended to avoid letting its hands be tied.

History left a legacy of deep-seated hatred between Korea and Japan. Korea had been harassed by Japanese pirates in the thirteenth and fourteenth centuries, invaded in 1592–7, subjugated from 1876 onwards and annexed in 1910. Under Japanese rule the national language was outlawed, peasants were dispossessed for the benefit of Japanese settlers, men recruited forcibly into the imperial army or deported to the mines and factories of Japan, girls sent all over Asia as 'comfort women' in the Japanese military brothels. Washington brought the two countries face to face in October 1951, but the negotiations broke down over the delimitation of territorial waters, the Tokdo islets, and the status of about 650,000 Koreans, many of whom had settled in Japan in the 1930s and did not want to go back to their war-torn country; the SCAP allowed them to stay with permanent resident status, to the great annoyance of the Japanese authorities. Talks broke up after six months and the two countries remained without official relations.

Relations with China were impassioned and ambiguous. Japanese culture had been enriched by contributions from China since the Yamato era. Since the Meiji Restoration China had been fascinated by Japan's success in the face of the West, and many revolutionaries had been trained there, starting with Sun Yat-sen who was venerated by Beijing as much as by Taipei. The Cold War anchored the two countries in opposed camps (China signed a Treaty of Alliance with the USSR in 1950), but neither presented a direct threat to the other. Trade between them never stopped and even in 1946, when its soldiers had only just left China, Japan exported goods worth 500 million yen there. But while Yoshida did not want to burn his bridges with Beijing, Washington demanded that he should recognise Nationalist China and threatened not to ratify the San Francisco Treaty until then. Tokyo had to give in and signed a peace treaty with Chiang Kai-shek on the very day of the end of the Occupation. Japan recognised the Taipei regime, which renounced all war reparations. But Yoshida got himself an escape route by explaining, in a public letter to Dulles, that Japan 'wishes to establish complete peaceful and commercial relations with China' and that the treaty signed with Taipei 'will be applicable to all the territories that are currently under its control' – which was a way of not committing himself regarding mainland China under Communist control.

JAPAN AFTER THE OCCUPATION

Japan recovered its independence on 28 April 1952 after ratification of the treaties. Six years and nine months of Occupation had changed it profoundly – too profoundly, the conservative élite thought. For the first time Japan found itself compulsorily included in the international game, on the Western side; the Left was fiercely against this. It was around those two themes that political confrontation was to crystallise in the ensuing period. The Japanese had just come through a time of unprecedented trauma. For the first time their country had known defeat. The certainty of Japanese superiority, a fundamental tenet of the national ideology, had been smashed to pieces. The whole *kokutai* system of values had been abruptly brought crashing down; denounced as archaic and oppressive, it had to give way to modern, democratic values imposed by foreign occupation.

Facing itself: the shattered image

The years of misery following the war destroyed the image of the nation as a family. Amid the ruins it was everyone for himself; people stole and bought and sold everything in order to survive. Peasants made starving city dwellers hand over their last family possessions for a bit of rice. Workers who were lucky enough to have permanent jobs excluded temporary workers from the unions. Around Hiroshima survivors of the bomb were driven away by villagers like bearers of plague. The *yakuza* underworld, confined until then to specific activities (mostly gambling and street trading), took advantage of the disruption and became a daily scourge. Gangs dealt in philopon, an ersatz cocaine spread by the GIs, and took over prostitution after it was banned. They subjected petty trade to protection rackets, and hired out their services for strike-breaking or to clear a space in ruined districts for the benefit of property speculators. But many respectable firms also hoarded basic necessities and devastated land. The brutality of political and social conflicts provided final proof that the *kazoku-kokka* much vaunted by the imperial ideology was just a myth. After frugality a long repressed zest for life broke out. Prostitution, strip-tease, gambling and dancing halls did a roaring trade. People jostled for entry to baseball matches, already very widespread before the war, and the cinema, which became the number one popular entertainment. 'Love-hotels' proliferated to offer couples a haven in spite of the housing crisis, and twelve million births in the five immediate post-war years were proof of the refound desire for life. This appetite for pleasure and consumption, rather contrary to the 'samurai spirit', was to be a major element in the economic recovery in the ensuing period, as much as the vaunted eagerness to work and save.

Facing freedom: a burst of creativity

Literature blossomed. While the great classical writers, Yasunari Kawabata (born 1899) and Junichiro Tanizaki (born 1886), went through a relatively fallow period amid the chaos, the young Yukio Mishima (born 1925), already famous and scandalous, found in that chaos an echo of his own tormented personality; he published in quick succession *Confessions of a Mask* (1949) and *Thirst for Love* (1950) in a satirical and popular vein. Jun Ishikawa and Masuji Ibuse (*The Clinic is Closed Today*, 1949) depicted the difficult daily existence of the small people of the cities. Osamu Dazai, who committed suicide at the age 39 leaving *No Longer Human* as his last work of a three-year career (1948), symbolised the disarray of the time. But this was above all the time of the heirs to the 'proletarian literature' which had been hounded by the pre-war censorship. The Communist Yuriko Miyamoto drew upon her own life to describe the transformation of a bourgeois girl into a militant in a long saga started in 1924 (*Nobuko*) and continued until her death in 1951; while Hiroshi Noma depicted the wretchedness of the bombed cities (*Dark Painting*, 1946) and the savage discipline of the imperial army (*Zone of Emptiness*, 1952).

The press became one of the pillars of the nation. In the 1930s the major dailies already had circulations of two or three million. The disappearance of all familiar landmarks and all traditional authority made the press the only compass for the public to find its directions. In 1946 there were 56 dailies published. It was no accident that the first major confrontation among trade unions, conservatives and the SCAP was over control of *Yomiuri, Asahi* and *Mainichi*. National debates over the emperor or the civil code were echoed with wide liberty of expression, often with calls for readers' opinions. Public opinion polls became the rage, but they were scarcely reliable, since the people questioned looked first of all for the 'right answer' in accordance with fashionable ideas – a failing that has still not disappeared even today. Journalists tended to misuse their new power. They assumed the right to give lessons on everything, and use this as authority to invade privacy – so much that one Akira Kurosawa film (*Scandal*) denounced those excesses in 1950.

The greatest liberty was found in the cinema. Before the war there were already three production enterprises (Nikkatsu, Tôhô and Daiei) and talented directors such as Kenji Mizoguchi and Yasujiro Ozu, both active from the late 1920s onwards. The industry blossomed from 1946. Film producers provided the best reflection of a society in the midst of revolution. They showed gangs of orphans wandering among the ruins, hunger (Yoshimura's *The Fellows Who Ate the Elephant*, 1947), the prolifer-ation of gangsters (Kurosawa's *Drunken Angel*, 1948) and prostitu-tion (Mizoguchi's *Women of the Night*, 1948). The first screen kiss was filmed in 1946. Many films denounced the oppression of wives in marriage (Mikio Naruse's *Repast*, 1951) and women's cruel fate in Japan's history (Mizoguchi's *The Life of Oharu*, 1952), or else depicted the breaking up of the traditional couple when confronted with new reality (Ozu's *Early Summer*, 1951). The responsibility of each person for his acts, the cornerstone of the Western system of values, was examined by Kurosawa in *Stray Dog* (1949) and *The Idiot* (1951). But in the face of a world crumbling around them, others took refuge in melancholy resignation, like Ozu's characters, or in the idea that all reality is just a point of view (Kurosawa's *Rashômon*, 1950). Only the war was – because of cen-sorship – not tackled head-on by any major film.

Facing the past: towards self-absolution

The collective unconscious of the Japanese made itself feel more or less at ease about the war by forging the so-called 'victim's mentality' *(igaisha isshiki)*. The press hid nothing of the horrors committed by the imperial army; the whole country condemned them unanimously. But an 'official truth', analogous to that which made it possible to clear the Emperor, soon appeared: the nation had been deceived by a handful of irresponsible extremists. Those people were vilified, starting with Tôjô, who did not even know how to die with dignity – he chose a pistol rather than the *seppuku*, and missed. But unlike the Germans, the Japanese had never brought the extremists to power through elections. In Japan itself there were never any horrors like those of the concentration camps in which the general population could feel that it had been an accomplice. Everything happened abroad, in the heat of battle – or at least it was thought so. The Japanese could thus consider that they hardly had any responsibility and that they had already paid in full by the destruction of their cities, especially by the atomic bombing that had been reserved for Japan alone. From that viewpoint Hiroshima and Nagasaki were a real godsend for the collective unconscious: there was absolution through nuclear destruction, and this provided a solid basis for the 'victim's mentality'. Characteristically, the films dealing with the war during this period were either 'weepie' melodramas where fate separates young lovers (Tadashi Imai's *Until the Day We Meet Again*, 1950) or touching idylls of Japanese officers and Chinese girls (*Escape at Dawn*, scenario by Kurosawa, 1950). Even so, there remained sincere detestation for the war and the army. It was especially deep-rooted among women, for they – unlike men who could feel a certain pride in having taken part in the epic of 'Greater Japan' – had only the grim memory of bombing and starving children. But very soon fascination for warlike exploits reappeared also. In 1950 Colonel Masanobu Tsuji, who had distinguished himself in the 'Death March' in the Philippines, emerged as a hero from the Burmese jungle where he had hidden to escape the punishment of war criminals. The account of his adventures was an instant bestseller. The Americans themselves contributed to this rehabilitation by de-purging and re-employing imperial officers for the National Police Reserve.

Facing the United States

The defeat and the Occupation created a complex and passionate relationship between Japan and its conqueror. There was inevitably resentment against the conqueror, and anti-Americanism was found as much on the right, where the corruption of traditional values was denounced, as on the left. But the ultra-nationalists themselves had to admit that only the United States protected Japan against Communism, while the Socialists had to admit that it had brought them freedom and social reforms. Among the population resentment was eclipsed by real admiration and recognition. The Japanese had expected a barbarian occupation; the military had promised that there would be wholesale rape and plunder if they let themselves be defeated. The disciplined kindliness of (most of) the victors was a miraculous surprise. Suddenly, everything American came to embody strength and progress. The tall blond GI became the girls' ideal. The Japanese language was filled with terms such as *pureboy* (playboy), *garu-furendo* (girl friend), *apâtô* (apartment) and, of course, *demokurashii*. The urban youth enthusiastically adopted baseball, jazz, Coca-Cola and kissing on the mouth. Japanese culture was never to shake off this American hold.

To the Americans farmers owed land, the Left owed democracy, conservatives owed power, the nation owed peace. The economic revival remained dependent on their goodwill, for they agreed to open their markets to Japan's exports while allowing it to protect its own. The United States was a protective big brother and MacArthur a venerated founding father. When he was recalled, Yoshida called him a 'wonder of History' before the Diet, the Emperor went out to greet him, and 250,000 Japanese lined the streets and shouted out thanks to him as far as the airport. The United States was to remain for long the country most loved by Japanese, the one in which they expressed most confidence in all opinion polls. Although it gradually decreased, the psychological dependence which resulted from this was not the least important legacy of the period which ended on 28 April 1952. It was only to end, partially, at the end of the 1980s, with the emergence of Japanese neo-nationalism on one side of the Pacific and of an American 'revisionist school' of Japan-bashers on the other.

3

LAYING THE FOUNDATIONS OF THE MIRACLE (1952–62)

POLITICS: FROM CONFRONTATION TO STABILISATION

No sooner had the Americans gone than demonstrations on May Day 1952 led to one person being killed and 1,400 injured. Yoshida introduced a law and order maintenance bill, but the JSP paralysed the Diet for 79 days before it was adopted (and the legal system did not dare to use it before 1974). This set the tone for a period of violent clashes – in the course of which, however, Japan's democracy gradually built up its structures.

Confrontation among conservatives – Yoshida vs. the Old Guard

As soon as they had been rehabilitated, purged politicians sought to retake the seats from which they had been removed by the SCAP. Public opinion expected Yoshida to respect his duty as a younger person (kôhai) under an obligation towards his elder and master (sampai), and give way to Ichirô Hatoyama. But he refused to do so, and sought to beat the old guard to it by calling a snap election in October 1952. His Liberal Party kept its absolute majority but lost 45 seats. The Reform Party (the former Progressive Party), under its new Chairman Mamoru Shigemitsu – a former member of militarist cabinets – made some progress. Despite their divisions the Socialists took advantage of the disappearance of the JCP and increased their strength from 48 to 111 seats, with 21.3 per cent of the vote. But the real danger for Yoshida came from the 124 purge survivors who got their old seats back. Whether they were Liberal or of the Reform Party, their aim was to remove him from power so as to get it back themselves. In November a no-confidence motion was passed against his right-hand man, the Finance Minister Hayato Ikeda, who had to resign.

In February 1953 Yoshida called a JSP deputy a 'fool' (*bakayaro*). A motion of censure was passed against him and he dissolved the House again.

The conservatives were now divided between the Liberals loyal to Yoshida, Hatoyama's Liberals who broke away to form the Japanese Liberal Party, and the Reform Party. Altogether they won 310 seats, while the Socialists won 138. Yoshida's supporters lost their absolute majority but they remained the most numerous, which meant that he could form a government again. But his days were numbered. The old guard leaders who had remained in the Liberal Party – Nobusuke Kishi and Tanzan Ishibashi – undermined him from within the party. Backed by the big employers' organisations concerned about instability, they launched the idea of a new conservative group advocating popular measures: more independence in foreign policy through conclusion of a peace treaty with the USSR, 'rationalisation' of the economy in depression since the end of the Korean War, a struggle against the 'excesses' provoked by liberal reforms (amoral life among the young, undermining of the traditional family), and protection of small businesses. Here can be discerned some of the favourite themes of the militarists and their allies the young 'anti-Zaibatsu' technocrats of the Kishi group. The shipyards scandal was the final blow to Yoshida. This was another case of bribes paid to politicians in return for subsidies, and the investigation implicated Yoshida's most faithful lieutenants, Hayato Ikeda and Eisaku Satô. He saved them by resorting to a procedure that allowed the Ministry of Justice to order a halt to the prosecution. Ikeda and Satô were later to be Prime Ministers, in 1960–4 and 1964–72 respectively, but public anger mounted against Yoshida.

The new conservative party was established in November 1954 under the name of the Democratic Party. Ichirô Hatoyama was its Chairman. 125 House members joined it; 185 remained loyal to Yoshida, but the Democrats reached an understanding with the Socialists who agreed with some of their aims, such as a peace treaty with the USSR. The JSP voted for a motion of censure in return for a promise by the Democrats to hold early elections, which it expected to bring it a few more seats, like those held in 1952 and 1953. Yoshida resigned, and Hatoyama replaced him on 7 December 1954. After seven years and two months in power, the man who presided over Japan's reconstruction retired to his

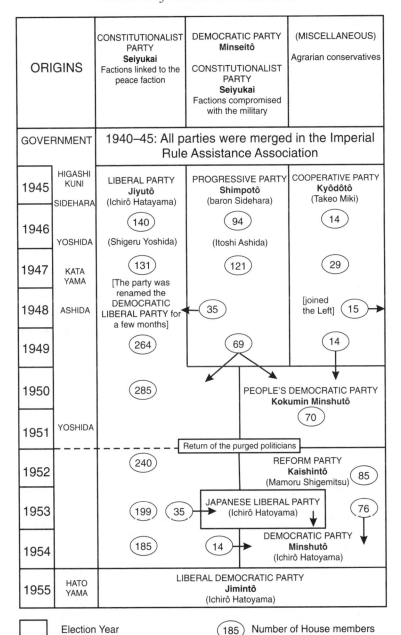

Fig. 3.1. THE JAPANESE CONSERVATIVE PARTIES, 1945–55

country house. Until his death in 1967 he remained a venerated master and a very powerful adviser behind the scenes. In essentials the generation trained by Yoshida was to rule the country from 1960 to 1987. But it was the old guard who returned to power immediately after him.

Stabilisation: the birth of the Liberal Democratic Party

The elections of February 1955 blocked the way to possible amendment of the Constitution. As agreed with the JSP, Hatoyama had dissolved the Lower House. The Democrats (185 seats) emerged much stronger than the Liberal Party, now without its leader (112). But the Socialists – just as they hoped – increased their share of the vote to 29.2 per cent and won 156 seats. This increase was decisive because it gave them a blocking third of the seats in the House, preventing the constitutional amendment of which the conservatives dreamed. From then on the conservatives were never to succeed in depriving them of the blocking third, until the JSP all but disappeared in 1996. The Socialists completed their victory by taking a third of the seats in the Upper House from 1959 onwards.

In the euphoria of this success, the Socialist right and left wings, separated since 1951, were reunited. The JSP was thus on the way to becoming the leading party in Japan again, if the conservatives remained divided. To prevent that happening, Japanese big business and Washington joined hands to persuade the conservative politicians to unify. The main employers' organisation, the Keidanren, decided to centralise all business political contributions through the medium of a single organisation, the Forum for Reconstruction (Kantankai), which made it clear that it would not fund anybody opposed to unification. The American CIA enrolled Kishi, who knew the Japanese conservative political world best, and provided him with abundant funds to convince the conservative Diet members to forget their past enmity. Yoshio Kodama and Ryoichi Sasakawa, two powerful *kuromaku* ('puppeteers' operating at the interface of political élites, businessmen, violent ultranationalist groups and the Mafia) also played their part in the process that led to the birth of the Liberal Democratic Party (LDP) in November 1955.

The creation of the new party made it possible for the conservatives always to present a united front in the Diet from then on. Their rivalries were to be settled within the confines of the party, whose rules, written or informal, were to govern the choice of the prime minister (who was always the Chairman of the LDP, elected at its biannual congress), the naming of candidates for elections, and the allocation of portfolios. Unity was to be maintained until 1993, except for the minor breakaway of the New Liberal Club (1976–86).

The two camps settled down to an ambiguous relationship. The Liberal Democratic Party and the Socialist Party had marked class characteristics (see pp. 142 and 145) and radical ideological differences concerning Japan's alignment in the Western camp and the problem of rearmament. In the Diet there were violent verbal and physical clashes; the police had to expel Socialist members and their secretaries who tried to prevent sessions from proceeding, in the voting on the law placing the police under centralised control again (1954) and the law abolishing elections for local education commissions (1956). The JSP, repeatedly overwhelmed in the House, turned to the Sôhyô, which called strikes and demonstrations against those laws and against the American bases. However, there were points of convergence. Both camps favoured normalising of relations with the USSR and the resumption of trade with China. The LDP carried out a part of the Socialist programme by gradually improving social welfare provisions, and the JSP could only approve of the LDP's numerous measures to help farmers and small shopkeepers and craftsmen. The LDP established a tradition of seeking consensus with the Socialists, and in June 1956 Hatoyama decided not to force through an electoral reform which could have caused fatal harm to them by creating single-seat constituencies.

Hatoyama retired after normalising relations with the Soviet Union. The agreement reached in October 1956 after sixteen months of very difficult negotiations was not a peace treaty; but the USSR stopped opposing Japan's entry to the United Nations, which took place on 18 December. Straight afterwards Hatoyama resigned, suffering from cancer. The main leaders of the old guard died in 1955–6; only Tanzan Ishibashi remained. He very narrowly defeated Kishi at the LDP Congress and succeeded Hatoyama. However, he too was so ill that he had to hand over to his rival after five weeks. On 23 February 1957, less than five years after the end of the Occupation, a former war criminal became Prime Minister of Japan.

National confrontation: the Kishi government and the 'Reverse Course' (1957–60)

Kishi remained in power for three years and four months. After that, in accordance with the LDP's informal rules, he never exercised government functions again but just had the title of 'adviser to the party' (*Jimintô kômon*). However, he sat in the House until 1983 and remained the mentor of all the reactionary wing of the party until his death in 1987.

The objectives of the right wing in the LDP and in the Japanese bureaucracy have hardly changed to this day. Constitutional amendment was sought to remove its most democratic aspects, to balance the list of citizen's rights with a list of duties, to abrogate Article 9 and to declare the Emperor head of state. If constitutional amendment were not possible, the idea was to whittle away in detail at local and trade union liberties and freedom of expression. Restoration of traditional Japan's values and symbols aimed to make the Emperor an object of almost religious reverence again; to give official status again to the Rising Sun flag and the *Kimigayo* anthem, both banned by the SCAP; to replace the Western calendar with the traditional system of imperial eras, re-establish moral teaching at schools, and give Shintoism a privileged position again. To wipe away the feeling of guilt arising from the war and restore national pride, the right wing considered it necessary to rewrite school textbooks, justifying Japanese expansion and minimising the attendant atrocities. Re-militarisation of Japan would proceed by broadening as far as possible the interpretation of 'self-defence'. A more active policy towards Asia and even towards the Communist neighbours was intended to bring in a counterbalance to the relationship of dependence on the USA, but without calling the precious Security Treaty into question. Lastly, a policy of state control over the economy was proposed, together with a social policy favouring the traditional popular electorate (farmers and shopkeepers); this showed the influence of the faction of young nationalist technocrats inspired by Kishi in the 1930s.

This right-wing tendency was powerful in the administration, which had been completely spared by the purges. It could count on the ultra-nationalist groups that were openly re-emerging and were traditionally linked to the powerful *yakuza* Mafia (see p. 97). But in the LDP the Right coexisted with a liberal, modernising wing favouring the big business enterprises, hostile to military spending and constitutional amendment; this was represented by the direct heirs of Yoshida, Ikeda and Satô. Another faction, typified by Takeo Miki and Ichirô Kôno, expressed popular rural feeling that was pacifist and favoured strict control over the world of business. One or the other tendency was to prevail in accordance with the changing situation, but the need to maintain the unity of the LDP forced them into a permanent compromise.

From the moment he took power, Kishi proclaimed a 'Reverse Course' (*Gyaku Kôsu*) and launched attacks on all fronts without fear of provoking confrontation with the opposition. But his increasing harshness was eventually to threaten national unity and provoke his downfall.

Trade union freedoms were curbed again. The last right still held by civil servants, the right to join a union, was abolished for some categories. The provision for retaining trade union dues at source was outlawed (but nevertheless remained in use in most big enterprises for 'lifetime' employees). Japan refused to ratify the International Labour Organisation convention on trade union freedoms; it went so far that even the highly anti-Communist ICFTU protested officially to Tokyo. The unions, however, exhibited great fighting strength. From 1952 the Sôhyô launched numerous strikes against reactionary bills. In 1959–60 the Socialist trade union body was able to bring in the other three (the Shinsanbetsu, Zenrô and Chûritsukai) and mobilise up to five million workers for general strikes in support of political demands. There were also hard-fought battles in the factories. Strike pickets clashed brutally with the police at the Oji paper works in September 1957. In January 1960 a plan for staff cutbacks set off a strike at the Mitsui coal mines at Miike in Kyûshû; this degenerated into the longest and most violent conflict in post-war history. Police from all over Japan were sent to Miike for tours of duty, while Sôhyô did the same with its militants during eleven months of clashes.

Resumption of control over the education system started in 1956 when governors and mayors were given the right to appoint local education commissions. Teachers were forbidden to take part in any political activity. Early in 1958 Kishi established a system of grading of teachers and reintroduced the teaching of the old Japanese mythology as well as 'ethics courses' centring around traditional values. The Teachers' Federation (Nikkyôsô) demonstrated all over Japan and defied the ban on strike action. The government strove to mobilise parents by blaming teachers for the mis-functioning of the education system caused by the Occupation reforms (overcrowded classrooms, uncertainty about programmes, etc.) and for the moral crisis of young people brought up during the years of defeat and ruin. The far Right and the *yakuza* attacked Nikkyôsô demonstrations (65 injured in August 1958 at Wakayama), and the federation's President was seriously hurt.

The strengthening of state power began with the law on maintenance of order in 1952 and the return to centralisation of the police in 1956. Kishi attacked local self-government. He abolished election of district mayors in Tokyo and sought to regroup regions under the control of appointed super-prefects, as in the military era; he failed in that, but he re-established the Ministry of the Interior in 1960 under the name of the Ministry of Local Autonomy (Jichirô). In 1958 he introduced a bill to allow any policeman to enter private property without a warrant to prevent 'an act which could constitute a danger to public order'; to oppose on his own authority an action that was not illegal (a demonstration or meeting) if he considered 'that it could lead to a threat to public order'; and to detain 'for their own protection' minors or people whom he considered liable to commit suicide (a classic pretext for arrest in the militarist period). But Japan had not forgotten the time when similar provisions had enabled the police to get rid of any opponent and the lowliest police officer was a local petty tyrant. The teachers' demonstrations and the Oji strike gave rise to police brutality and excesses committed against journalists. The press let loose its anger when an over-zealous policeman took three people discussing the bill on a Tokyo pavement to the police station (13 November 1958).

Public opinion rebelled. The four trade union federations formed a united front; the three major dailies attacked the police bill without any let-up; the intelligentsia mobilised. The groups which had the most to fear from a return to the old order – Christians, Buddhists, and women's movements grouped in the Shufuren (Housewives' Federation) – joined the movement. There was a special role for the Federation of Students' Organisations (Zengakuren). Founded in 1948, it claimed a membership of 300,000 and could mobilise nearly 20,000 trained activists. Communists were in a majority on its national council. Zengakuren activists, wearing helmets and armed with long bamboo pikes, manoeuvring at the blowing of a whistle, were the spearhead of the street demonstrations. The JSP coordinated the movement within a National Struggle Council. When Kishi tried to force the police bill through in the Diet, Socialist members boycotted debates and barricaded themselves in rooms. To overcome their obstruction Kishi extended the parliamentary session on 4 November 1958. The next day four million workers were on strike; Diet members came to blows; Ikeda and Miki threatened to walk out of the government. Kishi had to withdraw the bill.

The Security Treaty crisis and the fall of Kishi

Reinforcement of the armed forces began in 1952. The National Police Reserve, renamed the Security Force, was increased to 110,000 men and provided with an embryonic navy which served secretly in the Korean war. Washington called for a Japanese army of 350,000 men, and Vice-President Richard Nixon officially said Article 9 was a 'mistake' (November 1953). In 1954 the Security Force adopted its present name of Self Defence Forces (SDF), and a Defence Agency was set up; it did not have the rank of a ministry but assumed all the functions of one. An armed forces expansion plan provided for an increase in strength to 180,000 men, 170 vessels and 770 combat aircraft in 1960. In 1954 the military budget accounted for 14 per cent of the state budget (compared with 9 per cent devoted to Social Security) or 2.8 per cent of GNP. That was its culminating point in the whole post-war era. Ex-servicemen formed organisations which were federated in 1954 in the Veterans and Bereaved Families Association (Izokukai), which claimed more than six million members. It called for payment of pensions, forbidden by the Americans. But it also worked for the moral rehabilitation of the army. Present in every hamlet throughout Japan, Izokukai soon proved to be a very efficient electoral machine working for the LDP. Alongside this powerful lobby associations of extremist ex-officers re-emerged in broad daylight. But rearmament met very strong resistance from public opinion. Military expenditure was one cause of the Liberal Party's election defeat in 1954. Hatoyama and Kishi himself had to cut it; it fell to 11 per cent of the budget and 1 per cent of GNP in 1960. In the absence of conscription, recruiting was difficult; in 1957 40 per cent of the candidates did not sit the examination and a third of those who passed did not join up. In these conditions the aims of the armed forces expansion plan could not be achieved. Above all, the constitutionality of the SDF posed a major problem. In 1952 the JSP started the first of a long series of legal actions based on Article 9; the Supreme Court, however, always refused to make a ruling. But in 1959 a court of first instance accepted the argument that the Security Treaty was unconstitutional – only to be over-ruled by the Supreme Court.

Lastly, several tragic incidents revealed that the rehabilitated ex-officers had revived within the SDF the inhuman practices of the former imperial army. In 1957 the 'Hiroshima death march', in which two soldiers died after being forced by beating to march until they were exhausted, scandalised public opinion. For all liberals the army remained a nest of fascists and a major danger for the young democracy.

The presence of the American bases provoked repeated incidents. From the beginning about a third of the Japanese disapproved of the Security Treaty (*Ampo*). This hostility increased when the bases were established, with the attendant ill-effects: expropriation, deforestation, noise and prostitution. Protest became more and more violent. In October 1956 the police had to use armoured vehicles at Tachikawa in the suburbs of Tokyo, and 1,100 people were injured. Japan's allergic anti-nuclear reaction was aroused in 1954 when the trawler *Fukuryu Maru no. 5* suffered irradiation from the first American H-bomb exploded on Bikini atoll. The Japanese were terrified; housewives refused to buy fish; fishermen demonstrated in front of the American embassy. The shadow of the 'ashes of death' (*shi no hai*) hovered over the country, and the Emperor no longer went anywhere without a Geiger counter. A national petition was signed by twenty million people and led to the creation of the Council Against the Atomic Bomb

(Gensuikyô), controlled by the Socialists and Communists. It organised a big international conference at Hiroshima for the tenth anniversary of the atomic bomb (6 August 1955). The press and the opposition demanded loudly to know whether the US Army had stockpiled nuclear weapons in Japan, which the government unconvincingly denied.

The situation in Asia led to fears that Japan would be drawn into a war by its alliance with the United States. The Korean War was concluded only by a precarious armistice in 1953, and the Indochina War ended in a disaster for the French at Diên Biên Phu in 1954. In 1957 the bombardment of the Nationalist-held islets of Quemoy and Matsu by the Chinese Communists aroused fears of an offensive against Taiwan. America no longer seemed invincible since the USSR took the lead in the space race with the Sputnik in 1957. Was the Security Treaty really a protection for Japan?

This concern led to the 'Ampo crisis', the most violent in post-war Japan. During the May 1958 election campaign Kishi tried to win over anti-American feeling to his side by requesting renegotiation of the treaty. Eisenhower agreed and talks opened in July. But by reopening the debate on the treaty Kishi gave the Left an opportunity to revive its campaign for its abrogation. As soon as the struggle against the police law was over the 134 organisations that had taken part in it were mobilised again in a National Council Against Revision of the Treaty (*Ampo Jôkai*). The debate reached the whole country, transmitted by the press but also by television, which 35 per cent of households already had. The LDP, financed by a special employers' contribution of 300 million yen, spread a mass of literature in favour of the treaty, including even comic strips. On 1 October 1959 there was a national broadcast debate between Kishi and the Chairman of the JSP. Public opinion remained uncertain; only a minority (20 per cent) called for pure and simple abrogation of the treaty, but a majority considered it dangerous and wanted Japan to adopt a neutralist position.

Kishi obtained considerable improvements (see pp. 114-15), but the new treaty had to be signed and ratified by the Diet. The process lasted seven months, during which violence increased relentlessly (there were 223 demonstrations in Tokyo during the crisis). On 27 November 1959 15,000 demonstrators invaded the

Diet, led by the Chairman of the JSP, Inejirô Asanuma. On 19 January 1960 Kishi flew off to sign the treaty in Washington; he had to play a trick to escape the crowd. In February the treaty was presented to the House. There was an explosion of street protests while the Socialists paralysed the debates. The session seemed likely to end on 19 May without the treaty being approved; to stop it being extended, the JSP House members locked up the Speaker in his office, but the police dragged them out, the session was extended, and the treaty was ratified in thirteen minutes. The press denounced 'tyranny by the majority'. But there still remained ratification by the Upper House, and an official visit by Eisenhower was scheduled for 19 June.

On 4 June five and a half million workers went on strike. On 10 June James C. Hagerty, White House Press Secretary, trapped in his car between the airport and Tokyo by thousands of Zengakuren members, had to be rescued by helicopter. Kishi called on the far right and the *yakuza* to maintain order at any price. On 15 June the Upper House examined the treaty text, while a new general strike paralysed the country. Around the Diet building there was a night of scuffles between 100,000 demonstrators and the police backed by the gangsters. Michiko Kamba, a student at Tokyo National University, was killed, and her death shocked the country to the core, since she belonged to the élite of the élite. On 17 June the seven leading dailies published a joint editorial saying, 'We have never had so much fear for the future of Japan. Democracy will perish if society allows violence to become general.' Kishi asked Eisenhower to postpone his visit – which in the end never took place. Two days later the treaty was ratified by the Upper House.

Kishi resigned almost immediately afterwards. Hayato Ikeda succeeded him and dissolved the House of Representatives. During the election campaign the Socialist leader Inejirô Asanuma was stabbed to death during a televised meeting, by a 17-year-old secondary school boy, son of an ex-officer. The murderer conveniently cut short the investigation by committing suicide in prison.

NOBUSUKE KISHI (1896–1987) AND
EISAKU SATÔ (1901–75)

Kishi and Satô were brothers, despite their different family names. Their father Hidesuke Kishi, a sake manufacturer of Yamaguchi, took the surname Satô from his wife, the daughter of a samurai. Their mother's family had solid political connections; one of their cousins was Shigeru Yoshida's son-in-law. Nobusuke returned to the Kishi surname when he was married to his cousin Yoshiko Kishi and became the adopted son-in-law to continue his father-in-law's *ié*. The two brothers went to the Imperial University of Tokyo. On graduation Nobusuke joined the Ministry of Industry, Eisaku the Railways. Nobusuke was influenced by Ikki Kita, the ideologist of 'pan-Asian nationalism' and mentor of the extremist young officers who was condemned to death and shot after the failed coup of 26 February 1936. He became an activist leader of the young technocrats close to the military, who wanted to place the Zaibatsus under tight control in the name of the national interest. He was chosen by the army to be in charge of economic planning in Manchukuo, where General Tôjô was Chief of Staff (1936).

Tôjô took him back with him to Tokyo and secured his entry into the government in 1939. He became minister of Trade in 1941 and was placed in charge of war industries in 1943. But rivalry among the three armed services disrupted production; Tôjô asked him to resign. Sensing that the military had lost, he refused, and thus brought about the fall of the government in July 1944; this opened the way for the peace faction. Imprisoned as a war criminal, he was released without trial in December 1947.

At that moment Satô was administrative deputy minister of Transport, after a more discreet career. Shigeru Yoshida made this distant relation by marriage Secretary General to the Government. He was elected in Yamaguchi First District in 1949. Appointed Minister of Posts, then Minister of Construction, he became Yoshida's trusted lieutenant, and in 1953 Yoshida appointed him Secretary General of the Liberal Party. As soon as his brother had been amnestied, at the end of the Occupation, he secured his admission to the party and helped him to get elected in the same constituency as himself in 1953. Among the politicians rehabilitated after the purges, Kishi was an exceptional man of action. In Sugamo he established close relations with Yoshio Kodama and Ryoichi Sasakawa, two ultranationalist leaders whose organisations worked hand in hand with the most activist elements in the Army; after their liberation, both those men established themselves as *kuromaku* ('puppeteers'), and they were to help his career forward. In the Liberal Party Kishi quietly organised mobilisation against Yoshida under the cover of a 'Committee for Study of the Constitution', and then openly set up a council for the organisation of a new party. Expelled from the Liberal Party, he became Secretary General of the Democratic Party on its creation in November 1954, and then held the same post in the LDP after the fall of Yoshida and the unification of the conservatives. Thus he was launched on a new career.

The career of his brother, who remained loyal to Yoshida, went through an eclipse. Involved in the shipyards scandal of 1954, he was saved from arrest for corruption, but was charged with breach of the law on political funds after Yoshida's fall. He was amnestied in 1956 on the occasion of Japan's admission to the UN.

As Prime Minister Kishi appointed his brother as minister of Finance in 1958. After the fall of Kishi, Satô, supported both by Yoshida's former followers and by his brother's friends, became a key personality in the LDP again. Under Ikeda he was Minister of MITI. In 1964 he narrowly failed to obtain the Chairmanship at the LDP Congress, but he became the designated successor to Ikeda when the latter retired, suffering from cancer, a few months later.

Impact of the crisis; the Ikeda government takes over

The October 1960 elections showed that the crisis did not affect the heart of Japan, nor did it profoundly alter the balance of forces among political parties. The conservatives won 57.6 per cent of votes and added nine more seats, while the Socialists lost seven. However, the violence relayed by television had had a profound impact on a nation which, officially, regards harmony as the supreme virtue. So Ikeda tried to bury the political polemics by giving priority to economic development. For the elections he centred his campaign around a plan to double national income in ten years, and promised 'a welfare state and an epoch-making extension of social security'. Towards the JSP he adopted a conciliatory attitude, a 'low profile' (*tai shisei*). As soon as he had taken office he mediated to impose a truce at the Miike mines where clashes were threatening to turn into a bloodbath after the murder of a trade union leader by the *yakuza*. After two more years, punctuated by miners' marches on Tokyo, hunger strikes and an invasion of the Prime Minister's residence, 73,000 jobs were abolished in the coal mining industry; however, the government paid for costly retraining and redeployment measures. Avoiding provocative legislation, negotiating compromises, Ikeda succeeded in having three quarters of the bills he presented to the Diet adopted unanimously.

A new division in the Socialist ranks helped the Prime Minister. The 1955 unification had been precarious. The JSP remained divided between the right-wing faction of Suehiro Nishio which had returned to its ranks, the moderates led by Saburô Eda, the moderate Marxists under Kôzô Sasaki, and the far-left wing of the Socialist Studies Society (Shakaishugi Kyôkai). This division was reproduced at the trade union level, the Zenrô being linked to Nishio while the Sôhyô backed the Marxists. The crisis of 1957–60 heightened the tensions. At Oji and Miike the employers engineered the creation of house unions which joined Zenrô and were violently opposed to the strikers led by Sôhyô. In March 1959, at the height of the struggle against Kishi, the Chairman of the JSP, Asanuma, declared in Beijing, 'American imperialism is the common enemy of the people of Japan and China'. That was too much for Nishio, who had always approved of the San Francisco Treaty. He led a new breakaway with forty deputies who founded the Democratic Socialist Party (DSP) in January 1960. In the 1960 elections the DSP suffered a crushing defeat, winning only 17 seats, but it succeeded in strengthening the Zenrô, which became the Dômei in 1962. This split did not put an end to the internal clashes in the JSP. Saburô Eda proposed following the example of the German SPD, which had just adopted a moderate programme centred around the gradual attainment of a Welfare State. It sought to change the JSP from a 'class party' into a 'national party' aiming at the widest possible support. The majority of Socialist Diet members agreed with him, but the party congress was dominated by section delegates, who were more radical. Eda was elected Secretary General, but his proposals were rejected by the congress in 1962. At the very moment when Japanese society was about to start on rapid modernisation, the JSP was constrained by doctrinal rigidity which was to cause its decline – while Eda's programme was to be carried out bit by bit by the conservatives.

Despite their theoretical rigidity, the Socialists were caught in the consensus trap again. Even under Kishi the LDP often forced them to vote with it when it resorted to wide-ranging rewards for the traditional popular electorate in response to the economic crisis of 1957–58 (see p. 98). For farmers (with ten million votes) the guaranteed price of rice rose 43 per cent in five years, in spite of the Finance Ministry which had succeeded hitherto in maintaining it at the level of world prices. Subsidies were extended to cover almost all agricultural products. The Agricultural Law of 1961 promised the peasants 'a standard of life equal to that of other citizens', and made Japan's agriculture the most protected in the world. For small and medium-scale enterprises, which employed 75 per cent of workers, Kishi reduced profits tax to 25 per cent compared with 33 per cent for the big firms, and in 1960 accorded low-interest loans worth 20 billion yen. Big business, supported by the MITI and the Finance Ministry, prevented more radical measures from succeeding (restrictions on establishment of supermarkets, for example, and penalties for abusive practices by big firms towards sub-contractors). But they only put off the evil day, for the small and medium enterprises and industries had become aware of their electoral clout.

The first measures to improve social protection were also voted by the Diet unanimously. In 1953 health insurance and retirement pensions were introduced, but more than a third of Japanese were not yet benefiting by them. Kishi had laws passed extending health insurance and pensions; providing minimal allowances for the aged, for single mothers and for the disabled; and introducing a minimum wage of a sort. Ikeda extended health insurance to the whole population and improved old age benefits. But social security remained very far from Western standards; the pensions under the national system, the only one covering all workers, were only 15 per cent of the average wage and were only paid at the age of 65, while the actual age of retirement in the big firms was 55. Thus the political crisis ended up developing 'patronage democracy' benefiting most of all the archaic and poorly productive sectors – agriculture and small-scale distribution – and based on consensus between the two major parties. It also led the LDP to lay the foundations of a Welfare State that was to be improved continually from then on, and to ensnare the Socialists by taking over a part of their programme. So, in the long term, the crisis strengthened conservative power. But in the immediate future it also breathed new life into all sorts of extremism. The crisis revived the far right. Kishi encouraged ultra-nationalist organisations to regroup in a Council of Patriotic Organisations (Zen Ai Kaigi), led by two of Sugamo's former fellow prisoners, Yoshio Kodama and Ryoichi Sasakawa, who set up a link between the *yakuza* Mafia and the right wing of the LDP. The Council was staffed by former officers implicated in the ultra-nationalist terrorism of the 1930s and representatives of the main gangster groups. To prepare for the visit by Eisenhower 40,000 *yakuza* were mobilised to help maintain order, and fought side by side with the police in the bloody clashes around the Senate on 15 May 1960. The Zen Ai Kaigi was to embrace 440 organisations and 150,000 members. Although weakened by repeated splits, it was from then on a force ready to prevent expression of opinion 'disrespectful' towards the Emperor or towards traditional Japan – by all methods. The assassination of Asanuma was followed four months later by an assault on the home of the editor of *Chûô Kôron*, a liberal weekly publishing a serial story considered to be offensive to the imperial family; a maid was killed and the editor's wife injured. The magazine halted publication and made a public apology. In 1971 *Black Money*, an inquiry into Kodama's activities, was prevented from appearing by threats from the violent right wing.

On the left, new forces were emerging. The JCP, eliminated from public life since 1952, was admitted to the National Struggle Councils against the police law and the Security Treaty. Its activists, always dedicated to the work, gained a dominant influence in the Zengakuren and on the Council Against the Bomb. They infiltrated a number of Sôhyô trade unions. The JCP came back to the Diet by winning three seats in the House of Representatives in 1960 and to the Upper House in 1962. In those 1962 Upper House elections the Kômeitô, set up by the Sôkagakkai Buddhist sect, attracted attention when it made an entry on the political stage with 11.5 per cent of votes cast and nine candidates elected. Lastly, the crisis caused the emergence, on the fringes of the parties, of 'citizens' movements' (*shimin undô*) whose prototype was 'The Voices of the Voiceless', organised in May 1960 around a nexus of intellectuals outraged by the way in which Kishi had rammed the Treaty through the House. These groups were to play a considerable role in the following period. But these developments hardly aroused any attention immediately, since by then the country was, after some difficult years, laying the foundations for formidable economic growth.

THE ECONOMY: FOUNDATIONS LAID FOR THE MIRACLE

From 1952 to 1962 the economy progressed at a well sustained rate. The end of the Korean War was followed by a year of recession (1954) which helped cause the fall of Yoshida. But growth resumed, led by investment which increased by 39 per cent in 1956 and 25 per cent in 1957. The 'Jimmu Boom' of 1955–7 coincided with the Hatoyama government. The overheating and trade deficit caused by the boom later forced Kishi to put on the brakes. The 'depression where you can see the bottom of the pot' (*nabezoko fukyô*) led to 600,000 unemployed in 1958 and did much to worsen the political crisis engineered by Kishi's 'Reverse Course'. But the economy revived for four years of extraordinary growth with the 'Iwato Boom' of 1958–62, in which the growth rate reached a peak of 14.1 per cent in 1961. In all GNP was multiplied two and a half times in constant terms over the decade.

By income per head ($220) Japan still ranked only thirty-fifth in the world, the figure being only one-fifteenth of that in the USA. In the IMF and World Bank, which it had joined in 1952, Japan was still classified as a developing country, authorised to protect its economy. Its trade remained in deficit, even though its exports were beginning to worry its trading partners in shipbuilding, textiles and motor cycles. From 1959 onwards international organisations put pressure on Tokyo to open up its economy. In 1962 a feeling of crisis took hold of the country, which prepared itself – in the words of a MITI official – for 'a bloodstained battle between national capital and foreign capital'. Japan was well prepared for it. Since 1952 the government had implemented an industrial policy whose main goals were 'national security' through exclusion of foreign capital and goods and 'national cohesion' through control of 'excessive competition'. The techniques of piloting the economy, tested and perfected throughout the decade, were to give Japan a decisive advantage in international competition for more than two decades.

Financing, controlling, enticing

In the aftermath of the war, and until the 1960s, Japanese enterprises were critically short of equity capital. The former Zaibatsus had operated mostly with capital raised on the stock exchange. The measures taken by the SCAP altered the situation completely. Firms now chased after bank loans, which represented 70 per cent of their financing. Thanks to a record rate of savings (12 per cent of GNP, twice as much as in the USA) the banks had plenty of money. They loaned in ways unimaginable in the West, lending well above the value of the borrowing enterprises, because they were implicitly covered by the Bank of Japan, which thus had control in the last resort over the financing of business: it pushed for investment desired by the government, and in return for their cooperation no bank went bankrupt in Japan until 1993.

The abolition of the Reconstruction Bank did not put an end to direct investment by the state. Eight specialised state-owned banks took over. Their share of total investment declined from 38 per cent in 1953 to 20 per cent in 1961, but three quarters was concentrated in three priority sectors – coal, steel and shipbuilding. In addition, the provision of a loan, even a symbolic one, by public bodies was an unambiguous signal to private banks to commit themselves. Those public bodies were financed by the FILP (Fiscal Investment and Loan Programme) which loaned to them the funds deposited in post offices. To turn savings in that direction, the state exempted postal savings accounts credited with up to three million yen from taxes, and tolerated the opening of numerous accounts by one person under different names in different post offices. Thus it offered individuals a means of tax evasion within reach of everyone, but allowed the FILP to collect 40 per cent of national savings, which was managed without any supervision by the MITI and the Finance Ministry.

Direct subsidies to industry had almost disappeared following the return to balanced budgets in 1949. The state preferred to intervene through tax deductions and tax incentives. For the priority sectors purchases of technology from abroad were tax-deductible, and so was amortisation of new equipment for half of its value in one year. Business could also evade taxation by making provisions on the most varied pretexts, including lack of water and 'exceptional risks'. Profits tax was fixed at 33 per cent, but those measures reduced it to 20 per cent on average, and in the priority sectors many big firms paid nothing at all.

Foreign trade regulation and protectionism

The law on exchange control and foreign trade had since 1949 obliged exporters to sell to the state all the foreign exchange that they earned. With that foreign currency the MITI drew up an annual budget for imports; it fixed quotas for products and allocated licenses to business firms. This system led to high prices for imported consumer goods, and the allocation of import licenses produced corruption that benefited both MITI officials and politicians. It led to strange deals, such as that which obliged sugar importers to subsidise shipbuilding with 5 per cent of their profits in return for renewal of their licenses. But it made it possible to limit imports of consumer goods in favour of industrial equipment imports, and to exclude almost at will from the market any foreign produce. The big trading companies (*sôgô shôsha*) were privileged partners of the MITI for the implementation of this policy. Most foreign trade passed through their hands. They relieved industrial enterprises of the task of marketing, provided them with raw materials on credit in times of recession, and allowed small and medium-sized enterprises to enter the international market by concentrating their exports. They charged very modest fees – sometimes as little as 0.5 per cent on a deal. Such small percentages required handling of large volumes, but the quota allocation made it possible for the MITI to concentrate the *shôsha* as it wished; about 1962 ten of them cornered more than half of Japan's foreign trade.

The foreign capital law of 1950 subjected all share acquisitions by foreigners and all joint ventures to authorisation. Against foreign firms which were already manufacturing in Japan through local subsidiaries, the MITI resorted to direct pressure. Thus IBM-Japan was threatened with 'all possible obstructive measures' if it did not agree to grant licences at cut prices and voluntarily restrict its production. The firm gave in (1960). Because of the same concern for independence, calls on international sources of credit were kept within strict limits. At the beginning of the decade the electricity companies and steelworks resorted to the IMF, but that led to sharp controversy. Rather than resorting to foreign credit again, Japan strove to clear its debts; in 1962 Ikeda made a symbolic repayment of $470 million to the USA for GARIOA aid.

Despite all the protection, Japan's trade was chronically in deficit. The cover for irreducible imports of food and raw materials was scarcely 60 per cent, and Japan was buying technology abroad on a massive scale. In 1957 the balance of payments deficit forced Tokyo to borrow $137 million from the IMF, which insisted on vigorous deflationary measures that led to the 'bottom of the pot depression'. Correcting that imbalance was vital for national independence. A Supreme Council was set up in 1954 to boost exports. Profits made from exports were given an 80 per cent tax exemption in 1955. The Japan External Trade Organisation (JETRO) was given the task of studying overseas markets and organising the marketing of Japanese products in cooperation with the *sôgô shôsha*. But the MITI looked beyond mere mercantilism. The 1955–60 economic plan, inspired by Tanzan Ishibashi, was based on the idea that it was the domestic market – nearly a hundred million people, enduring privations for twenty years – that could provide an outlet for mass production, this being the only way to cut costs and ensure competitivity of exports, while import controls would stop foreign firms from profiting from that market. That doctrine of a dialectic between exports and the domestic market led to a massive reduction in income tax to encourage consumption. From then on the Japanese economy was to be piloted like a two-engined aircraft, with exports and the domestic market being activated each in turn as the other died down.

Regulation of competition, and encouragement of innovation

Government control over the distribution of raw materials and production quotas was abolished in theory in 1952, on the Americans' insistence. The Americans also left behind them the antimonopoly law, the ban on holding companies, the law on excessive concentration, and the Fair Trade Commission (FTC) responsible for enforcing them. These were all obstacles to the

MITI's determination to reduce the damaging effects of uncontrolled competition by organisation of cartels. But it got round them as soon as 1952 by using for the first time the procedure of informal administrative guidance (*gyôsei shidô*) to 'advise' textile businesses to cut their excessive production and to assign quotas to each of them, with the threat of not releasing foreign exchange for cotton imports. This procedure was to become an essential tool of Japanese industrial policy. But the MITI also worked on changing the law. In 1953 it became legal again to create a cartel to deal with a depression or to 'rationalise' a legally designated branch. In 1955 the law on excessive concentration was repealed. A bill to repeal the anti-monopoly law was lost in the political crisis in 1958; but despite that setback the MITI was able to impose 'constructive cooperation among firms' everywhere, without the FTC doing anything but make symbolic protests.

Protection and cartelisation would not have been enough if Japanese industry had not been able to create conditions for its technical superiority at the same time. Japan profited from the generosity of the United States where transfer of technology was concerned; the American electronics industry, for example, sold it no less than thirty thousand licenses between 1950 and 1975. But Japan's strong point was practical use of the patents. For example, Sony bought the patent for transistors for $25,000 from Western Electric, which had used it to manufacture hearing aids, and had the idea of using it for small portable radio sets, hundreds of thousands of which were to be taken back to the USA by GIs stationed in Japan.

Improvements in management were brought in under the auspices of the Council for Rationalisation of Industry. It made systematic the changes that were to become the original feature of Japanese human resources management (lifetime employment, training on the job, quality circles), and 'recommended' their adoption. Lastly, no fewer than 58 laws which the MITI had passed between 1952 and 1965 aimed at seeking out promising sectors for the future. They set out a programme for 'greenhouse cultivation' (*ikusei*) of branches of business on which the MITI concentrated its aid in exchange for cooperation among the firms concerned. Special aid was accordingly given to the synthetic textiles, plastics and petrochemicals, machine tools and motor industries, and lastly to electronics. In some cases the state was involved directly in mixed enterprises, as with synthetic rubber and the aeronautical industry.

The threat of liberalisation: 'Black Ships II'

From 1958 onwards Japan's trading partners began to get worried. Japan, like European countries, had joined the IMF and GATT under the protection of special clauses allowing protection for countries ravaged by war. Europe renounced this in 1959, leaving Japan isolated and subjected to strong pressure to do the same. The problem was politically very sensitive. Kishi took advantage of the last days of his government to make a decision: he had nothing to lose any more by having a plan agreed providing for liberalisation of 80 per cent of imports in three years, finishing with the most sensitive products (vehicles and electronic products). But a real feeling of danger took hold of the country. The press splashed headlines about 'the return of the black ships' – the American fleet which forced Japan to open up in 1853. To prepare for the battle the MITI drew up a bill to give it *carte blanche* to organise industry into cartels and guide the banks. That was going too far; the bill was opposed by employers and by the Ministry of Finance, legal supervisor of the financial system, and was buried by the Diet in 1963.

SOCIETY IN THE GROWTH PERIOD

The explanation of the 'Japanese miracle' also lay in social stability which ensured the continuation in power of the LDP (and hence continuity in development and industrial policies), and in the fact that business managed to reduce labour disputes to the minimum. Such disputes were still numerous and violent – at Oji and Miike for example – but it was at that time that methods were perfected which Japan was to use to manage the social consequences of its growth. Its effectiveness in doing so was to be one of its winning cards from then on.

Rising standards of living and the consumer revolution

Wage increases between 1952 and 1957 were slightly above inflation (between 4 and 5 per cent per year). But the 'Iwato Boom' started a very rapid increase. The trade unions adopted the slogan 'Wages at European levels!' From 1957 to 1960 wages rose twice as fast as prices, and the state contributed to the general improvement in incomes by considerable tax deductions and new social benefits.

The consumer frenzy was symbolised by 'the housewife's three sacred treasures': the washing machine and the refrigerator – which under 5 per cent of households had in 1950 – and the television, whose first broadcasts were in 1953. In 1962 more than three quarters of households had a television set, and almost 100 per cent a washing machine. The '50,000 yen revolution' put all goods in that price range (about $140) – like stereos and Western furniture – within the reach of consumers. Consumer habits changed rapidly. Western ready-made garments and synthetic textiles became essential. Rice consumption began to decline in 1962, while Western food – dried noodles, tinned soup, instant coffee – proliferated. Already industry was reorienting itself towards new consumer products, notably cars which were still owned by only 3 per cent of households. The first cheap private cars coming on the market were the Subaru and the Nissan Bluebird (1959).

That was the heyday of leisure. In 1962 22 per cent of a family budget was spent on restaurants and outings to hot springs (*onsen*) or to the cinema, which recorded one billion admissions in 1958. Pachinko, a sort of vertical electric billiards which was the number one popular entertainment, had a turnover of 240 billion yen in 1954, equivalent to half the value of Japan's exports. Traditional sumô wrestling, which had fallen into abeyance, became popular again when the four yearly tournaments (*basho*) came to be televised.

The problem of housing was acute because of demographic pressure following the baby boom. Hatoyama launched a programme of big state housing projects (*danchi*). They were inhabitant by modern-style families – a couple with two children – living in Westernised interiors. The *danchi zoku* (*danchi* tribe) were then a symbol of the modern Japan of young qualified people of the cities. But in the countryside most households still followed the *ié* model and lived in thatched wooden houses.

A job for life – within limits

The lifetime employment system emerged in the 1920s (see p. 28). At the end of the 1950s it became general for a portion of the big firms' staff. Labour supply was then tight because of the war losses and because the people born in the years of low birth rate between 1935 and 1945 were reaching adulthood at the very moment when growth was accelerating. In 1961 there were two job offers for each young person, and unemployment fell to the lowest possible level (1.4 per cent). Firms competed for manpower. The MITI sought to keep the situation under control with the help of the Rationalisation Council, whose task was to promote standards for the benefits offered to workers, in order to avoid 'excessive competition' for manpower among employers.

The standard system of lifetime employment became common to all the big firms. Recruiting took place once a year, in April; in theory, firms held back from prospecting for candidates on university campuses earlier. New employees, whatever their levels of education and future careers (as skilled workers, white collar workers or senior staff), had almost identical starting pay. Vocational training was provided during the three years of probation, when the new recruit was moved from one post to another. An appointment only became definitive at the end of that period. Every worker then had before him a career which offered a guaranteed minimum based on length of service and a maximum varying according to personal aptitude. Thus every skilled worker would rise at least seven grades in 35 years with a firm, but the better ones would get accelerated promotion after ten years, and could even progress twice as fast to reach the supervisory level. Wages automatically rose with length of service, but they also varied according to discretionary half-yearly appraisals by superiors. A portion was paid in the form of biennial bonuses, averaging three months' pay in 1962, that depended on the firm's performance. Wages reached a peak about the age of 45–50. Retirement was at 55; the employee then received an allowance equivalent to two or three years' pay, but no pension. Retirement pension systems (national or provided by the enterprise or branch) only took care of him ten years later. So 'retired' people took jobs again, most often with a sub-contractor of their former employer, with pay half of what they had been earning; or else they used their retirement allowance to start a small business, often a small shop.

Only people with lifetime employment enjoyed the social advantages offered by a firm: medical care, housing, organised leisure activities etc. Only they belonged to the union to which skilled and other workers and management staff up to the level of deputy head of section belonged. In principle they were never made redundant; if the situation so demanded, they were transferred to other branches of the firm, or to firms specially set up by the employer for that 'welfare' purpose.

This system seemed irrational to Western managers when they discussed it from 1970 onwards. Older workers whose productivity was declining and whose knowledge was out of date earned four times more than young people. And how could workers guaranteed against everything be motivated? In reality the twice-yearly appraisals, the opportunity offered to all to make a career, and the need for the older employees to count on their firm to be given jobs after retirement were powerful incentives. Furthermore, on top of the automatic rises in basic salary with length of service, the earnings of each worker depended for about one third on elements varying according to merit – promotion and overtime work, which were awarded by the foreman on a discriminatory basis. The system of bonuses – whose amount was linked to the earnings of the firm – made it possible to adjust wages down in bad times. The business had manpower adapted exactly to its needs and imbued with the culture of the firm, since the firm could train the staff itself feeling sure of holding on to the human capital to which it was giving added value. Lastly, unproductive or restive elements were weeded out by constantly marginalising them in laborious or degrading jobs until they 'asked to stop' (*yamete morau*). In 1965, for example, nearly 120,000 workers, about 4 per cent of the staff with lifetime employment, left the big firms before retirement.

Above all, the system only concerned a small minority. Even in the big firms – depending on the branch – up to a third of the labour force consisted of part-timers (*pâtô*) recruited under short-term contracts or on a daily basis, through the agency of labour dealers often linked to the *yakuza*. They had low pay and no trade union or social protection at all. In 1973 Satochi Kamata described in *Japan in the Passing Lane* the brutal exploitation of those temporary workers who made it possible to adjust staff numbers to the situation permanently. Above all, among the small and medium enterprises and industries which employed more than three-quarters of all workers lifetime employment was almost unknown, as were trade unions and even the legal minimum hourly wage.

Persistence of the dual economy

In industry, small and medium-scale businesses with under two hundred workers employed 66 per cent of the country's workforce about 1962, compared with about 40 per cent in the USA. Such businesses prospered in traditional industries (textiles, food, toy making) but also in precision mechanics and machine tools. The big motor manufacturing, shipbuilding and electrical industry firms had a pyramid of sub-contractors whose lower rung comprised family workshops where work was carried on in a lean-to attached to the house, with a few old machines. This structure allowed Japanese industry to benefit both from the big firms' advanced technology and from the cheap labour of the sub-contractors. Industry could also make the sub-contractors bear the brunt of recessions, by forcing them to reduce their prices or accept delayed payment. Bankruptcies and redundancies multiplied then among small and medium industries. But as their workforce consisted of family members or else of new migrants and peasant-workers, it was able to turn to the traditional solidarity of the *ié* in time of recession. The complete absence of trade unions made it possible to quell crises quietly. When activity resumed the workshops took the workers back. When necessary they changed over to new activity easily, because of their minimal capital and because they only needed rudimentary equipment.

A large rural population still

The agrarian reform only brought stability to the countryside for a time. In 1955 agriculture was still the leading employer, with 41 per cent of the national workforce compared with 36 per cent in the tertiary sector and 23 per cent in industry. But farms were too small to give peasants an improvement in their living standards comparable to that of city dwellers. Easy availability of work hastened the drift to the towns. One and a half million peasants left the land between 1955 and 1960, and then the movement accelerated to reach 700,000 departures per year. In 1962 the number of industrial workers drew level with the number of peasants at 30 per cent of the active population.

This flight from the countryside was a threat to social stability and to the LDP, which had its main base in the rural constituencies. But it had original characteristics that softened its impact. Almost none of those who left to look for jobs sold his land. It was still cultivated by the wife and grandparents: the mother (*kâchan*), the grandfather (*jiichan*) and the grandmother (*bâchan*) – this was called 'three *chan*' farming. The head or the first son of the family looked for a temporary job nearby, so as to go back to work in the fields at the end of the week. About 1962 one third of peasant families were already drawing more than half of their income from the wages of some of their members, and this percentage was to grow steadily during the next decades until it exceeded 75 percent in 2000. The growth of this type of worker-peasant made it possible to maintain a high rural population, which adapted to change bit by bit on the spot, and reduced the effects of crises. During the 'bottom of the pot depression', tens of thousands of temporary industrial workers were able to fall back on their farms.

Trade unions: weaknesses and adaptation

Four trade union federations emerged at the end of the violent struggles of 1945–52. In 1962 half of the trade union members belonged to the Sôhyô. But more than 50 per cent of its four million members were concentrated in the civil service – regional and municipal employees, teachers, employees of Japan National Railways – where they had no right to strike or to lead any other protest action. In the private sector the strongholds remained the railways and heavy industry. The Sôhyô succeeded in mobilising workers on a large scale in support of political demands against Kishi's 'Reverse Course', but it completely lost its fight against staff cuts in the coal and motor industries in 1960–2. Its leaders remained dyed-in-the-wool Marxists, but it steadily adopted a pragmatic line. Further to the left, the Shinsanbetsu tried to breathe life into a radical tradition in which Communism and Anarcho-Syndicalism were mingled. But it only had a few tens of thousands of members, especially railwaymen and seamen. The moderate wing was divided between the 'neutrals' of the

Chûritsurôren (founded in 1956) and the right-wing Socialists of the Dômei (founded in 1962 as heir to Zenrô). The latter, with about 1.6 million members, was the second largest federation in Japan. In the motor, electricity and metallurgical industries it was backed by the employers who saw it as the most effective weapon against the Sôhyô. Lastly, many house unions were not affiliated to any federation.

Behind a respectable rate of unionisation (35 per cent) there was still the same weakness. The privileged minority of civil servants and workers with lifetime employment was almost 90 per cent unionised, but temporary workers and the employees of small and medium businesses were left to their fate by the union federations. In addition, the federations had only a weak hold on house unions that were affiliated to them in theory. At the level of the individual firm, trade union representatives were often more or less co-opted by the management; they enjoyed the material privileges of senior staff and were included in the decision-making process. 'Mutual understanding' (*sôgô rikai*) was the rule, and nobody cared to see an outside body like a union federation getting involved in negotiations. In addition the law did not provide for collective bargaining by branch. The tactic of the 'spring offensive' (*shuntô*) was devised by the Sôhyô in 1955 to remedy that fragmentation. All pay negotiations were brought together in March, when companies drew up their balance sheets for the end of the financial year and got ready to recruit new staff at the end of the school year (31 March). A national objective was fixed. The most firmly established federations – those of railwaymen and steel workers – started action and tried to obtain the maximum. The agreements that they signed then served as an obligatory point of reference for other branches, for the labour shortage did not allow employers to let wages fall behind there. This characteristic tactic, still used until the 1990s, enabled Japanese trade unionism to overcome its structural handicaps.

The employers also knew how to present a united front. During the Miike strike at the Mitsui coal-mines, Mitsui's competitors drew up plans for regular supplies to its customers, and the latter willingly paid for coal at a higher price to finance the struggle against the Sôhyô. That period was still filled with conflicts whose class character was very clear. But new ways of thinking were already being established among the young.

NEW WAYS OF THINKING?

The 'Tribe of the Sun' – and others

The generation reaching adulthood in this period was born between 1935 and 1945. Too young to have been really drilled in the values of imperial Japan, witnesses to their fathers' humiliating defeat, educated by teachers hastily readapted to a foreign value system, subjected to harsh privations and fascinated by the wealth of America, these young people were disoriented and had the fantasy of being cynical, materialist and brutal. In 1955 a young writer of 23, Shintarô Ishihara, won the most famous Japanese literary prize, the Akutagawa Prize, for his second novel, whose original title meant 'Season of the Sun' (translated into English as *Season of Violence*). Its hero, a young boxer, has as his motto, 'I do what I want, as I want'; he leads a bourgeois girl who falls madly in love with him to her death, then goes to disrupt the funeral ceremony. Ishihara followed up the next year with *Punishment Room*, whose main attraction is the rape of a girl student drugged by a rebellious deliquent student. Eight films were made from his work in five years.

The new urban generation was thus given the name of 'the tribe of the sun' (*taiyô zoku*). Its thirst for action sometimes found expression on the political plane – Asanuma's assassin was 17 – and by the fashion for tough sports such as boxing and mountaineering. The media concentrated attention on these angry young men. But they represented only a minority and were to become pillars of conservatism in the following period, like Ishihara who was to make a career in the LDP: deputy for Tokyo from 1972, a minister in 1988, he became the spokesman for the ultra-nationalist wing of the party and Governor of Tokyo in 1999.

The average Japanese was far from that complacent violence displayed by the fashionable youth. In 1958 he was passionately aroused by the romantic idyll (in reality carefully woven by the palace) between Crown Prince Akihito and Michiko Shôda, the leading industrialist's daughter who was to be the first commoner to enter the imperial family. Right in the middle of the crisis caused by Kishi's bill on the police, the unfolding of what the press depicted as a touching modern affair of the heart kept the country in suspense, until the grandiose televised wedding ceremony on 10 April 1959.

Rich and diverse literature

Literary creativity seems to have been stimulated by the rapid changes and crises. The major pre-war writers sparkled brilliantly in works whose disillusioned eroticism caused as much scandal as Ishihara's violence: *The House of the Sleeping Beauties*(1960) and *Beauty and Sadness* (1961) by Kawabata, *The Key* (1956) and *The Diary of a Mad Old Man* (1961) by Tanizaki. In 1956 Mishima had a huge success with his sixth novel, *The Temple of the Golden Pavilion*. Seven years older than Ishihara – with whom he had something in common in his taste for violent action, his sado-masochism and his scepticism about any form of social action – he nonetheless produced work of a quite different breadth, probably more typical of the new Japan caught between its tradition and a modernity both fascinating and hated, between its pride and its defeat.

'Proletarian' literature forged ahead with the Communist Hiroshi Noma, who described the mechanisms of stock market speculation in *Sky of the Dice* (1959), and Tsutomu Minakami, a former door-to-door salesman whose detective stories dealt compassionately with the most destitute (*The Straits of Starvation*, 1962). Yasushi Inoue analysed pure and introverted personalities perpetually seeking love (*Wall of Ice*, 1956–7). Shusaku Endô, a Catholic writer who won the Akutagawa Prize a year before Ishihara, constantly posed the problem of individual responsibility and the confrontation between desire for the absolute and the compromises demanded by reality (*Wonderful Fool*, 1959).

There was less and less interest in the defeat and the war. An exception was Endô's *The Sea and Poison* (1957), which exposed the deadly experiments on American prisoners by the professors of Medicine at the Imperial University of Kyûshû. But now the far right was watching. Shichirô Fukazawa, who had won fame by depicting the tragic fate of peasants in Japan's Middle Ages (*The Song of Oak Mountain*, 1956), published in 1960 a book considered disrespectful to the Emperor; immediately he and his publisher were harassed and threatened. Then in 1961 came the attack on *Chûô Kôron* (see p. 97).

The heyday of Japanese cinema

It was in the cinema that work still reflecting the trauma of 1945 was to be found. SCAP censorship had prevented it from expressing itself fully on the subject. As soon as the Americans had left, the Nikkyôsô financed two films to depict the tragedy of Hiroshima. In *The Tower of Lilies* (1953) Imai described the forced suicide of a group of girls during the battle of Okinawa. Kon Ichikawa's *Fires on the Plain* (1959) showed Japanese troops reduced to cannibalism during the battle of Leyte. Masaki Kobayashi's blockbuster *The Human Condition* (1958–61) narrated in three episodes the Odyssey of a young intellectual of good will caught up in the war in China, whose chaotic fate ends in a Soviet camp in Siberia. These films clearly denounced the war, but others were ambiguous. In *Room with Thick Walls* (1953) Kobayashi put the Americans on a par with the Japanese where atrocities were concerned, and exposed the role of scapegoat played by several of the so-called war criminals. Keisuke Kinoshita's *Twenty-Four Eyes* (1954) emphasised with tear-filled sentimentality that it was impossible to stand against the course of events, even with the best will. Kon Ichikawa's *The Burmese Harp* (1956) depicted, through the story of an officer who becomes a monk, a Japan regretting and praying for all the victims. But already many films were showing the imperial army in a heroic light (Inoshirô Honda's *Eagle of the Pacific*, 1953) or else illustrating complacently the role attributed to Hirohito as a peace-loving sovereign by the official version (*The Emperor and the General*, 1967). The Americans were increasingly depicted as bestial brutes raping women and corrupting Japan, as in Shôhei Imamura's Grand Guignol-like film *Hogs and Warships* (1961).

Japanese cinema was then at its peak: in 1958 there were 500 films per year, 5,000 cinemas and a billion admissions. But its creativity was beginning to be constrained by the four big production companies, which imposed very repetitive successful genres: samurai films (*chambara*) which glorified heroism in war again; gangster films which showed the Japanese *yakuza* as positive heroes, defenders of traditional codes of chivalry against bad characters who were generally Korean; young people's films, playing on the desire for revolt seasoned with second-rate romanticism; monster films, launched in 1954 by the success of *Godzilla*, in which the forces of evil are woken up from a long sleep by some sort of atomic phenomenon but are subdued by the joint efforts of the Self Defence Forces and the scientific community; and 'social' films (*shômin-eiga*), dealing with the lives of ordinary people, the recurrent theme being that the poor can always be happy by help-ing each other with enthusiasm and optimism. This standardisa-tion was soon to bring about a general decline in the Japanese cinema.

FOREIGN POLICY: JAPAN RETURNS TO THE INTERNATIONAL SCENE

Even after the end of the Occupation Japan's freedom of action in international affairs remained limited. The Security Treaty was only one element in multi-faceted dependence on the United States. Japan was not then a member of any international organi-sation. It had not signed peace treaties, nor did it have diplomatic relations, with either Beijing or Moscow. So it was cut off from its Asian neighbours, with which the war reparations question had not been settled. Public opinion remained sharply divided between the Left, pacifist and neutralist, and those who saw America as the only protection against the Communist advance that threatened to overrun Asia. But the conservatives themselves were divided between those for whom the alignment with Wash-ington must be unconditional and those who wanted Japan to show caution towards the two Communist giants close by, and to renew contact with them so far as circumstances permitted.

Dependence on the USA and its limits

After 1952 Japan remained tied to the USA by the highly unequal Security Treaty. Its economy depended to a great extent on the goodwill of an America accepting one-way free trade and selling technology at a low price. On the diplomatic plane Tokyo could rely only on Washington to back its return to international organi-sations. The Americans had kept territorial pawns, the Bônin Islands and Okinawa, whose fate had not been settled by the San Francisco Treaty. Lastly, the defeat and the reforms under the Occupation had led to psychological dependence. In the Foreign Ministry, staffed with English-speakers who had served their apprenticeship dealing with the SCAP, many were plainly incapa-ble of imagining Japan outside the American orbit. The United States was determined not to let it leave that orbit. In 1952 it forced Yoshida to give up his idea of an approach to Beijing (see p. 75). In

1956, when Hatoyama was seeking to normalise relations with the USSR, his own diplomats, in close contact with the US embassy, went so far as to conceal Moscow's first overtures from him. In 1961 Tokyo willy-nilly had to sponsor with Washington, at the UN, the resolution that made the admission of Communist China an 'important question' requiring a two-thirds majority, and was to prevent that admission being agreed for ten years.

Japan, however, retained a margin for manoeuvre. In Korea war could resume at any moment. In Indochina the Geneva Agreements only secured a respite; guerrilla warfare resumed, the NLF was created in 1960, and in 1962 16,000 American 'advisers' were already operating in South Vietnam. The danger of a Chinese attack on Taiwan still lingered. To deal with these threats the US Army needed its bases in Japan, Japanese supplies and a stable conservative government in Tokyo. So Tokyo was able to secure the most favourable economic treatment from the Americans, while still refusing the massive rearmament that they called for. Rather than risk a crisis Washington preferred to pay up. When Hatoyama refused to increase the military budget by more than 5 per cent in 1957, giving public hostility as a pretext, the Americans compensated by increasing their aid for the Self Defence Forces from $12 million to $150 million. The Americans conceded to Kishi a revision of the Security Treaty very much in Japan's favour. Tokyo succeeded in getting the new text to mention twice the constitutional provisions limiting Japan's armed forces. The US forces lost their right to intervene to maintain order in Japan itself. There was provision for a consultation procedure before installation of new sorts of weapon at the bases and before any intervention launched from Japan by the US Army 'to ensure the maintenance ... of international security in the Far East'. There was to be lively controversy about that clause since no consultation ever took place, and even the boundaries of the 'Far East' were not precisely laid down; to calm public opinion the Japanese government gave an assurance that it covered only Taiwan and South Korea, but from 1962 the American forces conducted operations in South Vietnam from Japanese territory. These difficulties notwithstanding, Tokyo secured an agreement that gave it very cheap military protection in conditions more satisfying to its sovereignty. In addition, the new Treaty could be denounced by either party, with a year's notice, as from 1970. While Japan had not broken its dependent relationship, it had begun to make it more balanced.

Normalisation of relations with the USSR; UN membership

Japan still had no peace treaty or diplomatic relations with the USSR, not present at San Francisco. The Soviets occupied the four southerly islands of the Kuriles, a few miles from Hokkaido. Out of 600,000 prisoners of war held in Siberia, a third were missing. In the absence of a fishing agreement between the two countries, the Soviet Navy hunted down Japanese fishermen in the Sea of Okhotsk and the North Pacific. Moscow's veto prevented Japan's admission to the UN. Finally, détente with China, desired both by public opinion and by trading companies, involved first normalisation of relations with its Soviet protector. In his campaign against Yoshida, Hatoyama made use of this theme. Normalisation with the Soviet Union was promised to the Socialists to get their support, and was included in the Democratic Party's election programme in 1955. The situation was favourable; Stalin had died in 1953 and the war had ended in Korea and (provisionally) in Indochina. The conference of Non-Aligned States at Bandung in 1955 set a wind of peaceful coexistence blowing in Asia, and Moscow thought it could take advantage of this to neutralise some allies of the United States – and why not Japan, which was represented at Bandung?

Moscow made the first moves in 1954 through an interview given by Molotov to a Japanese newspaper, and then a joint Sino-Soviet statement proposing a non-aggression pact. Despite the reluctance of his Foreign Ministry, Hatoyama grabbed the olive branch. Talks opened in London in 1955; they collapsed in September, resumed in January 1956, and halted again in March. In June the Minister of Agriculture, Ichirô Kôno, scored a personal success with a fishing agreement, which made it possible to resume the dialogue in July. But after two weeks it was deadlock again. The question of the Kuriles held everything up. It was a complex one historically and legally. For Tokyo giving up the Kuriles would set a disastrous precedent while the Americans were still occupying Okinawa. Hatoyama's rivals sought to tie his hands by raising the bidding: all four islands or nothing! For Moscow the question of principle was no less important: no territory annexed in 1945 must ever be handed back. In addition the islands controlled the only ice-free passage allowing the Vladivostok fleet to enter the Pacific throughout the year.

However, the USSR finally agreed to hand back the two smallest islets, Habomai and Shikotan. But Japanese public opinion stood in the way of any partial solution. Then Hatoyama flew to Moscow himself and agreed to the least possible evil. The joint communiqué of 15 October 1956 put an end to the state of war and restored diplomatic relations, but did not constitute a peace treaty. The question of the Kuriles was left in suspense. The USSR agreed not to ask for war reparations – it had already seized all Japanese property in Manchuria – and Tokyo was satisfied with promises of 'clarification' on the fate of the missing prisoners. Two months later, Moscow allowed Japan to enter the UN, and Hatoyama retired. Kishi did nothing to push the rapprochement further and strengthened ties with Washington as much as possible. So when he renewed the Security Treaty, Moscow seized that opportunity to cancel the offer to return Habomai and Shikotan; nothing would be handed back while there were American bases in Japan. However, economic considerations made it possible for Ikeda to renew contact. Khrushchev had tried since 1959 to interest Westerners in the development of Siberia; he was cold-shouldered everywhere, except in Japan, whose first trade mission landed in Moscow in 1962.

Between two Chinas

Communication was never cut between Tokyo and Beijing. The Yoshida letter of December 1951 (see p. 75) contained a promise not to sign a bilateral agreement with Beijing, but also reaffirmed the will to achieve 'complete peaceful and commercial relations' with People's China. Socialists and progressive intellectuals regularly travelled to Beijing. In the LDP Tanzan Ishibashi and Kenzô Matsumura headed a pro-Beijing lobby. In 1954, and then in 1955 at Bandung, the Chinese People's Republic proposed a non-aggression treaty to Japan. In 1956 it invited Hatoyama to stop over on his way back from Moscow. He did not accept, but in 1957 a JSP delegation brought back a new offer of negotiations from Beijing – in vain. But while the situation was frozen at the political level trade made regular progress. China had the raw materials that Japan lacked, and Japan could supply China with the machinery that it needed. In 1956 Japan's trade with the People's Republic exceeded its trade with Taiwan. In 1957, following Britain, Tokyo relaxed trade restrictions imposed since the Korean War by Concom and Chincom. In 1958, for its second five-year plan, Beijing ordered turnkey refineries and thermal power stations from Japan; the Japanese exported goods worth $20 billion to China, 7 per cent of their total exports. However, tension rose again when the staunchly pro-Taiwan Kishi came to power. His first official visit in Asia was to Taipei. The People's Republic resumed shelling of Quemoy and Matsu, while Chiang Kai-shek talked again of 'liberating' the mainland. In 1960 Eisenhower went personally to assure Chiang of his support. In this situation Sino-Japanese trade plummeted to just one billion dollars in 1960. But contact was never broken; Matsumura visited Beijing again at the end of 1959.

Japan's return to South-East Asia

The Treaty of San Francisco was very ill received by the non-Communist Asian countries. Some were not represented (Burma, Korea). Others, which signed the treaty, did not ratify it (the Philippines, Indonesia). Everywhere the cruelties of the imperial army and Japanese contempt for the indigenous people had left a legacy of lasting hatred.

Korea was an extreme case. After the failure of negotiations in 1952–3, there were naval clashes between the two countries around the Tokdo islets (called Takueshima by the Japanese) when the Koreans landed and established a permanent police force there. Seoul also accused Tokyo of letting agents of Pyongyang organise the Koreans in Japan, and allowing those who so wished to return to North Korea (1959). The LDP was hampered in negotiations by the opposition, which rejected any prospect of a separate agreement with 'the puppets of Washington'. So Tokyo and Seoul remained without diplomatic relations, while opinion polls showed Korea as a whole coming just behind the USSR as the country most hated by Japanese public opinion. But Japan succeeded in settling the question of war reparations with other countries. In 1952 Burma accepted $250 million, including $200 million in the form of Japanese manufactured goods and machinery. In 1956 the Philippines settled for $800 million payable in twenty years, two-thirds in the form of goods and services, one third as loans. In 1958 Indonesia accepted a similar sum on very similar terms. The three countries of Indochina, which had signed the Treaty of San Francisco, only obtained $62.6 million. In all those six countries received about a tenth of what they had requested.

Settling the reparations question through supplies of Japanese capital goods and tied loans paved the way for Japanese firms to make a comeback in the region. Trade between Japan and Asia trebled in value from 1950 to 1956. Kishi blazed the trail for an Asian policy in a White Paper which emphasised 'the need to organise a regional association and intensify economic cooperation'. He provided the Import-Export Bank with a special fund and established an Asian Economy Research Institute. The idea of a regional development fund was put forward on the occasion of the talks with Washington on the repayment of GARIOA aid; Ikeda suggested using a part of this to finance a regional bank jointly with the United States, and this project was to come to fruition in the following period. However, trade with the Asian zone was only 14 per cent of Japan's external trade in 1960.

Anti-Japanese feeling remained strong, as was shown by many incidents during Kishi's regional tour in 1957. But in 1958 the Presidents of Indonesia and of the Philippines were received by Hirohito, and Japan played host to the Third Asian Games. In 1962 the bad feelings had subsided sufficiently for Crown Prince Akihito to go not only to India and Pakistan, but also to the Philippines, one of the countries most devastated by the imperial army.

The rest of the world

Japanese diplomacy was hardly active in other regions. While the Emperor of Ethiopia, Haile Selassie, was the first foreign head of state to be received by Hirohito (in 1956), this was above all a symbolic meeting between the two oldest reigning dynasties in the world. In Europe Japan's favoured partners were already Germany (Chancellor Adenauer went to Tokyo in 1960) and above all Britain. Besides being the first power to have renounced the unequal treaties, and having also concluded with Japan the alliance that gave it a free hand to attack Russia in 1904, Britain was also dear to Hirohito's heart as he had completed his princely education there in 1921. Prince Akihito took the risk of going to London in 1953 for the Queen's coronation, and the Queen's cousin Princess Alexandra visited Tokyo in 1961.

4

THE 'MIRACLE' AND ITS OTHER SIDE
(1962–72)

THE DECADE OF THE ECONOMIC MIRACLE

The High Growth era (Kôdo seichô)

Japan's growth rate in this decade was three times as fast as that of the Western powers. In 1962 its GNP was still only 20 per cent of that of the United States; in 1972, it was one third. Between 1964 and 1968 it overtook in succession the GNP of Britain, France and West Germany. While the Ikeda Plan forecast its doubling in ten years, in fact it doubled between 1960 and 1965, doubled again between 1966 and 1970, and increased 25 per cent between 1970 and 1972. In the West a series of books drew attention to Japan's growth for the first time – *Le miracle économique japonais* by Hubert Brochier (1970), *The Emerging Japanese Superstate: Challenge and Response* by Herman Kahn (1970) and *Japon, Troisième Grand* by Robert Guillain (1969) among others.

However, this success had not yet projected Japan to the front of the international stage. In 1972 its GNP per capita was still only half that of France, and its exports were only 6 per cent of the world total, compared with the USA's 19 per cent and Western Europe's 44 per cent. Its trade balance remained in deficit until 1964 and worsened again in 1967. Its surplus only really burst forth from 1970, when it rose in three years from $2 billion to $9 billion. At that time Japan was already number one in the world in shipbuilding, television sets, cameras, motor cycles and heavy vehicles. It ranked second or third for cars, steel and synthetic textiles. But its exports had not yet done serious damage to the corresponding sectors in its trading partners. The Japanese kept repeating in international fora that their country was only a small, poor archipelago, overpopulated and without resources, and the majority of economists considered that the 'Japanese miracle' was very fragile.

The growth was not without hitches. The Tokyo Olympic Games in 1964 produced a huge effort in infrastructure – building of the first Shinkansen (high speed train) and urban motorways in Tokyo. The completion of these programmes led in 1965 to a recession marked by the biggest bankruptcies in the post-war period. The government injected 940 billion yen into public works and tax concessions worth 310 billion yen stimulated consumption. There followed the 'Izanagi Boom' until 1970. It culminated in the Osaka Universal Exhibition with 62 million visitors and 680 billion yen turnover. But the balance was once again upset by the first trade conflict with the USA, over synthetic textiles (1969–71), and by the world monetary crisis of August 1971.

Standards of living improved at the same speed as production. The labour supply remained very tight. Japan refused to turn to foreign workers. The flight from the countryside gathered pace and proportion of the active population in the primary sector fell from 30 per cent in 1962 to 14 per cent in 1972. But in that year there were 1.7 job offers for every application. Pay rises were therefore considerable. They averaged 11 per cent per year between 1962 and 1965, compared with a 6.5 per cent rise for prices, and between 1968 and 1972 wages doubled while prices rose only by one third. In all purchasing power increased by 10 per cent per year, twice as fast as in France during the same period. The standard of living remained far from Western standards, but undoubtedly the whole population benefited by the growth. Households were equipped with the 'three C's': colour TV, car, cooler. Most social categories adopted the dress style of the white-collared salary-earners, and class consciousness became blurred; in 1970, according to opinion polls, more than half of the Japanese considered themselves as part of the middle class. This period saw the emergence of consumption habits such as costly receptions in hotels on the occasion of weddings and end of year parties, golf, and group foreign travel. State *danchi* were replaced in the dreams of urban executives by *manshion*s built by private promoters with keener aesthetic sense.

The recipes for growth

The recipes for growth remained the same. The pay rises that stimulated consumption were possible because productivity rose even faster owing to ever increasing investment – up by 20 per cent per year during the 'Izanagi Boom', with a record 57 per cent in 1967. Capital was always raised by loans, and indebtedness accounted for 80 per cent of companies' balance sheets in 1972, compared with 70 per cent in 1962. The state always covered lenders, as in 1965 when it saved Yamaichi Securities, one of the four big securities firms, from bankruptcy. The savings rate continued to increase: savings accounted for 12 per cent of GNP in 1960, 17 per cent in 1973 – compared with 6 per cent in the USA.

Small and medium industries showed more vitality than ever. They created twice as many jobs as the big firms and their productivity increased very fast. The law on modernisation of small and medium enterprises (1963) authorised the MITI to coordinate priority investments in them, benefiting especially the machine tool industry where those enterprises were at the forefront of progress – in 1960 Japan imported a third of its needs, in 1972 scarcely 7 per cent, and in 1982 it controlled half of the American market in digital control machines. The economy remained heavily protected despite Kishi's promises in 1960 (see p. 103). In 1963 Japan maintained restrictions on imports of 122 products, three times more than West Germany and six times more than Britain. Bans and quotas protected strategic sectors (computers, integrated circuits) and agriculture; imports of citrus fruits and beef were severely restricted, rice imports banned altogether. Even when there were no quotas, products able to compete with local manufacturers faced prohibitive tariffs, administrative harassment, impenetrable distribution systems, and nationalism – cultivated by official campaigns – among consumers.

Japan feared foreign capital even more than foreign products. Admission to the OECD obliged it in principle to lift bans, while weak capitalisation of Japanese enterprises made them easy targets for takeovers. But the 'liberalisation' announced in 1967 was deceptive. Seventeen branches were opened up to foreign capital – only ultra-traditional manufactures (sake, wooden clogs), product categories where Japan was not afraid of any competition any more (motor-cycles), others where there was no local market (cornflakes) or others for which the government controlled

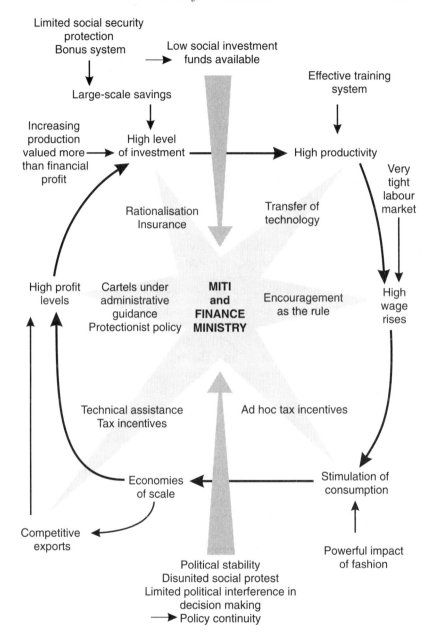

Fig. 4.1.   THE GREAT BOOM: THE LINKS IN THE CHAIN

outlets (railway equipment). Thirty-three other branches were half-opened; foreigners were not allowed to acquire more than 20 per cent of a firm, nor to have the majority in a joint venture, and the MITI's authorisation was still necessary 'if the operation involves introduction of new technology' – which meant always.

New elements: challenge to the MITI

The MITI's authority began to be challenged. In 1963 its special bill for promotion of priority industries was buried (see p. 103). Relaxation of exchange controls deprived it of the import licensing weapon. State loans played a decreasing role: 20 per cent of total investment in 1962, 10 per cent in 1972. But it still retained the essential part of its legislative arsenal, and 'administrative guidance' through informal directives, backed by bureaucratic retaliation against those not complying, turned out to be more practical than any law, for they largely escaped observation and controversy. They were carefully prepared in permanent concertation with the branches concerned, and were from now on the main mode action for the MITI.

To prepare the economy for liberalisation, the MITI 'advised' coordination of investment and sharing of markets. In 1965 it placed ceilings on the new production capacities for petrochemicals and synthetic textiles, and reserved them for already established firms. It sought to reconstitute giant firms whose size would put them beyond the reach of foreign would-be predators. It sponsored the reconstitution of Mitsubishi Heavy Industries, which had been broken up by the SCAP, in 1964, and the merger of the Prince and Nissan motor manufacturers in 1966. However, in 1970 the reconstitution of the former Nippon Steel met strong resistance. The major steel companies had always been refractory to 'administrative directives'. They resisted the plan for a merger between Yawata and Fuji (offshoots of the former Nippon Steel) because the new firm would control more than 30 per cent of the market. The Fair Trade Commission – trampled upon by the MITI for years – dared to take the case to court. The press, consumer associations and many economists took sides against the MITI. The merger was authorised but the new company, New Japan Steel, had to hand over two steelworks to competing firms.

The MITI also wanted to reduce the number of motor manufacturers from ten to a chosen couple: Toyota and Nissan. But the others rebelled and called on the Americans for help. Mitsubishi forestalled the official opening up of this sector to foreign investment by exhibiting the Colt produced in joint venture with Chrysler at the Osaka Expo. The MITI had to give in. The technocracy was attacked by the press, which called it an 'over-possessive mother' (*kyoiku mama*) or a gang specialising in blackmail rackets against companies (*sôkaiya*). The employers blamed it for its authoritarianism, consumer groups for favouring monopolies, for price manipulation and for pollution. Politicians began to make their authority felt. In 1963 the Minister of the MITI, Hajime Fukuda, violated tradition by imposing his choice for the post of Administrative Vice Minister (the number one bureaucrat in the ministry and its real boss). Kakuei Tanaka, the future Prime Minister, energetically forced Finance Ministry officials to pressure banks into improving their loans to small and medium enterprises (1965), and went over the MITI's head to resolve the textile crisis with the United States in 1971 (see p. 158).

New industrial groups emerged, less linked with the administration. Alongside the four *keiretsu*, heirs to the former Zaibatsus, two others were created around the Sanwa and Dai-Ichi banks, associated with the Nissho Iwai and C. Itoh trading companies. But the new consumer markets were often conquered by postwar newcomers, such as Matsushita which headed 560 companies in 1970, and Honda which became number one in the world for motor-cycles. This new generation of firms also included Sony and Canon, Omron (electrical and electronic goods), Pioneer and Akai, Komatsu (earthmoving and heavy plant machines) and YKK (zip fasteners, aluminium) – all future world leaders in their respective branches.

The government broke the rule of presenting a balanced budget that had prevailed since the Dodge Plan, when only the issue of short-term bonds to finance public works had been authorised. That taboo was broken for the first time during the 1965 depression. In 1972, to cope with the crisis caused by readjustment of the international monetary system, a budget for a deficit of 2,000 billion yen was presented. This was the beginning of accelerated growth of the public debt in the following period. But the newest element was a questioning of the ultimate purpose of growth, because of the impact of its negative side-effects – the 'other side of the miracle' – against which public opinion was mobilised with increasing force.

THE OTHER SIDE OF THE MIRACLE

Pollution, a national disaster: the 'four big cases'

Growth continued for fifteen years without any care about pollution. Yet a nervous disorder leading to hideous malformations and fatal paralysis was reported as early as 1956 at Minamata, a small town in Kyûshû where the Chissô Corporation had been dumping mercury into the bay since 1908. In 1959 the same illness appeared along the Agano river in Niigata prefecture, downstream from a Shôwa Denko chemical plant; a petrochemical complex was blamed for an epidemic of fatal asthma at Yokkaichi in Mie prefecture; and poisoning of the water by cadmium in Toyama prefecture led to the appearance of the *itai-itai* illness (from 'aye-aye', the cries of pain uttered by the victims). But attention was then diverted by the Security Treaty crisis. The victims were isolated by a coalition of the big firms, trade unionists mobilised to defend the factories and jobs, and the administration, which tucked away reports establishing the cause of the illnesses. The JSP hesitated to take up the problem, to avoid trouble with the unions. All tactics were employed against protesters – physical violence, arrests of leaders, 'mediation' by public authorities which offered meagre compensation to the victims in return for a promise to stop all protest action.

Most of the victims gave up, but action committees continued the struggle with press reports, demonstrations and hunger strikes. A succession of new scandals aroused the public: 7,864 babies were poisoned by arsenic-contaminated Morinaga milk, 1,614 people were either killed or rendered disabled by Kanemi oil containing PCB (polychlorinated biphenyls). In 1967 the government agreed to pass a law setting anti-pollution standards – to be applied in ten years and on condition that they were 'compatible with healthy growth of the economy'. But in the following year the Health Ministry had to admit officially the link between the Minamata disorder and the mercury waste. The river Agano victims finally dared to sue Shôwa Denko and the government, and were soon followed by the victims of Minamata, Yokkaichi and Toyama. The LDP hastily passed a law to extend assistance to 'officially certified' victims (1969). But it was not enough to save the companies responsible for the 'four big cases' from being condemned to pay enormous damages in first instance court judgments in 1971–2. This was just the beginning of a legal marathon, since the companies appealed again and again while trying by every means to reach an out-of-court settlement with the dispirited victims, who on their side tried to have the state's responsibility recognised for it to take over from companies ruined by the damages, such as Chissô. The government spun out the process and tried to exclude as many people as possible from the benefits of the 1969 law (2,000 certified out of 10,000 cases at Minamata). In 1992, forty years after the first signs of the illness at Minamata, proceedings were still continuing before the Kumamoto district court. Only after the LDP's temporary fall from power was a global settlement reached in 1995, through the efforts of the Socialist Prime Minister Tomiichi Murayama.

But the barrier had been breached; the media now scrutinised pollution cases. Lead was discovered in the blood of people living near the major crossroads in Tokyo, and PCB in young mothers' milk at Osaka. At Yokkaichi a firm was caught dumping sulphuric acid in the sea. In Tokyo many residents used small gas masks to protect themselves against photochemical fogs. Everywhere the local authorities used their autonomous power to lay down anti-pollution standards. The government beat a retreat. The Diet passed fourteen anti-pollution laws and repealed the clause making their application conditional on economic growth (1970). An Environment Agency was set up. The clean-up of the environment in the following decade was to be remarkable. But public opinion and industry were now divorced.

Hard life in the mega-cities
Growth had continued without any concern for planned development. Industrial combines and millions of migrants were crowded along the narrow coastal band along the Pacific shore. In 1970 the three conurbations of Tokyo-Yokohama, Nagoya and Osaka-Kobe-Kyoto had a combined population of 33 million – a third of the country's population living on 1 per cent of its

territory, at a density exceeding 9,200 inhabitants per square kilo-
metre. Under such weight the soil was sinking 20 centimetres per
year in some parts of Tokyo. With Sapporo, Hiroshima and the
Shimonoseki-Kitakyûshû-Fukuoka urban area added, more than
half the population was crowded into six over-industrialised
urban conglomerations, where nothing was done to organise
urban development and planning.

The quality of life there was often appalling. The small size and
discomfort of dwellings was to become proverbial when an EEC
report described them as 'rabbit hutches'. New migrants' families,
workers and young couples often lived in one single room of a
prefabricated dwelling, without central heating or sound proof-
ing. The wooden houses of the old urban middle classes were shut
off from the sun by blocks of flats, and shaken by motorways passing at rooftop level. The *manshions* of the city centres soon became
inaccessible to the average salaryman, who could only escape the
danchi for the distant suburbs. Everyday transport became steadily
harder to endure; on the most used railway lines in Tokyo and
Osaka the index of overcrowding during rush hours was nearly
300 ('the coach is stuffed full of bodies to the maximum, shouts
are heard and sometimes the windows are broken'). All basic ame-
nities – roads, crèches, hospitals, open spaces – were insufficient.
Government revenue was only 21.4 per cent of GNP, compared
with 32.8 per cent in France in 1969, and it was allocated as a priority to economic infrastructure. 'Japan has had to develop its
economy at the cost of living conditions. That could be called its
destiny', an official report stated coldly in 1959; the official view
had not changed in 1972.

Social security cover remained very mediocre. After the measures voted hastily in 1958 and 1962, the share of social benefits in
the state budget reached a peak of 14.5 per cent in 1965. But it fell
thereafter under pressure from the Ministry of Finance. Only
health insurance improved; the share of medical costs borne by
patients fell from 30 per cent in 1960 to 19.3 per cent in 1970,
thanks to the powerful Japanese Medical Association which contributed funds to the LDP in exchange for legislation favouring
consumption of medical care. But family allowances and unemployment insurance remained unknown. Retirement pensions
were derisory for those who only had the basic compulsory
system set up in 1959; they received the equivalent of $46 per

month in 1970, and those who had not been able to make contributions received a minimum old age pension of about $7 (2,300 yen). All over the country local authorities had to set up emergency complementary systems. The share of transfers to households in public expenditure was only 19.4 per cent in 1969, compared with 44 per cent in France. Not only that: social contributions accounted for 21.2 per cent of state revenue. So the system made a profit – profit that was not lost to productive investment.

Savings were therefore obligatory to face the prospect of illness and old age, or in the hope of buying a house, but also for children's education. Higher education had become a prerequisite for a lifetime job or a good marriage, and now more than two-thirds of pupils continued beyond secondary school. Competition for the best universities became fierce with the arrival of the baby-boomers at their doors. During their secondary school years pupils went to private supplementary lessons (*juku*) to prepare for university entrance, and fees were very high in the private universities which provided three-quarters of university education. Marriage was also very costly, with fashion dictating elaborate ceremonies that no respectable family could any longer do without. About 1970 an average household was saving 22 per cent of its income, aided by the system of bonuses which now accounted for a quarter of annual pay.

Disarray, uncertainty and the 'new religions'

Discontent and disarray were worsened by the conjunction of four phenomena. The flight from the countryside took millions of migrants away from the security of village solidarity and the *ié*. Often they had to renounce their inheritance in order to preserve the small family holding, and ended up in hard and insecure jobs. About 2 million women born around 1920 did not find husbands because of the losses in the war. Marginalised by society, they were often taken on as 'hostesses' by the leisure industry, or else made a living by running tiny bars or small trading businesses. Many craftsmen suffered from the modernisation of consumption habits. Lastly, people born in the years about 1900, who had borne all the burden of the first economic miracle, the war and reconstruction, were reaching old age, often with nothing, since after their savings were swallowed up by the post-war inflation, they did not have the time to build them up again or to make any significant contributions to retirement pension systems, which were too recent.

New religions (*shin sunkyô*) flourished among these vulnerable groups. They had already emerged in the Meiji era, when modernisation was destabilising society, but their proliferation had been halted by militarism. Now they blossomed freely. Around 1970 each of the more principal ones claimed several million followers. The most powerful was the Sôkagakkai ('Society for the Creation of Values'), derived from the sectarian and nationalistic Buddhism of Nichiren, the thirteenth-century monk (see p. 8), and claiming more than 10 million followers. All were founded on a charismatic leader, often considered as a messiah. They promised wellbeing on earth and preached brotherhood, peace, mutual aid, the precepts of virtue and the order of the past. Their deities were compassionate and consoling. Their rituals were very simple, often drawing on old village folklore. They organised the faithful into small groups meeting regularly for everyone to confide in and be encouraged by the others; reconstituting small warm communities in the harsh and chaotic world of the megalopolis was at the root of their success. They proselytised actively, sometime aggressively, especially the Sôkagakkai. They were very practical, and definitely did not turn their followers away from normal social life; thus they did not qualify as 'sects'. They accumulated vast property. Each one built its holy city in the form of huge complexes designed in baroque and garish architecture, with temples, hotels, universities and congress halls all together. To oppose the powerful Shintoist lobby they formed the Federation of New Religions (Shinshûren), with eighty affiliated religions; it secured complete tax exemption for them, an invaluable asset that they banded together to preserve as a very powerful political lobby, while the Sôkagakkai went so far as to found its own party, the Kômeitô.

Youth, cinema and revolt

The young were also troubled by uncertainty. The baby boom generation acutely felt the crisis of passage to adult life that also shook the American hippies and the May 1968 students in France.

NEW RELIGIONS

The new religions that emerged before the war can be divided into two families.

(1) The religions derived from the 'Sect Shintô' (*kyôha shintô*). Between 1876 and 1908 the Meiji government recognised three sects claiming to follow Shintoism but rejecting the association of the official 'Shrine Shintô' (*jinja shintô*) with the state. Today there are 130, claiming about 8 million faithful. The most important are:

- *Seichô ni ié* (House of Growth). Founded in 1930; 3 million followers. Its doctrine is a mixture of Shintô and Buddhism, Christianity, Freud and Western philosophy. It supported militarism and its founder was purged by the SCAP.

- *Tenrikyô* (Divine Wisdom). Established in 1838; about 2.5 million followers. Its founder, a peasant woman, claimed to be the Messiah sent by the father-god (Oyagami) to rid humanity of the 'eight layers of dust' (selfishness etc.) which prevented it from knowing harmony and joy. It was persecuted by the military. Its essential rites are performing of social services (a sort of daily good deed), purification dances, and repeated pilgrimages to the shrine where the deified spirit of the foundress resides. The *Tenrikyô* has a universal vocation. It was established in the United States in 1896. Its university, founded in 1925 to teach languages to its missionaries, has acquired a reputation in that field and for martial arts.

- *Perfect Liberty Kyôdan*. Founded in 1931, this sect was banned in 1937, even though the goddess Amaterasu (ancestress of the imperial line) was at the centre of its Pantheon. Recreated in 1946 under its present name, it claims 2.6 million followers. Its first precept is 'Life is an Art'. Its annual festival is famous for its fireworks. It has its own schools and hospitals.

- *Konkokyô* (the Golden Light), founded in 1859 by a peasant of Okayama; about 500,000 followers. A very primitive sect, it emphasises filial duty and magic aimed at obtaining material advantages.

- *Kurozumikyô* (from the name of its founder) is the oldest of all (1814). This regional sect of Okayama (200,000 followers) insists on traditional values: gratitude to parents and society, hard work, sincerity, etc., under the aegis of Amaterasu.

(2) Buddhist sects mostly deriving their ideas from the Sutra of the Lotus, which emphasises the virtue of faith 'simple as that of a small child'. They developed on the margin of established sects (Tendai, Shingon, Jodôshû etc.), who were in charge of the temples. Apart from the Sôkagakkai, the most important are:

- *Reiyukai* (Society of Companions of the Spirits). Founded in 1925 by a woman healer, Miki Kotami. Women play an important role in this sect. Its functioning is close to that of the Sôkagakkai: a hierarchical organisation based on neighbourhood groups, daily meetings of the faithful, active proselytisation, simplicity of ritual (reciting of the words 'I find my refuge in the Sutra of the Lotus' before the family altar). Its doctrine stresses social harmony and the effacement of the individual in the succession of generations. About 2.8 million followers, including Shintarô Ishihara, former *enfant terrible* of the 'Tribe of the Sun', praise-singer of Japanese neo-nationalism and Governor of Tokyo since 1999.

- *Risshô Koseikai* (Society for Justice and Personal Perfection). This sect, which broke away from *Reiyukai* in 1938, expanded rapidly thanks to the charisma of its foundress, Myôkô Naganuma, and claimed about 5.3 million followers. It remained close to the *Reiyukai* in belief, ritual and organisation. Very active on the international plane, it set up the World Conference for Religion and Peace in 1970. Its chairman was invited as an observer at the Second Vatican Council. It regularly conducts big anti-nuclear campaigns (32 million signatures in 1982).

- *Sekai Kyûseikyô* (the Religion for Salvation of the World). Founded in 1935; about 800,000 followers. It stands for the creation of an earthly paradise, organic agriculture, and the purifying quality of beauty (its museums contain treasures of

Japanese art). It rejects medicine and teaches that every believer has the gift of healing. Women play an essential role in its leadership.

The distinction between Shintoism and Buddhism fades away before the traits common to all these religions: syncretism, simplicity of the message of consolation, insistence on traditional values, solidity of the organisation, and, except for the Sôkagakkai, active political support for the LDP.

The Zengakuren, more or less dormant since the Security Treaty crisis, was still there, ready to mobilise once more young people who felt misgivings on the threshold of active life which was more constricting in Japan than elsewhere.

The 'new wave' in the cinema reflected this crisis of revolt. While the leading companies produced more and more stereotyped films, independent young film-makers established their own production firm, ATG. They made films about juvenile delinquents (Susumu Hani's *Bad Boys*), American Vietnam War deserters hiding in Japan (Hiroshi Teshigahara's *Summer Soldiers*), youthful nihilism (Yoshihige Yoshida's *Eros plus Massacre*), sexual liberation of women and violence inflicted on them by male society (Shôhei Imamura's *Unholy Desire*), and the student revolt (Shûji Terayama's *Throw Away Your Books, Let's go into the Street*). Nagisa Oshima was the most prolific. In his work can be seen the disillusion among militants after the Security Treaty struggle (*A Foggy Night in Japan*, 1960); denunciation of anti-Korean racism and the legal system (*Death by Hanging*, 1968) and of sexual taboos (*Sing a Song of Sex*, 1967); glorifying of popular revolts in the Middle Ages (*Ninja Bugeichô*, 1967); and re-writing of the entire history of Japan since 1945 through the saga of a traditional family whose patriarch is a transparent metaphor for the Emperor (*The Ceremony*, 1971).

Intellectuals in disarray and the return of 'Japanese-ness'

Literature also reflected the uncertainty of the times. Tanizaki kept quiet and died in 1965. Kawabata, Nobel prize winner in 1968, committed suicide in 1972. On 25 November 1970

Mishima, with some members of his 'private army', took the general commanding the Tokyo military region hostage; he demanded that the garrison should gather to hear him, and after a speech on 'the glorious tradition of our country', carried out the samurai *seppuku* before the press which had rushed to the scene. The uncertainty also affected the proletarian writers; Noma broke with the JCP and plunged into nihilism (*Ring of Youth,* 1971). Death and madness haunt the work of newcomers like Takehiko Fukunaga, who after translating several works of Jean-Paul Sartre published *The Farewell* (1962) and *The Island of Death* (1972). The most representative author of this period was Kôbô Abe, haunted by the vision of a society where man loses his identity, prisoner of an absurd fate (*The Woman in the Dunes,* 1962) or reduced to being a mere object (*The Box Man,* 1969). The war was still present, as in *Black Rain* (1966) in which Masuji Ibuse dealt with the drama of the Hiroshima survivors. But now revisionist works were appearing, as well as reminiscences by former prisoners such as the historian Yuji Aida, denouncing brutality by the Allies equally with those of the imperial army.

The intelligentsia remained fascinated by foreign thinkers; Jean-Paul Sartre and Albert Camus were mentors to several generations of students. But there was now a large-scale return to Japanese-ness. A whole school of essayists sought to define 'what is truly Japanese' in a culture where traditional forms and values were disappearing. 'Books about Japanese-ness' (*nihonjinron*) set out for the general public details of what was specific to the Japanese soul, and sold millions of copies, such as Shôten Yamamoto's best-seller entitled *The Japanese and the Jews* (two chosen races, both suffering exclusion). The anthropologist Chie Nakane in *Japanese Society* (1968), and the psychoanalyst Takeo Doi in *The Anatomy of Dependence* (1971), sought what was radically different in the social model or functioning of the Japanese unconscious. 'Modernist' criticism of the preceding period, which wanted to rid Japan of its 'feudal remnants' to get in line with the individualist Western model, gradually gave way to a positive reappraisal of the national heritage. At the same time national pride was boosted by a series of symbolic events: Japan's achievement of third place in the number of medals won at the Mexico Olympic Games and the award of the Nobel Prize for Literature to Kawabata (1968), the first ascent of Everest by a Japanese team, the launching of the

Osumi satellite into orbit, and the success of the Osaka Expo (1970), followed by that of the Winter Olympics at Sapporo (1972).

NEW STRUGGLES

Under the impact of social change, revolt took on a new appearance. Organisations that had led it in the preceding period under the aegis of the JSP gave way before newly emerging forms, new objects and new players in struggles.

Citizen, community and consumer movements

The term 'citizens' movements' (*shimin undô*) appeared in 1960 to designate the political struggle collectives that sought to mobilise ordinary citizens outside the parties' control. The most active were the Council Against the Atomic Bomb (Gensuikyô) and the Collective for Struggle for Peace in Vietnam (Beheiren) set up in 1965. But they were undermined by internal rivalries between parties of the Left. In 1965 the former split into two organisations, one Communist and the other Socialist. The Beheiren played a major role in mobilising opposition to American intervention, but it was overwhelmed by the violence of its far-Left militants who turned to terrorism about 1970.

The 'inhabitants' movements' (*jûmin undô*), whose prototype was the Minamata movement, numbered about four thousand around 1970. They were typically local and small-scale; most had less than five hundred members. Their favoured area of action was among closely knit traditional communities and in middle-sized cities. They operated very democratically, with an informal hierarchy and a rotating chairmanship. Women played a major part in them, because the protest was related to daily life, because the men of the villages were often absent – at sea, or in the city as temporary workers – and because women were less exposed to retaliation in their employment. Political militants were active in them, but the majority of the groups had no connection with the parties. Their methods of action were imaginative, often vigorous and more and more sophisticated as time went by. The most numerous movements were those directed against polluting installations or, in cities, against new blocks shutting out the sun from traditional homes. Many came from communities whose way of life and land were threatened by the building of factories or infrastructure – for example, most of the 162 plans for hydroelectric dams drawn up after 1966 were blocked or held up. But it was Sanrizuka peasants' struggle against the new Tokyo airport (Narita) which remains the symbol of this type of protest; it still continues today, for although the airport was opened to traffic in 1977, it still operates under strict police guard and has only one runway, while the government gave up any plan to build a second one after numerous attempts.

Consumer movements (*sôhisha undô*) proliferated at the end of the period . The Housewives' Federation (Shufuren) had been set up in 1948 to struggle against price increases and keep an eye on the quality of products, especially food. Its campaigns became more determined. In 1970 it launched a national boycott of Matsushita colour television sets when it found that they were on sale overseas more cheaply than in Japan; the firm reduced its prices by 20 per cent. In 1972 the Shufuren also secured a ban on the manufacture of synthetic protein-based livestock feed. The discovery of cadmium-contaminated rice (1966) and the Morinaga and Kanemi scandals also led to creation of numerous local consumer cooperatives distributing organic farming products. Around 1972 there were already almost a thousand groups with about ten million members.

Anti-discrimination movements

The Eta movement. The Eta, who number about 3 million, are not ethnically distinct from other Japanese. Discrimination against them has an occupational and religious origin: they specialised in butchery, tanning and other activities linked with death, seen as impure by Buddhism. The Tokugawa made them outcasts, living in special villages whose names were not put on maps – hence their other names, *Burakumin* ('the hamlet people') and *Hinin* ('non-beings'). Other people feared contact with them as a stain. The Meiji government abolished legal discrimination against them, but *de facto* discrimination continued. A Liberation Movement (Suiheisha) was founded in 1923, but its activism led rather to increased hostility against the former outcasts. After the war the movement reappeared under the name of Buraku Kaihô Dômei (Burakumin Liberation League). Around 1960 discrimination remained total. The great majority of the Eta lived in sordid ghettoes. It was difficult for them to get away to be absorbed into society, for their place of birth gave their origin away in the eyes of employers or potential parents-in-law, who did not hesitate to have enquiries made by specialised private detectives in case of doubt. However, the Eta vote began to carry weight in the cities where it was concentrated (Osaka, Kobe, Fukuoka) when the gap between the LDP and the Left narrowed. The League, dominated by the Socialists, played an important part in the election of the first progressive governors and mayors in Tokyo (1967) and Osaka (1971). The government then hastily released considerable sums to pay for rehabilitation of the ghettoes, loans to Eta enterprises, scholarships and subsidies to Burakumin associations.

The Korean community was a legacy of the war. Of 2 million forced labourers deported to Japan, about 600,000 chose to stay there in 1945 with the authorisation of the SCAP. At the end of the Occupation they were deprived of Japanese nationality – which they had held as subjects of the empire – and thus excluded from the social security systems and civil service jobs. The 1965 Treaty between Tokyo and Seoul (see p. 161) confirmed their right of permanent residence, but nothing more. They were the only significant ethnic minority in the country. Pushed to the margins, they produced highly combative gangs which challenged the *yakuza* in bloody clashes before establishing profitable connections with them. On the political level they reacted to their exclusion by joining, in their majority, an association favourable to North Korea (Chôsôren). But they did not wage any real battle for their rights before the 1970s.

Women's movements. The Occupation placed women on an equal footing with men, in theory. But in reality their situation remained very inferior. At school girls were obliged to take lessons in 'feminine manners'. As many girls as boys finished secondary schooling (90 per cent), but after that the vast majority of girls were directed to two-year pseudo-universities while awaiting marriage, which was still often arranged by the family. Women made up one third of the waged labour force – not counting those who worked without wages in small and medium-scale family businesses or on farms – but they almost never enjoyed lifetime employment, and 40 per cent of them worked in the lowest category of small enterprises (with under thirty employees). They got jobs in large numbers between the ages of 20 and 25, but the employer gave them no training, because he parted company with them when they married. They took jobs again when their children had grown up and the couple faced pressing financial needs again to prepare for retirement. So they did not benefit from wage rises linked to length of service; at 50 a woman only earned half as much as a man for equal work. Those who worked all their lives were usually forced to retire at the age of 50. In 1973 a judge declared that this practice was legal, giving the reason that 'the output of a woman of 55 is equivalent to that of a man of 66'. While the leading figures of feminism, Fusae Ichikawa and Shizue Katô, now in their 70s, were regularly re-elected to the Senate, there were only seven women in the House of Representatives in 1972. Ichikawa herself was defeated in 1971. In local assemblies only 1.1 per cent of elected representatives were women.

This condition was broadly accepted. Women thoroughly internalised their condition. In an opinion poll in 1973, 80 per cent approved the traditional separation of the roles of the two sexes, and more than half said their children were the most important thing in their lives. But women's consciousness was awakening. Women played a major role in inhabitants' movements. In 1971 village women of Kanazashi in Oita region protested against the building of a cement works by chaining themselves to the boat used for site surveys, until the company abandoned the scheme. In 1969 a woman worker sued Nissan over the age of retirement. Women's turnout at elections surpassed that of men – 72.4 per cent compared with 71 per cent in 1972 – and they went over to the opposition: in 1972 there were more women than men voting for the JSP, the JCP and the Kômeitô. The feminist movement in the narrow sense – Ûman Ribu (= 'women's lib') – emerged in October 1970 when two hundred young women demonstrated in Tokyo in the smart Ginza district. Its first national conference brought together about a hundred groups (1972). Abortion and contraception were the main issues on which it campaigned. Abortion had been unrestricted since 1948, but the LDP was trying to amend the law under pressure from some religious groups and from the employers, who were short of labour. Commercial sales of the contraceptive pill remained banned, under pressure from the medical lobby for which 2 million abortions per year were a goldmine. It was under the name of the Federation for Freedom of the Pill and Abortion (Chupiren) that the feminists came together.

The traditionalists' reaction was virulent. A well-known essayist publicly defined the wife as 'a domestic servant who has sexual needs'. But the LDP cautiously agreed to a law on women's work (1972), which 'encouraged' employers not to discriminate and to raise the level of qualification of jobs offered to women – but provided for no incentives or sanctions.

The student outbreak of 1968 and the terrorist movement

The violent discontent of the baby boom generation, as it reached adult life, affected most industrial democracies between 1965 and 1970. In Japan it took on spectacular forms. The theatres of 'exemplary struggles' – Vietnam and Mao's China – were nearby. The American forces operated in Vietnam from Japan without consulting the Japanese government, despite the provisions of the Security Treaty, and the continued American control of Okinawa, where B-52s took off, aroused nationalist feeling. The revolt against the 'consumer society', an element common to all the movements, was further inflamed by the excesses of growth that was much faster and much less controlled than elsewhere. As two thirds of this age group continued studies beyond secondary level, the universities were crammed; the private ones, which admitted three quarters of the students, were often unable to provide serious teaching, like the monstrous Nihon University which registered 100,000 students. There was a great mental gap between the young people trained in democratic principles and a caste of university staff imbued with the high prestige traditionally conferred on *sensei* (teachers). Lastly, the romanticism of violence and death that filled the samurai spirit was transmitted by numerous films and by personalities like Mishima; it was found, even if they were unaware of it, among young Japanese students of the far Left.

The struggle against the Vietnam War and for the return of Okinawa was the detonator, especially after the founding of the Beheiren in 1965. Networks of sympathisers hid American deserters. Street demonstrations were more and more violent. On 8 October 1967 students attacked the airport from which Prime Minister Satô was to take off for Saigon. On 18 January 1968 a call by the aircraft-carrier *Enterprise* at Sasebo near Nagasaki provoked several days of clashes and thousands of injuries and arrests. Protests paralysed the universities. The movement started in January 1968 in the Faculty of Medicine of the National University of Tokyo (Tôdai), where unpaid housemen protested against exploitation. It spread to the whole country in a few weeks and took on very violent forms, imitating the Chinese Cultural Revolution – looting of administrative offices, kidnapping and 'public trials' of professors before mass assemblies. The central building of Tôdai, Yasuda Hall, was occupied by far-Left activists who turned it into a fortress where they eventually held out for more than six months, from July 1968 to January 1969.

But the student movement did not carry the rest of society along with it. The far-left activists isolated themselves by violently denouncing Socialists and Communists. The workers – under the control of the unions – did not budge. Yasuda Hall was recaptured by 8,000 policemen after two days of very violent assault shown live before tens of millions of television viewers (18–19 January 1969). An emergency law provided for punishment of staff and closure of establishments for failure to restore order on their campuses. More than two thousand activists were arrested and sentences rained down, up to two years' imprisonment. Even those who got off with light punishment were most often excluded for life from the comfort of employment with big companies. By obtaining a promise of the return of Okinawa in November 1969 Prime Minister Satô partially disarmed the Beheiren, whose activity dwindled steadily as the American forces left Vietnam.

The movement then degenerated into terrorism. A few hundred militants went underground. They made contact with North Korea, the Palestinians and Cuba, and proclaimed the armed struggle. The most active group was the Red Army (Sekigun), led by a Kyoto student, Tsuyoshi Okudaira, and his wife Fusako Shigenobu. They raided armouries and banks, placed homemade bombs in police stations and the offices of big business, and hijacked a Japan Airlines aircraft to Pyongyang (March 1970). But the movement was torn by sectarian quarrels and undermined by suicidal tendencies. The militants of Sekigun executed fourteen of their comrades before the police decapitated the group after a spectacular televised battle lasting 218 hours around a mountain chalet (19–27 February 1972), in which two policemen were killed. Okudaira and Shigenobu fled to Lebanon. On 30 May 1972 three Japanese terrorists machine-gunned a crowd at Tel Aviv airport, killing 26 people.

The police were never able to defeat the terrorism completely. There were 166 terrorist outrages, 17 dead and 677 injured between 1971 and 1980. Even today far-left groups carry out attacks occasionally, for example 'on the imperial system' as when they detonated a bomb along the road followed by Hirohito's funeral cortège in January 1989. But essentially they exhausted themselves in sectarian vendettas, which have caused the deaths of some 150 militants since 1971.

The struggle against the building of the new Tokyo International Airport (Narita) developed in this context. The site at Sanrizuka, 66 kilometres north of Tokyo, was chosen in 1966 without any agreement with the local farmers. They resisted expropriation and set up the League Against the Airport (Hantai Dômei). The peasants were joined by several dozen students who settled in permanently, and a cinema crew which eventually made seven films of the struggle. Narita became for the whole world the symbol of resistance aroused by the High Growth Era. The peasants fortified the site 'in Vietnamese style' with small forts and tunnels. The first police attack left 1,400 injured in February 1971 and three policemen were killed in September. Six years of clashes with more deaths had to pass before the airport was opened in 1977. To this day it remains incomplete, with only one runway, and operates under heavy police guard.

PARTIES AND THE POLITICAL SYSTEM IN A TIME OF CHANGE

Outwardly, the political system was hardly affected by the protest activity. Eisaku Satô succeeded the terminally ill Ikeda in November 1964 and remained in power until July 1972 – seven years and nine months in power, beating Yoshida's record. The LDP retained its absolute majority in both houses of the Diet. But beneath the apparent continuity the balance was changing.

The Liberal Democratic Party: steady consolidation

The LDP's power was being eroded at every level. In parliamentary elections its share of the vote fell from 54.7 per cent in 1963 to 46.8 per cent in 1972. The conservatives still won an absolute majority of votes, thanks to their independent candidates, and held on to 282 seats out of the 500 in the House of Representatives. But in the Upper House their majority fell to a few votes after they lost eight seats in 1971. Their setback was all the more worrying at the local level. About 1960 the LDP had a near-monopoly of power there; only Kyoto had been held since 1950 by a Communist governor. But by 1972 the Left had taken control of 120 of the 636 large cities, including Yokohama and Osaka. At the regional level the election of the Socialist Minobe as Governor of Tokyo in 1967 was a major shock. The era of progressive local authorities (*kakushin jichitai*) began. Backed by coalitions that included the Socialist and Communist Parties, the new Kômeitô Buddhist party, and 'inhabitants' movements', they were to increase their strength continually over ten years, until they were administering 40 per cent of Japan's population.

The LDP's strength, however, was still overwhelming. In votes and in seats it remained twice as powerful as the JSP. It was the only 'catch-all party' in Japan. It aroused massive electoral support among farmers, small and big entrepreneurs, qualified staff, the liberal professions, and old people, among whom it enjoyed support rates of 50–65 per cent. But even in the categories most unfavourable to the conservatives *a priori* – workers and the under–30s – it won about a third of the vote.

The party's ability to win elections was based on three *ban*: its organised hard-core followers (*jiban*), its candidates' reputation (*kanban*) and an abundant election war chest (*kaban*). Its elected representatives were typically the heirs to local political dynasties, prominent people recommended by the chambers of commerce and cooperatives, former senior civil servants. They were backed by the mayors and governors (who could not be candidates themselves since Japanese law forbids plurality of elective positions). In face of all this the Socialist candidates often looked like lightweights.

The LDP's Diet members organised the voters in support associations (*kôenkai*). The LDP itself had scarcely 200,000 real members. Mobilisation depended entirely on those personal networks of clients which each representative jealously organised for his own interests, because of the voting system which obliged him to compete against other LDP candidates in every election (see p. 68). A *kôenkai* for a conservative Diet member had tens of thousands of members, up to a hundred thousand for leading figures in the party. It was based on local clubs promoted by petty local leaders at district or village level, with twenty-odd paid secretaries at constituency level. To set it up, the Diet member would bargain for the support of regional and municipal councillors who put their networks at his service, with rival *kôenkai* battling to attract support away from each other. Most of their activities were recreational: excursions, banquets, lectures, flower arrangement classes. People could go to them for an introduction to an employer or a little help in getting a child admitted to a better school, or even to arrange a marriage. They often provided rudimentary social security through a solidarity fund. Their members received gifts in cash on ceremonial occasions (weddings, funerals) and small presents at traditional times of year – summer and the end of the year. In exchange they promised 'their' Diet member unconditional loyalty which would be passed on to his heir. The total membership of conservative *kôenkai* was estimated at more than ten million people. Satisfying this patronage network cost a great deal. Around 1960 the average expense for campaigning for a Diet seat was estimated at 20 million yen ($55,000); in 1972 it was five times as much. But the LDP had almost unlimited financial backing from the employers' organisations and the big firms.

The LDP was further strengthened by the systematic use of the state budget for party political purposes. Its Diet members had the public works kitty in their hands, and those public works – being 'investment' financed from special state bonds – were not limited by concern to balance the budget. It was the Diet that decided how to share them out. So everyone could cultivate his constituency with dams and roads. For remote rural areas, a conservative deputy with connections to the public purse was an essential element of survival. The rural voters, who secured half of its seats for the LDP, benefited from generalised farm price support. Every year, when the Diet debated the budget, and the LDP's parliamentary 'rice tribe' engaged battle with the Ministry of Finance for higher agricultural subsidies. By 1972 the price of Japanese rice had become four times higher than world prices, and agricultural subsidies amounted to 12 per cent of the state budget, compared with 3.3 per cent in France. But in the rural areas the turnout at elections was over 80 per cent and the LDP swept three quarters of the seats.

The LDP's skill at wielding power was equal to its ability to win elections. When first created, the party seemed fragile. It was divided between pre-war politicians and the new generation schooled by Yoshida; between former Democrats and former Liberals; between professional politicians who climbed the ladder from local assemblies and former senior civil servants who entered politics by getting directly into the Diet, where they accounted for about a third of conservative deputies; between reactionaries like Kishi, liberals like Ikeda, and populists like Miki and Kôno; between the lobby supporting Seoul and Taipei (Satô, Kishi) and those who rather favoured placating Beijing (Ikeda, Kôno, Miki). Lastly, there were fierce rivalries between ten or so leaders who wanted to sit in the prime minister's chair. These rivalries led to the institutionalising of factions (*habatsu*), which consisted of twenty to fifty Diet members gathered around someone seen as a potential prime minister. They were held together by personal loyalty to the leader and by the election funds that he dispensed to his protégés. In 1962 there were five major factions (those of Ikeda, Satô, Onô, Kôno and Miki) and four smaller ones. The man who would head the Japanese government was in practice chosen every two years when the LDP congress elected the party president – who thereafter stood before the Diet to be officially elected prime minister. On that occasion the factions made alliances around the strongest candidates. The contest was often a close one: in 1958 Ishibashi only beat Kishi by seven votes, and in 1964 Ikeda, who was seeking a third term, was only four votes ahead of Satô. And yet the LDP remained united. The employers threatened to deprive any breakaway leader of funds. After Kishi's fall, the habit grew of distributing portfolios among all the factions in proportion to their numerical strength, changing the cabinet every year to distribute posts among the largest possible number of Diet members. The head of government took care to modify his alliances between congresses, and thus each faction found itself sometimes in the majority, sometimes in the minority. This sophisticated system of managing internal rivalry enabled the LDP to stay in power without splitting up. Governmental stability reflected this internal stability in the party. There were just two prime ministers in this period – Ikeda until 1964, then Satô. The latter's exceptionally long tenure of office is explained partly by his skill at manoeuvring, but also by the removal of his main rivals from the scene: Kishi was out of the running, while Ikeda and Bamboku Onô died in 1964 and Kôno in 1965. Those men's lieutenants quarrelled over their factions, which broke up and were then re-formed. The only stable factions were the Prime Minister's own and that of Takeo Miki, ideologically and historically marginal to the LDP. In 1970 the inheritances were finally settled to the advantage of Takeo Fukuda (heir to Kishi), Masayoshi Ohira (heir to Ikeda) and Yasuhiro Nakasone (heir to Kôno). At once pressure began to mount against Satô, and his government was not to last two years.

The Japan Socialist Party: gradual decline

The Japan Socialist Party hardly benefited from the LDP's relative decline, even though it was practically the only opposition party in 1962. It declined from 29 per cent of votes and 144 seats in 1962 to 21.9 per cent and 118 in 1972. The success of the progressive mayors and governors concealed a declining trend for the party in the big cities. During the decade it fell from 40 to 16 per cent of seats in Tokyo and Osaka, where the JCP and the new Buddhist Kômeitô, both insignificant in 1962, won a third of the seats ten years later. The Socialists let the potential electoral support among rural migrants, those left behind by the economic growth, and white-collar city dwellers slip away.

The JSP remained above all the party of unionised workers, civil servants and the labour aristocracy, of which more than two-thirds voted for it. But the small and medium-scale industries and other businesses escaped it, and it did not win half of the total working class vote, for which both the LDP and the JCP were competitors. In the rural areas, although it won no more than 20 per cent of votes, the electoral system often enabled it to take the last seat in a constituency. Therefore it defended the same ultra-protectionist agricultural policy as the LDP, and was gradually pushed towards compromises, if not a deal, with the government party. The power of the Sôhyô strengthened this concentration of support in one category of workers. The unions were officially affiliated to the JSP as 'support organisations' and carried the day at the party congress. The Sôhyô provided the party with almost all its 50,000 members, its six thousand permanent staff and its funds. Trade union apparatchiks accounted for more than half the local elected representatives and about 40 per cent of the Socialist Diet members.

The party was prevented by its doctrinal rigidity from adapting to a changing society. After the condemnation of his moderate ideas (see p. 95) Eda was removed as Secretary General in 1962. A confused struggle ensued between the strict Marxists of the Socialist Studies Society, Kôzô Sasaki's pragmatic Marxists, and the moderates. Two stormy congresses were held in 1964. Sasaki was elected Chairman and a document was added to the party's platform praising the USSR, condemning European Social Democratic parties, and calling for 'a class government when the proletariat has seized power'. The Society systematically spread its influence in party sections, and the party found itself cut in two with Diet members, generally moderate, on the one side and the sections, whose delegates held the majority at the congress which defined the official line, on the other side. The leadership was a precarious balance between the two, usually combining a leftist Chairman and a moderate Secretary General. The party got bogged down in quarrels and declined in the face of new rivals.

The Communist Party: revival

In 1962 the Japan Communist Party was barely emerging from a semi-undergound existence. It only had three parliamentary seats, and ten regional councillors out of 2,659. Sanzô Nosaka, expelled by Moscow in 1950, took over the party again in 1957, in association with Kenji Miyamoto as Secretary General. It had to deal with numerous factions. The Sino-Soviet dispute divided the party, which expelled first the pro-Soviets in 1964 and then the pro-Chinese, to adopt an independent and pragmatic line: neutralism and non-alignment, defence of the Constitution, improvement of social benefits and a minimum of nationalisation. In the Diet the Communists often voted with the LDP for measures to support the peasantry and small-scale enterprises. The party's grass roots were based around free consultation centres where doctors and lawyers helped people who found themselves destitute and uprooted – migrants, old people without pensions, women on their own. At elections it put forward the most respectable candidates possible. It thus became 'the party of the three *shi*': doctors (*isshi*), lawyers (*bengoshi*) and teachers (*kyôshi*). It was also the only party to put forward many women; in 1974 there were 10.5 per cent of women among its Diet members, compared with 4 per cent for the JSP and 2 per cent for the LDP.

This strategy won spectacular successes in the big cities. In 1967 the JCP won 14 seats, in 1972 38 (10.5 per cent of the vote), sweeping 27.5 per cent in Osaka, 24.6 per cent of the vote in Kyoto and 19.7 per cent in Tokyo. The number of its regional councillors rose tenfold and in 1967, for the first time, a Communist was elected mayor of a Japanese city. In the trade unions the Sôhyô succeeded in containing Communist infiltration, except among the teachers of the Nikkyôso. But in the 'citizens' movements' the JCP's action led to sharp divisions. The Council Against the Atomic Bomb split in 1965. In 1970 the Communists left the Burakumin Liberation League and founded a rival organisation, which clashed with the League over the subsidies beginning to flow in. Thanks to the prestige of Torazô Ninagawa, the 'Red Governor' of Kyoto who had started in his region a pioneer system of preferential loans to small-scale enterprises, the JCP exerted a dominant influence over the left-wing shop owners' federation (Minshô), whose membership rose from 80,000 to 200,000 between 1966 and 1972. However, the JCP remained the party of one sector. It won very few votes in rural areas. Its electorate was mostly working class and young, although it also penetrated the traditional urban circles of shopkeepers and craftsmen. Its audience was limited to the big cities, and it only had elected representatives in seven regions out of forty-six. But in the megalopoles it became an essential element in progressive fronts which won success after success from 1967 onwards. While it was not a mass party (200,000 members around 1970), its militants' activism and devotion gave it a clear advantage over the JSP which was both its partner and its rival within those fronts.

Buddhist politics: the Kômeitô

The Sôkagakkai sect was founded in 1937 by Tsunesaburô Makiguchi and Jôsei Toda. It was derived from the nationalist, popular and intolerant Buddhism preached in the thirteenth century by Nichiren. The sect was opposed to Shintoism and to state control of religion. It was suppressed by the military; Makiguchi died in prison and Toda was only released in 1945. The movement started up again in a modest way with only 5,000 followers in 1951. But the social upheavals provided the opportunity for phenomenal growth. The Sôkagakkai reached 3.5 million followers in 1963, maybe 10 million in 1972 – many more than any other 'new religion'. This success was due to aggressive proselytisation. Each of the faithful was supposed to convert three people per year; the faithful were trained in a persuasion technique called *shaku buku* (break and flatten). The message was simple: a family altar provided by the sect and daily recital of the Sutra of the Lotus would bring health, wealth and harmony in the home. The moral code tolerated alcohol and sex 'within reasonable limits'. The organisation was military: ten households formed a group, ten groups a section, ten sections a district, etc. The groups met regularly to encourage their members and prepare conversion campaigns. The sect had women's and young people's associations, and a powerful cultural organisation. Its wealth was considerable: in 1965 it collected 35.5 billion yen (about $100 million) in four days to build a grand temple. Daisuku Ikeda, who became its Chairman in 1968 and was still at the helm in 2000, was one of the most powerful men in Japan.

The Sôkagakkai went into politics in 1955, with 51 of its candidates elected to local assemblies, followed by three members of the Upper House in 1956. Its only avowed purpose then was to secure the erection of a national temple. But in 1957 Toda elaborated a theory of 'Buddhist democracy', which was a prelude to the creation in 1961 of the Clean Government Party, Kômeitô. The new party won 25 seats in the House in 1967 and 47 in 1969 (11 per cent of the vote), thus becoming the second opposition party. Until the end of the 1980s it continued to be led by the same men – Yoshitaku Takeiri as President, Junya Kanô as Secretary General.

The Kômeitô voters typified the disadvantaged and rootless classes in the megalopoles. Only 5 per cent of them had university degrees, 40 per cent were craftsmen or small-scale employers and their employees, 25 per cent skilled workers, 60 per cent women. Unlike the JCP the Kômeitô only presented candidates where they could win; it was absent everywhere except in the very large cities. The similarity between its strongholds and those of the Communists was striking, and that made them ferocious enemies. More than half of the Kômeitô voters had voted previously for the LDP, a third for the JSP; but it took seats mostly from the Socialists because their deputies were often elected in the last position, and thus vulnerable even to a limited loss of votes.

The Kômeitô's political programme was rid of religious references in 1970. It condemned 'private interests, the dehumanising principle of the economy'. It called for 'Socialism based on human dignity', action against obstacles to living 'a worthy existence' (the housing crisis, excessive taxes, etc.), strengthening of social security – including an allowance for 'family misfortunes' –, defence of the Constitution, and pacifism aiming at the establishment of universal peace. There were obvious points of convergence with the left-wing parties' programme. The Kômeitô thus joined the local progressive fronts in 1970, except where they were too clearly dominated by the Communist Party, as in Kyoto. But it retained its own very special colouring. It put itself forward as the champion of morality and denounced wholesale the corruption of all the established parties. From Nichiren it retained the idea that Japan had the vocation to convert the world, and cultivated nationalism; it called for disbanding of the Self Defence Forces, but respected the symbols of traditional Japan. Together with its militant aggressiveness, these anti-parliamentary and nationalist tendencies led to it being called 'fascist', while in fact it was like the Poujadists in France: 'for the small guys, against the big guys'. It seemed to most Japanese alien to 'normal' political life, and while its voters were exceptionally faithful, it provoked negative reactions, stronger than those against any other party, from the rest of public opinion, and above all among modern and educated voters.

The Democratic Socialist Party: stagnation

When Suehiro Nishio left the JSP in 1960 (see p. 95), he took forty deputies with him. But deprived of the support of the Sôhyô, they were reduced to 17 in the following elections. In 1972 the DSP still held only 19 seats, receiving 6.9 per cent of the vote. Except in some rural constituencies held by family dynasties going back to the pre-war Farmer-Labour Party, they owed their election to the combined support of the Dômei union organisation and the employers. They were often trade union officials coopted by management, which encouraged employees and sub-contractors to back 'the firm's candidate', especially in the big motor works. Its seats were concentrated in the industrial zone of central Japan (Nagoya, Osaka). However, the connection between the DSP and the Dômei remained fairly loose; less than half the union's members voted for the party, which remained wedged into a very narrow base. It depended very much on the personal prestige of its candidates; when Nishio retired in 1972 the party lost six seats altogether in Osaka, where he had been a historic figure in the workers' movement since before the war. As for the programme, the DSP clashed with the Socialists over the Security Treaty and the Self Defence Forces, which it accepted 'until a general disarmament agreement', and it called for social security 'ensuring a minimum standard of living from birth to death'.

PRESSURE GROUPS IN THE POLITICAL SYSTEM; NEO-CORPORATIST TRENDS

Besides of the political parties, the role of pressure groups increased during this period. Modernisation that threatened more and more numerous social groups impelled them to organise themselves on their own, especially as the opposition had little success in channelling new discontents – and not much will to do so, especially in the case of the JSP. When confronted with these movements the government typically sought to tame them. The LDP, in difficulty, needed more and more money and stable electoral support; it sought support from all the organisations capable of providing those resources, by inviting them to join consultative bodies and consulting regularly with them, by taking responsibility for their interests, and by providing them with financial compensation. Thus numerous lobbies were integrated semi-officially into the decision-making process, in near symbiosis with the administration and the government party. A sort of informal neo-corporatism took shape.

Employers' organisations: not all-powerful

Employers' organisations played a major role by the side of the LDP. The Keidanren (Federation of Economic Organisations) was the spokesman for the traditional establishment of big enterprises or *zaikai*. The Nikkeiren (Federation of Employers' Associations) dealt particularly with social and trade union relations. The Dôyukai (Japanese Management Association) was the organisation of the more liberal wing of the employers and took an interest in improving firms' management. The chambers of commerce network was a powerful agent of regional influence at election time. The employers' organisations accounted for 95 per cent of conservative politicians' funding. Thus they had considerable influence, which they used to push those politicians into uniting in 1955, and since then, where possible, they have brought their influence to bear in defence of their interests. They demanded economic growth protected from foreign competition, with as few social considerations as possible to hamper it, and maximum state aid to back it. In this they were backed by the MITI and the Ministry of Finance. However, the employers' organisations were far from having absolute power over the LDP. They were often kept in check by groups capable of delivering guaranteed votes, which were as precious as election funds.

Small-scale business: a growing force

Two organisations were set up in 1952. The powerful League of Small and Medium Enterprises (Chûseiren) maintained connections with the two major parties, while the Cooperative Movement of Shopkeepers' Associations (Minshô) was close to the JCP. Both called for a tax system and favourable loans for small and medium enterprises, a law against improper practices by the big firms (delays in payment, etc.) and against their intrusion into traditionally semi-craft branches such as production of tatami mats and *tôfu*, and restrictions on establishment of supermarkets. At first the employers' organisations, backed by the MITI, held them in check. But the 1960 crisis enabled them to secure a series of measures in their favour (see p. 96). In 1963 they won another victory when a bill protecting small and medium enterprises, rejected by the MITI, was presented as a members' bill by united LDP and opposition Diet members, and adopted. When the government saved Yamaichi Securities from bankruptcy in 1965, the small enterprises demanded for themselves the establishment of a system of unguaranteed loans. The Communist Governor of Kyoto granted this immediately. Others did the same, but the government refused to follow suit, and the MITI kept pushing for the creation of supermarkets on a large scale. In response the Minshô rose from 80,000 members in 1966 to 200,000 in 1972; the JCP and the Kômeitô made progress in the ranks of small and medium-scale business. In the LDP Kakuei Tanaka and Yasuhiro Nakasone rang the alarm bell. As Prime Minister Tanaka in 1973 was to extend the system of preferential loans for small and medium enterprises over the country as a whole.

Agricultural cooperatives: the pillar of the LDP's hegemony

The cooperatives were essential to control the rural constituencies, which were the LDP's strongholds. They could get entire hamlets out to vote, not losing more than a few votes. They made use of community solidarity but also of overt pressure such as ostracism (*mura-hachibu*), whereby a whole hamlet refused mutual aid to the recalcitrant until he was brought to apologise publicly before the general assembly. Nôkyô, the giant umbrella organisation for all the agricultural cooperatives, was a true *keiretsu*, which extended its activities with the backing of the state authorities which authorised it to act as a bank, an insurer and an estate agent, in addition to the marketing of agricultural produce, fertiliser and equipment. The cooperatives controlled more than 300 varying enterprises and supplied almost all the needs of 5.5 million rural homes. Closely associated with the management of subsidies that flowed into the countryside, they were at the same time real parastatal bodies and LDP election agents.

The farm lobby had the unanimous backing of all the parties. It secured a system of protection that made Japan's agricultural products the most expensive in the world. It was in vain that the Keidanren called for 'a cheap agriculture' (*yasuagari nôgyô*) in preference to a system that ate into consumers' purchasing power and kept in the countryside the labour industry needed. Because of their success the cooperatives were able to eliminate what was left of the rural leagues inherited from the Occupation. In 1958 the remnants of the left-wing organisations have been absorbed by the moderates of the Zennichinô (see p. 58); but that federation was now itself moribund. The Communist Federation of Agricultural Workers had no more than 10,000 members at its peak. Here and there communities threatened with expropriation showed a fierce combative spirit, as at Narita, but they did not encounter any solidarity in a rural world now under tight conservative control.

Religious movements

Even if the Sôkagakkai is an exceptional case, religious movements did not hesitate to intervene in political life. The Christian churches and certain Buddhist organisations took part in the struggle against the Security Treaty. Many recommended candidates for the Upper House elections; but the religious groups had very divergent interests.

Traditional Shintoism (*jinja shintô*) controlled nearly 80,000 shrines, run by professional priests who passed on the job from father to son, and together formed a caste of notables. *Jinja shintô* was nostalgic for the imperial system and very close to the right wing of the LDP (Kishi, Nakasone). It campaigned for the nationalisation of the Yasukuni shrine (see p. 44), which would restore a link between the state and the former official religion in defiance of the Constitution. It was supported by the Association of Veterans and Bereaved Families (Izokukai), 6 million strong, for which that nationalisation would be a solemn rehabilitation of the ex-servicemen. This campaign, begun in 1956, led to a virulent national debate. The massive petitions of the Izokukai were answered by those of the Buddhists and by left-wing demonstrations. The LDP procrastinated; a commission set up in 1959 eventually took six years to propose a bill that was to be buried by the Diet five times and dropped in 1974. Buddhism, the new religions and the Christian churches thus defeated the Shintoist lobby. But Buddhism itself also had a long tradition of collusion with state authority. It shared its following with Shintô since most Japanese practised one religion or the other according to the circumstances of their lives. Some Buddhist sects were active in the pacifist movement, but generally they avoided committing themselves. The new religions, members of the Shinshûren, were impressively effective at election time. Most of them backed the LDP, in return for the complete exemption from taxes that was awarded to all religious bodies. In any case they were fairly favourable to revival of the traditional Japan, except for the restoration of official Shintoism. The Christians, long persecuted and not belonging in Japanese tradition, rather took the opposition side; but they were only a million, fairly scattered around.

Other pressure groups

The new social movements like *jûmin undô* did not exert any real control over their members. Ideologically, they were multifarious. A big consumers' association like the Shufuren did not command the votes of the millions of members that it claimed. It took part in left-wing movements like the Council Against the Atomic Bomb, but it let itself be seduced by the administration into joining numerous commissions in which its female leaders were to be gradually integrated into the most outward circle of decision makers. Only the Burakumin League had real electoral power, because of the concentration and solidarity of the ghettoes. At first it backed the progressive fronts, but with the award of massive subsidies, the state authorities began steadily to win the movement over.

The Japanese Medical Association, supported by the pharmaceutical lobby, is the best example of a professional pressure group. It supported the LDP in return for exorbitant tax concessions, the right for doctors prescribing medicines to sell them to the patients themselves, and also an improvement in health insurance which guaranteed them an extensive solvent clientele. As a rule each ministry encouraged the professions under its supervision to organise themselves, for its own power in dealing with other departments – especially Finance – depended on its capacity for mobilising a lobby. Hence there was a close symbiosis between the government and the professional bodies, which made it possible to maintain privileges not always justified from the viewpoint of the public good.

All organised groups, from the volunteer firemen (numbering millions, because of the highly inflammable traditional wooden buildings) to schools of flower arrangement and martial arts, cultivated administrative and political protection. Thus the conservative government had an extraordinarily wide and diverse base, which made it difficult to shake and much more than the establishment's and big business' party.

FOREIGN POLICY

Tension with the United States: the 'Nixon Shocks'

The Security Treaty and the Okinawa question remained at the heart of Japanese-American relations throughout the decade. After the 1960 crisis the treaty was renewed for ten years. When it expired in 1970 the Japanese government feared a new explosion. The United States, engaged in the Vietnam conflict and worried about the reinforcement of the Soviet army in the Far East, wanted absolutely to retain its Japanese bases. In this situation the return of the islands placed under American administration in 1952 became a central element in negotiations, for it could make it possible for Satô to disarm the opposition, if he secured it in exhange for the renewal of the treaty. Okinawa occupied a key place in American strategy in Asia, with 50,000 troops, 117 military installations – including seven airfields from which B-52s took off to bomb Vietnam and U-2s to spy on the USSR and China – and nuclear missile bases. Even though the island lived off the bases, left-wing forces were dead-set against the US forces. In 1965 violent demonstrations erupted in Okinawa against the Vietnam war and Satô, on a visit to the island, declared that the postwar era would not be brought to an end before Okinawa and the Bônin Islands were returned to Japan. In 1967, after going to Saigon to show his support for the American intervention, he secured the return of the Bônin Islands and negotiations over Okinawa.

The formulation of the Nixon Doctrine (May 1969) made the negotiations easier. In a speech in Guam the US President announced his intention to transfer gradually to its Asian allies the responsibility for their own defence. This disengagement was due to the growing unpopularity of the Vietnam War in the United States, but also to the serious difficulties affecting the American balance of payments. The United States withdrew its forces from Vietnam, reducing them from 535,000 in 1969 to 27,000 in 1972. It brought a division home from Korea and reduced its forces in Japan from 41,800 to 25,500 in 1971 – not including the forces based at Okinawa. The Japanese government knew how to make use of the new situation. The Nixon-Satô communiqué of 21 November 1969 promised the return of Okinawa in exchange for a declaration by Tokyo that the security of Japan was tied to that of Taiwan and Korea. That could be interpreted as a commitment to take part in their defence, and to strengthen that impression Satô appointed as Minister of Defence the LDP's best known 'hawk', Yasuhiro Nakasone.

The prospect of a considerable increase in the Self Defence Forces seemed to arise from this. Since the 1960s crisis the military budget stagnated around 8 per cent of the national budget and fell from 1.2 per cent of GNP to 0.8 per cent. The third plan for development of the armed forces provided only for a modest increase in the land forces' strength, to 180,000 men – which had already been the target for 1960 – and 40 more aircraft. And Satô, to defuse the violent opposition which he sensed was coming over the nuclear weapons stockpiled in Okinawa, made a commitment to respect the 'three non-nuclear principles': no atomic weapon would be manufactured in Japan, bought by Japan, or allowed to enter Japan. But the debate rebounded. The first White Paper on defence, published in 1970 by Nakasone, stated that 'legally, Japan can possess nuclear weapons whose power would not exceed the minimum necessary for its defence'. In the same year Tokyo signed the Non-Proliferation Treaty, but refused to ratify it until it had secured some relaxation of its restrictive provisions, and guaranteed access to technology. The White Paper also defined a new autonomous defence doctrine; Japan must be able to repel on its own any conventional attack and manufacture all necessary armaments itself, including fighter aircraft. A new armed forces development plan, for 1972–6, provided for a 17 per cent increase in the military budget in 1971, and strengthening of the Air Force and the Navy as a priority to make active defence possible well away from the coasts – or maybe intervention still further afield in the Korea-Taiwan perimeter.

But Nakasone encountered strong opposition. In the LDP the 'doves' (Miki, Ohira) gave priority to the restoration of Japanese influence in Asia by economic and diplomatic means, and did not want to bring back bad memories. The army itself was too closely linked with the US Army and the American arms lobby to embrace the idea of autonomous defence. Nakasone lost the Defence portfolio after only one year. His plan was scaled down, and the idea of a Japanese fighter aircraft was dropped. In the meantime rapprochement with China had become the absolute priority.

America's U-turn towards People's China underlay the Nixon Doctrine. The Sino-Soviet clashes on the Ussuri river (March 1969) made it possible for the United States to envisage a rapprochement with Beijing, without which its disengagement from Asia would be too great a risk. But Nixon moved in that direction without telling the Japanese, not caring if he wrong-footed them. In 1971, while Henry Kissinger travelled secretly to Beijing, Washington asked Tokyo again to sponsor at the UN a resolution to block the admission of People's China, and when a communiqué announced that Nixon would go to China in 1972, Japan was only forewarned a few hours beforehand (15 July). This was the first *Nixon shoku* ('Nixon shock'). However, when Beijing joined the UN in October, Tokyo still agreed to sponsor an attempt to preserve Taiwan's seat by proposing, in vain, representation of both Chinas. This loyalty was ill rewarded. Tokyo was surprised again by the communiqué published at the end of Nixon's journey (27 February 1972). Washington did not officially recognise the People's Republic and did not break with Taiwan, but it 'acknowledged' Beijing's position that there was only one China of which Taiwan was a part, and promised to withdraw its forces from the island in due course. Japan was thoroughly shaken; it was afraid of being left isolated by a reversal of American alliances in Asia. It went on to react by making a rapprochement with Beijing on its own account, and go much further than Nixon had dared to go. Between Tokyo and Washington the era of trust was over.

Economic quarrels poisoned the atmosphere further. Since the end of the previous period Washington had been orchestrating pressure on Japan by GATT and the OECD to make it lift its protective measures. Tension mounted after 1965, when Japan recorded its first trade surplus with the United States ($100 million). The American deficit deepened to $1.5 billion in 1970. It was all the more unendurable because the Vietnam war, from which Japanese industry made handsome profits, upset the

American balance of payments. In 1965 Washington obliged Japan and the EEC to limit their steel exports. In the 1968 elections, in order to win the cotton-growing South, Nixon promised to protect it against Japanese textile imports. But the textile lobby was also powerful in Tokyo; the Diet voted unanimously against any concession to the Americans. At the Nixon-Satô summit of 1969 Satô promised to resolve this problem and speed up the removal of protectionist measures. But Japan was then going through a period of intense agitation. The LDP thought only of reassuring its electorate and blocked all concessions, while the opposition played the anti-American card for all it was worth. In 1970 the US House of Representatives adopted a bill introducing quotas for Japanese textiles and the Zenith company took legal action against dumping of Japanese television sets. In March 1971 Nixon rejected a Japanese non-binding proposal for voluntary restraint of textile exports.

The crisis widened when Washington pressed its trading partners to revalue their currencies. On 15 August 1971 the United States unilaterally suspended convertibility of the dollar into gold and imposed a 10 per cent surtax on all imports. This was the second *Nixon shoku*. The Europeans at once let their currencies float, but Tokyo held out until 28 August before agreeing to revaluation of the yen by 16.88 per cent – the biggest rise of all those that had occurred thus far. In October the new MITI Minister, Kakuei Tanaka, signed against the wishes of his own officials a three-year agreement limiting the annual increase in textile exports to the United States to 5 per cent for synthetics and 1 per cent for wool. The United States had won. Its trade deficit with Japan fell from $5.8 billion in 1971 to $3 billion in 1972. But the price, again, was tension between the two countries.

Even so, the bilateral relationship remained vital for both of them. A third of Japan's trade was with the United States, on which Japan's security also depended, while Washington had no firmer base in the region, where the spectre of defeat in Vietnam raised the threat of a collapse of neighbouring countries one after another (the 'domino theory'). In these conditions the return of Okinawa was agreed in June 1971 and took effect on 15 May 1972. Satô retired almost immediately afterwards. Kakuei Tanaka, who succeeded him, was to accept a series of commercial concessions to Nixon in the Hawaii Agreements (see p. 167).

Normalising relations with China

Trade relations with the two Chinas developed rapidly. As Beijing agreed to trade only with 'friendly firms', the *sôgô shôsha* split the two markets amicably among themselves, the markets being noticeably equal in size: trade with Taiwan was worth $662 million in 1968 and trade with Beijing $620 million in 1966. But the political question remained ultra-sensitive. The LDP was deeply divided. The Taipei-Seoul lobby was led by Kishi and his heir Takeo Fukuda, to whom Taiwan and South Korea were to pay hundreds of thousands of dollars to try to ensure his victory over Kakuei Tanaka in the succession to Satô. Beijing's supporters fell behind Tanaka, Takeo Miki and Masayoshi Ohira. The opposition was also divided; the leaders of the JSP and the Kômeitô often travelled to Beijing, but the Democratic Socialist Party supported Taiwan.

The Taiwan lobby had the upper hand until 1971. In 1964 it secured a ban on credits from the Import-Export Bank for trade with People's China, while obtaining a $150 million loan to Taipei. The Cultural Revolution (1967–8) checked trade with Beijing. In 1969 the Nixon-Satô communiqué linked the security of Japan with that of Taiwan. Even after the first 'Nixon shock' Tokyo pursued to the end the battle on Taipei's behalf at the UN, under the direction of Fukuda as Foreign Minister. But the reaction to the Sino-American communiqué of 27 February 1972 was very swift. It took only a few days for the Import-Export Bank to reopen its lines of credit for trade with Beijing and Fukuda himself suggested recognition of the People's Republic. Talks began behind the scenes, sometimes using emissaries of the JSP and the Kômeitô to bypass the too pro-American Foreign Ministry officials. Satô's replacement by Tanaka, with Ohira as Foreign Minister, removed the last remaining obstacles.

Tanaka flew to Beijing on 25 September. He went much further than Nixon, in recognising the People's Republic as the sole legal government of China including Taiwan, and broke off relations with Chiang Kai-shek. The two parties committed themselves to negotiating a peace treaty. China, showing great moderation, renounced war reparations and evaded the question of the Senkaku islands, a tiny archipelago north-east of Taiwan, which Beijing had been claiming since the discovery of oil in 1965. However, lines were not cut with Taiwan. Unofficial associations took over from the closed embassies and consulates. Japan became the leading investor in the island, where Washington was in the process of disengagement, and trade continued to develop, until it reached more than $800 million per year.

The Soviet Union: enduring antagonism

Tokyo had adopted an even-handed attitude to the Sino-Soviet conflict. Both the USSR and Japan showed a desire for détente: former inhabitants of the Kuriles were allowed to visit their family graves (1964), consulates were opened in Osaka and Vladivostok (1966), and an air link was established between Tokyo and Moscow. An Economic Cooperation Committee signed in 1965 the first agreement for exploitation of the Siberian forests, Japan providing $130 million, repayable in timber. In 1968 Japan's trade with the USSR exceeded its trade with China, at $624 million. However, political relations deteriorated from 1969 onwards. Moscow tried to prevent the renewal of the Security Treaty by proposing a system of collective security in Asia, on the basis of the withdrawal of all foreign troops. But since that manoeuvre coincided with the violent Sino-Soviet clashes on the Ussuri, it did not even win the support of the Japanese left. Then Moscow let itself be overtaken by the rapprochement between Tokyo and Beijing. Gromyko did go to propose negotiations for a peace treaty in January 1972, but nothing was done before Tanaka's journey to Beijing in September. The Sino-Japanese communiqué included a clause by which the two countries committed themselves to opposing any attempt by a third power to establish its 'hegemony' in Asia – which was clearly aimed at the USSR. Moscow then returned to an uncompromising position on the Kurile Islands, and the talks which began at in October got nowhere. But economic cooperation continued. At the beginning of 1972 Moscow put forward a series of plans for joint exploitation of oil, gas, coal, timber and nickel as far as the Urals – in fact offering Japan all the raw materials it needed.

Normalising relations with Korea

Tokyo and Seoul had remained without diplomatic relations since 1952. Even the coming of moderate leaders to power – Ikeda, and

General Park Chung-hee in Seoul – did not make any progress possible, because Ikeda sought to placate the JSP, which was hostile to any separate peace with South Korea. But the increasing dangers in Asia – the Vietnam War, and the explosion of China's first atomic bomb in 1964 – pushed the two countries into new talks.

By the Treaty of 22 June 1965 Tokyo recognised the Seoul government as the only legitimate government of Korea, in conformity with the UN's position. Seoul renounced war reparations in exchange for $800 million in economic aid. The right of permanent residence for the Koreans of Japan was confirmed. To defuse the conflict over limits of territorial waters, a common fishing zone was created; but both countries maintained their claim to the Tokdo islets. In both countries the treaty was greeted with violent protest, but Japanese investment in Korea began to increase straight away. In 1969 Seoul had more trade with Japan (36.2 per cent) than with the USA (34.6 per cent), and more Japanese than American capital flowed into South Korea.

The question of North Korea was raised again after the normalisation of Sino-Japanese relations. The JSP and the Kômeitô called for similar normalisation with Pyongyang. Within the LDP itself, a North Korea Friendship League was created. On his side Kim Il-Sung was afraid of being isolated and stopped calling for the abrogation of the treaty between Seoul and Tokyo as a precondition for any contact. In 1972 Diet members belonging to the League negotiated a trade agreement that was supposed to increase trade from $60 million to $500 million.

First Asian cooperation moves

Around 1970 Japan was selling 80 per cent of its exports to the countries bordering the Pacific and South-East Asia, and obtaining two thirds of imports from there. Tokyo could no longer avoid taking an interest in regional cooperation. But it had to act with care and keep a very low political profile since painful memories of the war still haunted the Asian countries and were combined with envy for the 'yellow Yankees' among peoples whose average income was only $106 per inhabitant compared with $1,500 in Japan in 1970.

An important first step towards regional organisation-building was the foundation of the Asian Development Bank in 1965 at the instigation of the United Nations. It had 27 member states, from Iran to Australia and Canada. Japan had 20 per cent of the capital, the same as the United States, and the post of Director was reserved to it. Almost at the same time, two cooperation bodies were set up. The South-East Asia Development Conference linked Japan with South Vietnam, Laos and Cambodia and the five countries that were then about to found ASEAN (Thailand, Malaysia, Singapore, Indonesia and the Philippines). It met annually to examine economic cooperation projects, which Tokyo was naturally entrusted with implementing. The Asia-Pacific Council (ASPAC), another interministerial conference, was more political. Against the background of the Vietnam war it brought together Washington's allies in the whole Pacific area: Taiwan, South Korea, South Vietnam, three ASEAN countries (Thailand, Malaysia and the Philippines), Australia and New Zealand. But Tokyo tried to make this, too, a forum for economic cooperation.

Satô's regional tour in 1967 symbolised Japan's return to the region. In a very calculated order he visited Seoul and Taipei, then Singapore, Rangoon, Kuala Lumpur, Bangkok, Vientiane, Phnom Penh, Jakarta, Sydney, Canberra and Manila, ending up in Saigon. All along the way, violent demonstrations reminded him that there was still little love for Japan in most Asian countries. Japan nevertheless pushed ahead for an increased regional role by promoting regional organisation. The informal PAFTAD (Pacific Organisation for Trade and Development), which was a mere 'private club' of academics and businessmen created in 1960 following a Japanese idea, was supplemented in 1967 by the PBEC (Pacific Basin Economic Conference). This new body – to whose birth Japan contributed greatly behind the scenes – brought together businessmen from about 1,000 enterprises from Japan, South Korea, Taiwan, the USA, Canada, Australia and New Zealand; civil servants also took part 'in their private capacities'.

The creation of ASEAN (August 1967) revealed smaller countries' mistrust of the powers, including Japan, whose rivalries were threatening the whole region. The Association of South-East Asian Nations grouped Indonesia, Malaysia, the Philippines, Singapore and Thailand. A permanent Committee and annual meetings of the heads of state or government ensured some degree of political cooperation within the group, which however was not very coherent. Japan had a twofold interest: Indonesia was its biggest regional supplier of raw materials, and it controlled, with Singapore and Malaysia, the Malacca Straits through which 95 per cent of Japan's oil imports passed. In the first display of ASEAN's assertiveness there was a mini-crisis between those three countries and Tokyo in 1971. When Britain gave up its Singapore naval base Japan showed a rather too obvious concern for the Straits by sending ships for an official call at Singapore; the three countries bordering the Straits then reaffirmed their sovereignty in a statement laying down that 'the Straits are not international straits'.

Japan's economic power was continually asserted. Credits and equipment supplies as war reparations paved the way for Japanese products throughout Asia. From bulbs to transistor radios, from fans to Honda motor cycles, they found their way in everywhere. Japan displaced the Westerners in their strongholds – the USA in South Korea and Taiwan, the British in Australia, where Japan became the first customer for exports. Japanese exports to South-East Asia rose from $1.8 billion in 1964 to $4.9 billion in 1970, and secured Japan a $2 billion surplus in that year. Official development aid took over from the reparations, and Japan became the fourth provider of such aid in the world in 1968, with a billion dollars which went essentially to the Asia zone, and first to Indonesia. Investment rose from $120 million in 1968 to $400 million in 1970. It was divided equally between large-scale operations aimed at getting hold of raw materials (Indonesian timber and oil, Australian iron ore) and a multitude of projects through which small and medium industries sought to penetrate local consumer markets.

The idea of anything like an 'Asia Zone' where Japan would have a privileged role was still difficult to raise; memories of the 'Co-Prosperity Sphere' were too fresh. But Takeo Miki, Foreign Minister in 1966, was already mentioning it then. And in 1970 the Defence Minister, Nakasone, wrote in the magazine *Kaigai Jijô*, 'Pan-Asianism has been one of Japan's great national aims since the Meiji era. It falls to us today to rethink the slogan "Asia is one!" in new terms.'

Limited role elsewhere

Europe was still far from Japanese preoccupations; it only accounted for around 10 per cent of Japan's trade. Sony's first attempt to establish a television set factory in Ireland was a failure, as was the launching of the first Honda cars in 1968. But the emergence of the European Community worried Japan, which feared that it would be surrounded by protective barriers. Trade negotiations were opened in July 1970, but failed because of Tokyo's refusal to accept the safeguard clauses envisaged by the EEC against some of the Japanese imports. On the political plane, Ikeda went on a European tour in 1962. On that occasion General de Gaulle – the French President – confided that the Japanese Prime Minister looked like a 'transistor radio salesman', an expression that shocked many Japanese. In 1964 Georges Pompidou was the first French head of government to travel to Tokyo. But Japan's preferred European partner was still Britain; Princess Margaret (1969) and then Prince Charles (1970) were welcomed with great pomp in Tokyo. In 1971 an official visit by Hirohito to seven European capitals showed that the page of the war had been turned. But Japan was still far from being seen by the old continent as anything like a great power.

Japan displayed little interest in Africa, which accounted for only 6 per cent of its trade, and relations remained limited at all levels. In the Middle East Tokyo carefully separated politics and economics; it bought 78 per cent of its oil from there, but always voted with Washington at the UN on the Israeli question. In Latin America (6.7 per cent of trade) Tokyo began to display a certain interest in the countries rich in raw materials, where the presence of Japanese immigrant communities (about 700,000 people) could provide it with bridgeheads. The Emperor received the President of Mexico in 1962 and the Crown Prince visited Mexico (1964) and then Peru, Argentina and Brazil (1967).

END OF THE SATO GOVERNMENT, JULY 1972

From 1970 onwards Satô's position weakened rapidly within the LDP, even though he was reelected for a fourth term as Chairman of the party. The leading factions were now in the hands of a new generation: Takeo Fukuda, Yasuhiro Nakasone and Masayoshi Ohira. By clinging to power Satô blocked their ambitions, at the risk of provoking splits. Aware of the danger, the Executive Committee of the party, where Satô's opponents now had the upper hand, altered its statutes to limit the chairmanship to two successive terms in the future.

The domestic political situation was continually worsening, with local election victories for the progressives, the government's rout in the pollution scandals, terrorism and the violence at Narita; so did the external situation, with the 'Nixon shocks'. In the Upper House elections of 1971 the LDP ended up balanced on a razor's edge. Satô was reduced to impotence by the LDP's backbenchers. They derailed the rearmament effort begun with Nakasone as Defence Minister, and blocked any negotiated solution in the crisis with the United States over textiles. The Prime Minister could not govern any longer. He threw in the sponge and promised to resign as soon as Okinawa was handed back, in May 1972.

Satô even failed to transfer power to the successor he had chosen, Takeo Fukuda. Two-thirds of his own faction decided to support Kakuei Tanaka. This son of a bankrupt carpenter clashed with the conservative establishment because of his relative youth (54), his populist style and the overt crudity of his ambitions, backed by a colossal fortune built up in public works. On the eve of the congress to choose Satô's successor he published *Building a New Japan*, setting out a grandiose vision for the archipelago's future development. This best-seller increased the popularity of the man nicknamed 'the bulldozer-computer' by the public. Fukuda, who was his elder at 67, a graduate of Tôdai and former official of the Ministry of Finance, embodied the traditional élite. But he was narrowly identified with the Taipei-Seoul lobby, which had lost momentum since Nixon's trip to Beijing. He stood for continuity with the two brothers Satô and Kishi, who had controlled the government since 1957. Tanaka, Ohira and Miki reached an agreement against him: whoever was in the lead in the first round of voting would get the benefit of the withdrawal of the other two.

Massive corruption marked the July 1972 congress, where the candidates were said to have spent altogether more than 17 million yen for a single vote. The delegates bargained over their votes in the corridors in front of the media. Fukuda received 400 million yen from Seoul, but Tanaka succeeded in buying Nakasone's support to take the lead in the first round, then defeated Fukuda in the second by 282 votes to 190. The ensuing 'Kaku-Fuku war' was to destabilise the LDP seriously in the following period.

5

A SHOCK-ABSORBER SYSTEM (1972–80)

Coming after the 'Nixon shocks', the oil shock of 1973 panicked the public, while hyperinflation threatened to destabilise society even more. The Tanaka government foundered in two years in a tidal wave of scandals. Rivalries intensified in the LDP, which in 1976 experienced its first breakaway. But the divided opposition was incapable of seizing the opportunity, despite a series of local election victories. The economy recovered in 1975, much quicker than in the West. Encouraged by this success the LDP, despite an internal crisis that led it to the verge of breaking up (1979–80), re-established its hold and regained the lost local authorities. In 1980 Japan was stabilised again, economically, socially and politically. Only one major shadow remained: the public deficit, which had been growing continually.

A NATION IN CRISIS (1972–76)

Trade crisis, oil shock, hyperinflation

The trade crisis arose from the confrontation with the United States, going on since 1968 and brought to a peak by the denunciation of the Bretton Woods agreements. Japan refused for four years to restrict its textile exports, and it was the last country to bend to US pressure and to revalue its currency. But in the end it had to give in. Tanaka, just after taking power, had to retreat again. On 1 September 1972, in Hawaii, he conceded to President Richard Nixon a general 10 per cent tariff cut, a 30 per cent increase in volume for imports subject to quotas, a voluntary limitation of Japanese television set exports, dropping of the project for a Japanese fighter aircraft in favour of the American F–15, exceptional imports worth $1 billion, and a commitment to limit the trade surplus with the United States to $3 billion before 1975 (compared with $5.8 billion in 1971). In 1973 the surplus fell dramatically to only $380 million. That did not stop Nixon from prohibiting the export of American soya beans the same year, at the request of the stockraising industry, concerned at seeing the price of that animal feed rocketing. In Japan, on the other hand, soya beans are an important part of daily diet, and the country was 98 per cent dependent on imports. The American embargo was seen as open blackmail. An agreement guaranteeing annual supplies of 11 million tons was eventually signed. But Japan had been thoroughly shaken by this crude revelation of its dependence.

The oil crisis following the Yom Kippur War (October 1973) came in the midst of all this. For energy Japan depended 90 per cent on oil, of which it was the world's leading importer. It bought 78 per cent of its imports from the Middle East, especially Iran (33 per cent) and Saudi Arabia (19 per cent). OPEC's decision to reduce output and then to quadruple prices led to a real panic. Housewives rushed to stock up on paraffin but also cooking oil, sugar, salt and toilet paper. The psychosis was aggravated by the big firms and distributors, which stocked up for speculation purposes. Here and there depositors rushed to the banks to withdraw their money, and the Bank of Japan had to intervene.

Inflation reached 18 per cent in 1973, 24 per cent in 1974. But those official averages concealed dramatic increases for basic necessities. Vegetables trebled or quadrupled in price, other food products doubled, clothing went up 50 per cent. The causes went well beyond the oil crisis. The world situation was inflationary, because of the policy of recovery at any price led by Nixon and the demand-stimulating measures taken all around as a result. In Japan itself the government responded to the reduction in exports by boosting consumption, massive public works, and assistance to sectors in difficulty, especially as 1972 was an election year. Just before quitting power Satô had presented a budget showing a 23 per cent rise, with a deficit of 2 billion yen.

Tanaka continued with the same policy. His grandiose programme for 'Building a New Japan' provided for huge investment in infrastructure, to relocate industries away from the overpopulated Pacific coastal strip, in the form of gigantic heavy industry combines. In 1973 he secured a budget showing a 25 per cent rise and approval of a five-year economic plan based on an annual growth rate of 9.7 per cent. That hypothesis had been reasonable in view of the economy's previous performance, but it was no longer so in the new situation. Frenzied speculation worsened inflation, and further tarnished the image of the big companies, following the pollution scandals. The legislation adopted for promotion of industrial relocation designated the zones to be developed, but the government took no measures to control the property dealings. The big firms rushed to those areas and in 1972 alone declared 15 billion yen of appreciation in property value. Speculation spread to the stock exchange (the Nikkei index passed from 3,000 to 5,000 yen between March and December 1972) and even membership cards at the leading golf clubs. The newspapers let forth against the firms, which were accused of creating artificial scarcity to keep prices up. The politicians and the MITI's rival government departments – the MITI being the big firms' ally as always – jumped on the bandwagon. In March 1973 the Planning Agency drew up a bill against market manipulation, which the MITI had refused to draft, and in February 1974 the Fair Trade Commission searched the oil companies' premises and charged 18 industrialists with restrictive practices. The following month the Diet examined the price increases in a special session; it summoned the leading figures among employers, and passed a law imposing a surtax on speculative profits. In this context, highly unfavourable to the employers, the spring wage offensive was a triumph: a 32.9 per cent wage rise.

GNP declined by 1.2 per cent in 1974, for the first time for twenty years, and the trade balance was $7 billion in deficit. The government cancelled development projects on a massive scale, but the deficit reached 15 per cent of the budget, compared with 4.4 per cent in 1973. More than 12,000 small and medium-scale enterprises went bankrupt, and the big firms laid off even permanent employees. The best-seller of the year was *Japan Sinks* by Sakyô Komatsu, which described the annihilation of the islands by monstrous earthquakes, volcanic eruptions and tidal waves. The economic crisis and the crisis of morale undermined the popularity of Tanaka.

Political crisis: the Tanaka government (1972–4)

When he took office Tanaka had an exceptional popularity rating, around 70 per cent. 'The Prime Minister that the people are waiting for', as *Mainichi* called him, took a series of popular measures. He flew to Beijing and 'overtook' the USA in recognising People's China. Against the opposition of the MITI and the Finance Ministry, he granted small and medium enterprises the system of preferential loans and the law against hypermarkets that they had been calling for, and allowed the agricultural cooperatives' banks to branch into loans to individuals and currency dealing. He made massive improvements in social legislation, copying most of the measures introduced at the local level by the progressive governors – family allowances, free medical care for the aged, a big increase in and index linking of retirement pensions. Then he quickly dissolved the House, to capitalise on his popularity.

However, in the December 1972 elections the LDP made losses again – 0.8 per cent of the vote and six seats. The JSP's representation rose from 90 to 118 and the JCP got its best score ever (10.4 per cent). Even though the left gained mostly at the expense of the Democratic Socialists, destabilised by the retirement of their founder Nishio, and the Kômeitô, entangled in the Fujiwara scandal (see p. 194), the election was a personal failure for Tanaka, who had called it but had not succeeded in reversing the LDP's downward trend (in percentage of votes cast) in all elections since 1960.

The political climate rapidly deteriorated in 1973, because of the economic crisis. The progressive fronts, with the help of the Kômeitô, took Nagoya, Kôbe and Kawasaki. Inflation and speculation triggered off attacks by the press, which began to blame the decline in public morality on the example given by Tanaka in the 'rotten congress' of 1972. The Prime Minister also faced difficulties from the employers' side, where the way the politicians turned discontent against the big firms was not appreciated. As for the MITI and the Ministry of Finance, Fukuda's fief, they disapproved of Tanaka's inflationary budget policies, his measures to help the small and medium enterprises, and his sensationalist way of promoting regional development through best-sellers. They were afraid of the rising power of new government agencies: the Planning Agency, where Tanaka got technical support to get the law against market manipulation drafted, and the National Land Agency, empowered to formulate basic land-use plans, which he intended to set up.

MOBILISATION OF PRESSURE GROUPS IN THE UPPER HOUSE ELECTIONS

The Upper House of the Diet has 252 seats, half of which come up for election every three years. Of the 126 seats contested each time, 76 are filled by elections in local constituencies, a majority of which (28) have only one deputy each. Until 1983 each of the other 50 seats was filled by a single-round election in a single national constituency; the voter had to choose just one name among more than a hundred candidates. To win, a candidate had to have considerable personal fame (like television, sports or showbusiness stars) or the backing of well organised pressure groups. Below are some examples of this organised backing from which conservative candidates officially benefited in 1974.

Ichirô Hatoyama

Tobacco Growers' Political Association; Sake Manufacturers' Union; PL Kyôdan (a new religion); Sumitomo Group; Dai-ichi Kangyô Bank; the Nomura securities firm; Bridgestone Tyres.

Hisatsune Sakomizu

Tobacco Distributors' Association; the Veterans and Bereaved Families Association; Tenrikyô (a new religion); C. Itoh Trading Company; Tôkyû Group (private railways, department stores, real estate).

Tatsomu Okabe (former Ministry of Transport official)

Shipbuilding Employers' Association; Entrepots, Docks and Harbours Association; Merchant Navy Captains' Association; Yamaha Engines; YKK.

Ken Saka (former police official)

Mitsubishi Group; National Association of Friends of the Police; Yuseiren (an oil group).

In 1983 single-member single-round voting in the national constituency was replaced by proportional representation under the list system.

In the LDP all the faction leaders had agreed to join the government after the elections, but this reconciliation was superficial. Nakasone, disappointed at not having been made Secretary General of the party, drew closer to Fukuda. They instigated the creation of the 'Association of Springtime Storms' (Seirankai) in which a leading light was Shintarô Ishihara (see p. 110), now a deputy for Tokyo, who turned his guns on the Prime Minister, accused of corrupting the nation. Tanaka and his closest ally, Masayoshi Ohira, responded by setting up the 'Council for Normalisation of the Party' (Tôrenkai) and promoted Miki to the rank of Deputy Prime Minister to make sure of his loyalty.

The technocracy and the factions hostile to Tanaka blocked the bill for creation of the National Land Agency throughout 1973. This personal failure for the Prime Minister was compounded in August by the kidnapping of the leader of the South Korean opposition, Kim Dae-jung, by Seoul's secret services in the heart of Tokyo. This affair was denounced on the Right as an affront to Japan's sovereignty, on the Left as proof of complicity with the dictatorship of General Park Chung-hee. The Korean Prime Minister apologised, and the National Land Agency law was at last passed in June 1974. But Tanaka was very much weakened. The opposition continued its local election victories, taking two new regions, Kagawa and Shiga. In this situation the Upper House elections of July 1974 promised to be perilous. The LDP had only had a majority of five votes, and the Upper House could block the whole legislative process since every measure that it rejects – except for the budget, the appointment of the Prime Minister and the ratification of treaties – must be passed again by the Lower House with a two-thirds majority, which the LDP did not have. The loss of five seats would be enough to force the government party to compromise with the opposition on every subject. Already the press was talking of 'the reversal of the balance of forces between the conservatives and progressives'.

To avoid this happening, the LDP made uninhibited use of its financial power. While the law laid down maximum expenditure of 29 million yen per candidate, the LDP spent on average 500 million for each one. The whole country chanted '*Gôtô yonraku*' (With five [hundred million] you win, with four you lose!). The employers' organisations were ruthlessly made to contribute. The banks loaned 10 billion yen which the LDP was never to pay back.

The big firms had to sponsor candidates officially; Toyota had to get a television presenter elected, Hitachi an actress, Mitsubishi a former police official, for whose cause it invested one billion yen. But these excesses alienated public opinion. The press invented a neologism which was to go far: *kinkenseiji* ('money politics'). The chairman of the National Election Commission publicly denounced the business candidates. The LDP barely escaped the worst – it lost only four seats and kept control of the Upper House by one vote. But the verdict of public opinion on *kinkenseiji* was clear. Many business candidates lost, including the Mitsubishi candidate. In contrast two independent candidates – the aged feminist Ichikawa and the writer Yukio Aoshima – who had conspicuously campaigned at bare-bone cost, not even putting up the miniumum number of posters nor distributing the leaflets authorised by law, were triumphally elected in the national constituency.

'Money politics' and the fall of Tanaka

The problem of political corruption was hardly new. It had its roots, at the end of the nineteenth century, in the forced transplant of democratic procedures on to a society whose culture was still feudal. The Occupation, by strengthening the government's control over the economy, created many more opportunities for bureaucrats and politicians to make power pay by peddling influence – something which is not clearly defined as illegal in Japan. The Shôwa Denkô scandal (1948) was the first in a long series. The second half of Satô's period in power, in particular, was covered with a 'black mist' (*kuroi kiri*) by the Kyôwa scandal (1966), the Osaka taxis scandal (1967), and Niitsu affair (1968). But no politician was ever sentenced. The crime of corruption is very difficult to define in Japanese law. It is necessary to prove that the accused 'was aware' that he was accepting a bribe, and that he had acted 'within the framework of his official duties'. Those two criteria are practically impossible to prove in a society where exchanging of gifts has been an essential element in social intercourse and decisions have commonly been made in an informal setting. In addition, the higher ranks of the magistracy often used their quasi-discretionary powers to halt proceedings.

There was also the problem of political contributions made by big business. Since its creation the LDP had been abundantly funded by the employers, in accordance with the 'Hatoyama formula'. Every year the Keidanren and the party reached agreement on a lump sum contribution. The employers' organisation shared this out among the various industries, then among businesses in each branch, in accordance with their profits. These sums collected were then paid into an umbrella organisation, the 'National Association' (Kokumin Kyôkai), which appeared as the sole donor in the LDP's official accounts. Besides this centralised contribution there were innumerable direct payments by enterprises to the factional leaders and Diet members on a case-by-case basis. The declared – very relative – figures reflected increasingly massive use of money by the LDP. In 1960 the conservatives declared that they had collected 3.5 billion yen, in 1972, three times as much; in 1974 they officially collected 17.5 billion in the six months before the 1974 Upper House election. Around 1960 a Lower House seat required investment estimated at 20 million yen; in 1972 it was *'ittô-nanaraku'* (with 100 million you win, with 70 million you lose!) The opposition tried to have payments by companies to the parties outlawed by arguing that they gave the rich influence contrary to the constitutional principle of equality among citizens. The plaintiffs won in the first instance in 1963, but lost in 1969 in the Supreme Court, whose *Yawata Iron and Steel* judgment definitively established that political contributions from business were constitutional.

But the indignation aroused by the excesses in the Upper House elections, after those of the 1972 congress, did not subside – especially as the average Japanese was suffering from speculation and pollution, allowed to continue unchecked by the collusion of the LDP and the employers. Citizens' movements attacked the firms too committed on the side of the government party. Thousands of consumers cancelled their standing orders for payment of bills to the Tokyo Electricity Company and took off a yen from payment to indicate their refusal to contribute to funding of the LDP. In August 1974 the company announced that it was suspending all political contributions. Other electricity companies and the private railway companies followed suit. The Keidanren hastily announced that it was halting payments 'while awaiting the establishment of morality in public life'. Tanaka was fatally destabilised. Miki and Fukuda left the government and threatened to break the LDP if he did not resign. In October the weekly *Bungei Shunjû*, which had very good sources in some government departments, exposed the details of Tanaka's personal enrichment through lucrative public works contracts and questionable land deals. His popularity rating plummeted to 12 per cent. The party's elders threatened to allow the opening of an inquiry. He preferred to resign, the day after a visit by US President Gerald Ford (26 November 1974).

The Miki government and the Lockheed scandal (1974–6)

A party congress to decide the succession to Tanaka risked tarnishing the LDP's image further, by repeating the murky battle of 1972. It was decided to resort to negotiation instead. But no agreement was possible between Fukuda who was backed by Nakasone, Ohira backed by Tanaka, and Miki. The aged Etsusaburô Shiina, Vice-Chairman of the LDP, was then called upon to arbitrate; he chose Miki. The new Prime Minister had been a member of the Diet since 1936. A founder of the Cooperative Party, a minister in the Katayama cabinet, he was placed in the centre-left of the party because of his good relations with the JSP, his avowed pacifism, and his rigorous denunciation of corruption in politics. He was a marginal figure within the LDP, where his faction did not carry much weight. But in the eyes of public opinion he was 'Mister Clean': never spattered by scandal, he was to leave 891 million yen of debts at his death in 1986. The LDP needed him to restore his image, and the weakness of his faction reassured the conservative establishment that it could get rid of him later. Meanwhile, he was only allowed to appoint two members of his own faction to the government.

The LDP only authorised Miki to make symbolic reforms to curb *kinkenseiji*. He wanted to outlaw companies' contributions, so that parties would be funded only by citizens' money; the LDP rejected his proposals in favour of others placing limits on companies' contributions according to their capital. But the maximum ceiling – 150 million yen per year including authorised payments to parties, factions and individual politicians – was more than any firm had ever officially paid to the LDP. All those who paid or received 'contributions' were supposed to declare them. But exceptions were allowed for 'subscriptions' and contributions under one million yen, and this made the law 'a bamboo bucket' through which money freely flowed. As for the electoral law, which placed a ceiling on expenditure and punished corruption of voters, it continued to tolerate all sorts of 'traditional social practices' (gifts), and the bodies responsible for auditing candidates' accounts continued to be designated by the very assemblies to which they were elected.

Nevertheless, as soon as these half-measures were adopted, public opinion seemed to be appeased by this 'symbolic purification' (*misogi*). The LDP's popularity rating rose again to 44 per cent. At once the employers declared themselves satisfied with the 'establishment of morality in public life' and resumed payments to the LDP, in preparation for the parliamentary elections of 1976. At the same time amendment of the anti-monopolies law, which Miki had promised in order to suppress speculation, was buried in the Upper House.

The economic situation improved. Inflation fell to 10 per cent in 1976, and wage increases were restricted to 8.8 per cent. The social consequences of the crisis were limited by a programme for retraining of 440,000 workers, and when the Sôhyô sought to take advantage of the tension to regain the right to strike for civil servants, the 'strike for the right to strike' failed amid public indifference, despite support from Miki, who was sharply disavowed by his party (November 1975). But a number of indicators were still in the red. The index of manufacturing output had not returned to its 1973 level, half of the firms listed on the stock exchange reported losses in 1975, investment and consumption remained stagnant. The government cut the discount rate and taxes for wage earners for 1976, an election year. But the steady increase in the budget deficit limited its margin of manoeuvre. Between 1974 and 1976 it rose from 15 to 29.4 per cent of the budget – the highest deficit of any industrial country.

The economic situation was partly responsible since revenue from company taxes kept falling. But the taxation system was structurally deficient (see p. 184). Ohira, the then Finance Minister, sought to open a debate on reform. But his concerns were to be swept aside by a sudden political storm.

The Lockheed scandal broke out in February 1976, following revelations before the American Senate. The firm admitted having paid $10 million to win two contracts in Japan in 1972, when the Tanaka government chose its P3C Orion anti-submarine aircraft for the Self Defence Forces, and the Lockheed Tristar to renew All Nippon Airways' fleet. The bribes were shared by Marubeni, one of the most prestigious *sôgô shôsha*, but especially by Yoshio Kodama, a former war criminal and a notorious 'godfather' on the borderline between the Mafia and the world of politics. The scandal again aroused public opinion and the media against political corruption. For Miki, thwarted in all his plans, this was the opportunity to take the initiative; he promised the whole truth, and personally asked President Ford for information in the hands of the American investigators. In an election year the opposition showed itself all the more aggressive because it had made progress for ten years and had hopes of finally ending the LDP's hegemony. Demanding a parliamentary inquiry, it paralysed the Diet by boycotting the budget session for seven weeks in March and April. Meanwhile the LDP experienced its first breakaway; the son of Ichirô Kôno founded the New Liberal Club (NLC) with four young Lower House members; it was to campaign for modernised conservatism among urban voters.

After Kodama (tax evasion) and the Marubeni executives (perjury), Tanaka was charged with corruption, with four other conservative Diet members. He was briefly imprisoned in July. The LDP elders thought Miki had gone too far. Ohira, Fukuda and Shiina had a petition signed by 277 Diet members calling for his resignation. Miki threatened to appoint a cabinet of loyalists, backed by the opposition, which would dissolve the Lower House and appeal to public opinion. In September the LDP was on the verge of a split. But its Secretary General, Nakasone, negotiated a compromise: the Prime Minister would stay in office and the elections would take place as scheduled in December.

The verdict of the elections of 5 December 1976 was ambiguous. The LDP had its worst post-war results with 41.7 per cent of votes cast (down 5 per cent). But with the independent candidates and the NLC, which made inroads into the big cities by winning 17 seats, the conservative bloc had 51.8 per cent, a slight rise. The LDP kept its absolute majority in the House, but it lost the working majority which had enabled it to control all the parliamentary committees until then. It had to give up the chairmanship of half the committees – including the Finance Committee – to the opposition, with the considerable powers of obstruction that went with those posts. The parties' strengths were thus nearly balanced in the Diet. Yet the opposition stagnated. The Socialist, Communist and Democratic Socialist Parties lost votes slightly. The Kômeitô, thrashed in 1972, regained 26 seats at the expense of the other opposition parties, especially the Communists, who lost 21 seats. There was not a clear condemnation of *kinkenseiji* since all incumbent deputies involved in the Lockheed scandal were reelected except one. In Niigata Tanaka won with 168,522 votes, against 54,302 for the candidate who came second, while the Minister of Justice who had had him arrested lost 24,000 votes and barely held on to his seat. Since the Prime Minister's faction lost eight of its incumbents out of 38, Miki could not claim the backing of public opinion. He resigned.

Tanaka remained the LDP kingmaker. He sat as an independent, because the party does not accept members facing prosecution, but his faction was to swell from 78 members in 1976 to 142 in 1986. It then controlled a full third of the votes at the party congress, and no government could last without his support. His court conviction at first instance (1983) made no difference. Paralysed after a cerebral haemorrhage in 1986, he was nonetheless reelected again that year, and sat in the House in theory until 1990. The opposition missed its chance. War among the leaders was to shake the LDP severely again, but it would not stop the conservative government re-establishing its power gradually, carried along by the spectacular revival of the economy.

ECONOMIC RECOVERY

Relaunching and restructuring the economy

The oil crisis imposed a threefold obligation on Japan: to reduce its dependence on imported sources of energy, to revive exports to pay the heavier oil import bill, and to reconsider the future of some branches of industry.

First of all, Japan sought to ensure the security of its supplies. It gave priority to its Asian suppliers, above all Indonesia (18 per cent of imports in 1973, 20 per cent in 1980) and the most stable Arab countries, such as Saudi Arabia (18 per cent in 1973, 33 per cent in 1980). But its overall dependence on the Middle East hardly diminished: 78 per cent of its supplies in 1973, 71 per cent in 1980. Tokyo also increased its stocks from 50 to 100 days, and sought to bypass the American 'majors' by negotiating direct agreements with the producing countries through a semi-state consortium. Replacing oil by other sources of energy was the big business then. The MITI planned to reduce oil's share in energy consumption to 33 per cent by 1990, by developing nuclear, hydroelectric, solar and geothermal energy. This plan was to come up against residents' movements mobilised against the dams and nuclear facilities. Technological shortcomings were revealed by the spectacular failure of the nuclear-propelled vessel *Mutsu*, rendered unserviceable on her first voyage by a reactor leak (1974). As a result, in 1980 oil still accounted for 65 per cent of energy consumption, nuclear energy for 10 per cent – but by 1990 oil's share was to be down to 45 per cent compared with nearly 30 per cent for nuclear energy, and 8 million homes were to be supplied with solar energy. The biggest effort was devoted to energy-saving in industry. A law laid down standards of consumption by branch, and made it obligatory to have an energy specialist in every big factory. In the five years after the oil shock, consumption of energy by unit of production fell by 43 per cent in the motor industry and 30 per cent in the steel industry. Japanese industry became the one that used energy most rationally, by far, going even further than the MITI had planned. At the Tokyo summit in 1979 Japan fought against its G7 partners for the right to import 6.9 million barrels per day until 1985; but it was only to need 4.5 million when that year came.

A surge in exports supported the resumption of economic growth. Exports rose from 11 per cent of GNP in 1970 to 17 per cent in 1981, and their value in dollars quadrupled. Japan was still exporting less than Germany or France as a percentage of GNP, but it accumulated huge profits. Between 1975 and 1982 it recorded $49 billion of trade surpluses, while the EEC and the USA recorded deficits of $297 billion and $244 billion respectively. Japan thus amassed a financial wealth of which it was to make full use in the following period.

The value added and technological level of the goods exported increased constantly. The share of textiles, steel and simple consumer goods (umbrellas, fans etc.) declined, while Japan wiped out the competition in photographic and optical products, watches, motorbikes and mass market electronics. In the United States it had by about 1980 occupied 40 per cent of the market in 16K computer memory and half the market in new digital control machine tools, while half of what it purchased consisted of raw materials and food products. Similarly, in sales of European goods to Japan the share of high technology goods constantly diminished in favour of luxury products alone. It was the motor industry that symbolised this new export boom. Production rose from 3 million units in 1970 to 7.4 million in 1980, including 2.6 million exported to the United States and the EEC. Their market share increased from 3 per cent to 21 per cent in the USA, and from 0.6 to 9 per cent in the highly protected European market. The Japanese offered models that consumed on average 8.4 litres of petrol per 100 kilometres compared with 13 for American models. They revolutionised production methods with the just-in-time system ('zero stocks'), multi-skilled operators, and permanent quality control on the assembly line ('zero defects'), which reduced time and cost considerably. And while lifetime employees in the big firms were now paid as well as their Western counterparts, sub-contracting and part-time employment still gave Japanese firms an advantage in wage costs.

The need to restructure industry flowed from the oil shock, which destroyed the profitability of industries consuming large amounts of energy and the petrochemicals industry. Japan also faced growing competition from the cheap labour of Third World countries for textiles and intermediate goods, and from the 'four Tigers' (Korea, Taiwan, Hong Kong and Singapore) for steel production, shipbuilding and mass market electronics. Rather than wasting its strength to prop them up, the MITI regrouped threatened industries into 'recession cartels' organised under a law of 1978. Some were virtually abandoned, for the benefit of a strategy of de-localisation and supply on a world scale. This happened with aluminium, whose imports were freed from restriction and whose producers were directed to link to the US giants; production fell from 1,188,000 tons in 1977 to 264,000 in 1983, and 60,000 jobs were lost; but there were neither strikes nor bankruptcies, and Japan was never to be short of aluminium. In other branches, reduction in production capacity and staff cuts (80,000 in the shipyards) were accompanied by aid to investment, to maintain a renovated 'hard core' capable of generating profits again.

But the expansion of the motor, electronics and capital goods industries more than compensated for the decline of the 14 branches legally recognised as 'in recession'. Growth averaged 5.1 per cent per year between 1976 and 1980, compared with 3.4 per cent in the USA and 3 per cent in the EEC. In 1982 GNP was half that of the United States, compared with a third ten years earlier. In GNP per inhabitant, a measure which until then had made its success seem relative, Japan was now hot on the heels of France and West Germany. The second oil shock, caused by the Iranian revolution (1979), passed almost unnoticed. Growth continued in Japan, while GNP declined in most of the other industrial countries. The rate of unemployment remained around 2 per cent, while it swung elsewhere between 6 per cent (West Germany) and 11 per cent (Britain), and the trade balance registered growing surpluses ($20 billion in 1981), which led to renewed tensions.

The other side of success: rising trade friction

Western trading partners' criticisms of Japan had been defused for a time by Tanaka's concessions (see p. 167) and by the return of surpluses in the USA's balance of payments. Tokyo had also lifted unilaterally many of the restrictions it had still been maintaining on imports until only 30 remained – fewer than in most Western countries – including 23 relating to agricultural products or politically highly sensitive ones such as hides and skins (used for activity reserved to the Burakumin). But when Japan bounced back before its trading partners had recovered from the first oil shock, its trade surplus with the United States swelled again, to $5.3 million in 1976. The EEC was then buying from Japan twice as much as it sold there. Western governments, struggling with rising unemployment, turned on Japan.

The range of criticisms widened considerably compared with the previous period. The traditional accusations – too low wages and protection – were increasingly hollow. But Japanese firms were now accused of every conceivable unfair practice, especially dumping and technological piracy. They were denounced for collusion with the administration and the judicial system, which, it was said, made it impossible for Western companies to defend their rights in Japan, to get their patents respected there or to get their products officially approved in a reasonable space of time to forestall their local competitors. The bureaucracy was accused of using unduly complex approval procedures and sanitary and security standards devised for the sole purpose of making difficulties for imports. These non-tariff barriers (NTBs) became the central point of friction. In 1979 the USA and the EEC presented a joint list of 99 procedures whose dismantling they demanded. The criticisms were not unfounded; examples of systematic administrative obstacles and denials of justice abound. But that does not alter the facts that Japan had been able to take a lead in productivity and technology, and that Western firms' efforts to penetrate Japan were insufficient. Many were satisfied with selling a small amount but at artificially high prices, through local importers with exclusive rights. They economised on distribution networks but were at the mercy of their local sole agent, who confined their products in the luxury range, and on occasion put them aside in favour of Japanese products. The immediate return on low investment was high, but penetration of the market remained limited and hazardous.

A new theme of criticism appeared: Japan's refusal to 'assume its international responsibilities'. The United States accused it of deliberately ensuring its security at the expense of American taxpayers, using the Constitution as an excuse. At the G7 summits, Tokyo was now summoned to make a contribution to world recovery by increasing its domestic demand and allowing the value of the yen to go up to make its exports less competitive.

Japan reacted on a case by case basis. It began talks on Voluntary Export Restriction Agreements (VERA), which had been started in the preceding period with the USA for textiles and steel. It appointed an Ombudsman to receive complaints from foreign businessmen, and set up a centre for import promotion. It promised to dismantle 67 NTBs on the US-European list. Before the 1979 G7 summit in Tokyo it allowed the yen to appreciate temporarily by nearly 30 per cent against the dollar and the ECU. But those measures had no concrete result; the trade surplus continued to rise.

UNFAIR COMPETITION: THE HOUDAILLE
-YAMAZAKI CASE (1976–83)

In 1970 Houdaille, an American machine tool manufacturer, authorised the Japanese company Yamazaki to use its technology under license for a ten-year period, on condition that its products were not marketed outside the Far East. In 1976 Yamazaki machines very close to those of Houdaille appeared on the American market. The Japanese firm claimed that the technology was its own, a qualitative improvement on the state of the art, and accordingly refused to continue to pay royalties.

Houdaille brought an action before the American International Trade Commission (ITC), which requested a Japanese administrative law court to permit Houdaille to conduct its discovery at Yamazaki's plants and offices. This routine legal request was initially granted. But the designated investigator had his visa cancelled on orders from the Japanese Foreign Ministry; then the Japanese government overruled the administrative judge who had granted the right to investigate.

Houdaille then initiated a private investigation of the Japanese machine-tool industry. He exposed the practices organised by the MITI to strengthen that sector: cartelisation (122 mergers in one year, 1968), exclusion of foreign suppliers from all public contracts, subsidies amounting to $985 million per year derived from betting on bicycle races, etc.

On the basis of this Houdaille presented a petition to President Reagan to ask for protection of American manufacturers (1983). Prime Minister Nakasone then personally sent two urgent messages to Reagan, who rejected the petition.

Threatened by the ITC with a ban on marketing of its products in the United States, Yamazaki accepted a financial compromise with Houdaille. But the Japanese from then on dominated the American market for numerically controlled machine tools.

Source: Marvin Wolf, *The Japanese Conspiracy*, Empire Books, 1983; New English Library, 1984, pp. 56–75.

The budget crisis and the debate on taxation

The budget deficit continued to increase and reached 6.3 per cent of GNP in 1979, a record year in which 36 per cent of the budget was financed by borrowing. Until 1975 the causes seemed to lie in the economic crisis, since the state was stimulating the economy, while the crisis reduced tax revenue. But now it seemed that even with an economy going at full speed the taxation system was incapable of generating revenue sufficient to cope with continually rising expenditure. Total state levies (taxes plus social security contributions) were far below those of the other industrialised countries at less than 36 per cent of national income, compared with 56 per cent in France, 51 per cent in West Germany and 48 per cent in Britain in 1982. Three-quarters of tax revenue came from direct taxation (compared with 40 per cent in France), including 30 per cent from company taxes (10 per cent in France). The companies paid 52.5 per cent of their retained earnings in taxes (compared with 43 per cent in France), at least in theory, since there were many legal loopholes and exemptions; economically and politically, it was difficult to tax them more. Income tax had reached the limit of what wage earners could endure. The tax thresholds were not raised with inflation, and abatements were reduced, to the point where total levies increased by a quarter in 1980, while the LDP's clients were spared. The press denounced the *ku-ro-yon* (nine-six-four) system whereby wage earners paid tax on 90 per cent of their income, small employers on 60 per cent and farmers on 40 per cent. The discontent was fuelled every year at the time of the budget debate, by the opposition which called for tax rebates for wage earners, taking advantage of its majority in the Finance Committee. So it seemed impossible to increase revenue within the existing taxation system. The Ministry of Finance had for long been calling for a general purchase tax, but the LDP was afraid that this would be unpopular. The debate on taxation, started by Ohira, was cut short in 1976 because of the Lockheed scandal.

However, irreducible expenditure mounted. Accumulated debt service ate up an increasing share of the budget, and social expenditure swelled under the impact of measures voted under the Tanaka government. Their share of the budget rose from 13 per cent in 1972 to 19 per cent in 1974. Retirement pension payments by the state-run systems shot up from 177 billion to 2,331 billion yen between 1969 and 1975. In a difficult political situation for the LDP no economies were possible. The conservatives needed all the pressure groups, and no subsidy could be reduced – on the contrary, on the eve of the Upper House elections of 1974 the guaranteed price of rice was raised by 30 per cent. Finally, the depressed state of private investment made it necessary to maintain state expenses at a high level; public works credits increased by more than 20 per cent every year, and a record 34.5 per cent in 1978. In these conditions the budgetary crisis became a central element in the political debate. From 1976 onwards the March-April budget debate polarised the confrontation between the opposition and an LDP which was to regain the advantage steadily in spite of the situation of 'nearly equal forces' in the Diet.

THE CONSERVATIVE COMEBACK (1977–80)

The opposition was demoralised by its semi-failure in the parliamentary elections of 1976. Its divisions and its structural weaknesses, masked by its successes at the local level since 1967, were plainly revealed. Although the LDP was still subject to fierce internal rivalries, it regained ground in elections, for the first time since its creation – from 41.8 per cent of the vote in 1976 to 44.6 per cent in 1979 and 47.9 in 1980. It lured the Kômeitô away from the 'progressive fronts', and with its help regained the lost local authorities, before firmly re-establishing its hold over the Diet.

The Fukuda government (1977–8)

The succession to Miki was settled by negotiation. Ohira gave way to Fukuda on condition that he would retire after two years. Then Ohira would succeed him; meanwhile he held the strategic position of Secretary General of the party, while Fukuda was confronted with four delicate tasks.

(1) He had to 'democratise' the LDP at least symbolically, to keep the pre-election promise to put an end to the obscure interplay of factions that favoured corruption. In 1977 he reformed the way of choosing the Chairman; from now on primary elections would be organised in which all party members would vote, and the congress would decide between the two leading candidates.
(2) He had to return to amendment of the anti-monopoly law. Buried in 1975, it could no longer be avoided in the face of new scandals and the demands of Japan's trading partners. The law was greatly strengthened, on the surface. The FTC was given the power to split up monopolistic enterprises, or to force them to shed a part of their productive capacity – but 'on condition that

this does not reduce their international competitivity'. And firms were given no less than ten years to conform to the new provisions of the law.

(3) He had to pass legislation in the situation of near-equilibrium with the opposition in the Diet. The 1977 budget had to be officially negotiated among the Secretaries-General of the six parties. The LDP agreed to three quarters of the tax cuts called for by the opposition. Fukuda succeeded in getting 85 per cent of the legislation he put forward adopted, but at the cost of intense negotiations behind the scenes.

(4) He had to win the Upper House elections of 1977, in which the LDP could not afford to lose a single seat. The media were already proclaiming 'the era of coalition governments'. But the LDP won an extra seat, while the JSP lost 12. As in 1974 the election was marked by success for independent personalities and for mini-parties, at the expense of the classical opposition. On the same day the conservatives regained a majority in the Tokyo Regional Assembly, which had been the Socialist Governor Ryôkichi Minobe's fief since 1967.

From the summer of 1977 onwards the LDP was on the up. It retook three of the nine regions governed by the progressives: Kagawa, Shiga, and notably Kyoto (April 1978), held for 28 years by the Communist Ninagawa. For the 1978 budget Fukuda made few concessions, thanks to the support of the NLC. He succeeded in opening Narita airport after six years of fierce struggle. Lastly, he signed a Treaty of Peace and Friendship with China (August 1978) which seemed to open up immense commercial possibilities. Strengthened by these successes, in November 1978 Fukuda sought re-election as Chairman of the LDP, in violation of his agreement with Ohira. The primaries were fiercely contested; the candidates recruited new 'party members' on a massive scale, and the membership rose at a stroke from 400,000 to 1.5 million. Ohira's faction had the full backing of Tanaka's, but Fukuda was not able to bring Nakasone over to his side, nor Miki's successor Toshio Kômoto, and both also stood. Ohira thus won by 80,000 votes. The Prime Minister resigned immediately; there was deep hatred between the two men from then on.

The Ohira government (1978–80)

Ohira's assumption of power was marked by a series of significant changes:

(1) The emergence of a new type of government structure, intended to strengthen the hand of politicians against the bureaucracy in the decision-making process. Amid much publicity, Ohira set up nine consultative councils (*kondankai*) attached to the prime minister's office, composed of intellectuals, businessmen, senior civil servants and some trade unionists chosen by him. These bodies on the fringes of the administration were entrusted with producing long-term 'visions' that were widely echoed in the media. They were to play an increasing role in the decision-making process and in public opinion.

(2) A determination to play a bigger international role in a situation worsened by the crises in Cambodia, Iran and Afghanistan. In 17 months Ohira had three summit meetings with President Carter and two with the Chinese leaders. He was host to the G7 summit in Tokyo in 1979, and made two regional tours of the South Pacific and North America.

(3) The final collapse of united action among the opposition, which was from then on incapable of taking any common stance against the LDP. In March 1979 Ohira had the budget bill rushed through a plenary session of the Chamber even though it had been rejected by the opposition-dominated Finance Committee. This assertion of the government's will showed that the LDP had got the initiative again. The next month, in local elections, it overran the last progressive strongholds. In Tokyo Minobe decided not to stand again, and the Kômeitô joined the LDP to get Sun'ichi Suzuki, a former conservative Deputy Governor, elected, defeating the Socialist-Communist candidate. In Osaka, however, the JSP allied with the conservatives and the centre against the outgoing mayor backed by the JCP. This was the end for the progressive local authorities.

Yet the LDP's internal rivalries were to lead it to the verge of a break-up. Ohira still had to grapple with Fukuda's resentment and the ambition of Nakasone, the only factional leader who had not yet been in power. After its local election victories the LDP's rating went up in opinion polls to its highest level in 15 years (52 per cent). The Prime Minister wanted to take advantage of this to put an end to the situation of 'near-parity' in the Diet, and to bring tax reform back on to the agenda. But when he spoke publicly of the need for a VAT, 214 conservative Diet members immediately formed a group to oppose it. When he brought the elections forward to October 1979, many LDP candidates campaigned against any new tax. Ohira retreated and promised 'restoration of public finance without tax increases'.

On 7 October the LDP gained votes but lost a seat, since many of its candidates, backed by rival factions, wiped each other out. The National Liberal Club was almost swept away, winning just four seats. The only party to gain was the JCP, which increased its representation to 22. Fukuda, Miki and Nakasone called for the Prime Minister's resignation. His refusal led to a month-long government crisis. All attempts at arbitration failed. On 5 November Fukuda ran against Ohira before the House, which had to elect a new head of government. Ohira won narrowly, by 135 votes to 125. The opposition had 254 votes, but it did not try to seize the opportunity; each party presented its own candidate, while the anti-Ohira factions resisted the temptation to break away and seek alliance with the centre.

The Prime Minister found it difficult to form his second cabinet. New scandals broke out. Koichi Hamada, a former gangster turned Diet member, had made one of the people charged in the Lockheed case pay enormous gambling debts for him. The KDD company, which had a monopoly of international telecommunications under parliamentary control, was accused of paying Diet members to shut their eyes to its prohibitive charges. Young members of parliament agitated in a 'League for Reform of the Party', led by Shintarô Ishihara and Ichirô Nakagawa. On 16 May 1980, the Fukuda and Miki factions abstained in a motion of censure put forward by the opposition. For the first time since the creation of the LDP the government was removed from office by the House. Ohira replied with a dissolution. He fixed the House of Representatives elections for the 22 June, to coincide with the Upper House elections.

Unity was maintained *in extremis*. Resentment subsided within the party after Ohira died suddenly of a heart attack on 11 June. The employers' organisations opposed a split with all their strength, and their contributions were vital for the candidates, whose war chests had been exhausted by the 1979 parliamentary

THE JAPANESE EXECUTIVE

Until the grand reform of the central administration on 1 January 2001, the Japanese cabinet had 19 portfolios; the list of these was fixed by law and unchanged since 1974. There were twelve ministries (*shô*): Justice, Foreign Affairs, Finance, MITI (Industry and Foreign Trade), Agriculture (and Forestry and Fisheries), Transport, Construction, Posts and Telecommunications, Health, Labour, Education and Home Affairs ('Local Autonomy'). Then there were seven 'agencies' (*chô*): Defence, Management and Coordination, Economic Planning, National Land, Science and Technology, the Environment, and Development of Hokkaido and Okinawa. The Secretary General of the Cabinet also had ministerial rank. Each minister was seconded by a 'parliamentary deputy minister' (a young member of parliament learning the ropes) and an 'administrative deputy minister' (the senior officer of the department, which selected him in a very independent way).

Under the Ohira government consultative councils reinforced the structure of the Executive:

(1) Study group on 'The garden city concept', under the chairmanship of the Director of the National Ethnological Museum.

(2) Study group on 'Economic policy towards foreign powers', whose chairman was a professor at the National University of Tokyo.

(3) Study group on 'Human values in a diversifying society', under the chairmanship of the Director of the Institute of Statistical Mathematics.

(4) Study group on 'Cooperation in the Pacific Basin', whose chairman was the Director of the Japanese Centre for Economic Research.

(5) Study group on 'Consolidation of the family as the basis of society', whose chairperson was a professor at the Women's Christian University of Tokyo.

(6) Study group on 'The strategy of global security', under the chairmanship of the Director of the Institute of Peace and Security Research.

(7) Study group on 'The era of culture', under the chairmanship of the owner of the Yamamoto Library.

(8) Study group on 'Economic performance within the framework of the era of culture', whose chairman was a professor at the National University of Tokyo.

(9) Study group on 'The historical evolution of science and technology', under the chairmanship of the Director of the National Institute for the Environment.

elections. All LDP incumbents signed a promise to maintain unity, and were re-selected together.

The 'double election' of 22 June was a triumph for the LDP. Its score of 47.9 per cent of the vote was the best since 1963. It gained 36 seats in the House and nine in the Senate, thus securing complete control over the Diet. It benefited from a 'sympathy vote' following Ohira's death. But the restoration of its monopoly of power was above all the result of the chronic weaknesses of the opposition and the conservative development of society as a whole.

AN IMPOTENT OPPOSITION

The Socialist Party: paralysed by divisions

The Japan Socialist Party was still divided between moderate Diet members and a base controlled by die-hard Marxist factions. The most dynamic and most sectarian was still the Socialist Studies Society (Shakaishugi Kyôkai), which called for the dictatorship of the proletariat and aggressively set up its cells in local party federations. Until 1977 a precarious balance was maintained by a neutral leadership – Tomomi Narita as Chairman and Masashi Ishibashi as Secretary General. Fairly good election results favoured this status quo at first, since the Socialists regained 28 seats in 1972, and Socialist-Communist-Kômeitô united fronts went from one success to another at the local level. In 1976 they controlled the five big special status metropolitan areas (Yokohama, Nagoya, Kyoto, Osaka and Kôbe), half of the cities of over 500,000 inhabitants, and a third of medium-sized cities. At the regional level they held Tokyo, Saitama and Kanagawa, almost the whole of central Japan (Shiga, Kyoto, Osaka, Kagawa and Okayama) and Okinawa; furthermore, in Hokkaido, Nagano and Fukuoka the LDP no longer controlled the regional assemblies. In all the progressives administered 40 per cent of the population, and the most advanced regions, accounting for 60 per cent of GNP. They turned these areas into 'show cases for Socialism', introducing advanced social policies and exemplary anti-pollution regulations.

But the Socialist Party, while remaining by far the leading opposition party, was linked with partners that were too dynamic for it. From the end of the preceding period the Kômeitô did better than the Socialists in the parliamentary elections in Tokyo and Osaka. So did the JCP in Osaka in 1972 and in Tokyo in 1980. There was a fierce conflict between the Socialist and Communist Parties for control over the Burakumin movement (see pp. 136–7) and over the subsidies allocated to the ghettoes. In 1974 activitists of the Socialist-led Liberation League beat up 22 Communist teachers at the Yoka secondary school in central Japan. In 1975 the JSP withdrew its support from the governor of Osaka, who was subsidising associations close to the JCP, and Minobe refused to seek a third term in Tokyo because of that dispute. He stood again *in extremis*, but he only won 352,000 votes more than the LDP candidate, Shintarô Ishihara, whereas he had been 1,250,000 votes ahead in 1971.

From 1976 onwards the almost equal strength of the parties in the Diet obliged the JSP to suggest a formula for the alternative government that was coming within the bounds of possibility: should it be a union with the Communists, or a centre alliance with the Kômeitô and the DSP? But the Socialists were too divided to make up their minds. They clung to the slogan 'A united front of the whole opposition', which the centre parties rejected. Their inability to propose a credible alternative government went far to explain why the voters did not place their trust in the opposition in the Upper House elections of 1974 and 1977, or in the parliamentary elections of 1976.

At the same time local governments were going through an acute financial crisis. They received two thirds of their revenue from the state, in the form of tax rebates and subsidies. The budgetary crisis therefore hit them, and especially hit the progressive regional authorities, whose social expenditure was the heaviest, and whose subsidies were reduced systematically by the LDP government. After 1975 Minobe was no longer able to finance any new policy in Tokyo. In addition the progressives' social and anti-pollution measures were taken over by the LDP at the national level. They lost their electoral appeal in the face of conservative candidates who highlighted their 'direct contact' with the government that provided the subsidies. The taking of the Kanagawa regional authority in 1975 was the progressives' last local government victory.

The Sôhyô, the Socialist Party's principal backer, was also having a hard time. After the failure of the 'strike for the right to strike' in November 1975 it was put on the defensive by the budgetary crisis, which enabled the LDP to arouse public opinion against the two most powerful Sôhyô federations, denouncing the 'excessive wages' of local government employees and the 'chronic deficit' of the national railways.

This situation revived the confrontation between Left and Right. The Shakaishugi Kyôkai called for an end to automatic reselection of incumbent members of the Diet, suggesting that candidates should from now on be chosen by the party's federations. In February 1977 Saburô Eda and four members of parliament left the party and formed the Social Democratic League (Shaminren), a moderate party. Four months later the Socialists lost 12 seats in the Upper House elections. Narita and Ishibashi resigned. A common anti-Kyôkai front offered the chairmanship to Ichiô Asukata, the popular Mayor of Yokohama; he refused it for three months, until the Kyôkai, isolated, gave up its attempt to control the parliamentary Socialist group. Asukata wanted to make the JSP 'a people's party with a million members', but it was difficult enough to increase membership to 70,000 in 1983. It remained incapable of deciding on a political line. In 1978–9, while the conservatives were taking all the progressive-held regions one by one, in Kyoto and Okinawa the Socialists allied with the Kômeitô against the LDP and the JCP; in Osaka they allied with the LDP and the centre against the JCP; in Tokyo, with the JCP against the LDP and the Kômeitô. Often the JSP did not even put any candidates forward. So as not to cut itself off from the centre, the party started reconsidering its position on the Self Defence Forces and the Security Treaty. But under pressure from the left wing it went no further than unconvincing compromises; it reaffirmed its determination to abrogate the Treaty, but only with Washington's consent, and replaced 'abolition' of the Self Defence Forces by 'reorganisation and reduction, taking account of public opinion' (1980). This made it possible for Asukata to move to the centre by signing an agreement with the Kômeitô preparing the way for a coalition government, but in 1982 he reverted to the left by trying to impose a Secretary General close to the Kyôkai.

Around 1980 the JSP appeared as an increasingly sclerotic party. Unable to broaden its support among the new categories of the urban population, it was the 'civil servants' party', prisoner of the Sôhyô which was losing speed. Supplanted in the megalopoles, it got its candidates for the Diet elected mostly in rural and semi-rural constituencies. But as it remained the only opposition party with a strong nationwide structure and a broad electoral appeal, it maintained its supremacy over the whole anti-LDP camp, and in so doing condemned the opposition to impotence.

The Kômeitô: from opposition to collaboration

Between 1967 (5.4 per cent of votes) and 1969 (10.9 per cent) the Kômeitô doubled its electoral support. In 1972 it fell back to 8.5 per cent. It recovered in 1979 to 10.9 per cent but declined in 1980, and finished the decade with 33 House members, fewer than at the start of the decade. The Kômeitô's weakness, like its strength, lay in its identification with its mother sect. Its supporters were exceptionally disciplined: more than 90 per cent of them backed it 'firmly', compared with an average of 60 per cent for the other parties. But the Sôkagakkai's intolerance aroused public hostility. In 1970 the party and the sect solemnly parted company. The Kômeitô removed religious references from its programme, and its leaders gave up their posts within the Sôkagakkai but to no avail, since the party and the sect remained lumped together in the eyes of all Japanese.

In its early days the 'Clean Government Party' had attracted floating voters receptive to its denunciation of public immorality. But its mother sect compromised it in a series of scandals. In 1970 it tried to stop publication of a critical book by violent and corrupt means (the Fujiwara scandal). Then it was convicted of having tapped the JCP Chairman's telephone. In 1976 the Sôkagakkai Chairman was implicated in extra-marital affairs with two Kômeitô women members of the Diet. Lastly, he had to admit that he had paid one of its former advisers to prevent compromising revelations (the Yamasaki affair). Infringements of liberties, corruption, doubtful morals – the party's image was irreparably damaged.

The sect and the party had prospered because of the social disorganisation in the big cities during the boom period, but their attraction was very slight where the social fabric held. The Kômeitô concentrated its strength in no more than sixty constituencies in the megalopoles, where all its Diet members were elected. But it remained confined to that narrow base, with disadvantaged and poorly educated voters. As a consequence, it did not develop a real political programme adapted to modern Japan. Instead, it gave priority to seeking local government power, because they would enable it to provide material help for its clientele. It was essentially an opportunist party. At the beginning of the decade it was the natural ally of the progressive fronts, which improved social security. Despite its bitter rivalry with the Communists, the Kômeitô went so far as to sign a 'peaceful coexistence pact' with the JCP in 1975. But when the financial crisis strangled the progressive regional governments, the Kômeitô made an alliance with the LDP to bring it back to local power, and thus ensure the subsidies needed for the social programmes. It drew close to the conservatives on the burning question of the armed forces, by recognising 'the right of self-defence' in 1978, and later accepting the continuation of the Security Treaty 'until the time when the international situation makes it no longer necessary'.

However, the Kômeitô always put itself forward as an opposition party. In 1980 it signed two separate agreements with the JSP and the DSP, the blueprint for a socialist-Centre coalition government, and 21 Lower House members and ten senators were elected with the joint backing of the Kômeitô and either the Socialist or the DSP. But as an ally of the LDP at local level and opposition party at national level, the Kômeitô lost a bit more yet of its credibility.

The Communist Party: solid but marginal

The Japan Communist Party carried out a thorough ideological *aggiornamento* during this decade, under the guidance of Kenji Miyamoto, Chairman of the Central Committee, and Tetsuzo Fuwa, Secretary-General. It abandoned reference to the dictatorship of the proletariat, and even the term 'Marxism-Leninism' was dropped in 1976. It made itself out to be ultra-national, defended the principle of a Japanese army independent of the United States, put Mount Fuji on its campaign posters and called on the USSR to restore all the Kurile islands as far as Kamchatka. It vigorously combated student far-left activism and denounced 'the four sins: violence, sex, drugs and gambling'. Its organisation was consolidated. With a membership of 400,000 in 1980, it had more militants than all the other opposition parties together. Its organisations of women, youth, and small and medium-scale enterprises ('The Three Big Families') controlled more than a million sympathisers. Its daily *Akahata* had 3.5 million readers. Its declared revenue, 90 per cent of which came from its publications, rose from 4 billion yen in 1969 to 21.4 billion in 1980. Officially it was the richest party in Japan! It ranked third among the Communist parties in the 'free world', after those of Italy and France.

Its electoral fortunes fluctuated. In 1972, with 10.5 per cent of the vote and 38 House members, it became the third opposition party. In 1976, with 10.4 per cent, it had only 17 seats, but with the same percentage of votes cast, it went up to 39 in 1979. As most of its deputies were elected in the last position in their constituencies, with a small margin, a few hundred votes were sufficient to make them win or lose, according to the year. The JCP's electoral map was copied from the Kômeitô's. In 1980 it obtained 15.2 per cent of the vote in Tokyo (Kômeitô: 17.3 per cent), 19.9 per cent in Osaka (Kômeitô: 20.1 per cent) and 11.2 per cent in Fukuoka (Kômeitô: 14.5 per cent). But it artificially enlarged its electorate by putting candidates forward in the whole country, because in the rural constituencies those who rejected the LDP and the Socialists often had no other choice but a symbolic Communist. The JCP held about 5 per cent of the seats in the municipal and regional assemblies. Thanks to the united fronts it shared local power for a time. But when those fronts fell in 1980, there remained only five Communist mayors in Japan's 3,325 local governments.

At the end of the decade the JCP was marginalised when the JSP signed a pact with the Kômeitô. In the Diet it was no longer associated with joint opposition moves. The press abused the party; in 1976 it uncovered the murder of a police informer in which Miyamoto was said to have been involved around 1930. Despite the party's care to distance itself from the USSR, the increasingly frosty relations between Moscow and Tokyo (see p. 209) also contributed to its isolation. Democratic freedoms were not really guaranteed for the Communists. *Akahata* was excluded from the press clubs which collect information from the administration, and could not be sold on news stands. The police illegally kept a watch on the party's offices and leaders (telephone tapping, video recordings) and no complaint ever led to conviction. Admitting Communist sympathies remained dangerous, socially and professionally – so much so that there were always four times fewer declarations of intention to vote for the JCP in opinion polls than actual votes cast for it in the secrecy of the polling booth.

Democratic Socialists, Shaminren and the New Liberal Club – desperately waiting for a role

The nearly equal balance of parties' strength in the Diet before 1980 raised the prospect that at some time the LDP would need reinforcements. That meant that the forty-odd seats of the House held by the DSP, the Shaminren and the NLC were important. However, they did not succeed in forming a united, autonomous and credible Centre grouping. The DSP barely managed to retain about thirty seats thanks to the Dômei, as its share of the vote fell below 7 per cent. The party had two irons in the fire: it signed an agreement with the Kômeitô (which was also allied to the LDP), but it also prepared a programme for governing with the LDP. Ideologically, it was now very close to the conservative right wing. Linked with the armaments industries, it rejected the limiting of the military budget to 1 per cent of GNP, and one of its Upper House members was the former Chief of Staff of the Self Defence Forces. It called for 'ideological neutrality in education' (in opposition to the Socialist Nikkyôso), peaceful use of nuclear energy on a large scale, and 'Japanese-style' social security leaving a big role to traditional family solidarity. Because of this move to the right the DSP failed to bring in those who left the JSP with Eda in 1977. They formed the Shaminren, which saw itself as a new sort of party, inspired by the 'citizens' movements'. Shaken by the death of its founder, it was taken in hand again by the popular Senator Hideo Den. But it only got three members of the Lower House and three of the Upper elected in 1980, and it sought salvation in plans for union with the New Liberal Club.

Six months after their breakaway Yôhei Kôno's neo-liberals won 4.1 per cent of votes and 17 deputies in December 1976. But the urban floating voters' enthusiasm quickly died down. In the Upper House elections of 1977 the NLC only won three seats. It split up; Kôno wanted to form a centre party with the DSP and the Shaminren, while the Secretary General, Takeo Nishioka, wanted to rejoin the LDP. Nishioka defected on the eve of the 1979 elections, in which only three of the founders and one of the newly elected representatives of 1976 kept their seats. The NLC bounced back to 12 seats in 1980, but now the LDP did not need an ally any more.

Mini-parties: a new political force in the making

The end of this decade witnessed the upsurge of small political groups which only ran candidates in the Upper House elections, where anyone gaining as few as 1 per cent of the votes cast could hope for a seat in the national constituency. In 1977 the Lockheed scandal and the impotence of the opposition encouraged the formation of the Liberal Reformist Union. Led by a hundred-odd intellectuals and artists, it aimed 'to transfer politics to the pure hands of amateurs'. It got a comedian elected, and then a female television star in 1980. In 1977 the Wheelchair Party also won a seat. These mini-parties were in a sense an extension of the 'citizens' movements' of the 1960s, but in a non-ideological form since they were mostly foreign to traditional leftist ideals. Significantly the historic *shimin undô*, the Council Against the Atomic Bomb, finally collapsed amid its divisions and abandoned the anti-nuclear ground to local movements and to religious groups linked to the conservatives, such as the Risshô Kôseikai.

CONSERVATIVE TRENDS IN SOCIETY

The conservative trend in society was due to a number of causes: the general improvement in living standards, pride aroused by economic success, the tendency to close ranks against outside dangers (oil shocks, tensions over trade, international tension) and the depressing impotence of the opposition. The social movements lost vigour, conservatives had the upper hand in most national debates, conformity and cynicism increased and nationalism revivied.

Social movements: division and recovery

The 'inhabitants' movements' continued to proliferate. They jeopardised the grandiose programme for nuclear power stations and dams drawn up after the first oil shock. But they remained confined to local objectives, sometimes as selfish as a struggle against the building of a 'too noisy' kindergarten. Without coordination or political objective, they sought financial compensation above all, and the authorities had learned how to buy them over. But the government accepted no compromise with those who had embarked on open struggles in the preceding period. Narita Airport was forcibly opened at the price of more dead, and the Minamata plaintiffs were dragged into an endless legal Marathon.

The consumer movements remained very active. There were 4,300 local cooperatives around 1980. But the big consumer federations did not confront the establishment any more. The Housewives' Federation now preferred to sit on MITI councils than to organise national boycotts, and launched into production of cosmetics. It cut itself off completely from the politicised feminists, who derided its leaders as 'kitchen cockroaches'.

The feminist movement did not succeed in taking root in Japan, although the pink-helmeted activists of the League for Freedom of Abortion and the Pill (Chupiren) at first won notoriety for their campaigns targeted at executives of firms accused of ill-treating female employees. In 1977 its founder, Misako Enoki, founded the Japan Women's Party (JWP) and ran ten candidates for the Upper House elections. She campaigned for improvement of material conditions for divorced women, and against professional discrimination. But she insisted that her candidates learned karate 'to fend off their male colleagues in case of need'. Half of them gave up before polling day. The JWP only won 0.3 per cent of votes cast; Ms Enoki wound it up, closed down the Chupiren, and retired from public life.

The Burakumin movement was undermined by an internal struggle between the Socialist and Communist Parties. After the fall of the progressive governors, the movement gradually joined the clientele of their conservative successors, who distributed the subsidies. Many Japanese were still instinctively repelled by the former outcasts, and the ghettoes did not disappear. But the continuation of those discriminated-against closed communities was also the best way, for the associations representing them, to keep their power as pressure groups going indefinitely.

The Korean community began to organise against the discrimination excluding its members form state employment and most social security systems. The first lawsuits were brought against Hitachi (in 1970) for discrimination in recruitment, and against the state, which refused to admit a Korean who had passed the test to the Legal Training and Research Institute (1976). The plaintiffs' victory in both cases aroused the community's consciousness. It was to mobilise actively after 1980 against the obligation for Koreans to be fingerprinted for identification – something reserved for criminals and foreigners.

Conservatives on the offensive

On most subjects that had been dividing opinion and mobilising the opposition in the previous period, the conservatives now made decisive progress. They owed this to changes in public opinion, but also to the backing of the Supreme Court, whose 15 judges appointed by the government were die-hard conservatives, since there had been no alternation of parties in power.

The existence of the Self Defence Forces and the Security Treaty was now accepted by more than 80 per cent of public opinion. The Kômeitô and the Socialists had to follow the trend. This acceptance was made easier by the policy of improving relations with China and the USSR (see pp. 208–9), which implied a low military profile. After Nakasone's failure at the Defence Ministry in 1970, the military budget steadily declined from 7.2 per cent of state expenditure to 4.9 per cent in 1980. With the international détente prevailing until 1978, the United States no longer called for reinforcement of the SDF; rather it wanted Tokyo to shoulder costs like the wages of Japanese employees at the bases and the renovation of barrack buildings there – measures which attracted relatively little attention.

In four judgments in 1952, 1960, 1967 and 1973 the Supreme Court refused to make a clear ruling on the constitutionality of the SDF. Thus it left the government with a free hand, while appeasing public opinion which remained overwhelmingly attached to Article 9. Miki made new concessions to pacifist sentiment in 1976, when he needed the opposition to remain in power. He secured ratification of the Non-Proliferation Treaty, stalled since 1968, in spite of the 'hawks' of the LDP. He strengthened existing administrative directives so as to ban the export of all materials and technology for military use. He secured approval for 'Standards for National Defence 1977–1987', which limited the SDF's task to repulsing 'a small-scale invasion' on its own and laid down that the military budget should not exceed 1 per cent of GNP (a limit already in force since 1967). After Miki's fall the 'hawks' counter-attacked, while international tension rose again. Two bills – to facilitate action by the army 'in case of exceptional circumstances' (a euphemism for 'in time of war') and to punish the divulging of military secrets – gave rise to lively polemics but got nowhere and are still debated today.

The highly sensitive debate about constitutional amendment remained dormant so long as the near-parity of forces prevailed in the Diet. But the majority of LDP deputies and members still favoured it. In 1977 Fukuda refused to celebrate the Constitution's 30th anniversary. And when the LDP had a free hand again, in 1980, its 'Constitution Study Committee' was revived after 16 years' hibernation.

Even without amendments to the Constitution restrictions on liberties went on. The left was completely defeated in its long battle against the ban on trade union and political activity by state employees since the Supreme Court confirmed that they did not have the right to strike in any form (1973, 1976, 1977), nor the right to distribute election leaflets (1974), nor even the right to carry a placard in a demonstration (1980), while public opinion did not back the 'strike for the right to strike' in 1975. The Court also legalised the seizure of press documents to identify participants in a demonstration (1969, 1978), and the Court condemned a journalist who revealed a secret clause in the treaty for restoration of Okinawa (1978), despite the absence of a law defining state secrets. Step by step Shintô came back as the quasi-state religion. In 1977 the Supreme Court recognised a municipal authority's right to finance a Shintoist ceremony to purify the land before the start of construction work. The argument of this important ruling – that the ritual was a 'social custom' which did not have any 'really religious meaning' – opened the way to financing of all sorts of Shintô ceremonies from public funds. Polemics surrounding the Yasukuni temple continued. In 1974 no less than five attempts were made to push through the bill for nationalisation of the shrine. After they failed, the LDP adopted an indirect strategy. In 1975 Miki went to Yasukuni for ceremonies commemorating the dead (on 15 August), ostensibly as a private citizen. In 1978 Fukuda went there also, 'in his private capacity' but in his official car, and the shades of the war criminals executed after the Tokyo trial were enshrined along with those of all the soldiers fallen in the service of the Emperor.

Restoration of the symbols of traditional Japan made good progress. The LDP did not dare to make the *Hinomaru* flag, still less the highly controversial *Kimigayo* anthem, the official national flag and anthem. But in 1977 the Ministry of Education 'stipulated' their use in school ceremonies. In 1978 Fukuda gave government patronage to the 'Nation's Foundation Day' (11 February), a revival of the former 'Anniversary of the Founding of the Empire' commemorating the coronation of the legendary Emperor Jimmu. In 1979 the traditional system of dating by eras, which was now no more than a 'custom followed in practice', was given legal force again for all public acts. The Imperial Household Agency kept a close eye on anything that seemed to affront imperial dignity – even the issuing of stamps with Hirohito's picture was forbidden to prevent 'sacrilegious misuse'. But public opinion did not follow. Among people under 30 indifference towards the Emperor was predominant in the opinion polls, and hardly more than 5 per cent of Japanese wanted to see his prerogatives increased – a central point in the constitutional amendments dreamed of by the LDP's right wing.

The debate over 'normalisation of education' (*kyôiku seijôka*) continued to rage fiercely between the Ministry of Education and the Nikkyôso. The leading figures in the LDP regularly restated

JAPAN'S NATIONAL SYMBOLS

The Kimigayo anthem: 'The Reign of His Majesty':

> *Thousands of years of happy reign be thine;*
> *Rule on, my lord, till what are pebbles now*
> *By age united to mighty rocks shall grow*
> *Whose venerable sides the moss doth line.*

This tenth-century poem, by an unknown author, was set to music at a very early date, for various instruments. In 1880 the Ministry of the Imperial Household selected a version proposed by Hayashi Hiromori, which was played for the first time on 3 November 1880, on Emperor Meiji's birthday. After that the song had semi-official status. In 1893 the Ministry of Education made playing of it obligatory at school ceremonies. The habit of playing it on official occasions spread; however, it was never decreed to be the 'national anthem'.

Hinomaru: 'the Sun flag'

It is not known when the banner depicting the circle of the sun was used for the first time. According to some accounts the monk Nichiren gave one to the Shogun leaving to fight the Mongol invasions of the thirteenth century. Several parties used it on battlefields in the feudal period. Hideyoshi used it when he invaded Korea in 1592 and 1597. The Tokugawa Shoguns hoisted it on their ships. In the middle of the nineteenth century, when there were increasingly numerous naval incidents off Japan, they made flying the flag obligatory on all Japanese ships. The *Hinomaru* was declared to be the 'national flag' by the Meiji government on 27 June 1870. Outlawed by the SCAP, it came gradually back into semi-official use *de facto*.

In July 1999, the *Kimigayo* and *Hinomaru* were made the national emblems by law.

their determination to 'put an end to the post-war order in education'. In 1977 Fukuda praised 'the ethical values' of the Imperial Rescript on Education of 1890. Debate raged around the flag and the *Kimigayo*, which the majority of teachers refused to hoist during school ceremonies, and around censorship of school textbooks. More and more openly the censorship commission set up by the Ministry hunted down opinions critical of the founding myths, 'disrespect' towards the imperial institution, and reports of atrocities committed during the period of colonial expansion. This censorship was challenged in court by Professor Saburô Ienaga, whom the commission ordered to make 323 corrections in his textbook; but in 1980 an ambiguous judgment by the Supreme Court left the censors' hands free. Rehabilitation of the militarist period in the textbooks was to go on, and would cause repeated diplomatic crises with China and Korea in 1982 and 2001.

The 'new middle-class masses': conformity, 'my-homeism', and the decline of ideologies

According to annual polls by the prime minister's office, Japanese society was now composed simply of one vast middle class; 90 per cent of people questioned now placed themselves in one of the three categories 'lower-middle', 'middle-middle' and 'upper-middle'. Fashionable expressions spoke of a 'post-Marxist society' of 'new middle masses' and the 'majority tendency of a hundred million people' (*ichiokunin sochunya*), which recalled the militarist slogan 'a hundred million people, one single mind'. Those expressions reflected the general rise in the standard of living and the absence of ostentatious signs of great wealth. But that vision of a society made totally equal by increasing comfort, promoted to be the quasi-official ideology and taken up by the greater part of the press, also recalled the 'family-state' of the imperial period.

The ideology of the 'new middle-class masses' was expressed in opinion polls by the weakening of traditional values, those of the left as well as the right, and the corresponding promotion of a vaguely defined 'modernity'. Between 1973 and 1978, among the priority objectives in the eyes of the Japanese, 'social security' declined (from 48.5 to 32 per cent), as did 'the people's rights' (from 11 to 9 per cent), while there was a rise for 'economic development' (from 10.5 to 21 per cent) and 'order and social peace' (from 12.5 to 17 per cent). But at the same time, individualism and rejection of traditional hierarchical structures were in fashion. Around 1980 less than half of young men said they were attracted by the classic 'lifetime employment' (compared with 70 per cent in 1970), and a quarter of girls said they did not wish to marry. Actual behaviour was different – 98 per cent of girls did marry – but the polls showed that personal development was becoming more fashionable than unconditional devotion to the firm or the traditional mother's role. This desire to retreat into a vaguely modernised private sphere (*my-home shugi*) was accompanied by a materialistic cynicism displayed, for example, by girls who sought first and foremost a husband 'with a car and without a mother-in-law' (*kâ-tsuki baba-nuki*) and growing scepticism regarding partisan ideology. Around 1980 more than a third of voters had no fixed partisan allegiance any more. This new mentality was basically conservative and led to the rejection of radicalism and the abandonment of the will to 'change the world'. In 1980, 46 per cent of the young thought that no general improvement in life was possible (compared with 36 per cent in 1970), while three quarters of Japanese said they were 'content' with the present state of society.

The decay of the cinema reflected a society turning away from dramatic questioning and tensions. ATG, which had produced many protest films of the 'new wave', went bankrupt in 1975. The loss of flavour and standardisation of films produced reached a peak with Yôji Yamada's *Tora-san* ('Mr Tiger') series, starting in 1969. In this an engaging peddler wanders with infectious good humour around ultra-conventional versions of provincial Japan and popular residential areas of Tokyo. This amusing but rather insipid version of the *shômin geki* (film about the lives of small people) had prodigious success, and only ended in 1996, after its 48th episode, with the death of the actor who played Tora-san. Erotic films had made their scandalous beginning in the previous period, notably with *Love behind Bars* shown in 1965 at the Berlin Festival without its producers' consent. The conservative establishment indignantly denounced 'the shame of the Japanese cinema, displayed before the eyes of the world', and struck back in 1972 by having three members of the commission responsible for watching over morals in film production arrested. Erotic films soon sobered down in the form of 'romantic porn', the speciality of Nikkatsu, whose directors were experts at juggling with the law banning the showing of pubic hair. Two-thirds of the 300 films produced in 1980 were cheap erotic productions, while the leading directors no longer found producers. Kurosawa produced

Dodeskaden in the USA in 1970, *Derzu Uzala* in the Soviet Union, and *Kagemusha* ('the shadow warrior'), winner of the Palme d'Or at Cannes in 1980, with money from Francis Coppola. Oshima turned to French directors for *In the Realm of the Senses* (1975) and *In the Realm of Passion* (1978), which were disfigured by the censorship and caused him prolonged trouble with the law in his country.

The few strong films of this period often depicted personalities gone adrift, without any aim in life (Yoichi Higashi's *The Third Base,* 1978) or engaged on fatal moral decline punctuated by orgies of violence (Shôhei Imamura's *Revenge is for Us,* 1979). In literature *Nearly Transparent Blue* by Ryû Murakami, who won the Akutagawa Prize in 1976 at the age of 24, echoed those films. He describes, through the downhill descent of young drug addicts around the American bases, 'the drama of a generation which no longer believes in anything'. But generally, this period was rather allergic to tragic art.

Japan and the outside world: distrust vs. superiority complex

Between Japan and the West, the relationship was now becoming more tense. While some Western writers made panegyrics of Japan (like Ezra Vogel in *Japan as Number One,* 1979), many bestsellers denounced more and more violently the 'Japanese Conspiracy' (the title of Martin Wolf's book in 1983) to dominate the world. The expression 'Japan Incorporated' became popular and gave credit to the myth of a secret headquarters where the MITI and the Keidanren were planning the systematic destruction of their Western competitors. Fantasies of the 'yellow peril' and 'Asiatic treachery' were exploited by best-sellers like *The Ninja* by E. Lusbader (1980), in which a Japanese killer is sent to New York to murder an American industrialist. In all respects Japanese businessmen were depicted as like samurai warriors. Denigration of Japan was as fashionable as attempts to copy its recipes. In 1978 an EEC study called the Japanese 'workaholics' living in 'rabbit hutches' – causing an uproar in Japan.

On the Japanese side, Vietnam and the 'Nixon shocks' produced a psychological break. Comparison between Japan's economic performance and those of its partners fed an increasing feeling of superiority. More than half of people questioned now asserted that 'the Japanese are superior to Westerners' (compared with 20 per cent in 1953, 47 per cent in 1968). Some authors even claimed superiority for Japan in areas where it was considered traditionally behindhand, such as social security (*Japan, The Welfare Superpower* by Y. Nakagawa, 1979). The expression 'the English illness' (*eikokubyô*) became popular to describe the decline in the Western countries, undermined by the excesses of social security and cosmopolitanism. Europe seemed more and more like a museum, and the best-seller devoted to it during this decade was a collection of odd local customs (*Things of the West* by Y. Fukuda, 1976). In contrast, *nihonjinron* continued to glorify Japan-ness by comparison with the French (1972), the Germans (1977) and the Americans (1980). The first books in the form of neo-nationalist appeals now appeared: 'Japanese! Don't sell off your cultural heritage!' (Yûjirô Shinoda, 1980) and 'Japan! Be a State!' (Ikutarô Shimizu, 1980). But McDonald's fast food, Seven Eleven supermarkets, pizzerias and French bakeries proliferated, even in small provincial towns.

FOREIGN POLICY

A new posture: 'all-round diplomacy'

The primacy of the relationship with the United States was not questioned, even if the relationship became one of conflict. Economically, the USA still accounted for more than a third of Japan's trade and provided most of Japan's trade surplus. Politically, the Security Treaty hardly presented a problem any more. In 1974 Gerald Ford made an official visit to Japan – the first American president to do so – without incident. The following year the Emperor went to the United States. The G7 meetings from 1975 onwards, extensively covered in the media, went far to strengthen the feeling of belonging to the Western camp, which neither the left, now in retreat, nor Japanese neo-nationalism seriously challenged. The Japanese found that their prime minister cut a poor figure beside Western leaders linked by long familiarity, but they were proud to see him admitted to the club of the great. Anyway they adopted a conciliatory position at those meetings, out of concern to avoid tension, and this favoured their acceptance.

However, the decade saw a major change: Japan rediscovered its vulnerability. The Vietnam débâcle showed that Washington's military shield was not unbreakable. The oil shock revealed the danger involved in the economy's dependence on the international environment, against which the US Army was powerless. Tokyo was thus forced to deal in a more and more independent way with its three major foreign problems: its relations with the two neighbouring Communist giants, its position in the Middle East and with regard to conflicts that threatened its supplies, and its position in an Asian environment that was still violent and unstable, but also marked by the emergence of new developing economies. This new diplomatic style was reflected in expressions like 'all-round diplomacy' (*zenhoi gaisho*), 'resources diplomacy' and 'diplomacy separated from ideology'.

This increased independence involved friction with Washington, when 'supplies diplomacy' openly prevailed over Western solidarity. At the time of the first oil shock Tokyo was hastily converted to the Palestinian cause. A month after OPEC's decision to reduce its supplies except to 'friendly' countries, the Tanaka government officially gave its backing to the Arab case. Deputy Prime Minister Miki, armed with blank cheques, toured eight Arab capitals, and Japan was soon classified as a 'friendly country'. However, Tokyo was able to shelter behind European countries, such as France, which also favoured dialogue with the Arabs, and it was spared at the conference of oil consuming countries in Washington in February 1974, where the clash was polarised between France and the United States. After the invasion of Cambodia by the Vietnamese in 1978, Tokyo showed its solidarity by suspending its economic aid to Hanoi and voting at the UN for maintenance of the Khmers Rouges as the government of Cambodia – its economic interests being clearly on the side of ASEAN in this case. But at the time of the Iran hostages crisis starting in November 1979 Japan, which was heavily involved in the building of a petrochemical complex at Bandar Khomeiny, secretly bought 12.5 million barrels of oil, while Washington had decreed a total embargo on Iranian oil. Japan did not make up its mind to boycott Iranian oil until April 1980. After the Soviet invasion of Afghanistan in December 1979, Tokyo suspended the granting of credits to the USSR and cultural exchanges. But it waited for the Chinese decision to boycott the Moscow Olympic Games (1980), and in

1981 it again provided a cheap billion-dollar credit for Siberian development projects. However, it also did good work for Western solidarity by increasing greatly its aid to the countries most threatened by the Afghan War (Pakistan and Turkey).

Between Beijing and Moscow: how to deal with unquiet giants?

The USSR and China were at the same time a formidable politico-military threat to Japan, impressive reserves of raw materials and vast potential markets close at hand. But their fierce quarrel forced Tokyo into a difficult diplomatic balancing act, especially as Beijing and Moscow had almost the same assets. Around 1970 the value of Japan's trade with each country was on the same scale, around $1 billion. There was a traditional sympathy for China among Japanese public opinion, but the pro-Taiwan lobby remained very active in the LDP. The USSR was the arch-enemy, but it held a pawn – the four southern Kurile Islands – which made it necessary to treat it with consideration. When he recognised People's China Tanaka committed himself to establishing normal trade and negotiating a peace treaty. But there were numerous obstacles. The opening of air links caused a crisis in the LDP and a clash with Taiwan, which closed its air space to the Japanese. For the peace treaty, Beijing demanded inclusion of an 'anti-hegemony clause'; this figured in a mild form in the communiqué of 19 September 1972, but its anti-Soviet meaning had become perfectly clear since then. Japan resisted this demand, especially as the USSR was now making many overtures.

In 1972 the two countries decided to open talks on a peace treaty, and Moscow proposed five giant joint development schemes in Siberia. The most important related to the Tyumen oil field, from which the USSR promised Japan up to 40 million tons of oil per year for twenty years. In 1973 Tanaka agreed to study the scheme, and in return, Brezhnev agreed to discuss 'problems outstanding since the war', and unofficially offered to hand back the two smallest islets of the Kuriles on the signature of a peace treaty. Beijing counter-attacked on oil, with a contract for 7.8 million tons at cut price (1975), while increasing the political pressure with a campaign over Japanese war crimes and the Senkaku islands (see pp. 328–30). The Tyumen project took a worrying turn when the Soviet Union called for building of a second Trans-

Siberian Railway, whose strategic implications did not escape either Beijing or Washington, which put pressure on Tokyo. When Brezhnev suggested to Miki an immediate friendship treaty pending a peace treaty, Miki did not follow the idea up. The balance tipped definitively in favour of Beijing after the death of Mao Zedong in September 1976. Prime Minister Hua Guofeng wanted to develop heavy industry on a massive scale, paying for it with oil. 'Chinese fever' seized the MITI, which hoped to see China supplying Japan with 15 per cent of its oil in 1990 (0.4 per cent in 1972). The Keidanren went ahead of the politicians and signed a trade agreement in February 1978. On 12 August 1978 Fukuda signed a Treaty of Peace and Friendship, including the anti-hegemony clause. There followed an official trade agreement, for the supply of fifteen turnkey petrochemical plants and a giant steelworks at Baoshan near Shanghai. The USSR hit back by setting up military bases in the Kuriles and moving SS-20 nuclear missiles near Vladivostok. In 1979 a defecting KGB officer in Tokyo revealed the extent of Soviet spy networks in Japan (the Levchenko affair). Relations reached their lowest point with the Soviet invasion of Afghanistan. But trade continued, to the advantage of Japan which recorded a $1.2 billion surplus in 1981. On the other side, the 'Chinese fever' did not last long. At the beginning of 1979 Beijing embarked on a worrying armed confrontation with Vietnam. The quality of China's oil was poor and exports of it stagnated. In September 1980 Hua Guofeng fell from power, and China turned to a development programme centred on light industry and agriculture; Beijing cancelled Japanese contracts worth $1.5 billion without compensation. This failure and the Soviet military threat were to make Japan more circumspect towards its Communist neighbours – which, after all, accounted only for 6 per cent of its foreign trade.

From Asia to the Pacific Basin: broadening vision

In Asia, Washington continued its disengagement in conformity with the Nixon Doctrine. South Vietnam, overwhelmed by the North, was left to its fate in 1975; the bases in Thailand were given up in 1976; SEATO was wound up in 1977 and the security treaty with Taiwan was denounced in 1978. So Japan, here too, was forced to act more independently, in a region plagued by confrontation that obliged it to make difficult balancing acts. But because of the importance of the economic stakes it could not remain passive. Around 1980 the Asia Zone (excluding China) received almost 30 per cent of Japan's outward direct investment, twice as much as Europe. A quarter of Japan's exports went there and the region had become its main supplier (15 per cent of its imports in 1970, 23 per cent in 1980), because of the priority given to the nearest sources of energy and raw materials after the first oil shock.

Relations with Taipei and Seoul remained strained on the political plane. Japan's rapprochement with Beijing caused an open crisis with Taipei over air links, and the smallest gesture towards Taipei caused severe tension with Beijing, as in 1975 when Miki sent condolences on the death of Chiang Kai-shek. In relations with Seoul the Kim Dae-Jung affair (see p. 172) was followed by the attempt on President Park's life by a Korean resident in Japan, who killed the President's wife (1974). South Korea, in addition, did not appreciate Tokyo's friendly approaches to the North under the policy of 'all-round diplomacy': increased trade ($50 million in 1970, $570 million in 1980), visits by members of the Pyongyang parliament to Tokyo in 1977, and a Japanese proposal to recognise North Korea if China and the Soviet Union recognised the South, which would confirm the division of the country. But South Korea and Taiwan were now achieving a spectacular economic take-off. The OECD classified them as 'newly industrialised countries' in 1978. They were already competing with Japan in certain medium-technology industries – shipbuilding, steel manufacture. But they also imported increasing amounts of Japanese equipment and technology, and welcomed Japanese factories moving there in search of cheap labour or to flee anti-pollution regulations. Economic interdependence increased. During the decade those two countries' share of Japanese exports rose from 8 to 10 per cent, their share of Japanese imports from 2 to 5 per cent.

In South-East Asia Japan was caught between ASEAN and Indochina, which came under Communist rule in 1975 and was the theatre of violent confrontation between China and the USSR through Vietnam – the invasion of China's protégé Cambodia in December 1978 and China's military riposte against Hanoi in February 1979.

Relations with ASEAN were rather strained at the beginning of the decade. In 1971 student riots 'against Japanese economic imperialism' shook the military regime in Thailand. In January 1974 Tanaka set out on a regional tour which went awry; he had to be airlifted from his besieged hotel in Bangkok, and he left behind him ten dead and hundreds of burned Japanese cars in the streets of Jakarta. But the fall of South Vietnam altered the situation. ASEAN closed its ranks, and to compensate for the American withdrawal, it appealed to Japan by inviting Fukuda to its second summit, in Kuala Lumpur in 1977. Regular ministerial consultations began, and a treaty on the Straits of Malacca was signed the same year. Tokyo wanted to respond in a way that did not alienate Hanoi, having normalised relations with it very quickly after the fall of Saigon and planning for economic cooperation. Hence the three points of the Fukuda doctrine, set out explicitly before the Kuala Lumpur summit: Japan 'will not in any way be involved militarily to maintain the balance of power in the region'; it would maintain 'a certain balance' between ASEAN and Communist Indochina; within those limits it would back ASEAN 'with firm determination' by economic means. For the immediate future Tokyo granted $1 billion for implementation of five industrial schemes, and promised to double its official development assistance (ODA) in three years. Since the last payments linked to war reparations, in 1976, Japan was falling behind in ODA, which accounted for only 0.21 per cent of its GNP in 1976, compared with an average of 0.31 per cent for the OECD countries. Asia, which received 70 per cent of Japanese aid, and especially ASEAN (36 per cent) were the main beneficiaries of its increase. This led to a noticeable improvement of the image of Japan in South-East Asia, where several governments began to praise it officially as a model to follow, with the 'Learn from Japan' campaign launched in Singapore, imitated soon afterwards in Malaysia (the 'Look East Policy', 1982).

Beyond Asia, Tokyo took an increasing interest in the concept of the 'Pacific Basin'. The cooperation organisations set up previously in the context of the Cold War (see p. 162) were succeeded by more informal networks developed by the business world and by academics, with discreet government support. The Pacific Basin Economic Cooperation Council (PBEC) was extended to cover South-East Asia and Peru. Numerous regional cooperation projects were discussed in that discreet forum. In 1980 it was supplemented by the semi-official Pacific Economic Cooperation Committee (PECC) with senior officials now attending officially rather than 'in their private capacity'. Within that framework Japan strengthened its ties with Australia, despite occasional crises over Australian beef quotas and the price of Australian sugar imported into Japan. An economic relations study programme paved the way for a Treaty of Friendship and Cooperation (1976) which was meant to make the two countries 'stable and faithful markets and suppliers'. The establishment of foundations and research centres contributed to forging of closer ties, although Canberra strengthened its control over foreign (Japanese) shareholdings in mining companies. Ohira made this broadening of Japan's geopolitical vision official policy, by setting up a consultative council to explore the 'Pacific Basin' concept. Early in 1980 he visited Australia, New Zealand and Papua New Guinea, and then Mexico, Canada (he was the first head of government of a non-Commonwealth country to address Canada's House of Commons) and the United States, where he held talks with Carter on a project for a second Panama Canal.

Elsewhere in the world

The economically integrated Europe in the making proved a difficult trading partner, increasingly joining American recriminations. But Japan was able to shelter behind Europe or to play on economic differences between Europe and Washington in the G7 (see p. 208). Taken individually, each European country only had meagre trade with Japan – its most important European partner, West Germany, accounting for no more than 1.3 per cent of Japan's exports and 3.3 per cent of its imports. In 1973 Tanaka became the first Japanese head of government to visit Europe for nine years. He discussed cooperation schemes like joint ventures with Britain for North Sea oil and with France for exploitation of Africa's natural resources, and partnership with Germany in the Siberian projects. But nothing came of all this. Crown Prince Akihito made visits to the royal families of Spain, the Netherlands and Belgium. In pursuit of 'all-round diplomacy' President Ceausescu of Romania paid a visit to Tokyo (1975) and the Prince went to Romania and Bulgaria (1979). But it required Marshal

Tito's funeral for a Japanese Prime Minister to go to Europe again (1980). Britain still had the best rating – the Queen visited Japan in 1975 – but Germany was becoming the essential partner in technology following an agreement on scientific exchanges in 1974. President Walter Scheel also visited Tokyo, in 1978. However, France, which was very strict about imports of Japanese cars, was regarded by Tokyo as a hostile power.

Africa had to wait until 1974 for its first visit by a Japanese Foreign Minister, who went to Egypt, Nigeria and Zaire. In 1980 Japan only had diplomatic representation in 22 countries of the continent, but it provided official aid to 40, which received 11.4 per cent of total Japanese ODA in 1980.

Tanaka in Brazil and then President Geisel in Tokyo (1976) spoke of big development schemes for timber, aluminium and steelworks. But the continent's political instability held Japan back from taking a real interest in that backyard of the USA. Latin America received only 6 per cent of Japanese aid in 1980.

As the only non-white member of the G7, Japan was beginning to pose as a power mediating between North and South. In 1979 Ohira was the only head of government of an advanced country to be invited to the United Nations Conference on Trade and Development (UNCTAD) summit in Manila. He took there technical assistance programmes and scholarships, but no spectacular promise to open up the Japanese market to manufactured products from the Third World. Development aid structures were established – most noticeably the Japan International Cooperation Agency in 1974 – but the effort remained modest; the Japanese Overseas Volunteer Corps (JOVC) only sent a few hundred technicians into the field every year, and in 1979 Tokyo was still awarding only 1,300 scholarships to foreign students, mostly from Asia.

6

THE DILEMMAS OF POWER (1980–92)

POLITICS: 'THE CONSERVATIVE DECADE' (AND HOW IT ENDED)

After its triumph of July 1980 the LDP's hands were free again. Helped by the environment of the 'second Cold War', the conservative right wing achieved some of its major objectives under the governments of Zenko Suzuki (1980–82) and Nakasone (1982–87): 'administrative reform' inspired by ultra-liberal notions, restoration of order in state finances and introduction of a purchase tax, an increase in military expenditure, assertion of authority over teachers and rewriting of history in a nationalist sense, and confirmation of the special relationship between Shintô and the state. But a reaction followed among public opinion, encouraged by a new wave of scandals. In 1989 the LDP lost its Upper House majority. From then on it had to come to terms with the opposition in order to govern through what amounted to an 'informal coalition' system. This return to a balance of power and an uninterrupted succession of politico-financial scandals gradually paralysed the conservative governments (Takeshita, November 1987 to May 1989; Unô, May-August 1989; Kaifu, September 1989-October 1991) and opened the way to restructuring of the political system.

Back to the LDP's hegemony

In 1983 the LDP did not repeat its 1980 electoral success; it lost 2.2 per cent of votes cast and 24 seats. To retain absolute control of the Diet it had to offer a portfolio to the NLC. But the 'double election' in 1986 was a triumph. The LDP obtained 49.4 per cent of the vote (54.4 per cent with independents added). It made a marked recovery in the megalopoles by regaining the support of the young, with support verging on 50 per cent among people between 20 and 25 years old. With 304 seats in the Chamber and

214

142 in the Upper House, it achieved its best score ever. The NLC fell to a miserable 1.8 per cent, and it decided to return to the bosom of the government party, in return for symbolic measures of 'cleaning up public life' (ministers were obliged to declare their personal wealth). At the local level there were now no more Socialist governors except in Fukuoka and Hokkaido, and even there they did not have the support of a majority of the regional assemblies. The LDP and independent conservatives monopolised more than 70 per cent of seats in the regional assemblies. Only in the megalopoles did they still need an alliance with centre parties. Their domination was even more overwhelming in the city councils, where the Kômeitô, the JSP and the JCP each held scarcely 5 per cent of seats. In these conditions a form of consensual political life prevailed at the local level, favoured by the absolute ban on plurality of public positions. The JSP joined the conservatives and the centre to back the most popular governors in fifteen-odd regions of the 47. At the municipal level, out of the 650 large and middle-sized cities, one in six was run by a mayor elected with the backing of all the parties, including the JCP, most often without any opposition.

The factional infighting died down in the LDP. With Ohira's death, most of the feelings of hatred between contenders disappeared. His successor was chosen by length of service from within his faction, through consensus with the other clans. Zenko Suzuki – elected since 1946 and a dull personality – was supposed only to be a transitional prime minister, and did not ask for another term of office in 1982. In accordance with the party by-laws as revised in 1977, the LDP then organised primary elections. Backed by the powerful Tanaka and Suzuki factions, and the only one among the generation of faction chiefs that emerged in the late 1960s not to have held power, Nakasone easily defeated Fukuda's son-in-law and heir Shintarô Abe, Miki's successor Toshio Kômoto and the young Nakagawa, who tried to create his own faction with neo-nationalist Diet members. His attempt ended tragically; ruined by his primaries campaign, Nakagawa committed suicide. The factional struggle stabilised. The dominant Tanaka faction which controlled more than one third of congress votes was now able to choose the prime minister almost at will through an alliance with the small Kômoto clan plus any of the three others. No coalition could last long without it. The choice of a prime minister was now made in negotiations behind the scenes, in which each clan tried to win the favour of Tanaka and his increasingly influential right-hand man, Noboru Takeshita. After 1980 there were no more primaries and no more disputed congresses. Passion and rancour among the LDP's power houses finally died down in 1986 when the highly controversial Tanaka himself was removed from the political scene – paralysed by a cerebral haemorrhage, he was unable to prevent Takeshita from taking control of his group the next year.

In 1984 Nakasone secured a second term of office without opposition. He was supposed to retire in 1986, since the LDP, badly burned by the experience of the too long Satô government, had limited the number of terms to two. But the new generation of faction leaders (Abe, Takeshita, and Suzuki's successor Kiichi Miyazawa) was not yet fully in control. As 'thanks' for he election triumph in 1986, Nakasone got a fifth year in power. But in November 1987 he had to make way for Takeshita, supported by Abe to whom he had promised the succession.

Conservative achievements, 1: 'administrative reform' and the neo-liberal offensive

Administrative reform (*gyôsei kaikaku*) was grafted onto the debate set off by the budget deficit. Suzuki solemnly declared it to be his priority objective. He made Nakasone head of the Management and Coordination Agency, in charge of the reform of the civil service, and Nakasone said he 'was ready to commit suicide' to make it work. An alarmist public opinion campaign was organised around the burgeoning budget deficit, the need for Japan to avoid 'the advanced countries' disease' (that is, the excesses of the welfare state), and the need to prepare for 'an ageing society' (see pp. 234–5). The neo-liberal ideas and experiments applied in Britain under Thatcher and the United States under Reagan were echoed widely. A special consultative council was set up under the chairmanship of Toshiwo Dôko, former Chairman of the Keidanren. After publishing its final recommendations in 1983, it was succeeded immediately by a 'Council for Implementation of the Reform'. But behind the general wording of *gyôsei kaikaku* lurked several different objectives.

A return to balanced budgets was planned 'between 1985 and 1995'. The deficit was reduced from 33 to 25 per cent of the budget between 1980 and 1984 by economy measures, enhanced tax pressure on enterprises, and action against the most blatant tax privilege abuses. Since Ohira's resounding failure in 1979, establishment of a general indirect taxation device has become a taboo subject. In the 1986 elections the LDP promised again not to create any new tax. But the size of its victory was such that Nakasone, in the last year of his spell in office, dared to take the plunge. He presented to the Diet a bill for a modest purchase tax (3 per cent), with numerous exemptions for small and medium enterprises. The opposition, encouraged behind the scenes by many of the LDP's backbenchers, stalemated the bill after highly tumultuous debates, but Takeshita secured the neutrality of the Kômeitô and the DSP to get it through in March 1988. From then, the deficit fell in 1992 to a minimum of 9.5 per cent of the budget and 1.5 per cent of GNP, before swelling to unprecedented heights as a result of the economic crisis.

Privatisation was aimed in the first place at the railways (Japan National Railways, JNR), whose 37.5 billion yen debts burdened the budget. Despite the ferocious opposition of the Sôhyô railwaymen's federation (Kokurô) and the JSP, JNR was divided into six private regional companies, which assumed about 40 per cent of the JNR debt. The rest was taken over by a state liquidation company, responsible for realising a portion of the land assets and retraining about 60,000 employees who were not re-hired. Privatisation was also extended to the tobacco monopoly, the National Theatre, the telecommunications corporation (NTT) and Japan Airlines. Their monopolies were abolished by the creation of new rival consortia and the opening up of international air traffic to domestic airlines such as All Nippon Airways. In all, 750,000 jobs were transferred to the private sector.

This was the opportunity for the government to strike a very hard blow at the Sôhyô. The Kokurô, to which 70 per cent of JNR employees belonged, was decimated. When railwaymen were re-engaged the new private companies systematically excluded Kokurô militants. Fearing for their jobs, they deserted *en masse* to the moderate federations. The Kokurô's membership fell from 180,000 to 60,000, of whom the majority were entrusted to the liquidators for retraining.

The deficit was the best possible excuse for pay reductions in the civil service. In 1982, for the first time, the government froze pay in this Socialist stronghold, against the opinion of the arbitration body responsible for acting as intermediary between the state and civil servants who were denied the right of collective bargaining. The campaign was also directed against the privileges granted previously by progressive local governments to their staff in terms of pay, bonuses and retirement pensions. On returning to power the conservatives aimed to have local communities' budgets balanced again, but also to destabilise the very powerful Sôhyô local government staff federation (Jichirô), which played a major role in Socialist candidates' election campaigns. The denunciation of 'bureaucrats' excessive privileges' was popular with voters. Directives were issued by the Ministry of the Interior, combined with financial reprisal measures (refusal to authorise some loans) and political ones. On the eve of the local elections of 1983 the ministry published a list of 33 municipal authorities which had not followed its 'advice' for reduced retirement pensions for their staff. Under this pressure local government workers' collective bargaining agreements were revised slightly downwards all over the country.

Downward revision of social benefits was also on the agenda. The government praised a social security system 'based on traditional values' – a codeword for children taking charge of aged parents. Regarding retirement pensions, the age from which a retired person began to draw his pension varied between systems, from 60 to 65. The government sought to bring all pension funds gradually into line with the least generous – pension drawn at 65. For health insurance, despite the opposition of the Medical Association, a 10 per cent patient's contribution (30 per cent for family members) was introduced. Free medical care for people over 70 – the most symbolic of the reforms initiated by the progressive local authorities during the 1970s – was now placed in doubt with the introduction of a 300 yen payment by patients. Conditions for obtaining family allowances were made harsher. The share of social expenditure in the state budget, which had peaked at over 19 per cent in 1983, declined to 17 per cent in 1992 despite the ageing of the population.

Modernisation and rationalisation of the administration were aimed at abolishing bodies that had become useless, transferring posts from ministries whose utility was declining because of social and economic changes (Agriculture) to those whose importance was growing (Foreign Affairs), and pruning the wild growth of regulations. The aim was also to strengthen the organs depending directly on the prime minister's office – of which the Economic Planning Agency, the National Land Agency and the Coordination and Management Agency were the most powerful – at the expense of major ministries jealous of their independence, like Finance and the MITI. The changes begun under Ohira continued when Nakasone created in turn numerous consultative councils – on administrative reform, fiscal reform, education, long term economic policy – with the avowed goal of bypassing the bureaucracy.

The employers sought to regain ground lost in the preceding decades to inhabitants' movements and the pressure groups of the cooperative movements and small and medium enterprises. Among the Dokô committee's proposals were reduction of subsidies to pollution victims, relaxing of authorisation procedures for building of nuclear power stations, regulation of dangerous industrial facilities by the private sector itself, facilitating the opening of hypermarkets, and reduction in subsidies to the peasantry and small enterprises. The private sector also sought to limit competition from public bodies, by restricting the activities of those responsible for low-cost housing in Tokyo and Osaka, banning pension funds from building cheap leisure complexes, and obliging the Post Office to reduce the interest rate for savings-bank books to avoid excessive competition with private banking – among others. But the pressure groups dug their heels in: out of 2,800 subsidies in the state budget, only one (!) appeared in the committee's final report as 'to be abolished'. Only thanks to very strong American pressure were the protection established by the LDP for its clientele of farmers and shopkeepers, and the whole system of administrative regulation of the economy, challenged gradually towards the end of the decade.

Conservative achievements, 2: rehabilitation of the military and the neo-nationalist offensive

The determined expansion of the defence budget from 1981 onwards contrasted with the trend in the previous period. A

consultatve committee set up by Ohira put forward the new concept of 'global security' (*sôgô ampô*): the globalisation of the Japanese economy meant that the nation was now living 'in symbiosis'
with the international environment in all its aspects. Its security
had become inseparable from the harmonious development of the
whole planet, which it had to aid by positive intervention in the
most varied field – not only development assistance, but also protection of the environment and cultural activity. The report also
stressed that Japan's security had a military aspect which had been
too much neglected, especially in the context of the 'second Cold
War' prevailing since 1979.

On an official visit to Washington in 1981 Suzuki pronounced
for the first time the word 'alliance' in reference to ties between
the United States and Japan. He suggested that the Self Defence
Forces could intervene far from the home islands to ensure security of sea lanes over a radius of 1,000 nautical miles, in cooperation with the US Seventh Fleet. His successor Nakasone was the
most famous 'hawk' of the government party. In 1982 a revised
five-year military equipment plan broke with the standards fixed
by Miki for 1977–87. Military credits escaped from the austerity
measures of the 'administrative reform'. While the state budget
was theoretically frozen in 1984 and 1987, military spending
increased in those years by more than 6 per cent. Its share of
public expenditure rose from 5.1 per cent in 1981 to 6.5 per cent
in 1987. The institutional safeguards established by Miki were
dismantled. The three principles regarding armament exports
were abandoned in practice in 1983, when the government
authorised the transfer of technology for military use to the
United States under Reagan's 'Star Wars' project. In 1987 the
threshold of 1 per cent of GNP for military expenditure was officially exceeded, by a minuscule but highly symbolic 0.1 per cent.

In the same year Miki's standards were replaced by a new document, *Strengthening Defence for the Future*. The mission assigned to
the SDF was now to repel any sort of classic aggression in a battle
waged far from the Japanese coasts. The Forces were to be
equipped with weapons systems capable of detecting approaching
air or sea forces over the horizon (the AWACS flying radars) and
very long range sea-air and sea-sea defence vessels (AEGIS
destroyers). The SDF also acquired Patriot missiles, which Japan
was the only country to manufacture under license, and they were

to be allowed to use satellites for 'peaceful purposes'. Lastly, returning to his pet idea of 1970, Nakasone planned for Japan to develop itself 'the fighter aircraft of the twenty-first century', christened the FS-X. Tokyo was only to give up that idea after a two-year tussle with Washington, on condition that the aircraft would be developed jointly.

The conservative right stepped up its ideological offensive. In 1980 Suzuki went to the Yasukuni temple accompanied by almost his entire cabinet – albeit still in his own 'private capacity'. In 1982 the censorship commission advised school textbooks to use a new vocabulary: the Korean revolts against Japanese occupation were to become 'riots', the 'invasion' (*shinryaku*) of China in 1936 a mere 'advance' (*shinshutsu*), and the massacres in Nanking in 1937 (possibly 300,000 dead) were to be presented as 'insufficiently established' facts. In 1985 Nakasone broke the ultimate taboo by going to Yasukuni in his official capacity – causing outrage in Beijing and Seoul. Nakasone retreated and suspended his visits to the shrine in the following years. But neo-nationalist academics published in 1986 a textbook of their own giving a positive view of Japan's role as defender of Asia against the white race and the driving force for decolonisation, and describing the Pacific War as a historical necessity. Around 1992 this history textbook was the third most-used in Japanese junior high schools. The senior leaders of the LDP made repeated statements asserting, in the words of Nakasone himself, 'that it is still too soon to judge whether the Pacific War was an error with regard to history'.

Nakasone's departure did not halt neo-nationalism. In 1989 Shintarô Ishihara published *The Japan that Can Say No*, a best-seller which denounced Hiroshima as a racist crime, asserted the superiority of the so-called 'Japanese model' of capitalism and hinted that Japan might switch alliances and supply military technology to the USSR in order to erode America's hegemony. In the same year Professor Ienaga lost a third legal case against the censors. In 1990 new directives from the Ministry of Education made the use of the *Hinomaru* flag and the *Kimigayo* mandatory at school ceremonies, and introduced 'making the pupils aware of the principles of the Imperial Rescript on Education' (of 1890) into the education curriculum. The Nikkyôso bent under pressure and adopted a line of 'cooperation' with the Ministry. In 1992 the JSP recognised the *Hinomaru* as the national flag, while still rejecting the *Kimigayo*.

The cause of Shintô continued to make progress. In 1988 the Supreme Court ruled against the Christian widow of a member of the SDF who had died on active service and been enshrined as a *kami* in a Shintô sanctuary against her will; the court argued that while society had to show 'tolerance' towards the plaintiff's faith, she had also to show it towards 'prevailing social customs', and Shintô was such a custom. In January 1989, on the death of Hirohito, the Shintô ritual which was in principle supposed to be the private affair of the imperial family was in practice merged with the national funeral ceremony before an audience of foreign heads of state. The religious rites of enthronement of his successor Akihito were financed from public funds without much controversy. The far Right remained watchful against anything 'un-Japanese'. It led a terrorist campaign against the major daily *Asahi*, the one closest to the pacifist Left, one of whose journalists was killed in the Osaka region (1987). When Hirohito died it tried its best to prevent a reopening of the polemics about his responsibility in the war. The (conservative) Mayor of Nagasaki was 'condemned to death' by the right-wing groups for having (mildly) criticised the late Emperor, and was seriously wounded in January 1990; then he was discarded as an LDP candidate and beaten in the next election.

Return to balance of power from 1989

Resistance to the neo-liberal policy was at first limited. In the Upper House elections of 1983 it was shown in the proliferation of mini-parties encouraged by the adoption of proportional representation in the national constituency. The new Salaryman Party stood up for average wage earners by denouncing tax discrimination against them and opposing all tax increases; it won 2 million votes and two seats. Together a dozen atypical political formations – including the UFO Party – won 12.5 per cent of the vote, thus becoming the third political force in Japan after the LDP and JSP. They succeeded above all in the big cities, among the modern, educated voters. On this first occasion when Japanese were voting for a party and no longer for personalities, the LDP's mediocre score in the national constituency (35.3 per cent) was a first warning for the government party. But the traditional opposition remained impotent. The centre groups and the JCP struggled to maintain their positions. The JSP was in disarray. The Socialists lost four seats, and Asukata handed back the chairmanship to his predecessor, Masashi Ishibashi. The not-so-new leader succeeded in softening somewhat the party's Marxist platform dating from 1955. That did not stop it falling to a historic low – the lowest yet – in parliamentary elections of 1986, with only 17.2 per cent of the vote and 85 seats (a decline of 27). Ishibashi then made way for Takako Doi, a Professor of Law and the first woman to lead a Japanese party.

Discontent suddenly crystallised in 1988–9, under the impact of six factors in conjunction. The introduction of the purchase tax in April 1988 mobilised housewives. The peasantry and small-scale shop-owners were threatened with dismantling, under American pressure, of the protection which the LDP had given them (see p. 233). The reduction in social benefits and the increase in military spending inflamed public opinion in general. The excesses of the speculative economy (see pp. 230–1) antagonised middle-class wage-earners, driven out of the city centres by the explosion of property prices. Trade unionism, badly hurt by the privatisation programme, countered with the gradual unification of all the major confederations within the Japanese Confederation of Labour (Rengô), which decided to put forward candidates of its own for the elections, in cooperation with the JSP. Lastly, the Recruit scandal brought to light the extent of influence-peddling and corruption, linked to the speculative economy, and led to Takeshita's resignation in May 1989. As all the faction leaders were compromised, the government was placed in the hands of the very little-known Sosuke Unô.

The Upper House elections of 23 July 1989 were a triumph for the JSP and Rengô, which made common cause. The JSP won nearly 10 million votes in the national constituency, where it crushed the LDP with 35 per cent of votes compared with 27.3 per cent in 1986. In the local constituencies the LDP lost 28 of its 48 seats being contested. In the new Senate the LDP had only 109 seats against 143 for the opposition in the new Senate; this was the first time since the war that it lost its majority in one of the two houses of parliament, and it never regained it in the Senate until today. Victory went to the JSP, which won 24 seats, and Rengô, which got 12 out of its 13 candidates elected, while the other opposition parties lost nine seats and 4 million votes. While the centre groups were compromised by the vote for the purchase tax and the Recruit scandal, the JSP was carried forward by the unexpected popularity of Miss Doi, who mobilised women voters. It put forward many 'amateur' candidates coming from the associations movement, including several women whose new style attracted the young and modern urban vote.

The LDP reacted by calling on a 'new man' to restore its image. Toshiki Kaifu, though not really young (58) and a veteran – elected ten times to the Diet – was to perform that task. He was said to have a good media image and to be a skilful debater. Affiliated to the Kômoto (formerly Miki) faction, reputed to be the 'cleanest', he emerged unscathed from the Recruit scandal. He promised to fight against corruption by a radical reform of the electoral system. That was enough to win the parliamentary elections of February 1990, where the LDP retained a 70-seat majority – partly because the conservative candidates spent on average 500 million yen each. The JSP repeated its Upper House election performance, gaining 57 seats and over 6 million votes more than in 1986. But the most of its gains were at the expense of the centre (which lost 23 seats) and the Communists (who lost ten), and the LDP again won a majority of votes cast (52.5 per cent with the independents).

So the political system was threatened with paralysis. The Japanese Upper House is constitutionally in a position to block the whole legislative process, except for the appointment of the prime minister and the voting of the budget. Its opposition could only be overridden by a two-thirds majority of the House, which the LDP did not have. Thus Japan entered into a *de facto* era of coalition governments. The Kômeitô, which held the keys to the Upper House with its 21 seats, quickly made overtures to the conservatives by denouncing the agreement linking it with the JSP since 1980.

Towards reshaping the political system

The LDP continued to govern, making agreements sometimes with the centre, sometimes with the JSP, to build up majorities in the Upper House. It even continued to score points. It did not go back on the consumption tax, nor on the cuts in social benefits. The neo-nationalist offensive continued. Kaifu took advantage of the Gulf Crisis to send the Self Defence Forces outside national territory for the first time, in the form of a flotilla of minesweepers whose task was to clear up part of the Gulf after the conflict (April 1991). In June 1992 Miyazawa forcefully pressured the centrists into passing the PKO (Peace Keeping Operations) Law which broke the official taboo against sending any Japanese military man abroad, by authorising the SDF to take part in UN missions – albeit under very restricting conditions. This was a severe defeat for the Socialists, fiercely hostile to the law. The JSP did not retain the support it had mobilised among undecided voters, and remained paralysed by the struggle between its left and right wings. The local elections of 1991 were catastrophic for it, especially in Tokyo, where its candidate for governor finished last with a miserable 6.5 per cent of the vote. The old guard of Sôhyô apparatchiks took advantage of this to get rid of the too popular Miss Doi. But the new Chairman, the right-winger Makoto Tanabe, only defeated his left-wing rival by 54 per cent of votes to 46 per cent; the party remained hopelessly split in two.

Nevertheless, reshaping of the political landscape seemed inevitable. At the end of his first term of office Kaifu was thrown out by the LDP faction leaders, and replaced by one of them, Kiichi Miyazawa (November 1991). But scandals came one after another. The Prime Minister's right-hand man was arrested for corruption over the Kyôwa affair. The Sagawa Kyûbin affair exposed financial links between the *yakuza* underworld, the politicians and the business world. The securities firms scandal revealed how they colluded with each other to take advantage of the speculative economy through manipulation of the stock market in favour of 'privileged' clients among politicians and the Mafia. The press and public opinion now clamoured for 'political reform' (*seiji kaikaku*) in which the main element should be electoral reform.

Such a reform would have to correct the imbalance in representation between the countryside and the under-represented big cities, to make elections less expensive and reduce corruption. Minor changes had already been brought in, most noticeably the introduction of proportional representation in Upper House elections in the national constituency (1983) and the transfer of seven Lower House seats to the cities (1986). Kaifu proposed a completely new system for parliamentary elections: two thirds of the members were to be elected from small single seat constituencies as in the British system, one third by proportional representation. But he encountered fierce resistance from both the LDP and the opposition. The Kômeitô, DSP and JCP knew that they would have almost no chance of winning in the single-seat constituencies. The conservative deputies feared that new constituency demarcation would disrupt their costly electoral machines. For trying to get his bill through with a threat of dissolution, Kaifu was abruptly removed from power after his two-year term as LDP chairman.

PARLIAMENTARY ELECTIONS, 1946–90

	Conservatives		Socialists Shakaito		Minshato		Kômeitô		Communists		N.L.C.		Independents and small parties	
	% of votes	seats	% of votes	seats	% of votes	seats	% of votes	seats	% of votes	seats	% of votes	seats	% of votes	seats
1946	46.3	248	17.8			92			3.8	5			32.1	119
1947	58.9	281	26.2			143			3.7	4			11.2	38
1949	63	347	13.5			48			9.7	35			13.8	36
1952	66.1	325	9.6	54	11.6	57			2.6	—			10.1	30
1953	65.7	310	13.1	72	13.5	66			2	1			5.8	17
1955	63.2	297	15.3	89	13.9	67			2	2			5.6	12
1958	57.8	287	32.9			166			2.6	1			6.7	13
1960	57.6	296	27.6	145	8.8	17			2.9	3			3.1	6
1963	54.7	283	29	144	7.4	23			4	5			4.9	12
1967	48.8	277	27.9	140	7.4	30	5.4	25	4.8	5			5.7	9
1969	47.6	288	21.5	90	7.7	31	10.9	47	6.8	14			5.5	18
1972	46.8	282	21.9	118	7	19	8.5	29	10.5	38			5.3	14
1976	41.8	249	20.7	123	6.3	29	10.9	55	10.4	17	4.2	17	5.7	21
1979	44.6	248	19.7	107	6.8	36	9.8	57	10.4	39	3	4	5.7	21
1980	47.9	284	19.3	107	6.6	32	9	33	9.8	29	3	12	4.4	14
1983	45.7	250	19.5	112	7.3	38	10.1	58	9.3	26	2.4	8	5.7	19
1986	49.4	300	17.2	85	6.4	26	9.4	56	8.8	26	1.8	6	6.8	13
1990	46.1	275	24.4	136	4.8	14	7.9	45	7.9	16			8.9	26

In 1990 the 'independents' consisted of 16 conservatives and 6 socialists; the 'other parties' of the 4 Shaminren deputies.

THE ECONOMY: EXPLOSION OF POWER

Japan as Number One?

Japan's GNP in 1990 was equal to those of Germany, France and Britain put together. It was getting near two-thirds of that of the United States. Expressed in dollars, income per head ($23,000) was the first among the major industrial countries, even though it remained below those of the Americans and many Europeans in purchasing power parity at $17,810. With an annual average growth rate of 4.9 per cent between 1986 and 1991, compared with 2.8 per cent in the EEC and 2.2 per cent in the USA, some economists even speculated that Japan's GNP could exceed that of the United States by the end of the century.

Trade surpluses kept increasing: $20 billion in 1981, $96 billion in 1987. None of the responses imagined by the West – from Voluntary Export Restriction Agreements (VERA) to negotiations on the Structural Impediments Initiative (SII) – succeeded in reversing this trend. Even an 85 per cent revaluation of the yen against the dollar between 1985 and 1989 caused only a moderate drop in the surplus, to $78.2 billion in 1991.

Thanks to this formidable rise in the value of the yen and the accumulated surpluses – plus a still fairly high rate of savings – Japan became the premier financial power in the world. The ten leading banks in the world were all Japanese in 1988. Japan used this new power for massive direct investment overseas (purchases of firms, relocation, property speculation). It rose to the first rank among lenders on the world financial market, the first rank of Official Development Assistance donors in actual amounts, and the second rank of contributors to the budgets of the United Nations and the IMF.

Japan's domination of the world economy was no longer expressed solely in market shares. Japan also acquired a monopoly or near-monopoly of some sophisticated technologies and manufactures – especially in electronic components – which placed many foreign producers in a situation of dependence on it, including American arms manufacturers. Research and development was integrated into the concept of 'global security', and promotion of technologies of the future became one of the main areas of action for the MITI, which actively tried to carve a new niche

for itself, since its power over the big firms was declining as they
became more and more 'internationalised'.

The Japanese economic machine confirmed once again its
remarkable capacity for adaptation to the uncertainties of the
world situation. Confronted with protectionist barriers in the
form of Voluntary Export Restriction Agreements, it bypassed
them by moving plants and starting production in the USA and
the EEC. Confronted with the massive rise in the value of the yen,
it took advantage of this to invest overseas, while offsetting the
negative effects on exports by new improvement in productivity.
Confronted with the threatening hostility of the United States
and the risk of seeing a 'Fortress Europe' emerge after 1992, it very
quickly redirected its commercial and financial flows, first from
the United States to Europe, then to Asia. On the domestic side,
the policy of almost free credit following the Plaza Agreements of
1985 led to a wave of stock market and property speculation, the
so-called 'bubble economy'. The financial logic of short-term
profit seemed to prevail over productive logic, whose prevalence
characterised the Japanese model of capitalism. As it ebbed away
from 1990 onwards the wave of speculation left behind it
resounding politico-financial scandals, which contributed to the
LDP's loss of its monopoly of power. But it was to take two more
years before the financial shock caused by the bursting of the
bubble would spread to the whole economy. Finally, the system
of production had to confront one more challenge in the form of a
growing labour shortage and a change of mentalities which called
the lifetime employment system into question and posed a new
problem: immigration.

Japan's trading partners tried all sorts of counter-measures to
cope with the increase in their trade deficits. The United States
was the most concerned. Its deficit rose from $40 billion in 1980
to more than $150 billion in 1987, nearly 40 per cent of it on trade
with Japan. It led the offensive against Tokyo, while the EEC,
whose foreign trade steadily recovered after the second oil shock
until it went into surplus again in 1986, appeared less virulent at
first. To reduce the trade imbalances without completely repudi-
ating the rules of the market economy, the Westerners were to use
three strategies.

Voluntary export restraint – and ways round it

'Managed trade' through VERAs was imposed on Japan under threat of reprisals (quotas, anti-dumping penalties, etc.). In 1981 it agreed to limit its car exports to the United States to 1,680,000 units per year for three years. This agreement remained in force until the end of the century, while the limit was gradually raised to 2,300,000 vehicles. The trade in cars and car parts, albeit 'managed', was to remain the cause of many conflicts during the next decade. West Germany obtained a similar agreement, while France clung to unofficial but stiff quotas (3 per cent of the market). Other agreements followed – on tape recorders, photocopiers, etc. – and it reached the point where one-third of Japan's trade with Westerners was 'managed' in this way. In 1986 the Americans imposed a new type of agreement, on microchips, which limited Japanese exports but was also meant to guarantee 20 per cent of the Japanese market for US products in 1993. In 1990 the agreement with the EEC on the vehicle trade limited Japanese imports to 8 per cent of the Community market until the end of the century (plus 8 per cent for production by Japanese firms working there).

The Japanese response was to set up production units in the 'protected' zones. The first made-in-USA Honda came off the production line in 1982. In 1990 a dozen Japanese factories produced 1.3 million vehicles per year in the United States. With imports, they were well set to conquer a third of the market. In the EEC Nissan set up production in Britain and Spain in 1982, followed by Toyota (Britain), Suzuki (Spain) and Honda. Other branches of industry followed. When the Americans and the EEC imposed quotas of locally manufactured parts for all the cars assembled in the delocalised Japanese factories, Japanese firms brought along their subcontractors, more than 300 of which established themselves around their car plants in the USA. Meanwhile, the VERAs had advantages for the Japanese. The exporting firms were able to take advantage of the artificial shortage of their products to sell them with substantial margins. And the relocation made it possible for them to make a game of changes in the local economic environment and protectionism, for example by exporting made-in-USA Japanese cars to Europe to get round the agreement of 1990.

Revaluation of the yen and the 'bubble economy'

The massive revaluation of the yen and the European currencies against the dollar was the result of the Plaza Hotel agreement in September 1985. The yen's value rose from 238 to 128
to the dollar in 1988, before stabilising for a time around 140.
Japan's partners expected that its exports would lose their com-
petitiveness and their imports to Japan would be made easier.
Indeed, Japan's trade surpluses declined, but with the United
States it fell very slightly: $58.6 billion in 1986, $55.5 billion in
1988. Many Japanese high technology products had no competitors, regardless of their prices. As for consumer products
imported by Japan, their price did not fall, as the exchange gains
were retained by the distributors, and thus they registered only
very modest growth. Furthermore, since the reduction in the
American trade deficit, which fell from $161 million to $109
million between 1987 and 1989, was made mostly at the
expense of the EEC, the Plaza Agreements contributed to
dividing the West and weakened the EEC more than Japan.

The rise of the yen (*endaka*), combined with exchange gains
from imports, gave Japanese firms the means to invest massively
overseas. Direct investments multiplied almost fivefold in five
years – $10.2 billion in 1985, more than $47 billion in 1988 –
before stabilising. Japan became the world's first lender. In 1989
Japanese bought 30 per cent of American Treasury Bonds and
covered 40 per cent of the international loans issued in London.
And the revenue from these investments was beginning to credit
Japan's balance of payments.

The revaluation also led to a rush of relocations and investment
abroad, aimed at reducing production costs. It boosted Japanese
industry's penetration in Asia, and its long-term productivity. But
it also set off a formidable wave of speculation. To offset the effect
of the *endaka* and facilitate investment the Minister of Finance,
Kiichi Miyazawa, reduced the discount rate to 2.5 per cent in
1985, in fact making credit almost free. The Nikkei stock
exchange index rose from 12,000 to 39,900 between 1985 and the
end of 1989, while the index of real estate prices rose from 150 to
380 (against a base of 100 in 1980), and very much more in the big
cities. All those who had some land, starting with the big firms,
borrowed from banks on the security of the land, invested the
money on the stock exchange, and started over again when the

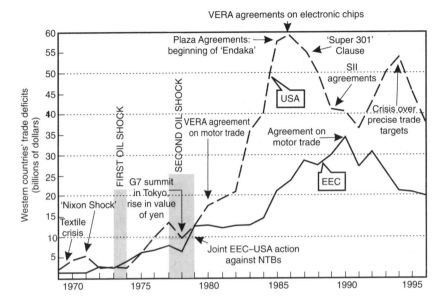

Fig. 6.1.   TRADE CRISES BETWEEN JAPAN AND THE WEST

value of the land increased and made it possible for them to borrow again. Banks' property loan commitments reached 44,000 billion yen, 11 per cent of GNP. In the absence of legislation making insider trading punishable, and with four securities firms passing 70 per cent of orders, doubtful practices had a free run. To attract big-time customers brokers guaranteed them against any fall in prices (the securities firms affair, 1991). When making initial public offerings of shares, firms distributed some in advance to politicians, ensuring a profit for them at the first quotation (Recruit affair, 1988). The Mafia, traditionally very present in the property market, received fat loans from the most respectable banks, and passed on a portion to politicians (Sagawa Kyûbin affair, 1992). All these scandals broke out when the speculative bubble burst at the end of 1989. The government was worried about the overheating and the political consequences of too blatant speculation, which had contributed to its defeat in the Upper House elections in 1989. It tightened credit, raised the discount rate, froze the property loans, unleashed the prosecutors against a few businessmen – and left to their fate the small shareholders, victims of the collapse of the Nikkei which fell by 46 per cent in only nine months from January 1990. The small shareholders – many of them housewives who invested their 'secret treasure' without telling their husbands – joined the middle-class salaried workers, whose dream of buying a home has been shattered by rising property prices, as victims of the 'bubble'.

Japan-phobia, IIS talks and new modernisation

Negotiations on structural obstacles to trade in the Structural Impediment Initiative were the ultimate stage of the pressure put on Japan by the United States. With tariff protection gone, non-tariff barriers mostly dismantled and the yen revalued, the American deficit remained. Even worse – Japanese capital was beginning to 'buy up America', including even its cultural symbols (CBS Records, Columbia Pictures, Universal Studios). A powerful anti-Japanese current of opinion developed, exemplified by a series of best-sellers with resounding titles: *America vs. Japan* (1986), *Yen! Japan's New Financial Threat* (1988), *Selling out: How We are Letting Japan Buy Our Future* (1989), Karel van Wolferen's *The Enigma of Japanese Power* (1989) and Pat Choate's *Agents of Influence: How Japan's Lobbyists Manipulate America* (1990). Some Congressmen smashed Toshiba products with hammers on the steps of Congress, amid full media publicity, when the company was caught selling machines prohibited by COCOM to the USSR. In 1988 new US trade legislation (the Super 301 clause) obliged the administration to identify countries guilty of 'unfair practices' and take retaliatory measures within one year if the 'culprits' did not amend their behaviour. In 1989 Japan was the first to be designated an 'unfair' country, together with Brazil and India. President Bush proposed negotiations which would go to the heart of Japanese economic and social practices. Tokyo agreed, only trying to save face by demanding that the structural weaknesses of the American economy – insufficient savings, insufficient productive investment, ineffective educational system – should also be discussed. The SII talks ended in a series of Japanese promises and concessions in June 1990:

– Reduction in 'excessive investment' both abroad and at home. Tokyo promised to spend 4,300 billion yen in ten years for social infrastructure, 90 per cent more than in the preceding decade. Private consumption was to be encouraged, at the expense of savings, by a reduction of the working week from 48 to 40 hours, multiplication of credit cards, extension of hypermarkets' opening hours, etc.

– Modernisation of distribution abolished the veto that small shop-owners' associations had over establishment of hypermarkets, which the Americans considered better suited for distribution of imported goods than small shops stuck in routine and held captive by exclusive connections with suppliers. At the end of 1991 Toys'R'Us of the USA opened in Japan the first toys supermarket, overcoming strident opposition by local retail outlets.

– The Americans accused the *keiretsu* of monopolistic practices, price fixing, rigged tenders, and many other misdemeanours. Tokyo promised to strengthen the FTC, stiffen penalties, stimulate competition and help consumers to defend themselves – but very few actions followed.

– Excessive property prices were also listed as 'structural obstacles'. The government agreed to prepare a law to tax land frozen for speculative purposes. But too many parties had an interest in the speculation. The LDP whittled down the text to inoffensive taxation at 0.2 per cent with 1.5 billion yen tax-free

– Dismantling of the last measures of agricultural protectionism: all the remaining quotas (notably for beef and citrus fruits) were immediately increased, and were supposed to end in a few years. But rice – loudly praised as 'the soul of Japan' – remained protected: Japan only promised to open 10 per cent of the market by the year 2000 and secretly hoped that the negotiations on global liberalisation of farm trade in the new WTO round would somehow be stalemated, giving it a fine excuse for not keeping its promise.

In fact many of these 'concessions' were advocated for a long time by the Keidanren, part of the economic ministries (especially the Economic Planning Agency) and some 'enlightened' LDP representatives. Since 1980 there had been successive reports proposing to the public 'a historic transformation in matters of economic management and life style' (the Maekawa Report, 1986), improvement in the quality of life, stimulation of consumption, better consideration of external criticisms, and introduction of less costly agriculture. But the more than ten million organised votes of peasants and small shop-owners put the politicians under very strong pressure. 'Foreign pressure' (*gaiatsu*) was thus a convenient argument widely used by the authorities to overcome that resistance, in the name of the national interest.

A society on the turn: problems and prospects

Thus Japan embarked on a new stage of its economic and social modernisation – one which would impact brutally on many people. Removal of protection from archaic sectors threatened about 3.5 million farmers, 1.5 million owners of small shops (with less than three employees), and their families – altogether about 16 million people. But the majority of peasants had already made their own redeployment; less than 25 per cent of those whom official statistics classified as 'farmers' derived their main income from the land, while the others spent only a few weeks a year tilling the soil and earned wages as factory or construction workers. As for small-scale shops, run to a great extent by elderly people, their numbers were to be reduced by natural wastage. Thus the risk of social unrest was minimal.

The ageing of the population was much more worrying. In 1990 people aged 65 or over amounted to 12 per cent of the population, and the proportion was projected to rise to 16 per cent in the year 2000, 18 per cent in 2005 and 23.5 per cent in 2020. Meanwhile the number of active people would start declining from 1996, and fall from 61.3 million to 51.5 million in 2025, when there would be only 2.5 workers for each retired person. The reason was a low fertility rate (1.53 children per woman in 1985) combined with a record life expectancy improved by healthy diets, reaching 75 years for men and 81 for women. The long-term economic consequences were obvious. Social security expenditure would eat up an increasing proportion of GNP – 14 per cent in 1985, perhaps 29 per cent in the year 2000 (however, for France, Germany and Italy the proportion was then over 35 per cent) – at the expense of productive investment. Savings would decline, as the aged consumed what they had built up during their lives. They could decline from 16 per cent of disposable income to half that amount (but in the USA the proportion was then under 5 per cent). The main risk is perhaps loss of motivation among active workers, who would have to make higher social security contributions.

The ageing of the population reflected on the labour market. In 1990 there were on average 3.5 job offers for a young science graduate, 2.9 for an Arts graduate, and 1.4 for a girl leaving secondary school. With an ageing population and an already very high rate of female employment (57 per cent between 20 and 64 years of age) the question of immigration arose. Officially, there was still no question of allowing the entry of foreign workers, and penalties were reinforced in 1990. In reality several hundreds of thousands of Pakistanis, Sri Lankans, Iranians and Chinese 'students' worked with hardly any concealment. Firms were able to bring in Asian workers as 'trainees' under the heading of development aid. And from 1990 onwards the law accorded permanent resident status with the right to work to foreigners of Japanese origin, which allowed thousands of South American *nisei* (descendants of Japanese emigrants) to go and work in Japan.

Changes in the employment system were the response to these various constraints. The shortage of manpower made it possible for workers to choose. The jobs described by the 'three K's' (*kitanai, kitsui, kiken*: dirty, hard and dangerous) did not find takers any more. The young found the traditional constraints of lifetime employment – low starting wages, endless overtime, authoritarian and interfering superiors, transfers to other locations taking no account of family circumstances – increasingly irksome. 'Death from overwork' (*karoshi*) was no longer accepted as inevitable, and gave rise to an increasing number of lawsuits. Highly specialised technicians, as well as engineers, designers and experts in international finance, allowed themselves increasingly to be enticed away by higher salaries. These constraints altered the employment system. The big companies, short of manpower, kept their salaried staff up to the age of 60 instead of 55, and if possible even longer; in 1992, 41 per cent of men over 65 still had jobs. This was counterbalanced by capping increments according to seniority at the ages 45–48. To retain young staff, a higher proportion of their salaries was related to competence and results. To take account of changes in outlook, the firms proposed two ways ahead when taking on new staff: the 'élite senior staff career' (*sôgôshoku*) for those committing themselves to unlimited availability as regards hours and location, and the 'general type of employee' system (*ippanshoku*), with few constraints and less promotion. The trend was to reduce the hard core of people with lifetime employment, so as to call on a flexible workforce of subcontractors and temporary workers. Lastly, relocation was the ultimate remedy.

SOCIETY

Going for change – quietly

The traditional image of Japanese society as one single middle class was shattered, but without major tensions. The neo-liberal policy and the reduction in protection for agriculture and small shops showed again that clashes of interests among social categories did exist in Japan, but the country did not return to the violence of the years 1945–60. The speculative economy brought to the fore ostentatious *nouveaux riches* who would eat *sushi* rolled into gold foil and spent fortunes on Western works of art. The internationalisation of the economy and the proliferation of new services (leisure, design) gave rise to yuppies, salaried staff with highly specialised qualifications or young bosses of small and medium-scale enterprises foreign to the classical enterprise culture. While the movement towards uniformity of life styles in town and country was being completed, new differentiations were thus emerging 'from the top'. At the same time the salarymen – the very icon of the 'Japanese miracle' – had the feeling of relative pauperisation, because of the explosion of property prices which made landed property inaccessible. They felt equally cheated when the prices of imported consumer goods did not fall despite the rise in the value of the yen. The image of a quasi-egalitarian society became less credible when all those who had land doubled or trebled their fortunes between 1985 and 1988. In opinion polls the slippage from the 'middle-middle' to the 'lower-middle' category testified to this new discontent, which in part explained the success of the JSP in 1989–90.

Trade union unification was also a major factor contributing to this success. It was a response to dangers threatening all the central trade union organisations: the fall in rates of unionisation, from 35 per cent in the 1970s to 25 per cent around 1990, and the neo-liberal offensive. In 1987 the moderates of the Churitsurôren and

Dômei joined to form the Rengô; in 1989 they were joined by the Sôhyô. The strength of the new confederation, with 9.3 million members, was shown in the Upper House elections of 1989. But the Rengô intended to use it to become a fully fledged negotiating partner of the state authorities, not to wage the class struggle. In the elections it was on the side of the opposition, but showed its independence by putting up candidates on its own ticket. It showed its commitment to dialogue by inviting the Minister of Labour to its celebration of May Day in 1990, and by giving up the confrontation with the Ministry of Education. It raised itself above purely trade union problems and put forward a 'programme for the overall welfare of wage-earners', including the welfare of their children (educational reform), their wives (crèches, etc.), and retired people (creation of special housing), and even organisation of leisure activities. It called for the widest possible participation in management of enterprises (*keiseisanka*) and in major national decisions (*seisakusanka*). Thus began the reintegration of the wage labour force into the circle of decision makers, in parallel with the loss of influence of the LDP's more antiquated clientele of supporters.

Reassertion of local identities and autonomy was linked to a variety of factors. Prosperity gave municipal and regional authorities a more independent financial basis. The trend towards a uniform way of life produced a nostalgic reaction, the *furusato boom* ('home village fashion'), reflected in the inexhaustible success of the *Tora-san* series and the unrestrained vitality of village and district festivals (*matsuri*). Local authorities and the LDP aimed to put a brake on the depopulation of rural areas. The government pushed the deconcentration of high-value-added industries to outlying areas and launched programmes for 'revitalisation of local communities' (1989) based on development of traditional crafts and production, linked with tourism.

'Internationalisation' provided an excellent field of action for local autonomy. All around Japan, municipal authorities set up their own international departments and looked for sister-cities (710 by the end of 1990). Many cities started aid programmes for development of their Asian twinned towns, or even carried on 'quasi-diplomacy' on their own, such as Niigata with North Korea which was quite near, and Fukuoka with South-East Asia. Local communities also asserted their independence in the conflict between foreign residents and the government over fingerprinting. Immigration officers, who are local civil servants under the jurisdiction of city mayors, often preferred to compromise with the protesters rather than follow the harsh directives of the National Police Agency and Home Affairs Ministry. More and more governors got themselves elected as 'independents' in opposition to official candidates designated by national party headquarters. In 1991, in Tokyo, the 80-year-old Governor Suzuki, whom the LDP, the Kômeitô and the DSP refused to back for a fourth term, crushed their candidate with a margin of 880,000 votes, after a campaign centred around defence of local autonomy, and despite criticisms of his management of the city.

This empowerment of the regions and cities typified the transition to a 'society of small masses' (*shôshû shakai*), in which campaigning movements could remain lively but were always kept within limits. Near to Tokyo the inhabitants of Zushi led a very tenacious struggle against deforestation for building of new US Army officers' quarters. The opponents of the scheme won seven municipal elections in a row between 1984 and 1990, but the environmentalists remained the most insignificant of the mini-parties, and failed to enter the Upper House. The Koreans' struggle over fingerprinting aroused little echo outside the foreign community. For the new generation of *shinjinrui*, this was rather the time to take what life had to offer.

'New human beings' and 'internationalisation'

The Japanese born in the 1960s, starting active life during the 1980s, had known only a Japan in full growth, well protected, where social confrontations disappeared. The labour market opened its arms to them. They were rocked to sleep with slogans of the quality of life. The world was at their feet; travel abroad had become a common initiation rite for students, and a considerable number of 'office girls' (unskilled women workers in their 20s) still living with their parents flew to Paris or Rome for bargain sales at Hermes or Gucci shops. Young people had before them a ready-made social mould – school examinations, near-obligatory marriage which was often arranged, lifetime employment – which provided them with security, and they just tried to make the best of the time that passed. Great enthusiasms were alien to that generation, which was 'like crystal' as the title of a successful novel by a young student, Yasuo Tanaka, put it in 1981: fragile and transparent. The young 'bamboo shoots' (*takenoko*), dressed in delicate colours, spent their Sundays among the parks of Tokyo, and tidily put away their clothes and make-up at the end of the day. The biggest best-seller of the decade (12 million copies) was *Totto-chan, the Little Girl at the Window*. These reminiscences of a television star marked the peak of the *kawai* genre (sweet and mawkish), with a touch of modern dreams added, since the heroine went to a school based on 'freedom, joy and love', the exact opposite of the system which all Japanese children had endured. The key values of the *shinjinrui* were elegant consumption and a hedonism that found it somewhat difficult to fit in with the work ethic but was eventually resolved into 'comfort-conservatism'. They were great connoisseurs of Western brands, saved less than their elders, and, unable to afford their own flats or condominiums, bought a BMW or a personalised car from a limited production run. They readily married in Christian churches, real or fake. One craze (*boomu*) followed another: the fashion for pandas offered by Beijing was followed by the fashion for Australian frilled lizards, and the gourmet boom made fortunes for importers of *Beaujolais nouveau* and then for 'ethnic' restaurants specialising in South-East Asian or even African food. Materialism and the desire to consume could push the young towards criminal behaviour: 51 per cent of reported crimes involved minors – mostly shoplifting – and 22 per cent were committed by girls. Young women's taste for chic and cynicism was shown in their search for 'three K's' jobs – planning, public relations, and international (*kikaku, kôkô, kokusai*) – and for 'three K's' husbands: tall, rich and trained at the good universities (*kôshinchô, kôshuûnyû, kôgakureki*). When entering the 'real world' of business, these young people felt the shock acutely, and 11 per cent of them left their first jobs after three months. But the *shinjinrui* generation, with little inclination to protest activity, was eventually absorbed into the social mould.

'Internationalisation' (*kokusaika*) was the key word of cultural modernisation. From the time of the Nakasone government it was presented as a national obligation, to avoid the rise of anti-Japanese feeling and 'know how to behave' in a world where contacts with foreign countries had become the rule. In the name of internationalisation *toruko* ('Turkish baths': sauna and prostitution) became *soap-lands*, and Black people shown as comic disappeared from children's books and advertising. Under the JET (Japan Exchange and Teaching) plan the Ministries of Education and the Interior brought thousands of teachers from the English-speaking world to Japanese secondary schools, and thousands of foreign trainees for local authorities. American universities opened campuses in Japan, even in the provinces. Language schools proliferated, as did organisations for reception and advice for foreigners. The 'Ron-Yasu relationship' between Yasihiro Nakasone and Ronald Reagan, ostensibly based on warm friendship, was portrayed as the example of what an international spirit could achieve. In 1990 the marriage of the Emperor's second son, back from Oxford, to the daughter of a university professor educated in Australia and the United States, Kiko Kawashima, also testified to this change, which made 'internationalisation' a major sign of recognition of the *shinjinrui*.

But internationalisation went together with neo-traditionalism and neo-nationalism, Nakasone being an emblematic figure of that too. The anthem and the flag were brought into schools at the same time as foreign language assistants. For the state authorities strengthening of national identity and pride were indispensable for the country to 'remain itself' while opening up to the world. In the eyes of public opinion the Western countries had ceased to be a model to follow. Japan had overtaken them; it must seek inspiration inside itself, in the values that had brought about its success. Since Ohira's time the concept of 'Japanese-style social security' based on 'strengthening of the family' as the basis of society had extolled three-generation households, for which some developers built specially designed houses. Women's situation hardly changed at all. The law on gender equality in the workplace (1985) did not provide for any sanction against employers guilty of sex discrimination, but lifted some measures that had protected women in the workplace until then, such as the ban on night work. In 1989 Kaifu hastily appointed two women to his first government, to respond to Miss Doi's popularity, but he dropped them as soon as the 1990 elections were over. The image of the career woman (*tonde-iru onna*), in fashion for a moment, did not compel acceptance. In 1988 the traditional division of roles between the sexes was still approved by 80 per cent of people questioned, with a record percentage among girls of 22. The traditional ethic of perseverance and solidarity was extolled by the most popular television series, but also by *manga* magazines for the young, of which the one with the biggest circulation – *Shônen Jump*, selling 6,500,000 copies per week – had as its motto 'Friendship, Effort, Success'. The 'home village vogue' also followed the direction of this reassertion of Japanese values, at the time when Japan's increasing power forced it to redefine its international role.

JAPAN'S SEARCH FOR A ROLE IN THE NEW WORLD ORDER

1980–5: return to the West

The 'Second Cold War', until Gorbachev came to power in 1985, led Japan to fit into the Western system again. The Soviet military threat seemed to hang heavily over the archipelago. The Red Army was reinforced in the Far East and the Kuriles, and the Soviet Navy established itself in Vietnam, from which it could cut the route to the Straits of Malacca at will. On its side Japan declared 6 February to be the 'Day of the Northern territories' in 1981. Tension reached its peak in 1983, when a Korean Airlines Boeing was shot down over the USSR with 360 passengers including many Japanese. Diplomatic relations were frozen; for a decade, between 1976 and 1986, the two countries' foreign ministers did not meet.

The idyll with China came to an end. Trade relations recovered from the 'Baoshan Shock', and Japan made increasing profits – $5 billion in 1985. But political relations were damaged because of Japan's neo-nationalist upsurge and the struggles in Beijing between the moderate Deng Xiaoping and the Communist Party's hard-line (anti-Japanese) wing. In 1982 the revision of school textbooks led to Chinese protests against 'the rebirth of militarism', in which Seoul joined, and Prime Minister Suzuki had to make an embarrassed explanation during an official visit. In 1984 Nakasone travelled to Beijing without incident. But the following year his visit to the Yasukuni shrine in his official capacity led to anti-Japanese demonstrations, which obliged him to cancel a second trip. Tension flared up again in 1987 after a Japanese legal ruling against Beijing in a property dispute involving People's

China and Taiwan. A new feature was that Japanese officials reacted more and more firmly to Chinese criticisms. In 1986 the Minister of Education declared, 'Those who criticise our textbooks would do well to look first at theirs', and in 1987 the Foreign Minister suggested that Deng Xiaoping was 'getting pig-headed with old age'.

These tensions with the two Communist giants led Japan to reaffirm its solidarity with the West by all means: strengthening military preparedness, joining in the RIMPAC manoeuvres with the US Seventh Fleet and the Australian Navy from 1982 onwards, description by Suzuki of the relationship with the US as an 'alliance', and financial aid to the countries most threatened by Soviet expansion, such as Pakistan and Turkey. At the 1983 G7 summit at Williamsburg Japan's solidarity with the West in security matters was solemnly reaffirmed. But Japan was now thinking in terms of 'global security' (cf. p. 220), against the background of commercial tension with the West. It diversified its international strategies. As North-South problems were superimposed on the East-West confrontation, Japan sought to position itself as a mediator for developing countries with the club of great white powers. From 1983 onwards Tokyo consulted ASEAN countries and Korea before every G7 meeting. On the 40th anniversary of the United Nations, Nakasone made a plea on behalf of small nations, while renewing the request for a permanent seat on the Security Council which Japan had been making since 1967.

Japan and the 'New World Order': is Asia the solution?

The sudden changes in the world order between 1985 and 1992 confronted Japan with the need to break out of the role of 'political dwarf' which it had more or less been playing since the war, and to act on its own to find its place in the new international setting.

There was a noticeable deterioration in relations with the United States. The Security Treaty remained the basis of Japan's security, but with the collapse of the USSR and the strengthening of the Self Defence Forces to a level at which it could confront any regional aggressor, it lost some of its raison d'être. Bilateral trade relations remained vital for both sides. In value they represented about 25 per cent of the United States' foreign trade and 30 per cent of Japan's. But the chronic imbalance increased anti-Japanese feeling to an unprecedented level in the US Congress (Clause Super 301 in 1989). Among the intelligentsia the 'revisionist school' held that Japan was irremediably alien to the common values of the West and that the position to take towards Japan must be 'revised', to exclude it from the rules of the liberal game that it did not practice itself. It reached the point where some authors even predicted *The Coming War with Japan* (G. Friedman and M. LeBard, 1991). Tokyo responded with an intense lobbying and public relations campaign. The Keidanren advised Japanese firms established in the USA to conduct themselves 'as exemplary members of the community' and to avoid too blatant acquisitions. The flow of investment and goods was gradually turned aside. The American deficit on trade with Japan fell from $55.5 billion in 1988 to less than $40 billion in 1991, while investment in the USA fell from more than 50 per cent of Japan's direct outward investment to less than 30 per cent.

Anti-American feeling (*kembei*) spread through all sections of Japanese opinion, from the average salaried employee who criticised the moral laxity of a country living beyond its means to the farmers fiercely defending protectionism. In some opinion polls the United States was now seen as the main threat in the eyes of Japanese people, ahead of the former Soviet Union and Korea. 'Unfortunate words' (*shitsugen*) regularly slipped from the mouths of the most senior politicians. The Speaker of the House of Representatives once said that 'one third of American workers are illiterate', and Prime Minister Miyazawa himself suggested that they had 'lost the ethic of work'. At the end of 1991 the rumour went around that the United States, freed from the Soviet threat, would redirect a part of its missile strike force against Japan. The resounding failure of George Bush's visit to Tokyo in January 1992 symbolised this deterioration in Japanese-American relations. But between two countries representing together about 45 per cent of world GNP, those relations remained one of the main pillars of the international order.

Japan had the same problem with Europe, up to a point. To establish a position in the EEC before the establishment of the Single Market in 1993, when it feared that protectionist barriers would go up, Japan redirected a growing proportion of its investment (less than 25 per cent in 1988, more than a third in 1991) and its trade towards the EEC, whose deficit on trade with Japan rose from \$27.3 billion in 1989 to \$36 billion in 1991. Anti-Japanese feeling grew in parallel. In 1991 Japan was for the first time named as the principal danger for their country by a majority of French people in an opinion poll.

The Gulf Crisis of 1990-1 and the collapse of the Soviet bloc confronted Japan with the problem of its responsibilities and its international status. In both cases it was called upon by the Westerners to pay for policies decided without it. Apart from the Arab countries it was Japan that made the biggest contribution to the war against Iraq (\$13 billion), while public opinion and many among the élite disapproved of this. Similarly, while Japan did not want to give financial aid to the CIS as long as Moscow retained the Kuriles, it was difficult for it to break solidarity with the G7, which had decided to help Yeltsin. If Japan was obliged to fall into line, it was because it had no authority at the international level. In the face of Westerners bearing values for universal use (human rights, freedom, democracy), Japan appeared like a power unable to use its wealth in a way benefiting the whole human race. This negative image was a major handicap. But Japan had been aware of it since the Nakasone government. One of the aims of 'internationalisation' was to put this right, using a many-sided strategy:

– On human rights, Japan strove to follow Western policy. It announced that it was officially making its ODA conditional on progress of democracy in the countries receiving it. But the increase in tension on this subject between the Westerners and the Asian countries, headed by China, Singapore and Malaysia, placed it in a delicate situation. After the Tiananmen Square massacre on 4 June 1989, Tokyo expressed reservations about the sanctions decided upon by the G7 (suspension of economic aid and high-level diplomatic contacts). It resumed its financial aid unilaterally in July 1990, and Kaifu travelled to Beijing in 1991.

– On disarmament, Japan was wrong-footed by the reduction of arsenals on which the great powers had embarked after the end of the Cold War. For a country posing as 'the most pacifist in the world' owing to its Constitution, it was difficult not to follow that movement. But that would mean abandoning the effort made since 1981 to strengthen the SDF, and annoying the United States, which was to supply AWACS and AEGIS systems for a

handsome profit. However, Miyazawa had to promise to reconsider the ongoing (1987–97) arms programme.

– Participation in UN peacekeeping missions by Japanese troops
was made possible by the PKO Law passed in June 1992 in the
wake of the Gulf War.

– Regarding overseas aid, Japan had become by 1990 the first
donor in the world in absolute cash terms. Its effort was still
modest as percentage of GNP, but Tokyo planned to increase it
continually. For humanitarian aid a law of 1987 created a 'Disasters Emergency Aid Corps' along the lines of Médecins sans
Frontières, which made its appearance at scenes of international
disasters. Significantly the two United Nations bodies headed by
Japanese were the World Health Organisation and the High
Commission for Refugees.

– Protection of the environment was seen as an important element in the 'global security' of a nation that drew all its resources
from the rest of the planet. Having for a long time opposed any
international regulation, Japan modified its stance and grudgingly
accepted restrictions on the hunting of whales. The Keidanren
published an Environment Charter, and Tokyo promised $2.3
billion in three years for conservation in developing countries at
the 1989 G7 summit in Paris. Japan had the most energy-saving
production system of the whole world, and technical skill tested
since the 1970s in action against pollution. It wanted to appear as a
nation at the cutting edge of the struggle for worldwide environmental protection.

The prospect of a tripolar world order began to emerge, with
the integration of Europe and the gradual establishment of the
North American Free Trade Area (the United States, Canada and
Mexico). Japan was afraid that these two blocs would be made into
protected economic areas endowed with all that Japan lacked: raw
materials, food security, and armed forces capable of intervening
all around the world. Faced with this prospect Japan seemed to be
tempted by the idea of a 'return to Asia', both political and economic – or, as Prime Minister Nakasone once wrote, 'Rethink the
slogan "Asia is one!" in new terms'. It invested $30 billion in that
region between 1986 and 1990 (though this was still only 15 per
cent of its direct outward investment). In 1991, for the first time,
its exports to Asia exceeded exports to the USA and to Europe in
value. Japan seemed like a model for Asian countries embarking

on the road to rapid development which it had taken before them. Anti-Japanese feeling was fading, and Emperor Akihito visited Thailand, Indonesia and Malaysia without incident in 1991.

However, despite its spectacular economic growth, Asia still remained an unstable area, rich in territorial disputes – notably in the South China Sea – and simmering guerrilla campaigns (the Philippines, Burma, East Timor). The future of the Korean peninsula, Taiwan and Cambodia remained uncertain. There was a wide variety of political regimes: still fragile democracies (Taiwan, Korea, the Philippines), semi-authoritarian systems (Malaysia, Singapore, Indonesia), bloodstained dictatorships (Burma), and the last Communist regimes on earth. Tokyo remained ill-at-ease in this company. The disproportion in income per head between Japan and some of its neighbours was as much as one to a hundred. Developing Asian countries accused Japan of big power egoism over its refusal to stabilise prices of raw materials, its closing of its market to their cheap manufactured goods, and accumulation of trade surpluses at their expense. China, freed from the constraints of the Cold War, was going through spectacular economic growth which was beginning to reawaken nationalist nostalgia for its historical hegemony over the region. And the prospect of a united Korea, with nuclear capability – however remote – openly worried Tokyo.

Against this background Japan's 'return to Asia' remained very cautious. It still preferred the concept of the 'Pacific Basin'. In 1989 Tokyo keenly supported the Australian proposal leading to the creation of APEC (Asia-Pacific Economic Cooperation) whose members were the United States, Canada, Mexico, the two white powers of the South Pacific, the six countries of ASEAN, the three Chinas (PRC, Taiwan and Hong Kong), South Korea and Japan. In contrast Japan gave a cool reception to the Malaysian proposal for an exclusive grouping of Asian countries in an East Asia Economic Caucus (EAEC) – a regional grouping in which Tokyo feared it would be isolated and caught between the growing power of China and the distrust of the developing countries of Asia.

7

THE END OF THE 'JAPANESE MODEL' (1992–2000)

From 1992 the financial shock caused by the bursting of the speculative bubble spread to the industrial sector and affected consumption, and unleashed the longest economic crisis that Japan had known since the war. After a short lull in 1996, the economy fell badly into recession again, the situation being worsened by the Asian crisis that broke in July 1997, and still remained stagnant four years later. This crisis threw fundamental doubt on the famous 'Japanese model' on which prosperity and social stability had rested since the 1960s. Everything had to be rethought, from the 'Toyota' system of production and lifetime employment to the basic principles of industrial policy applied under the aegis of the MITI. The protectionist and anti-competitive logic of an economy under administrative guidance gave way bit by bit to the logic of the Anglo-American model of the market economy, which had been spreading around the world since the end of the Cold War. 'Deregulation' became the key word, and Japan was opened up as never before, not only to foreign products but also to foreign capital investment and to foreign economic operators in industry, finance, distribution and services of all sorts. But numerous lobbies put up dogged resistance to these changes.

Attacks on officials' supervision of the economy were extended to challenge the 'straitjacket society' (*kanri shakai*), authoritarian and 'vertical' (*tate shakai*), as a whole. After the comfort-conservatism of the 1980s, protest activity revived. Networks of associations and voluntary movements proliferated in a reinvigorated civil society, while the élite of the 'Iron Triangle' – as the alliance between the LDP, the bureaucracy and big business is often described – lost its legitimacy and cohesion in a succession of scandals. Local communities increasingly took up opposition to the central government and the administration. The leadership crisis, and the stress which it caused in society, reached a peak in

247

1995, the year marked by the deadly Kobe earthquake and the Aum sect's sarin gas outrage.

The political system was shaken. In 1993 the LDP, then forming the government, split and lost its majority in the House of Representatives. In 1994 it returned to power at the price of accepting a seemingly unnatural coalition with the Socialists. The 1996 elections enabled it to form a government on its own again, albeit a minority one. In 1997 the disintegration of the opposition gave the LDP back an absolute majority in the House. In 1999 it finally regained control of the Upper House through an alliance with the conservatives of the Liberal Party and the Buddhists of the New Kômeitô. But the party system had been severely shaken. The voters, put off by splits, defections and U-turns, swung between despondency and revolt, between abstention and protest voting. The upsurge of political cynicism undermined the legitimacy of the system and was a bad augury for the governability of the country.

On the international plane, Japan's positions became progressively less comfortable, while definition of its foreign policy continued to encounter the same obstacles: constitutional constraints and divisions among public opinion and among the élite. Until 1997 the rapid development of Asia made it fashionable to think of changing Japanese foreign policy to centre it on Asia, 'the first pole of world power in the twenty-first century'. But that development also implied, eventually, a major shift in the balance of forces in the region, especially to the advantage of China, and this posed the question of leadership and regional security in new terms. The entire region was pregnant with potential conflicts, including territorial disputes never settled since 1945 between Japan and its immediate neighbours. Meanwhile, since the end of the Cold War had made Japan less essential to its security, the United States no longer hesitated to apply stronger pressure than ever on Tokyo to make it submit to the rules of the market economy as conceived by Wall Street. Japanese opinion responded by fits of anger and the revival of a Protean nationalism of which Shintarô Ishihara's election as Governor of Tokyo in 1999 was just one symptom. Furthermore, the polemics between Westerners and Asians over human rights and so-called 'Asian values' from the late 1980s placed Japan in an uncomfortable position between the two camps.

From July 1997 the financial and economic crisis that hit developing countries of Asia made the regional situation even more unpredictable, with threats of disintegration in Indonesia, nuclear escalation between India and Pakistan, multiple provocative actions by a North Korean regime on the verge of collapse, among others. This worrying context forced Japan to modify its defence posture ever more clearly, increasing the capabilities of its armed forces and giving them wider tasks within the framework of a renegotiated and broadened Security Treaty with the USA. But the crisis also gave Japan, whose economic and financial power remained out of proportion to that of its neighbours, the opportunity to play the role of saviour and thus to gain the political authority it lacked.

In 2000, the economic and political situation seemingly reached its nadir. The then Prime Minister Yoshirô Mori, widely seen as a mere puppet in the hands of the LDP's 'dons' and derided by the media as a feeble character, saw his popularity ratings plunge to a single-digit level, forcing him out in April 2001. His successor Junichirô Koizumi, a maverick politician from outside the LDP's mainstream with a reputation as a strong-willed champion of reforms, was greeted with cheers – possible opening a new era in Japanese politics.

JAPAN AND GLOBALISATION: CHALLENGE TO THE ECONOMIC AND SOCIAL MODEL

Banking crisis, scandals, paralysis of the government

The havoc caused in the financial system by the bursting of the speculative bubble was enormous. The Nikkei index reached its peak at 39,985 on 31 December 1989; it fell 46 per cent in nine months, to 21,591 on 1 October 1990. It continued to collapse, falling below 15,000 in August 1992; by then it had lost almost two thirds of its value. Then it hovered between an annual average of 17,000 and 20,000 until 1997. The year 1998 was an *annus horribilis*: at its minimum the Nikkei fell to 11,787. Property values fell even further, to the point where transactions were almost paralysed in the big cities because nobody wanted to sell at prices which had lost up to 75 per cent of their 1980s value. Overall this collapse in share and property prices reduced national wealth by about 12 per cent, or 800,000 billion yen ($6,734 billion),[1] according to the most pessimistic calculations. The banks which had fed the speculation by lending wildly and securing loans on land or shares found they had a mountain of bad loans. Non-banking credit bodies were even harder hit, especially the *jusen* specialising in property loans, because they had engaged in the riskiest operations which banks were forbidden to undertake themselves. Their difficulties had repercussions on insurance companies and agricultural cooperatives which had entrusted considerable funds to them to get a good return. In 1999 estimates of the total amount of bad loans weighing down the banking system were around 110,000 billion yen ($926 billion) – about 22.5 per cent of GDP. On their side life insurance companies had a hole in their books estimated between 19,000 and 34,000 billion yen ($160-286 billion). By way of comparison, the total bad debts in the saving-and-loan mess in the USA (1988–92) did not exceed $250 billion, less than 4 per cent of GDP.

The Ministry of Finance, which supervised the banking sector, bore full responsibility for what happened and thus sought to minimise the problem. The real figure for the bad loans was not revealed for a long time. In 1994 official figures were still giving a figure of only 13,000 billion yen ($109 billion) – scarcely 10 per cent of the amount calculated by the banks themselves, which was to be revealed gradually year after year – and they never exceeded 38,100 billion. The Finance Ministry sought at any price to avoid bankruptcies, and this held up stabilisation measures. But in December 1994 it had to resign itself to the first bankruptcies of mutual credit bodies (Tokyo Kyôwa and the Anzen Credit Union). In August 1995 the first bankruptcy of a regional bank (the Hyôgô Bank) led to rush of panic-stricken depositors to bank counters. In 1996 all the *jusen* had to be liquidated. In 1997 life insurance companies began to fall in their turn (Nissan Mutual Life went bankrupt), and then, in November, in two big blows, the Finance Ministry abandoned to their fates the tenth largest bank in the country, Hokkaido Takushoku, and the second largest securities firm, Yamaichi Securities, whose debts to its subsidiaries amounted to 6,000 billion yen ($50.5 billion).

The crisis set off a wave of scandals. Many loans had been made to companies or groups of speculators linked to the *yakuza*, especially the two main 'families', Inagawa-kai and Yamaguchi-gumi. According to some estimates those loans to Mafiosi accounted for about 40 per cent of the total bad loans, which led the press to splash headlines about the *'yakuza* depression'. Determined to pay nothing back, the gangs murdered several bank staff and carried out numerous attacks on businessmen to intimidate them – senior staff, chairmen and their families. Every investigation revealed the links between the Mafia, business and politicians. In 1990 the first scandals related to securities firms, when the public found that they compensated for the losses of some privileged customers – companies, public bodies and trade unions, but also notorious *yakuza* – while ordinary investors, including many women who had gambled on the stock exchange with savings they had accumulated without their husbands' knowledge (the 'housewife's hidden treasure'), lost all their investments with the collapse of the Nikkei. The investigations soon revealed collusion between securities firms and some *yakuza* speculators on whose behalf they manipulated the Stock Exchange – notably the collaboration of Nomura Securities and Nikko Securities with Susumu Ishii, of the Inagawa-kai family, in his effort to corner the shares of Tôkyô Dentetsu, a railway and department store operator, and Honshû Paper. Soon afterwards it was the turn of the top banks to be tarred by scandal. Sumitomo Bank had placed on the board of the Itoman trading company a gangster who literally plundered it. The Fuji, Tôkai and Saitama Kyôwa Banks had issued fake certificates of deposit which were used by *yakuza* to get loans. The Industrial Bank of Japan, the élite's bank, had done the same for the benefit of a lady owning bars in Osaka, for the colossal sum of 240 billion yen ($2 billion).

This scandal and the Itoman case had ramifications extending to the LDP's leading figures – in particular Noboru Takeshita, heir to the Tanaka clan and former Prime Minister, and his brother-in-law Shin Kanemaru, who controlled the LDP's financing networks among the construction companies. Then, in 1992, came the Sagawa scandal which struck a body blow to the party (see pp. 253–5). This affair with many ramifications revealed once again the collusion between financial circles and *yakuza* in speculation in the 'bubble', but also a disturbing intimacy between some of the most important personalities in the LDP and underworld figures whom they readily met for face-to-face talks. The scandal led to fierce infighting within the government party. A group of former senior civil servants surrounding Prime Minister Miyazawa sought to 'purify' the party by reducing the influence of Takeshita and Kanemaru. This infighting eventually led to the arrest of Kanemaru in March 1993 and splits that forced the party out of power for ten months soon afterwards. Thanks to the fall of Kanemaru investigations were extended to Public Works circles. Eighteen of the main enterprises in that sector were investigated; the Governors of Miyagi and Ibaraki were arrested, as was the Mayor of Sendai. From then on an endless succession of scandals hit all sections of the élite. Hardly had the LDP been removed from power than the coalition replacing it was accused in its turn and Prime Minister Morihiro Hosokawa (see p. 287) was smeared by the Sagawa case. The administration lost what remained of its aura of integrity. The Minister of Health was discredited by the scandal of blood contaminated by the HIV virus, and then by a bribery scandal relating to retirement homes (the Orange-kai affair). In 1998 the scandals reached the Ministry of Defence, many of whose senior officials were convicted of collusion with the electronics giant NEC in a case of over-pricing. The Ministry of Justice was not spared; in 1998 the nation's number two prosecutor resigned, after being convicted of entertaining his mistress on the taxpayer's money.

The media took on the duty of hunting down the smallest cases of misconduct among officials, including one police superintendent who was harshly punished for having a few traffic tickets set aside, and army officers suspended from duty for letting some friends fire a few rounds in army training areas (2000). But it was the Ministry of Finance that became the *bête noire* of public opinion and the main target of investigations. As the banking disaster was exposed in its full extent, the Finance bureaucrats were collectively accused of laxity in supervision or even complicity with the speculators. Thus, when the Daiwa Bank was nabbed in the United States in 1995 for fiddling its books to hide $1.1 billion speculative losses, it appeared that the ministry, informed confidentially by the bank's management, had hidden the news for six weeks. Caught in the crossfire of the foreign press and Japanese public opinion, the ministry's staff became the favoured target for investigations. In 1998, 1,050 were interrogated, three committed suicide, four were charged and 122 were subjected to internal

A TYPICAL SCANDAL: THE SAGAWA KYÛBIN AFFAIR

The Sagawa Kyûbin affair, which broke in the summer of 1991, was the one whose multiple ramifications give the best picture of the secret goings-on linking the worlds of politics, business and finance among themselves and with the *yakuza*. By showing several of the 'godfathers' of contemporary Japan in action, it set off the crisis within the LDP leading to the party's temporary loss of power between August 1993 and June 1994. It also marked the beginning of the end of the tolerance shown to illicit activities; the media showed more boldness in their investigations and more vehemence in their condemnations. So this scandal is the best prism for examining the multiple facets of daily life in what Japanese call 'the clandestine districts' (*ankoku gai*) – the networks where the traditional élites rub shoulders with the underworld – in the early 1990s.

The political aspect of the affair was very indirect, but its consequences turned out to be devastating. It revealed in broad daylight the relations between the LDP, the far-right terrorist groups (*uyoku dantai*) and the *yakuza* gangs. In the mid–1980s an *uyoku dantai* based in Shimane, the electoral stronghold of the LDP heavyweight Noboru Takeshita, set off a bomb at the offices of the socialist teachers' union, the Nikkyôso, which is a *bête noire* to all the Japanese Right. After being arrested the head of the group committed suicide; Takeshita sent neither a representative nor a wreath to the funeral. In 1987 another ultra-nationalist group, the Nihon Komintô, used that 'insult' as justification for blackmailing Takeshita, who was then on the point of becoming Prime Minister. To do this the far-rightists used the traditional technique of 'smothering the enemy with praise': the entire Japanese far Right began to sing Takeshita's praises. It was encouraged from within the LDP by Kakuei Tanaka, who had just had his leadership of his clan in the party stolen by Takeshita. To negotiate an end to the blackmail, on the advice of Shin Kanemaru, the LDP elders sought the mediation of the 'godfather' Susumu Ishii, head of the Inagawa-kai, the second biggest gangster family in Japan. According to press revelations the talks that followed were face-to-face talks between the *yakuza* and the cream of the government party, including Ryûtarô Hashimoto (Prime Minister 1996–98) and his successor Keizô Obuchi (1998–2000). The financial terms of the settlement which made it possible for Takeshita to get the campaign against him halted, so that he could become Prime Minister, have never been revealed.

This affair illustrates both the vulnerability of the conservative political élite to blackmail and its easy access to channels of communication with *yakuza*. The same sort of relations were often found on a smaller scale. A year after Takeshita a town councillor at Yoghiumi, a small town in the Ehime region, was grappling with a local far-Right group. He got the Minister of Transport, whose constituency the place was, to intervene; the minister contacted a *yakuza* to arrange a deal worth 9 million yen (then about $75,750).

On the business side, the main actor in the scandal was the Sagawa Kyûbin company, the second express trucking company in Japan. The affair had three principal aspects, well illustrating the major factors giving rise to the 'illicit business' market:

1. Administrative controls over the economy: transport companies are a favourite target for administrative control. They have to negotiate operating rights prefecture by prefecture, and follow drastic safety rules. So they often ask the politicians to help them obtain the innumerable permits needed, in return for cash, and also pay the officials responsible for checking safety. Locally, Kakuei Tanaka himself ran the corruption game in his stronghold of Niigata. At the national level it was his right-hand man Shin Kanemaru who received from Sagawa Kyûbin sums to pay to more than a hundred LDP Diet members, about 500 million yen (then about $4.2 million).

2. The inadequacies of the Japanese legal system, which is poorly developed, very slow, very expensive and not very efficient. To deal with problems with customers and road accidents, the Chairman of Sagawa preferred to use Aizu-kotetsu, a 'family' of the Kyoto region comprising about 55 local gangs.

3. The absence of controls over Stock Exchange operations (until 1992), which left the field clear for speculation. The area manager of Sagawa for Tokyo worked on speculation with Inagawa-kai, the 'family' headed by the godfather Susumu Ishii. He lent him 8 billion yen (then about $60 million) to help him in his attempt to corner the shares of Tôkyû Dentetsu. On that occasion Ishii also received technical assistance from two of the leading securities firms, Nomura and Nikko, who helped him make a discreet purchase of two big blocks of shares; and help from several banks

which lent him considerable sums for that purpose. As for Sagawa's area manager for Tokyo, he also made generous loans to numerous companies linked to the *yakuza* (the so-called 'sister companies' or *kigyô shatei*). Thus he loaned the equivalent of $28 million, notably to golf clubs. It was a tax inspection of one of those clubs that set off the whole scandal.

disciplinary measures; the Minister resigned with his Administrative Vice Minister and his permanent secretary, as did the Governor of the Bank of Japan. As for the business world, it was shaken by an endless series of revelations. Investigations into bankruptcies – notably that of Yamaichi – revealed a world of fraudulent accounting practices, to which the administration seemed to have closed its eyes. In addition investigators unravelling the tangle of relationships between *yakuza* speculators and the financial establishment threw light on steady relationships maintained by the biggest firms – Nomura (again!), the Dai-Ichi Bank, the Asahi breweries, Japan Airlines – with the world of professional racketeers (*sokaiya*). The sight of offices searched and senior staff resigning publicly with grovelling apologies, or taken away by the police, became an almost daily feature on television. The political world was of course not spared; in 1998 an opposition House member was arrested and charged with corruption after the lifting of his parliamentary immunity (which had happened only once before in the whole post-war period), and one of his LDP colleagues committed suicide the day before he was to be arrested also.

This damaging climate deprived the élite of the legitimacy needed to resolve the banking crisis rapidly at the taxpayer's expense as was done in the United States, France and Norway in the same circumstances. The government waited until 1996 – six years after the onset of the crisis – to draw on the state budget to settle the liquidation of the *jusen*, which had built up 9,700 billion yen ($81.6 billion) of irrecoverable debts. The bill was paid partly by the banks and agricultural cooperatives which had financed them, but the taxpayer was also made to contribute, to the tune of 685 billion yen ($5.7 billion). On that occasion the Diet was the scene of violent confrontation, with boycotting and fist-fights.

The LDP paid for the taxpayers' discontent by failing to get an absolute majority in the October 1996 elections. That made it difficult to repeat the operation. The government had to wait two years more before the Asian crisis and the dramatic deterioration in Japan's economic situation enabled it finally to get public opinion and the opposition to accept a rescue plan for the 20 major city and long-term credit banks and trust banks. These were to receive 60,000 billion yen ($505 billion) of public funds. In return they had to follow the administration's instructions to stabilise their balance sheets and restructure by regrouping and reducing their staff. The two worst affected, the Nippon Credit Bank and Long-Term Credit Bank, were placed under direct state control. In return for public funds the others had to hand over to a Financial Reconstruction Commission securities which the commission could convert into shares to take over control of those not following its orders. But there remained more than 120 local and mutual banks and nearly 500 credit associations, mostly in a bad state, and cleaning up and restructuring are much more politically sensitive for them than for the biggest ones.

During the eight years when the state authorities had procrastinated, the whole economy had plunged into recession. The banking disaster was not the only cause of this. Its effects were combined with the repercussions of the world economic situation and the increasingly apparent dysfunctioning of the 'Japanese model'. This multiplicity of causal factors led commentators to speak of the 'complex recession' (*fukugô fukyô*).

Fukugô fukyô – the 'complex recession' (1992–2001)

The financial crisis had an impact on the industrial sector from 1992 onwards. Many companies had joined in speculation on a large scale in the 'bubble years', and losses forced them to reduce their investments. The banking crisis added uncertainty and a credit crunch for small and medium enterprises. The ensuing decline in activity had repercussions on employment and reduced overtime for workers, which led to a fall in purchasing power, whose decline in turn worsened the crisis. All this was combined with the effects of the world economic situation. In the late 1980s growth was marking time in all the advanced countries, following the sharp correction that occurred on Wall Street in October 1987

much easier to implement than structural reforms of the economic system, which would threaten many lobbies in the LDP patronage network.

This Keynesian policy was not totally ineffective. Helped by the fall in the value of the yen which greatly aided exports, it allowed growth to resume in 1996. But the Ministry of Finance and the government then committed a pilot error. To reduce the budget deficit, which had been increased to 80 per cent of GDP by six years' massive pump-priming, the purchase tax was raised from 3 to 5 per cent, and social benefits were reduced. This tightening of the tax screw, together with the onset of the Asian crisis, derailed the recovery. The government responded by new injections of 52,000 billion yen in 1997–8. To these were added measures to help small and medium enterprises, through loan guarantees for a total of 20,000 billion yen ($168 billion), to retrain several hundreds of thousands of workers facing redundancy, and even distribution of consumption vouchers to the aged and to families.

This massive spending only brought about GDP growth of a mere 0.5 per cent in both 1999 and 2000, at the cost of considerable budget deficits. Between 1992 and 1999 the crisis reduced tax revenue by 24.6 per cent, while expenditure rose by 13.4 per cent. While the United States budget, target of all Japanese criticisms over the preceding decade, now enjoyed surpluses and the countries of the European Union brought their budget deficits to less than 3 per cent of their GDP, Japan's reached 9.2 per cent of GDP in 2000, and the cumulative total debt of the state and local communities neared 140 per cent of GDP, while 60 per cent is considered as the 'alert threshold' by the IMF. The problem will worsen in the short term, because Japan will face the growing expense of retirement pensions because of its ageing population; public money will also be needed for more rescue plans – especially for local banks and for life insurance companies. Thus the public debt is a major problem for the future, serious enough for the US rating agency Moody's to downgrade the Japanese debt provisionally in the autumn of 1998, and again in 2001.

Anyway, even if the government's policy has achieved a modest degree of short-term results, the return to growth will only be sustainable if pump-priming from public funds is supplemented by private investment and consumption by individuals. So profits and confidence need to be restored – which requires structural reform measures, or *risotura*.

Risotura – 'reconstruction'

Ceaseless American strong-arm pressure pushed Japan ever further along the road to a more open market. The SII agreements (see pp. 235–6) merely encouraged the Americans. In 1992 George Bush, Tokyo's preference, was defeated in the presidential election by Bill Clinton, a supporter of strong measures influenced to some degree by the revisionist school. Inspired by the success of the 1986 agreement on semiconductors, which allowed American manufacturers to take over a significant share of the Japanese market, the new administration insisted on numerical targets in figures to measure the opening up of Japan – in other words, guaranteed market shares for American firms. Washington's first demands related to cars and car parts, which accounted for more than half of the US trade deficit with Japan. Japan resisted with the support of the European Union, which feared that the USA would get unilateral advantages at its expense. In February 1994 the Japanese cut off negotiations; in 1995 the Clinton administration finally dropped the demand for numerical targets. But the struggle continued. Negotiators engaged in successive confrontations over photographic films, the right of foreign lawyers to practice in Japan, the share-out between the two countries' airlines, the exorbitant costs of cargo handling at Japan's ports – an ultra-sensitive sector run by the *yakuza* – and the deregulation of the financial products market and insurance. All this brought results: American exports to Japan increased by 27 per cent per year between 1992 and 1995, while the bilateral deficit fell 25 per cent. However, it went up again after 1996 in the wake of the declining value of the yen, and this led to new tensions. In 1998, at the APEC summit in Kuching, Japan thwarted market opening measures proposed by the Americans for fisheries and forest products. In 1999 the US administration once again used the Super 301 trade clause to target specific Japanese industries – cars, car parts, flat glass, steel, rice, government procurement and insurance – in which unfair trade practices were liable to retaliatory measures.

But market opening also responded to the needs of numerous Japanese firms whose competitivity was declining because of Japan's excessively high costs for wages, services and land. In 1992, with hourly wages equivalent to $19 in Japan compared with $14.5 in the USA, and equivalent productivity, the cost of producing the same car was 20 per cent cheaper in Honda's American plants than in Japan. According to *The Economist*, in 1993 Japan's manufacturing sector productivity matched the USA only in three sectors (transport equipment, electrical machinery and basic metal products); on average, Japan's productivity was no more than 80 per cent of the USA's, and in sectors like food and drink it lagged behind by more than 60 per cent. In 1996 the OECD report on the competitivity of the major industrial countries rated Japan only 14th, far behind the USA (ranking third) and even after Chile. Very high technology, in which the Japanese had few competitors, resisted well. But the rise of the Newly Industrialising Economies (NIEs) created fierce competition in sectors such as the steel and motor industries, components and mass market electronics. Samsung of Korea became the leading producer of DRAM (direct random access memory) electronic chips, in which Japan's world market share plummeted from 90 to 40 per cent in six years (1990–6). Kia, also of Korea, elbowed the Japanese out of the Indonesian 'national car' scheme (before being bankrupted by the 1997 crisis).

The blame for this decline in competitivity was laid first of all on the traditional system of human resources management, based on the idea that employees are a precious and scarce resource which a company must look after at any cost, rather than a cost factor. Lifetime employment, promotion by seniority and trade union participation in management were no longer the 'three sacred treasures'; they were now denounced as 'three sacred cows' which stopped firms adapting. The model of organisation of work which experts from the whole world had come to study in Japanese factories in the 1970s and 1980s was also criticised. Just-in-time production was now accused of congesting traffic all over the country, making transport ever more expensive, and being excessively vulnerable to mishaps such as the Kôbe earthquake. Under-use of the most expensive and high-tech production facilities reminded everyone that robots are less flexible than human labour, and in a situation where workers were demoralised, it was realised that use of robots deskilled the workforce and deprived it of motivation; small teams of workers with many-sided skills became fashionable again. Also questioned now was the principle that big firms must do as much as possible in-house – from staff training to marketing of their products through design and the perfecting of manufacturing software. Outsourcing was now the fashion, and firms specialising in services to companies should be one of the biggest sources of future jobs according to the MITI's *Vision for 2010*. A third object of criticism was the Japanese companies' strategy of basing their growth – notably for export – by doing everything to satisfy the consumer's smallest wish, even at the cost of short-term profits. Motor manufacturers, in particular, based their reputation on short lines aimed at the smallest corners of the market, an infinite variety of options for all consumers' tastes – up to 67 different steering wheels for one single model! – and a short life span for each model. But in a situation where the domestic market was depressed by the consumption crisis, and where competition was becoming keener with the Americans coming back a large scale and the rising NIEs, market shares could hardly be increased any more – rather the opposite. The only possible expansion strategy was to increasie profits by cutting costs. So the Japanese converted to 'lean production': using the same parts for many different models and limiting options offered to the consumers.

Consequently the whole logic that gave priority to production over finance and to the engineer over the shareholder had to be reconsidered. That was the logic of a system where heads of companies came from the production rather than the finance side, obtained funds from friendly banks rather than on the stock exchange, and gave priority to production by reinvesting profits to improve the equipment rather than redistributing them to shareholders. But as part of the total reform of the financial system – the 'Big Bang' promised by Prime Minister Hashimoto in 1996 (see p. 285) – legislation was adapted little by little to give shareholders more power. It was made easier for them to sue heads of companies (1997), and their right to question them publicly at annual general meetings, without being silenced by the shouts of hired *sokaiya* gangsters, was upheld by the courts. Since the early 1960s, Japan's growth and stability had been based on a system in which 'the company exists first for its workers, then for its customers, and for society, but not for its shareholders'. But in April 1999, when Sony announced that it was going to cut 17,000 jobs (admittedly most of them overseas) at a time when the firm's profits reached a record, it was obvious that the old model had had its day, and was being replaced by a logic giving more importance to financial profits.

Shizen tôta (natural selection): keiretsu and 'convoys' in decline
This new logic weakened the forms of solidarity that had provided cohesion in the world of industry. The trial of strength between big and small enterprises became more violent. To restore their profits, principals exerted pitiless pressure on their sub-contractors to cut their prices – in that way Toyota managed to secure reductions of half a yen or a yen for 20,000 different parts. When the sub-contractors could not cut prices any further, the big firms abandoned them for cheaper ones, elsewhere in Asia, or else bought them up. Caught between banks that were not lending to them any more, orders that were drying up and principals cutting prices, small and medium enterprises were going under at the rate of 18,900 per year in 2000 (bankruptcies of less than 10 million yen not being registered) – the third highest in the post-Second World War era. Among many others, out of about 11,000 die and mould makers, producing plastic and metal moulds for cars, electronics and the food industry, which were operating in 1990, 20 per cent had collapsed during the decade.

The cohesion of the *keiretsu* has thus been put to the test. Increasingly firms have entered into joint ventures outside their groups or supply firms belonging to rival *keiretsu*, like Toyota (Mitsui) whose plants in Thailand supply engines to Isuzu (Dai-Ichi) and Nissan (Fuyô). In 1998 Toyota refused to help its *keiretsu*'s bank, the Sakura Bank, to recapitalise, and Fuji Bank met a similar refusal from the big firms of its *keiretsu* (Fuyô) – Canon, Hitachi, Marubeni and Yasuda Life. When Nikko Securities (Mitsubishi) decided to sell 25 per cent of its capital, it preferred an American partner, the Travelers Group, rather than the Bank of Tokyo-Mitsubishi in its own group. With the collapse of the stock exchange many companies now see the cross-holding pattern that characterises the structure of capital within a *keiretsu* as a costly obligation. But the deregulation of the financial sector and the lifting of the ban imposed on holding companies since 1947 are expected to allow the *keiretsu* to reorganise themselves by merging their banking, insurance and brokerage activities in monster finance companies which would play the role of holding companies at the centre of the group.

Generally speaking, the logic of the 'convoy' (*gosô sendan*) – whose aim is that all enterprises in one sector should advance at the same speed under the guidance of the administration, to protect those that perform less well – is being replaced gradually by the logic of 'natural selection' (*shizen tôta*). There have been more and more instances of merger and acquisition: 950 in 1998, twice as many as in 1995. In the motor and electronics industries the most dynamic and profitable firms (Toyota, Honda, Sony, Matsushita) part company with the ones doing less well.

Similarly, gigantism is now out of fashion. The new, fashionable model of an enterprise adapted to the new economic order is now a small or medium-scale start-up launched from scratch by a young adventurer in high-tech or finance, or a young woman following up an innovative idea in the field of services. The self-made men reappeared. The stars of the crisis years were Masayoshi Son, son of a destitute Korean immigrant, who became the 'Japanese Bill Gates' by creating a software distribution empire (Softbank), then branching into financial services; Yasuyuki Nambu, since 1976 pioneer of temporary employment with his Pasôna agency, who went into sales of cars and of cut-price Italian designer clothes in his Designer Collezione chain; Yasumitsu Shigeta, who set up Hikari Tsushin, a successful mobile phone retailer; and Tomoko Takasugi, an estate agency employee who set up her own business, offering to companies the service of managing their company housing in their place. The new social attitudes also value small-scale enterprises breaking free through technological performance from the principals providing contracts, and eventually imposing their own conditions; and others which join forces to compete with the big firms in tendering for contracts, such as the Hurricane group, in which 50 small-scale suppliers of software systems banded together. Even the giant groups adopt the 'small is beautiful' principle. Hitachi (300,000 employees), overwhelmed by losses of 250 billion yen in 1998, carried out a reorganisation into ten divisions which enjoy complete management autonomy, and Mitsubishi Chemical reorganised its R&D into numerous small laboratories with a staff of no more than 20–30 researchers, under the guidance of a professor at the Massachusetts Institute of Technology – one among many foreigners called in to help the *risotura*.

Foreigners come into play

Foreigners are now becoming full participants in Japan's economic system. Attracted by low share prices, the fall in the value of the yen, ultra-cheap credit and deregulation of foreign exchange, foreign investment in Japan rose by 50 per cent, and then doubled again to reach a record $10.8 billion in 1996 in 1998. This was still not much compared with what other developed countries were receiving ($68 billion in the USA in 1995); and Japanese investment overseas, although in decline, still amounted to four times that sum. But the trend is towards operations on an increasingly large scale; two deals concluded in the first half of 1999 – the $5.16 billion investment by Renault of France in Nissan, and acquisition of control over Nippon Leasing by General Electric Capital for $6.5 billion – amounted on their own to a sum exceeding all foreign investment in 1998. In 2000, several big life insurance companies went bankrupt, thus offering golden opportunities to foreign companies that rushed to pick up the pieces. The crisis also attracts foreign speculators. Several buy-out funds specialising in purchase of bankrupt companies were set up in the USA to operate in Japan, and 'vulture funds' specialising in bad debts have been reported buying up large amounts of them, at 10 per cent of their face value, from distressed Japanese banks.

On their side, Japanese firms are getting rid of their insular mentality. In senior staff careers, experience of other countries is no longer a handicap but a 'plus'. The leading firms no longer hesitate to resort to the services of foreign service enterprises, like Fuji Bank which had a portion of its accounts audited by Ernst and Young (1998), and Sony, which shifted the management of some of its pension plans from local to foreign companies, including Goldman Sachs. In 1999 the government itself entrusted the Morgan Bank with looking for a foreign rescuer for the reorganised Long Term Credit Bank. The firms most in difficulty, abandoned by their *keiretsu*, no longer hesitate to turn to foreign saviours. In the car industry, by 2000 Mazda, Nissan and

Mitsubishi Motors had sold controlling shares of their capital to Ford, Renault and DaimlerChrysler respectively, and were chaired by a Scotsman, a Frenchman and a German. Carlos Ghosn, the French 'cost killer' sent to Nissan in 1999 with full powers, managed to restore profitability in only two years, and became a celebrity in Japan. In the banking sector, the Nippon Credit Bank and the LTCB, before being placed under state supervision in 1998, vainly sought help from the Bankers Trust of the USA and the Société de Banque Suisse; after cleaning their books, the government looked to foreign consortia for taking them up. Even the old national preference reflex is giving way to the logic of profit. In an exemplary case concerning the highly sensitive telecommunications sector, Cable and Wireless of Britain took control of International Digital Equipment in 1999 after a two-month battle with NTT. The foreign bidder defeated the 'quasi-official' operator thanks to two other 'establishment' firms, Toyota and the Itôchu trading firm, which sold it their shares rather than accept a lower offer from NTT. While this was a case of a hostile takeover – the first ever to succeed in Japan – a very large number of tie-ups were negotiated amicably. NTT itself collaborated with American Telegraph and Telephone. Sumitomo Rubber allied itself with Goodyear to form the first pneumatic tyres venture in the world. In the chemicals industry the alliance of Teijin and the US company DuPont had the same effect for polyester film.

Even in distribution, one of the most protected LDP constituencies, Toys 'R' Us – which had been the first foreign retail chain to force open the gates of the archipelago in 1992 – became the leading distributor in Japan seven years later, with 78 shops. Retailers and foreign restaurant chains have been popping up, in the wake of the very sharp drop in land prices and the relative weakness of local competition. Japanese distribution chains, handicapped by three decades of protection of small-scale shops, are underdeveloped compared with foreign competitors: Daiei, the biggest, only had 383 stores compared with 1,000 for the French firm Carrefour – whose first steps in Japan aroused intense media coverage (2000) – and 3,600 for Wal Mart, number one in the world, which is due to land in Japan in the near future. These new arrivals obtain supplies directly from abroad, and sometimes sell by mail order, bypassing local wholesalers and middlemen, whose number fell by 20 per cent between 1991 (470,000) and 1998 (391,000). Similarly, after the amendment of the law protecting small-scale trade in 1992, the number of retail shops fell by 10 per cent every three years.

Kûdôka – '*hollowing out*'

Opening the door to foreign business made the 'nationalist postulate' on which industrial policy was based obsolete. The MITI had always sought to ensure that Japan produced all that it could on its own soil, so as to preserve national independence. In 1995 Japanese firms only carried out 6 per cent of their production overseas, compared with 24 per cent for their American competitors and 20 per cent for Germany. But when neighbouring countries offer much lower hourly wage costs, currencies that were stable in relation to the dollar until 1997, and sub-contractors whose quality continuously improves, relocation becomes an inescapable necessity. By 2000 Japanese firms were expected to carry on at least 15 per cent of their production overseas. This implies job losses in the archipelago, and increased imports. Thus, on the market for television sets, the share of 'imports' rose from 10 per cent in 1990 to 80 per cent in 1995. But these were essentially reverse imports (*gyaku yunyû*) of sets manufactured in other Asian countries by Sony, Matsushita or Toshiba. The increase in 'imports' of cars (31 per cent up in 1996) also owed something to reverse imports from Japanese plants in the United States. *Gyaku yunyû* now accounts for 20 per cent of goods imported into Japan. But while relocation is thus good for the big firms, it is a danger for jobs in industry and small-scale sub-contractors. The word *kûdôka*, which was all in vogue in the media around 1995, is a rather brutal word meaning something close to 'disembowelling'; it helped increase social anxiety.

The United States still remains by far Japan's leading trading partner, with a 26.8 per cent share in 1999, compared with 12.1 per cent for China (second) and 16 per cent for the whole European Union. But it was in Asia as a whole that trade has made the biggest progress during the period, despite a temporary drop due to the regional economic crisis in 1997. In 1991, for the first time, Japan exported more to Asia than to the USA (30.6 per cent of its total exports, as against 29.1 per cent), and this trend has never

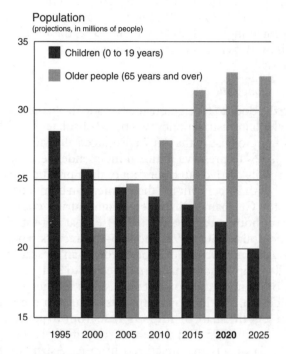

Fig. 7.1(a)   PREDICTING THE WORST: DEMOGRAPHY AND ECONOMIC GROWTH (1995–2025)

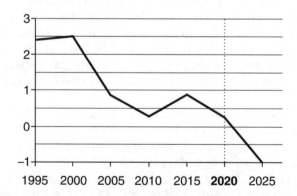

Fig. 7.1(b)   PREDICTING THE WORST: RATE OF POPULATION GROWTH (1995–2025)

If the average number of children to whom one woman gives birth in her life does not rise again from the present 1.34, the Japanese population will decrease from 2007 onwards. In 2020 people aged 65 years old or older will constitute 25 per cent of the whole population – the highest percentage in the world. This aging population will weigh heavily upon the labor force. If no comprehensive reform is undertaken, the pension system and the State budget will crash together.

If the structural economic reform fails, the growth rate will diminish from year to year until the GNP declines from 2020 onwards. The current-account balance will fall in the red in 2025 and Japan will suffer from both trade and budgetary defecits.

Source: Sanwa Research Institute, published in *Nihon Keizai Shimbun*

been reversed – on the contrary, Asia's share of exports rose to 37.3 per cent in 1999. From 1990 to 1996, Japan's trade surplus with Asia grew steadily from $27.7 billion to $51.4 billion – having exceeded for the first time the surplus with the USA in 1992. The crisis in 1997 led to a redirecting of Japan's trade, whose surplus with Asia declined 51.8 per cent in two years (to only $33.8 billion in 1999) while growing 34.5 per cent with the booming USA (from $41 billion to $63.3 billion) and a full 400 per cent with the less booming but politically less resilient EU (from $8 billion to $32.7 billion). Nevertheless, despite this temporary setback, Asia as a region is now firmly installed as the most important partner in Japanese external trade overall, with a 38.5 per cent share.

In Japan's direct outward investment, Asia's share rose from 12.4 per cent in 1990 to 24.2 per cent in 1995. From 1994 that proportion exceeded the proportion directed towards Europe (16.7 per cent), but remained well below investment in the United States (43.8 per cent). Investors were encouraged to go to Asia by a better return on investment than anywhere else, about 6 per cent. In 1997, despite seven years of financial crisis, Japan was still the number one foreign investor in Korea, Taiwan, Indonesia and Thailand; in addition it devoted 60 per cent of its official development aid to Asia. But as with trade, after crisis struck Asia Japan redirected its foreign investment, of which only 16 per cent went to Asia in 1998 compared with 34.4 per cent to the USA and 25.3 per cent to Europe.

JAPAN, EUROPEAN UNION, U.S.A.:
BASIC STATISTICAL DATA

Demography, 1999

	Japan	EU	USA
Area (km.²)	377,500	3,236,180	9,363,120
Population	126,506,000	374,818,000	276,200,000
Population growth 1991–8 (%)	+2.1	+3.6	+9.3

The economy, 1998

	Japan	EU	USA
GDP¹ billion$	4,092	8,290	8,076
GDP per capita¹ ($)	32,350	22,119	29,240
GDP per capita, p.p.p.² ($)	23,257	20,352	29,605
Investment % of GDP	26.1	20.2	20

¹ calculated at current exchange rate   ² p.p.p. = purchasing power parity

Source: all data adapted from *L'État du monde*, Paris: La Découverte, various years

---

Data relating to the GDP and per capita GDP calculated at the current exchange rate are to be used with caution. Since they vary parallel to the exchange rate, they cause some countries – especially Japan – to 'weigh more' or to 'weigh less' from year to year while in fact they stagnated, and their people to appear 'richer' or 'poorer' while their standard of living hardly changed.

In comparative purchasing power parity, Japan surpassed every European Union country in 1998 – except Luxembourg. The Japanese were more or less evenly matched with the Belgians (23,223) and the Austrians (23,166). Despite eight years of economic crisis, they still surpassed the German (22,169), French (21,175) and British (20,336) rates.

Growth, 1991–98

		Japan	EU	USA
GDP growth		+23%	+28.6%	+43%
Comparison (EU = 100)	1991	51.6	100	87.6
	1998	49.3	100	97.4
GDP per capita, p.p.p.		+20.3%	+22.2%	+33.7%
Comparison (EU = 100)	1991	116.4	100	132.8
	1998	114.2	100	145.5

Trade, 1999

		Japan	EU[1]	USA
Imports	billion $	280.3	821.6	1,030
	% of GDP	6.8	9.9	12.7
	$ per capita	2,215	2,191	3,729
Exports	billion	403.7	795.4	685.3
	% of GDP	9.8	9.6	8.5
	$ per capita	3,191	2,122	1,821
% of world's exports		7.2	14.2	12.3

[1] Trade with non-EU countries   customs clearance basis

Comparison: Japan and the EU 'Big Three' (Germany, France, UK), 1999

		Japan	'Big Three'	USA
Population		126,506,000	199,800,000	
GDP	billion $	4,092	4,866	
GDP per capita	$	32,346	24,476	
GDP per capita, p.p.p.	$	23,257	21,340	
Trade in goods				
Imports	billion $	280.3	1,063.3	
Exports	billion $	403.7	1,108.9	
Trade in services				
Imports		115.1	274.4	197.5
Exports		61	431.7	274.7
Current account	billion $	+69.3	+202.9	−267.5
balance	% of GDP	1.7	4.1	3.3

But even though Japan's GDP is still about 1.5 times the total of other Asian countries including China, and it provides them with a high proportion of the equipment needed for their rapid development, its position in Asia is far from one of hegemony. For the emerging Asian economies, it is the United States – not Japan – that represents the buyer of last resort, a huge, wide open export market. By comparison the Japanese market has not opened up much, especially for the four NIEs, which sell only about 10 per cent of their exports there. Except for China and Indonesia, all the Asian countries have heavy trade deficits with Japan; those of South Korea before the 1997 crisis, and Taiwan even after it, used to be in the $14–15 billion range, at times higher than the whole EU's deficit on Japan trade. The NIEs, especially South Korea which joined the OECD in 1996, have become serious competitors for Japan in areas such as the motor, steel, components and mass-produced electronics industries. They have accused Japan of keeping its market closed, refusing them transfers of technology, or even wanting to wreck their budding industries – for example when Tokyo threatened to take Indonesia to the World Trade Organisation (WTO) over the measures introduced to protect its infant national motor industry.

Generally speaking, before the crisis, Asia's growth was increasingly self-sustaining. Cross-investment and trade developed very rapidly between China, the Korea and Taiwan 'Tigers' and ASEAN. Most of the foreign capital invested between 1990 and 1995 in China and in the ASEAN countries came neither from Japan, nor from the USA, nor from Europe. The emerging Asian countries traded more and more among themselves, and ASEAN planned to establish a free trade zone gradually from 2003 onwards. Even if relocation has made it difficult to say whether an investment or a product is 'Korean', 'Thai' or 'Malaysian', it is obvious that Japan, although it still carried considerable weight, was not hegemonic in an Asian region whose development, on the eve of the 1997 crisis, seemed more and more self-sustaining. And it is still not so since the crisis struck its neighbours.

Paths to the future

After ten years of crisis it seems that Japan has been able to avoid major social disruption. The crisis brought much misery in its train. The number of suicides shot up by 30 per cent in 1998 to a record 33,000 – including many bankrupted small businessmen, laid-off employees and jobless people. 'Cardboard cities' set up by homeless people became a commonsight around some railway stations and parks in Tokyo. In 2000 small and medium enterprises went bankrupt at the rate of about 1,600 per month, compared with only 500 in 1990 – but it was the older businessmen who gave up, while others struggled to adapt. From 1992 to 1998, 209,000 small shops disappeared, but it was the 'pop and mom stores' owned by people in their seventies that went first. This natural attrition produced human tragedies, but not social disturbance. For wage earners, the fall in pay due to the reduction of overtime and bonuses was more or less compensated by the fall in prices; the collapse in property prices even gave them back their dream of buying a home. While companies sometimes used all sorts of pressure to push some employees out through the door, overall staff cuts were more limited, more gradual and socially less traumatic than in most Western countries. Social cohesion was therefore less affected, the crime rate and the proportion of poor people among the population remained very low, and no Japanese town ever witnessed police chasing after rioting demonstrators. This is certainly an asset for tomorrow's Japan.

The routes for large-scale redeployment of the economy towards new sectors had already been traced, notably by the 'vision' published by the MITI in 1994 under the title *An Industrial Structure for the Twenty-First Century*. This document lists twelve growth sectors for the future. Some are characteristic of an ageing society with a high standard of living: personal services, leisure, silver industries and improvement of the quality of life. Others are brought in by the new logics of a restructured and globalised society: services to companies, international trade management – for example, import-export services provided by the mammoth Japanese trading companies to emerging economies – and financial engineering backed by the biggest mass of savings in the world, estimated at about $12,000 billion, of which a large part is still dormant in post office savings banks. Others are centred around very high technology, for which Japanese companies never sacrificed R & D even at the worst point of the crisis; they still devoted 3 per cent of GDP to it in 1995, then kept increasing this amount despite the recession (by 4.7 per cent in 1997) to establish successive all-time highs in 1996 and 1997. High-tech hopes focus upon the space industry, new materials, software and the range of activities derived from the merger between electronics and biology – biotechnology and artificial intelligence applied to fully automated production processes and all kinds of robots. These twelve sectors are expected to ensure most future growth, while traditional sectors are expected to be renovated (steel, elec- tronics) and concentrate on top of the range consumption (luxury cars, fashion). The outlines of this change were already discern- ible in the results of Japanese firms for fiscal year 1998–9, when the ranks of the ten most profitable companies in the country were joined by a consumer credit firm (Takefuji) and a mobile telephone operator (DoCoMo). In contrast the traditional manu- facturing giants declined – Mitsubishi Heavy fell from fifth posi- tion to 53rd, Matsushita from sixth to eleventh – or else disappeared from the rating altogether, like NEC (ranked eighth in 1997–8).

To lead these changes a new breed of managers emerged, imbued with the culture of profit and liberated from the old reflexes. The self-made man, as we have seen, came back into fashion, with figures like Masayoshi Son or Yasuyuki Nambu. But the phenomenon also affects the established big firms. In 1995–6 all the six car manufacturing firms changed their chairmen, and Toyota's Hiroshi Okuda was the first ever not to come from the founding dynasty, having leap-frogged six candidates with more seniority. Toshiba's new Chairman, Taizo Nishimura, who has spent a large part of his career abroad, also elbowed nine more senior top executives out of his way. These new managers do not hesitate to display a measure of hedonism, nor to abandon the dark blue suit; still less to declare to the media that 'the Japanese model is completely obsolete'. Also, many big companies' boards, which had traditionally comprised dozens of aged and dozy direc- tors (59 for the Bank of Tokyo-Mitsubishi), have now been sharply cut back – to only ten members at Sony, Nissan and Toshiba (including Nissan's three French ones).

These new entrepreneurs call above all for the freedom to com- plete their schemes without bureaucratic obstacles. Even the officials of the MITI, in the conclusion to their 'vision', emphasise that structural adjustments will be carried out by the free play of economic actors, rather than under administrative guidance. *Kiseikanwa* (deregulation) was the key word for all this period and still is.

Kiseikanwa – 'deregulation'

Deregulation is a highly political subject, because of the enormous interests at stake. The theme had already appeared in debate at the end of the 1970s under the name 'administrative reform'. But the reform had come up against stubborn opposition from bureaucrats and ground to a halt after the end of the Nakasone cabinet in 1987 (see pp. 216–19). With the crisis, however, a true national consensus emerged in support of the view that Japan's adaptation to the new world economic game must involve general deregulation and the curtailing of administrative power. Only a handful of politicians dare oppose it openly, even though many still are very reluctant to agree to any concrete measure. Each government surpassed the one before in 'deregulatory rhetoric'. The ephemeral prime minister Hata (May–June 1994) promised to make prices come down by 30 per cent through deregulation; his successor set up no less than three *ad hoc* bodies which formulated in 1991 a Deregulation Plan in 1,091 measures. The bureaucracy was lambasted and assailed from all sides – by public opinion, but also by politicians, employers and foreign trade partners – as being mainly responsible for the crisis and an obstacle to reforms. The wretched results of its 'economic guidance' and the scandals deprived the bureaucracy of legitimacy for resisting plans which aimed to reduce its powers and its staffing. Even so, it still had plenty of ways to defend itself – starting with its very close ties with the government party and the quasi-monopoly it exercised over the drawing up and implementation of the budget. In addition, those who clamoured for deregulation were divided by antagonistic interests while seemingly pursuing the same goals.

Their first objective was to end the administration's supervision of the economy. In 1989 the number of permits in force was 10,054. Ministries were ordered to reduce that number. But in 1995 there were in fact more (10,760). In the face of this ill will on the part of the bureaucratic fortresses, the idea of breaking them up took shape and became the essential objective. In the 1996 parliamentary election campaign all the parties outdid each other, and the LDP itself proposed reducing the number of central government ministries and agencies from 21 to 10. The Ministry of Finance was made the scapegoat for the whole crisis, and thus was the priority target. There was talk of depriving it of all the power that it had exercised so badly over financial policy, and of the supervision of the banking system, to give that task to an independent agency. The Ministry, it was suggested, should also lose control of fiscal policy, to retain only budgetary power. The Ministry of Posts and Telecommunications was another favourite target, for it controlled two vast kitties which aroused envious looks all round: the fast-expanding communications market and the enormous mass of savings deposited in post offices.

The struggles between the ministries and the lobbies were behind closed doors, but fierce. In 1997 the Ministry of Posts mobilised postmasters – who are very important election agents for many Diet members – to force the government to abandon a plan to privatise the post office savings banks. Finally, a detailed plan provided for the administration to be reduced to just 13 departments on 1 January 2001 (see Fig. 7.2). The Ministry of Finance was symbolically stripped of its name *Okurashô* – meaning literally 'Big Storehouse' and going back to the fifth century – and was reduced to *Zaimushô* (Treasury Ministry). It lost its control over monetary policy to the Bank of Japan, supervision of the banking system to a newly-created Agency of Financial Affairs, and fiscal policy to an Agency of Fiscal and Economic Policy – both under the direct supervision of the Prime Minister's Cabinet Office. The Finance Ministry, however, retained the right to intervene in financial policy 'in case of crisis', and staffed most of the two newly-created agencies. The Ministry of Posts emerged as the big loser. It was – strangely enough – merged with the Management and Coordination Agency and the Ministry of the Home Affairs, thus losing its independence and coming under more direct control by the cabinet. The trade unions, much weakened by the economic crisis and the near-disappearance of their political arm – the Socialist Party (see p. 297) – were unable to prevent 'their' Ministry of Labour losing its independence and being merged with the Ministry of Health and Welfare. The merger of Construction with Transport, the National Land Agency and the

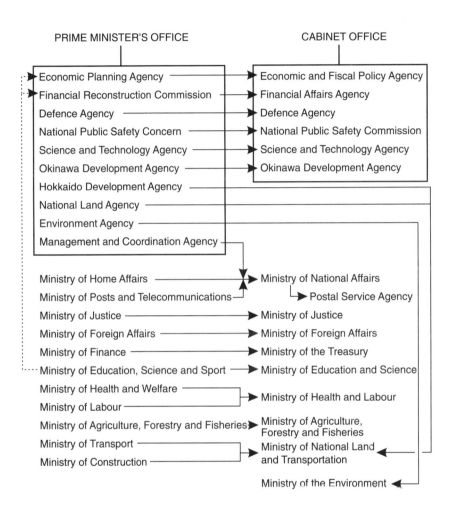

Fig. 7.2.   THE REORGANISATION OF THE NATIONAL
GOVERNMENT (1 JANUARY 2001)

Hokkaido Development Agency was ostensibly aimed at breaking the lobbies and cleaning up corruption in that sector; it created a mammoth Ministry of Land, Infrastructure and Transport so vast that its efficiency might be in doubt. Lastly, Education was joined to the Science and Technology Agency. To crown it all, the number of civil servants is to be cut by 25 per cent before 2010, but many functions are to be transferred to 'independent administrative corporations' whose staff would have the status of civil servants. And the idea of setting up an independent inspection body to conduct audits of administrative work, on the lines of the French Cour des Comptes, was abandoned.

For the politicians the civil servants were the ideal scapegoat to divert voters' anger. But beyond that short-term objective there was also a determination to reclaim the decision making power confiscated by the bureaucracy. This was strongly asserted by Ichirô Ozawa, the man who precipitated a general shake-up in the political system in July 1993 (see p. 283). In his view the bureaucrats do not have the capacity nor the imagination to cope with the pressing situation created by the coming of a new era since the end of the Cold War, still less the legitimacy to call for 'blood, toil, sweat and tears' in order to conduct drastic and painful policies necessary for the Japanese economy to face globalisation. This determination to restore the supremacy of political power was expressed in a series of more or less important measures. Officials were forbidden to answer questions in their ministers' place before Diet commissions. The number of deputy minister posts was increased from one to two, to give young Diet members experience of face-to-face work with civil servants. Lastly, efforts were made to strengthen the powers of the Japanese prime minister, who had traditionally been one of the weakest holders of executive power in the world.

For big business – as during the 1980s – the ultimate aim of deregulation was to open up fields of activity which political patronage had closed to it. Among other developments, the amendment of the Retail Trade Law in 1992 enabled supermarkets to wipe out small-scale retailers, and there is even talk of opening up the most important LDP constituency, agriculture, to big business, by encouraging small landowners to regroup themselves in order to lease large pieces of land to entrepreneurs. But the main objective is the two most profitable sectors of the economy in the twenty-first century, which deregulation will make it possible to restructure completely. One is the strategic telecommunications sector where NTT, the former state monopoly which remained the favourite child of the Ministry of Posts even after its (incomplete) privatisation, still retained an ultradominant position. The other is the financial sector, where the protection granted by the LDP to small banks, and the stringent regulation imposed by the Ministry of Finance prevented concentration and caused Japanese financial enterprises to lag behind their foreign competitors to their cost, even though they had the biggest mass of savings in the world at their disposal.

In 1997 Prime Minister Hashimoto promised to carry out a radical reform of the financial sector – the 'Big Bang', whose slogan was 'Free, Global and Fair'. Financial bodies were permitted to combine banking, brokerage, insurance and consumer credit – and the profits accruing to them. Interest rates and the prices of services were to be deregulated. Strict regulations ostensibly intended for depositors' protection, which had enforced restrictive management of pension funds and prevented proposing high returns to savers, are being removed bit by bit. To put an end to the situation prevailing throughout the post-war period, when the financial sector was more or less required by the state to provide cheap funding for the manufacturing sector without being able to exercise any control, holding companies – outlawed since the Occupation – were authorised again, and restrictions on banks' acquisition of stakes in companies were removed. The big banks have been encouraged to absorb the small ones and merge into new banking giants, while newcomers have been welcomed into the field: the government made a point of selling the Nippon Credit Bank to an American consortium after taking it over and 'cleaning it up', and the retail chain Seven Eleven started its own banking business in 2001. Lastly, to make full integration into international financial circuits possible and reassure foreign investors, the prevailing international norms for accounting and auditing were gradually introduced in Japan, and since 1992 a Stock Exchange Supervisory Commission has been in charge of enforcing a code of conduct more or less similar to those common to most Western countries.

But from the citizens' point of view, 'deregulation' can also mean 'democratisation'. Citizen-consumers expected it to bring a fall in prices, but their criticisms were also directed increasingly at the lack of transparency of decisions by the administration, its arbitrariness, its systematic withholding of information, its unaccountability. Thus the theme of deregulation was inseparable from challenging of the whole authoritarian model of society. It went together with calls for 'the right to information' (*jôhô kôhai*) – which politicians and big business did not want any more than the bureaucracy. It was inseparable from the re-awakening of civil society after the 'conservative 1980s'. Amidst the crisis, a new sense of citizenship expressed itself through volunteer work, networks and associations of all kinds which rose in arms against the 'straitjacket society', and newly-elected mayors and governors who dared to challenge Tokyo, while the political system was going through a period of chaotic recomposition.

POLITICS: THE END OF THE '1955 SYSTEM' AND THE UNFINISHED RECOMPOSITION

Neo-conservative boom and the 1993 elections

From the late 1980s the LDP was confronted with the demand for 'political reform' (*seiji kaikaku*) aimed at wiping out corruption through sweeping electoral reform and a change in the system of political funding. In 1991 Toshiki Kaifu had failed to overcome the opposition of conservative House members, fiercely hostile to any re-demarcation of constituencies and any limits on fund-raising. His successor, Kiichi Miyazawa, was soon paralysed by the Sagawa affair (see Box, pp. 253–5), while the economic situation stirred up discontent. But the traditional opposition parties were incapable of taking advantage of this. The Socialists, back under the thumb of trade union apparatchiks after the removal of Miss Doi from leadership, lost all the popularity that she had acquired among floating voters. New parties were to emerge to respond to the call for change.

In May 1992 Morihiro Hosokawa, Governor of Kumamoto prefecture and former LDP senator, created the New Japan Party (Nihon Shintô). He recruited support among local conservative elected representatives, especially members of prefecture assemblies wanting to get elected to the Diet, whose ambitions were blocked by the proliferation of 'family seats' serving LDP deputies (in 1992 nearly 60 per cent of Liberal Democratic Diet members were *nissei* or *sansei*, whose seats had been in their families for two or three generations). In this respect the creation of the NJP was one sign of the revolt of local communities against the Tokyo establishment, characteristic of the whole period. The new party seized upon all the fashionable themes: electoral reform, bringing new and younger faces into politics, promotion of women and 'amateurs' in public life, decentralisation, deregulation and defence of consumers. In July 1992, in its first appearance on the electoral stage, it obtained more than 8 per cent of votes and two seats in the Upper House elections. Hosokawa had a reputation of being a 'model governor'; heir to a leading aristocratic family and a likeable and media-friendly person, he became the fashionable politician, greeted by the media as 'Japan's Kennedy'.

The Japan Renewal Party (Shinseitô) was created in 1993 by Ichirô Ozawa, a heavyweight of the LDP; a protégé of Kakuei Tanaka and then of his right-hand man Shin Kanemaru, he was one of the key men in the secret funding networks which linked the LDP with the business world and particularly with construction and public works companies. He had been Minister of Science and Technology, Chief Secretary to the Cabinet and government spokesman, Minister of Home Affairs, and finally Secretary-General of the LDP in 1989. After 25 years in the House he was in a position to become prime minister, on condition that he became the head of one of the party's five factions. But his arrogant and bruising personality and his avowed neo-nationalism – he called openly for revision of the Constitution and strengthening of the Self Defence Forces – made him firm enemies. He belonged to the former Tanaka faction, then led by Noboru Takeshita. When the Sagawa scandal forced Takeshita to relinquish the leadership in December 1992, Ozawa sought to succeed him but the majority of the faction chose Keizô Obuchi in a vote. In March 1993 a series of public works scandals enabled Ozawa's enemies to secure the arrest of his mentor Kanemaru. The investigation spread until it threatened Ozawa. He then counterattacked; in June he left the LDP and created the Renewal Party with the 35 members of the faction who backed him. They were mostly younger members. To wrong-foot his accusers, Ozawa made political reform and moral standards in public life his rallying cry.

Immediately after this breakaway, ten other Diet members left the LDP to set up the Harbinger Party (Sakigake). They were all young House members who had only been elected once, twice or three times. Their leader was Masayoshi Takemura, former Governor of Shiga prefecture, a member of the Diet only since 1986. He was a stranger to the Tokyo élite, and had a reputation as a 'model governor' recalling Hosokawa's. The founders of the Sakigake were made of centre-left, liberal and pacifist material. Nearly all were *nissei* who had inherited family seats, secure seats that made them independent of the party. The archetype was Yukio Hatoyama, deputy for Hokkaido and grandson of the first LDP head of government; with his brother Kunio, deputy for Tokyo, he had inherited one of the biggest fortunes and one of the most extensive networks of contacts among the Japanese élite.

These two breakaways deprived the LDP of its majority in the House. Miyazawa dissolved it. In the elections of 18 July 1993 the LDP won 39.5 per cent of votes cast again, and 223 seats (one more than before). Only the megalopoles clearly rejected it; it lost 35 seats in Tokyo-Yokohama and Osaka-Kobe. The three neo-conservative parties won a total of 22.5 per cent of the vote and 103 seats (57 more than before). Together they became the second political force in the country, and the first in the big cities – winning 29 per cent of the vote in Tokyo and more than a third in the neighbouring prefectures where the typical urban 'salarymen' live in big housing estates. But their gains were not at the expense of the LDP; nearly all their new seats were taken from the Socialists, who were the big losers. The old left-wing party had its worst results in the post-war era (15.4 per cent) and plummeted from 140 seats to 72; in Tokyo ten of the 11 Socialist incumbents were defeated. The Centre parties gained a little: the Kômeitô gained 6 seats (making 52) and the Democratic Party of Japan five (making 19). The JCP held on to its 15 seats. But a record abstention rate (32.7 per cent, 6 points up) showed that public opinion was sceptical about the 'renewal' it was being promised.

The LDP out of power (1993–4)

As the LDP remained by far the leading party, it should have been responsible for forming a government again. But all the other parties, except the JCP, formed a coalition. Together they had a small

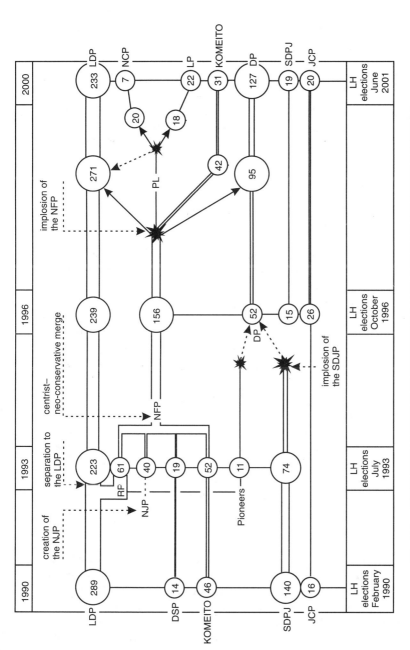

Fig. 7.3. CHANGES IN THE PARTY SYSTEM AND PARTIES' REPRESENTATION IN THE LOWER HOUSE, 1990–2000 (simplified)

majority of 18, but they did not agree on anything. The Renewal Party wanted to strengthen the Self Defence Forces and increase the purchase tax from 3 to 10 per cent, while the Socialists wanted to abolish both – at least in principle. But all had promised the voters to put an end to the LDP's reign; so they were obliged to assume their responsibilities by governing, or lose their credibility. In addition Ozawa, who was the architect of the coalition, knew his former Liberal Democratic colleagues well; he thought that by depriving them of the sweets of office, he would provoke new breakaways that would eventually destroy the LDP. And indeed, during the nine months when the LDP was out of power, about twenty House members left it to start small parties – the Reform Group, the New Future Party, the Liberal Party, etc. – in order to wait and see.

The coalition chose Hosokawa as Prime Minister. The popularity rating of 'Japan's Kennedy' was around 75 per cent. But his NJP only had 35 House members, almost all inexperienced and poorly funded. His position was precarious and his partners knew they could get rid of him when they no longer needed him. The new government's first mission was to carry out the 'political reform' which the media and public opinion were clamouring for. The electoral system in use since 1947 for Lower House elections was accused of causing all the ills affecting the body politic. It was now altered radically. The 147 medium-sized multiple-seats constituencies were replaced by 300 small local constituencies on the British model (a single seat, a single round of voting, first past the post) and 200 seats filled by proportional representation in eleven regions. Each voter had two ballots and so was free, if he wished, to choose the LDP candidate in his local constituency and the regional Communist list. A party could put a candidate forward both in a local constituency and on the regional proportional representation list. These 'double candidacies' were authorised at the pressing request of the incumbents, for whom they offered the best possible guarantee of re-election.

The LDP had for long wanted single-seat constituencies, because such a system always favours the most powerful party, and all political pundits agreed that the formidable conservative machines would be unbeatable in a face to face fight with poorly funded and divided opposition candidates. On the traditional opposition side the Socialists would have preferred to retain the existing system, but they could not admit it. The Communist Party and the Kômeitô inclined towards a complete proportional representation system. The neo-conservative parties were divided on the question, but having made the reform a major argument of their election campaign, they could not get out of it. Hosokawa at first favoured a perfect compromise – 250 local seats and 250 filled through proportional representation. This proposal was adopted by the House, but a Socialist minority blocked it in the Senate, in the hope of burying all reform. The result, however, was the opposite of what they had hoped for; Hosakawa reached agreement with the LDP on a version more in conformity with the latter's wishes, reducing the number of proportional-representation seats to 200 against 300 local seats. The reform was finally adopted in January 1994.

As regards political funding, the most radical proposals favoured banning companies entirely from making political contributions, and financing the parties wholly from public funds. Most opposition legislators also wanted to prohibit all donations to individual politicians, and to confine the right to handle political funds to parties as such. Their LDP colleagues were strongly against such restrictions. Both those radical proposals were put aside. The new law contented itself with reducing the maximum amount of permitted contributions and increasing the obligation of transparency by obliging politicians to identify donors of all sums exceeding 50,000 yen (compared with all over 1 million yen before). So reform was restricted to 'strengthening' the system in force since the Miki reform of 1975, although it had already proved its complete ineffectiveness. State funding of parties was introduced, but in accordance with the LDP's wishes it remained minimal – no more than 30 billion yen, scarcely 3 per cent of what elected representatives at national level spent every year.

As soon as the reform had been voted, the coalition was divided. Since the budget deficit swelled amidst the economic crisis, the Renewal Party wanted to increase the purchase tax; the Socialists refused. Hosokawa, now implicated in his turn in the Sagawa affair, preferred to retire from the scene. Ozawa then tried to break the LDP by offering the post of prime minister to Michio Watanabe, heir to Nakasone, a neo-nationalist like him, and head of the second faction in the LDP. But Watanabe refused. The Renewal Party then had no alternative but to form a minority cabinet with the Centre parties and the NJP (29 April 1994). Ozawa's right-hand man, Tsutomu Hata, became Prime Minister. But on 30 June the LDP, the Socialists and the Sakigake signed an agreement to govern in alliance; they had a 50-seat majority. Hata resigned immediately.

The LDP–Socialist–Harbinger coalition and the traumas of 1995

The coalition of the LDP and its former Socialist opponents was only half a surprise. Forty years of shared parliamentary life had woven a number of complicities between the two old parties. Miss Doi's successor at the head of the JSP, Makoto Tanabe, was so notoriously linked with Ozawa's mentor Shin Kanemaru that he resigned straight after Kanemaru's disgrace, in December 1992. The Socialists had long since stopped contesting the social order, and based their 'opposition' on largely symbolic issues such as the *Hinomaru* flag and the *Kimigayo* anthem. The hard core of their electorate – the civil servants and Sôhyô trade union members – belonged to the protected Japan, just as much as the privileged patronage circles of the LDP. Consequently those two parties nourished the same suspicion of the deregulation policy advocated by the neo-conservatives, and they had a common interest in preserving their share of the 'political market' against those newcomers.

The Socialists had already moved their policies well towards the right since Sôhyô joined the moderate unions in the new Rengô confederation in 1989 (see p. 237). While they remained hostile in principle to the Security Treaty and the Self Defence Forces, they made the hoped-for end to the Treaty conditional on Washington's prior agreement, and accepted that the SDF was 'legal ... although non-constitutional' (!). In March 1993 Tanabe's successor, Sadao Yamahana, went as far as breaking the supreme taboo by envisaging 'creative evolution' (*sôken*) of the Constitution. The party even changed its name to a watered-down 'Social Democratic Party of Japan' (SDPJ) in 1992, but in English only – in Japanese it retained its old name Shakaitô. But this ideological sell-out disoriented the Socialist voters. The JSP paid for that in an unprecedented defeat in the elections of 18 July 1993. It was still the second party in Japan, but its popularity was collapsing, its militants were deserting and its leaders were at daggers drawn. After the election disaster, Yamahana was removed from the leadership and replaced by a historic figure beyond reproach, Tomiichi Murayama, who was in his 70s and had been in the Diet for 33 years. Yamahana then threatened to leave the party with his followers. In this débâcle governing – even in alliance with the Devil – was the Socialists' last chance. The SDPJ secured the post of Prime Minister for Murayama, and five portfolios. The Sakigake received the sensitive Finance Ministry. But Yôhei Kôno, the Chairman of the LDP, became Deputy Prime Minister, and his party had 13 ministries including the MITI, Home Affairs, Foreign Affairs, Defence and Justice. In an attempt to block the coalition's way when the prime minister was to be elected by the Diet on 30 June, Ozawa enticed to his side the former Prime Minister Kaifu, who left the LDP and stood against Murayama with the support of the Renewal Party, the New Japan Party and the centre parties. In the first round Murayama won only 241 votes in the Lower House out of 511, when 36 LDP members, 24 Socialist ones and eight of the Sakigake defected. But after he was elected in the second round, those defectors returned quickly to the fold to share in the benefits of power. In the end only ten LDP Diet members followed Kaifu to join the Renewal Party.

To oppose the LDP-SDPJ-Sakigake coalition, Ozawa then set about unifying the neo-conservatives and the centre. It took six months for the New Frontier Party (Shinshintô) to come into being in December 1994. It became the second party in the lower house. The Renewal Party, the Kômeitô and the DSP disappeared, merged into the new party. The New Japan Party split; 22 of its Lower House members followed Hosokawa into the NFP, but 13 refused. With reinforcement from ten LDP defectors, the new party started with 176 Diet members. Ozawa was its Chairman and controlled its finances.

This merger was aimed first at presenting a united neo-conservative-Centre front at the Upper House elections in 1995, and still more at the next parliamentary elections. Many of the neo-conservative and Centre deputies had been elected in the same big city constituencies in 1993. If they wanted to survive in the new system of one-seat constituencies, it was imperative for them to come to terms among themselves so as not to compete with each other in the face of LDP candidates. But beyond that common electoral interest there were very deep ideological differences. Ozawa's avowed neo-nationalism clashed with Hosokawa's and the Buddhists' pacifist principles; his Thatcherism was hard to reconcile with the Kômeitô's Poujadism and the DSP's base of support among trade unions. In addition, its authoritarianism weakened a party which counted in its ranks three former Prime Ministers (Kaifu, Hosokawa and Hata) and suffered from a 'surfeit of ambitions'. Ten per cent of its deputies eventually left in the 18 months following its creation.

There was a great deal of public and media scepticism about the Murayama cabinet. However, it was to last 19 months, until January 1996. Its longevity was due in part to the dramatic events that traumatised Japan in 1995 and made a power vacuum unthinkable. On 17 January 1995 the Great Hanshin Earthquake which struck Kôbe was a tragic reminder to Japanese of the fragility of their islands. The disaster left 5,478 dead and more than 26,000 injured. More than 277,000 houses and flats were destroyed or damaged, leaving 316,000 people without shelter. The disaster greatly increased the crisis of confidence in the élites. The state authorities had shown themselves incapable of reacting with the necessary speed; 24 hours had to pass before relief work began to get organised. The Ministry of Construction was discredited by the ineffectiveness of anti-earthquake building standards, and the wide-ranging malpractice revealed by the collapse of numerous structures confirmed the impression of general corruption among construction companies and in the ministry.

On 20 March the terrorist attack with sarin gas in the Tokyo underground railway, carried out by the Aum Shinrykio sect, killed twelve people; 5,500 had to be treated in hospital. Japan was horrified by this indiscriminate violence, and stupefied to learn that the sect's members included students at the best universities – including the National University of Tokyo. Public opinion was perplexed by the attitude of the police, who had let Aum manufacture weapons and accumulate tons of poison, who had botched the investigation after a first sarin attack which had killed nine people in 1994 in the town of Matsumoto, and who were unable to prevent the unexplained murder of the sect's number two (by a *yakuza*) after arresting him. Equally disconcerting were the attitudes of some of the youth, who made a hero of the smart young lawyer who acted as a spokesman for the sect, and of the media, which gave him a disproportionate amount of attention. Japan discovered its 'lost children of modernity', and the bankruptcy of its value system. To complete the traumatising of public opinion, the sudden rocketing in the value of the yen in the spring of 1995 seemed to demonstrate the country's impotence in face of monetary manipulation supposedly orchestrated by the United States, and the first bankruptcies of credit unions in the summer caused panic among savers.

Amid all this, the governorships of Tokyo and Osaka were at stake in local elections in May 1995. All the political establishment parties, except the JCP, agreed to support two common candidates coming from the higher ranks of the civil service. But these 'quasi-official' candidates were crushingly defeated. A strong protest vote elected two independents, Yukio Aoshima in Tokyo and 'Knock' Yokoyama in Osaka. Both had built up their popularity as television stars, in comic acting roles ('Knock' was a clumsy boxer and Aoshima played in drag in a successful series entitled *The Nasty Grandma*). Although both had had long careers in the Upper House, they stood ostensibly as amateurs; Aoshima did not campaign at all and remained at home 'to study to be a good governor', while Yokoyama cycled in the rain to stick up his own posters. Both put themselves forward as 'sons of the local people' and promised to give back to the cities' inhabitants the voice taken away by the élites. They attacked corruption and scandals; Aoshima promised that not a single yen of the Tokyo taxpayer's money would be used to rescue bankrupt financial institutions, and that he would cancel the gigantic Exhibition of the Cities of the World scheme, which thinly concealed lucrative property development deals. The decisive victory of the two 'amateurs' shook the entire world of politics, and the ripples went further; the English-language press had the headline, 'Bring on the Clowns' (*Far Eastern Economic Review*, 20 April). In the same elections little-known young candidates defeated eminent conservatives in many cities – even small ones – and the number of independents elected to prefecture assemblies rose from 409 to 587, out of a total of 2,548. The Communists took control of a town hall for the first time without any alliance, and narrowly failed to win the mayoralty in Kyoto. By this voting local communities clearly manifested their rejection of the establishment and their determination to take affairs back into their own hands.

Two months later, the Upper House elections were a victory for the New Frontier Party, with 34 per cent of the vote and 49 seats (an increase of 21). The LDP only had 22.4 per cent of votes cast, although it increased its seats by 16 at the expense of its ally the SDPJ, which collapsed, getting just 16 per cent of the vote and losing 25 of its 41 seats falling vacant on that occasion. But the most significant fact was probably that the majority of the electorate (55.5 per cent) did not vote. It was the first time that had happened since the war in a national election; that was a measure of the deep discredit into which political life had fallen.

The coalition did not succeed in overcoming this public distrust. Tension rose within the Murayama cabinet. A political crisis was narrowly avoided in August, at the time of the fiftieth anniversary of the end of the Second World War, when the SDPJ insisted that the government should finally make an official apology to Asian countries and admit that Japan had well and truly committed 'aggression' against them in the past. The LDP refused. Murayama threatened to resign and on his own initiative, on the occasion of the official ceremonies marking the anniversary of 15 August 1945, he pronounced the taboo words 'apology' and 'aggression' in a speech in the presence of the Emperor. The LDP made haste to declare that the Prime Minister was not speaking in the name of the government. Finally the Diet adopted by the narrowest majority – 251 votes out of 500 – a motion expressing 'deep remorse' and declaring ambiguously: 'Considering the innumerable cases of colonial domination and aggression in modern history, we acknowledge that Japan also committed such acts.' But the conservative rank and file were furious. In September 1995 the moderate Yôhei Kôno was removed from the chairmanship of the LDP. He was replaced by Ryûtarô Hashimoto, a confirmed nationalist and Chairman of the powerful Association of Veterans and Bereaved Families (Izokukai), who then became Deputy Prime Minister.

It was more than Murayama could bear; he threw in the sponge in January 1996. Hashimoto succeeded him as Prime Minister. His aim was to take advantage of a period when the economy seemed to be bouncing back to dissolve the House as soon as possible. But first he continued the coalition, so that the SDPJ and the Sakigake shared responsibility for several unpopular measures – increasing the purchase tax to 5 per cent to reduce the budget deficit, and voting credits to liquidate the bankrupt *jusen* (see pp. 258–9). The SDPJ was completely adrift; it even accepted the Finance portfolio, which put it in the front line against public protests. After the budget vote Hashimoto had to settle the crisis in Okinawa over the American bases (see p. 332). He dissolved the House immediately afterwards, on 27 September.

Birth of the Democratic Party and the 1996 elections

The prospect of elections panicked the SDPJ and the Sakigake parliamentarians, who lost their souls and their voters in the alliance with the LDP. Even the trade unions now refused to back them. They were ready to grab any lifebelt, and one was thrown to them by two Sakigake parliamentarians: Yukio Hatoyama, the conservative heir, and Naoto Kan, who was from the alternative Left. A veteran of the 1968 student uprising, Kan had taken his first steps in politics during the 1970s as secretary to the leading feminist Fusae Ichikawa and to the then young 'amateur' Yukio Aoshima, who was to become Governor of Tokyo in 1995. A representative for Tokyo since 1980 on the ticket of the small centre-left group Shaminren, he joined the Sakigake in 1993. As Minister of Health and Welfare in 1996, he won instant popularity by forcing his department to open the files on HIV-contaminated blood, which the victims had been requesting in vain for years, and having the people responsible in the ministry and the pharmaceutical groups charged. Hatoyama was born in 1947 and Kan in 1946. They shared the same desire to 'give power to the post-war generation' and the same aversion to a 'straitjacket society'. One week before the dissolution they launched the Democratic Party (Minshutô). Hatoyama brought to the new party a considerable wealth and networks extending all over the élite; Kan brought unrivalled popularity. Socialist and Sakigake House members rushed to join. Hatoyama and Kan closed the door of the new party to senior old-timers, including Takemura and Murayama himself, and the old guard's troops abandoned it without hesitation.

THE DEMOCRATIC PARTY (MINSHUTÔ)

[The preamble to Minshutô's political platform may certainly sound strange to the ears of Western politicians. It looks like a collection of the images and concepts common to the Japanese alternative movement.]

Rejection of the 'vertical' and hierarchical society

For a hundred years, we have had a system built on the centralised and vertical state. Democracy has developed from under bureaucracy's wing. But ... it is now time to build a multipolar, horizontal and cooperative society centred on citizens.

The desire to build a 'brave new world' from the point of view of individuals

Enough with viewing things in a line which only prolongs the past! ... We have decided to act to totally reform this country's social structure ... A hundred years have passed, but the new century is yet to begin. Hence our feeling that society, politics, the economy, foreign affairs, everything is in deadlock.

In modern times ... human beings are treated as a homogeneous mass which may be measured. Capitalism and socialist egalitarianism – the two main ideas which have influenced the world – are rivals in appearance, but they both consider men and women as a faceless mass, and so does Japanese bureaucratic 'egalitarian capitalism'.

A political structure of interactive cyber-networks

Centralised parties are relics of the 20th century. The Minshutô's basic idea is ... to develop a political structure of horizontal networks. In this structure, if someone discovers a problem and proposes a solution, responses will come from all around the web, thus creating 'crossroads'. Once the problem has been solved, the structure will revert to its inital shape. It will resemble the human body's immune system ... In this system...the differences of opinion will be actively debated, each person will confront his/her ideas with others' in order to reach new consensus ... To manage this open political network, we will make massive use of computers. We will be the first generation to practice cyber-democracy as global citizens.

The call for active participation of all citizens

Global citizens will be involved in decision-making at the local, national and global levels, according to their affinities and interests ... The population subjected to politics only votes from time to time. But the citizen who is an actor of politics ... seeks information and thinks for himself; he devotes his money and energy to the attainment of a better life.

A decentralised society of self-reliant communities, a welfare based on voluntary participation, and a new type of 'civic economy'

We advocate a small government, a small parliament, powerful and efficient local authorities ... the transfer of sovereignty from the State to the regions. Social welfare will be strengthened through the active participation of citizens ... The massive industrial production, consumption and pollution generated by the cult of runaway growth ... will give way to the development of ... creative and knowledge-rich small businesses, independent farmers and a civil economy – NGOs and cooperatives.

A 'symbiotic' society, environmentalist version

The spirit of fraternity must underlie future society. Freedom tends to degenerate into ... the law of the jungle and equality into a twisted egalitarianism ... While fraternity is free from these failings, it has been neglected in the last hundred years ... We are all diverse, irreplaceable beings. That is why we have the right to choose our own fate, and the duty to face up to our choices.

We must aspire to symbiosis with others, while respecting each person's autonomy and differences; empathise with others, while cooperating to seek areas of agreement. Autonomy and symbiosis are important also for relations between Japan and the world, and even between human beings and nature. The Christian concept of fraternity neglects the latter relationship. It teaches love of one's neighbour ... but Eastern wisdom teaches us that human beings are part of nature. Trees and animals are as irreplaceable as we are. It is therefore possible to achieve a meaningful exchange between nature and human beings. This is the East's own type of fraternity ... based on empathy with nature and the appreciation of life.

[*This document, then unpublished, was made available to the author in September 1996 by Banri Kaieda, Minshutô's Lower House member for Tokyo. The author takes responsibility for the translation from Japanese and for any faults in it.*]

Public opinion watched these games with distrust. On the eve of the elections more than 80 per cent of citizens declared that they did not trust politicians, and 60 per cent had become 'floating voters' who no longer supported any specific party. The new electoral system was complicated, the boundaries of constituences had been redrawn, and confused voters kept phoning electoral commissions, but also newspapers and even academics, for explanations. Two of the three major contending parties – the NFP and the DP – were completely new. The organisations which had traditionally backed the conservatives – agricultural cooperatives, business groups, doctors' organisations – were divided between the LDP's candidates and the NFP's, and on the unions' side Rengô backed the DP but also some NFP candidates.

Confusion was worsened by the difficulty of seeing any difference between the positions of the contending parties. Yet there was no lack of issues: the economic crisis, deregulation and administrative reform, the growing budget deficit, the purchase tax, the outstanding bill from the years of speculation which taxpayers were refusing to pay, and social security reform to cope with the ageing population. Even the antiquated polemics over the Security Treaty were suddenly revived by the Okinawa events (see p. 332). But public opinion did not trust the politicians any more, and especially not Ozawa, who was now campaigning against the increase of the purchase tax to 5 per cent whereas he had favoured raising it to 10 per cent when his RP was in the government. To complete the confusion, the issues telescoped: deregulation threatened many interests, but the public loved the anti-bureaucracy rhetoric; citizens shrank from tax increases, but wanted the budget deficit cut. Now all the candidates had themselves photographed cycling like 'Knock' Yokoyama and shouted 'Rejuvenate! Deregulate! Decentralise!' – while spending as much money as ever.

The elections took place on 20 October 1996. As in the Upper House elections the preceding year, there was massive abstention; at 40.3 per cent it had risen 14 points over two elections to reach its post-war record for parliamentary elections. It reached its peak in the big cities, and this was a failure for the DP, which had betted on the urban floating vote. However, Hashimoto did not win his own bet that he would regain an absolute majority for the LDP: with 239 seats (a rise of 28), it was still 11 short. Thanks to the solid patronage bases established by its incumbents, the government party carried over 169 of the 300 local constituencies, but it won only 32.8 per cent of the proportional representation vote – less than 20 per cent of the electorate, with abstention taken into account. The NFP, which had campaigned for nothing less than winning a majority, was brought down to earth with a bump; it lost four seats, leaving it with 156, and only won 28 per cent of the proportional representation vote, compared with 34 per cent in the 1995 Upper House elections. This was a crushing personal defeat for Ozawa who, in a style completely new to Japan, centred the whole NFP campaign around his person. The DP barely managed to keep its 52 seats. It had been created too short a time before polling, and was unable to field candidates in more than half of the local constituencies, where it won only 17 seats, while its rather poor showing in the proportional representation vote (16.7 per cent) disappointed hopes. The SDPJ only had 15 survivors, the Sakigake two. The protest vote gave the Communist Party an unprecedented success; it increased its share of the vote from 7.7 to 13 per cent. But as it was almost impossible for the JCP to win in the local constituencies, it only had 26 deputies, an increase of 11. Because of double candidacies, incumbents succeeded very well: 88.5 per cent of LDP deputies seeking re-election won – even more than under the former electoral system. The hope that proportional representation would bring new blood into the body politic was disappointed. The parties drew up their lists with incumbent members, notables supported by farmers' cooperatives, Chambers of Industry or trade unions and a few apparatchiks – except for a few symbolic figures such as Kyokudôzan, a popular sumô wrestler, who ran for the NFP, or the leader of the haemophiliacs contaminated by HIV for the DP. And in contrast with what had happened in the Upper House elections since 1983, no small protest party succeeded in taking advantage of the new system to get into the House.

After the polls, Hashimoto formed a homogeneous LDP government with the 'support without participation' of the remnants of the SDPJ and the Sakigake. Although the LDP was still in the minority in both houses of the Diet, it could count on the impotence of the opposition. In the DP, Kan and Hatoyama disagreed on strategy. The former favoured negotiating support for the government on a case-by-case basis in exchange for some reforms, while the latter feared that the party would lose its soul by doing so. As for the NFP, it soon began to disintegrate. Five of its deputies set up Group 21, 12 others the Party of the Sun (Taiyotô) led by Hata, while others began to drift towards the LDP.

The LDP on the way back to hegemony?

In the June 1997 elections for the Tokyo Regional Assembly the NFP lost all its seats. The party could not keep going, and it soon officially disbanded. It gave birth to no less than five groups – the Liberal Party, the New Peace Party, the Voice of the People, the New Party of Harmony and the Reform Club. After months of confusion, 22 former NPP legislators joined the LDP, which thus regained an absolute majority in the House; 41 joined the DP, which became the leading opposition force with 93 deputies; 42 resurrected the Kômeitô under the name of New Kômeitô. Those faithful to Ozawa formed the Liberal Party, with 43 seats. This confusion further increased public distrust of politics.

Having regained control of the Lower House, the LDP hoped to retake the Senate in the 1998 elections. But contrary to predictions, it lost 15 seats, ending up with 103, and won only 25 per cent of the proportional representation vote, with the DP hard on its heels (21.7 per cent). This failure was all the more significant in that there was a fairly high turnout of 58 per cent, compared with 44.5 per cent in 1995. The urban voters and the young mobilised against the government party, which was trounced in the big cities, winning no seats at all in Tokyo, Yokohama, Nagoya, Osaka or Kobe, and was saved from the worst only by the rural prefectures. But the opposition had no cause to celebrate. With 47 seats (a rise of only six) the DP still controlled less than 20 per cent of the Senate and no more in the House. All the other parties lost ground except the JCP, which continued its steady progress since 1993 by winning 13.8 per cent of the vote and 23 seats, nine more than before. The disenchanted voters also leaned towards independent candidates, who made it their business to denounce the political establishment.

This setback forced Ryûtarô Hashimoto to resign. The LDP then chose Keizô Obuchi, not quite a charismatic politician. After an American journalist derided him for having 'as much pizzas as a cold pizza', the phrase became popular around Japan, and the new cabinet started with a popularity rating of no more than 30 per cent. But the new Prime Minister showed himself to be very skilled at manoeuvring. In three months he succeeded in securing the DP's support for the much awaited rescue plan for the banks. In accepting the use of taxpayers' money in this way, the main opposition party reneged, and its divisions deepened between its right wing coming from the LDP and the former neo-conservatives and its socialist-leaning left wing. In the May 1999 local elections the Democrats joined in the traditional game of Japanese politics by allying everywhere with the conservatives to support common candidates. Only in Tokyo did they dare to put forward their own candidate – Hatoyama's own brother, who won only 15 per cent of the vote. Hatoyama's prestige was badly damaged as a result, while Kan's was tarnished by the revelation of an extramarital affair – another novelty in a country where politicians' private lives had traditionally been a taboo subject. The DP lost its credibility and its support among the public collapsed from 28 per cent in the summer of 1998 to just 7 per cent in May 1999, while the LDP's rose in the same period from 28 to 36 per cent.

Obuchi had broadened his parliamentary base by reaching an agreement with Ozawa's Liberal Party and giving it the Home Affairs Ministry (January 1999), but this coalition was still ten seats short in the Senate. Obuchi then successfully wooed the New Kômeitô, which had 24. The Buddhists entered the government in September. The opposition was thus reduced to the DP and the JCP, with less than 25 per cent of the seats in the Diet, and the LDP became master of the game again. At the price of merely cosmetic concessions, the conservatives were now able to get the most controversial bills through. In only four months the Diet passed new guidelines for wider military cooperation with the USA, introduced a hotly contested bill creating a national identification number for all Japanese citizens to give the public authorities better access to information on anyone, and authorised the police to resort to telephone tapping. The government even felt strong enough to tackle the most sensitive subjects head on: in July 1999 the *Hinomaru* and *Kimigayo* were made officially the national emblems by law, and the House set up a permanent Research Council to study amendment of the Constitution.

The LDP may have shown overconfidence, as at the time of triumphant conservatism under the Nakasone government. The alliance with the Kômeitô embarrassed many Diet members who knew well that public opinion disliked the Sôkagakkai. Ozawa was trying every trick to push the government to the right, to the dismay of the LDP's moderate wing and many in his own Liberal party, which broke up: Ozawa led 18 Liberal Diet members out of the coalition, while 20 others set up the New Conservative Party (NCP) which remained in the government. Amidst this uncertainty, Obuchi had a sudden brain haemorrhage in April 2000. The public was kept in the dark while party elders arranged the succession in top secrecy. This return to the old 'smoke-filled room politics' infuriated the media. To make things worse, Yoshirô Mori, the new Prime Minister, born in 1937, quickly showed how far he was out of touch with contemporary Japanese society. To the utmost astonishment of many, he boasted publicly of 'Japan the Land of Gods, with the Emperor at its centre', and of the country's *kokutai* (national essence) – a term typical of the militarist era, which no politician had ever dared use since 1945. In a single month his popularity rating collapsed from 40 to 19 per cent, and it never rose again.

The parliamentary elections of 25 June 2000 were a clear repudiation of the governing coalition. The LDP lost 38 seats, the (not so) New Kômeitô 11 out of 42, and the NCP 13 out of 20, while the Democrats swept two thirds of the seats in Tokyo and got 127 in all. Even though the coalition remained well in control, it had been badly shaken. The Prime Minister's popularity rating kept sliding until it reached the single-digit level. Under pressure from the media and the LDP's backbenchers, the party bigwigs finally discarded the beleaguered Mori in April 2001. They had planned for Hashimoto to come back as his successor, but the party's local chapters and rank-and-file Diet members rose in revolt and chose the maverick Junichirô Koizumi through primaries. A divorced man with an avowed liking for rock music and flashy neckties, an expert at playing the media game and a forceful advocate of pro-market structural reforms, Koizumi had run for the premiership twice without success, in 1996 and 1998. His image as a 'lone wolf' and a 'Don Quixote' had made him very popular, and he was greeted by a massive 80 per cent popularity rating – the highest ever in the political history of Japan.

Koizumi might eventually reconcile the LDP and the urban, modern electorate. But even if the LDP manages to keep its control over the central government, it has to confront a growing movement for autonomy among local communities where citizens fed up with the parties try to deepen democracy in their own way.

Towards a new political equilibrium: the challenge of local communities

In Japan the local and national élites have been kept separate by the ban on plurality of public offices and by the large number of quasi-hereditary seats in the Diet, which stopped local politicians getting in there. The rivalry between the two groups played a major role in political change when Hosakawa exploited it by recruiting NJP candidates for the 1993 elections widely among local conservative assembly members. Masayoshi Takemura, the founder of the Sakigake, also embodied the prototype of the provincial leader full of common sense and good will, tested in the field as Governor of a disadvantaged prefecture, who did not hesitate to challenge the national élites as far as Tokyo. However, the two new parties' success was short-lived. The NJP broke up as early as 1994, the Sakigake disappeared following the 1996 parliamentary elections, and Takemura and Hosokawa both retired from politics.

Having thus failed to 'go up to Tokyo', local politicians tried to bring the power down to them. Like deregulation, decentralisation became a highly popular theme, which no party dared to oppose head on. It came just after electoral reform in the Hosokawa government's programme. On returning to power the LDP could not bury it. It had to get a (carefully toned down) decentralisation law passed, which allocated no new tax revenue to local communities while transferring new responsibilities to them, and giving them, at least in principle, more freedom to organise their administrative departments according to their own convenience. This very timid law was not to end the debate, and the LDP had to bring in a new one – hardly more innovative – in 1998. But it did not succeed in defusing the movement of citizens who were displaying with a new determination their will to assert vis-à-vis the central government their will to run their own affairs, using the most varied means to do so.

The weapon of the local referendum began to be used. As early as 1988 the Hokkaido anti-nuclear movement mustered more than 900,000 signatures of voters in the region, much more than were necessary legally to force the prefecture assembly to pronounce on a petition for a referendum on a nuclear plant. The assembly only refused by a majority of one vote. But in August 1996 the inhabitants of the small town of Maki, in Niigata prefecture, voting on their Mayor's initiative, made headlines by rejecting the building of a nuclear power station in their district. The following month, the whole of Okinawa island was summoned by its Governor to vote on the American military bases there – and asked that they be removed by an overwhelming majority (89 per cent). In December 1997, also in Okinawa, the inhabitants of the town of Nago rejected a plan to build a new heliport for US forces despite intense pressure from the conservative town council and from the Ministry of Defence, whose officials went from door to door to urge voters to back the project. Between 1996 and 2000 there were ten local referenda in the country, almost all about environmental questions. Such a referendum can be organised by the local executive as in Maki and Okinawa, or on the initiative of voters who present a petition calling for it to the local assembly – if the assembly accepts it. They have no binding force; at Nago, despite the negative vote, the mayor restated his determination to build the heliport. But they give local protest a legitimacy that forces the state authorities to give in to them as at Maki, or else to negotiate: Okinawa did not succeed in removing the US army, but it won a comfortable package of subsidies and a promise that one of the biggest bases would be moved. The increasing number of such referenda has put the establishment in a cold sweat – to the point where the mere mention of a village referendum caused the powerful Kyûshû Electricity Company to drop a plan for a nuclear plant altogether (1997).

Another weapon available to local authorities is adopting regulations to satisfy demands that the central government refuses to consider. That strategy had already been used by progressive local authorities during the 1970s, especially in social policy and against pollution. In the 1990s more and more prefectures and big cities made studies of the impact of major projects on the environment compulsory, to the dismay of the MITI, or recognised residents' 'right to information' by agreeing to communicate the most varied administrative documents to them. As in the 1970s the government was obliged to follow suit, and a law on the right to information was passed in 1998. Also, following the authorisation given by the Ministry of Health and Welfare for marketing of genetically modified vegetables in 1996, more than 2,000 of the 3,233 local authorities petitioned against it, thus obliging the government to pass hastily a law making ingredient labelling mandatory.

Some communities went over to open disobedience. In 1985 the progressive city government of Kawasaki had shown the way when it refused to continue fingerprinting foreigners, despite repeated orders from the Police Agency; similarly it rejected the government's objections to the employment of foreigners as local government staff. In 1996 the Governor of Okinawa followed suit by refusing to act as a substitute for the recalcitrant landowners who refused to renew the leases of their land for the American bases; he rejected repeated orders from Prime Minister Hashimoto, who had to get a Supreme Court order to make him give in. As the crisis and the scandals undermined the legitimacy of the national élites, the local communities' challenge became more and more resolute. In 1995 the election of Yukio Aoshima and 'Knock' Yokoyama as Governors of the two biggest prefectures in Japan was a striking sign of their inhabitants' refusal to be governed by representatives seconded from the central government. In 1999, during the long parliamentary debate on the extension of military cooperation between Japan and the United States (see pp. 334–5), the government had to cope with the intrusion of local bodies even into foreign policy, when a number of assemblies in coastal regions adopted resolutions banning the bringing of nuclear weapons into their territory – meaning, by the ships of the US Seventh Fleet.

Nonetheless, at the end of the decade, the government party seemed to be containing the local protest movement. In 1998 its candidate defeated the outgoing Governor of Okinawa, who had organised the referendum against the American bases, and the two most important petitions ever seen for referenda – against the building of an international airport in Kôbe and a dam at Yoshino (Tokushima prefecture) – were overwhelmingly rejected by the local assemblies, even though they had collected hundreds of thousands of signatures. In Tokyo and Osaka Aoshima and 'Knock' Yokoyama were under siege by local assemblies still dominated by the conservatives, so much so that Aoshima decided not to run again in 1999. Yokoyama got re-elected, but soon afterwards he was trapped in a *sekuhara* (sexual harassment) scandal, and resigned in disgrace. Because of the economic crisis and falling tax revenue, most regions and big cities were on the verge of bankruptcy, and since they needed the central government's authorisation to raise loans, their protest impulses seemed bound to decline.

But the protest campaigners proved indomitable. In Kôbe the opponents of the airport took their case to court. In Yoshino the anti-dam protesters won a hard-fought battle for a majority in the local assembly in 1999 and a referendum followed, which resulted in 90 per cent of the 113,000 voters saying 'No' to the scheme and left the Ministry of Construction fuming. Furthermore, the move of local voters towards populist, independent governors vowing to 'get rid of political parties and central government interference' and 'give back power to local people' continued unabated: Tokyo went to Ishihara Shintarô in 1999 (see p. 318), then Nagano to the writer and famous womaniser Yasuo Tanaka; three of the seemingly most secure LDP fiefs – Tochigi, Akita and Chiba – had also fallen by the end of 2001.

These local communities' efforts at emancipation were just one expression of a wider phenomenon. After the relative decline in militancy in the 1980s, protest action rose up again with new forms and new aims in Japanese civil society, and is still rising, despite some setbacks.

RETURN TO CONTESTATION AND CHANGES IN THINKING

The right to know, the right to act

What the rush for local referenda and populist governors revealed was the determination of citizens to express themselves directly. In polls conducted by the media on the occasion of the 50th anniversary of the Constitution, in 1997, the two amendments most often desired by people were those that would allow direct expressions of popular will: national referenda on popular initiative (as in Italy) and choice of the prime minister by popular election (as in Israel). Meanwhile citizens went to court with increased determination, sometimes successfully, while even if unsuccessful their lawsuits gained media attention. Even the old-fashioned direct action came back into fashion in 1992 during the campaign against the Peace Keeping Operations (PKO) law, whose opponents spoke out in the streets and organised demonstrations and sit-ins on a large scale. The same methods were used by the haemophiliac victims of HIV-contaminated blood, and in the 1995–96 campaign against the American bases – whose spontaneity and strength were a complete surprise (see p. 332).

The right to information (*jôho kôhai*) was the issue in a number of actions begun by citizens to obtain access to administrative documents, ranging from school report books to medical records and – above all – local community budgets. In 1995 the courts granted citizens, for the first time, the right to know details of the implementation of prefecture budgets. Self-styled 'citizen ombudsman' organisations sprang up all over Japan, and the result was a flood of revelations about officials' expensive meals and local representatives' luxurious 'study trips' at the taxpayer's expense. The Governor of Akita resigned after the discovery of serious abuses, while in Hokkaido and Tokyo the prefecture administration hastily refunded considerable sums. As Health and Welfare Minister in 1996, Naoto Kan built his popularity on the opening of administrative files relating to the HIV-contaminated blood case. Even the closed and ultra-conservative world of sumô wrestling had to promise in 1998 to unveil the list of those who held the very profitable rights to serve as stablemasters. Against this background many local communities enacted ordinances of their own that gave their inhabitants a more or less extensive right to information. The 'citizen ombudsmen', including a number of lawyers, extended their demands to the most sensitive items on the local budget – tenders for public works. The LDP was forced to get a bill which has been 'under study' for twenty years passed in 1998. This law took great care to limit freedom of information in a number of very vaguely worded cases – for example, if it could 'be prejudicial to the legitimate profit of a private enterprise', or 'impair frank discussion among the official concerned' or 'interfere with the action of government institutions'. It also placed obstacles in the way of judicial proceedings against a government department refusing access to documents. Thus the new law did not put an end to the movement for *jôho kôhai*, while reinforcing its legitmacy.

Consumer protection also made progress through the courts. In 1994 Matsushita Electrics was condemned to pay damages to the victim of an implosion in a television set, even though the plaintiff had not been able to prove formally that the manufacturer had been guilty of bad workmanship. This decision was a revolution, since the jurisprudence had until then laid the entire burden of proof on victims. Here again the government had to follow suit, despite the reluctance of the MITI and the employers' organisations. In 1995 a law strengthened the principle of the manufacturer's responsibility, while avoiding making it too easy for the consumer to go to court – encouraging him rather to turn to 'conciliation commissions' where the producers are over-represented. But the consumer was learning to defend himself by other means. In 1999 an ill-used customer forced the Vice-Chairman of the very powerful Toshiba group to apologise to him publicly, after spreading his complaints over the Internet to six million people in a few weeks. In 2000 Mitsubishi Motors had to face a similar action, which ended with the firm being punished by the administration and its market share plunging.

Against discrimination: women and foreigners

The struggle against discrimination revived. Leaving the great battles behind, women's movements now attacked everyday sexism, like the traditional practice of girls being listed after boys in school roll-call books. They demanded the right to keep their maiden names after marriage, and were supported on this point by the government Administrative Council which worked on a revision of the Civil Code in 1996; however, the issue has been stalled in the Diet since then. The first conviction in a sexual harassment case was pronounced in 1991. That did not stop a popular daily from publishing in 1996 a successful series of 140 articles entitled 'I love sexual harassment', with no legal problems; but legal actions multiplied, and the highest damages awarded reached 7.7 million yen in 1999, prompting the government to issue anti-sexist directives which banned officials from asking their women colleagues to serve them tea, as well as from asking them about their sex lives. Then, in 2000, Osaka's Governor resigned because

INTERNATIONALISATION

The number of foreign residents in Japan grew from 941,000 in 1988 to 1,556,000 in 1999. Koreans who willingly or forcibly came to work in Japan before 1945 and gained permanent resident status after the war for themselves and their offspring amounted to 72 per cent of the whole foreign population in 1988; they now account for only 40.9 per cent (636,000). The Chinese community became the second largest during the 1990s – about 294,000 people (19 per cent). The South American of Japanese ancestry are almost as numerous, since they can freely enter Japan to work; most of them are from Brazil (224,000, as against only 4,000 in 1988).

Most of the other foreign residents are Asian, especially Filipinos (115,000, or 7.4 per cent). The Caucasians account for no more than 7 per cent, about half of them American (43,000) or British (15,000). The number of Japanese marrying foreigners in Japan multiplied during the 1980s – from 7,000 a year to more than 25,000 – but it levelled off afterward (29,500 in 1999). Still, it represents almost 4 per cent of all the marriages registered in Japan. In more than half of the cases, bride or groom is either Korean or Chinese.

About 100,000 people now enter Japan every year for the first time, for the purpose of work, many of them Asian trainees under the supervision of the Japanese International Cooperation Agency.

Nakasone's grand plan for raising the number of foreign students in Japan from 25,000 in 1988 to 100,000 by the year 2,000 failed, because fellowships are scarce, cost of living high and academic standards below those of many American or European universities. In 1998 there were only 51,000 foreign students in Japan, 75 per cent of them Chinese or Korean – part of whose came to Japan to work illegally under the guise of studying Japanese language in private schools.

Source: Japan Almanac 2001, Asahi Shimbun.

of a *sekuhara* scandal and was replaced by the first-ever female governor in Japan. Lastly, women's movements rose in revolt when the Ministry of Health, which had been 'studying' the question of the contraceptive pill for almost half a century, took less than six months to authorise putting Viagra on the market. The outcry, extensively relayed in the media, forced the bureaucracy to finally give the go-ahead to the pill.

On the political level, from 1993 onward women were now in the government almost as a matter of course – but only one at a time, except for Hosokawa's and Hata's cabinets which each had two, and in minor posts – and Takako Doi became Speaker of the House in 1993. In the 1999 local elections, an unprecedented number of women were elected: 6.2 per cent of the total, compared with only 3 per cent in 1991, and a record 14 per cent in the city councils of the 12 biggest cities. In 2000 the first ever woman was elected governor, in Osaka, and was soon followed by two others, and 33 women entered the House, compared with 12 in 1990. Lastly, Koizumi appointed five women among his 17 ministers in April 2001, and gave the prestigious Foreign Ministry to the popular Makiko Tanaka, daughter of the late Kakuei Tanaka.

The number of foreigners living in Japan increased regularly (see Box, p. 307). In 1999 there were officially 1,556,000, or 1.22 per cent of the population – plus illegal immigrants estimated to number between 200,000 and 400,000. Permanent foreign residents won their long fight over fingerprinting, and after the Kawasaki city council opened some local government jobs to them the central government was forced gradually to follow suit, and notably to authorise the employment of Korean residents as full-time teachers at state schools. In 1999 the pupils of foreign schools in Japan – mostly the Korean ones – were allowed to take the national universities' entrance examinations. Even giving foreign residents the right to vote in municipal elections was considered; a Finn naturalised as a Japanese citizen became in 1995 the first foreigner to be elected a municipal councillor, and then ran unsuccessfully for the Diet. Even the Ainus of Hokkaido, to whom Japan had always refused any recognition so as to preserve the myth of its 'ethnic homogeneity', secured a law which recognised them as a separate group – although it does not provide any protection for them as such – after one of them had been elected to the Upper House in 1995.

Environmental protest: a new spirit

The struggle for protection of the environment continued unabated. Between 1991 and 1997 five lawsuits pending since the late 1970s against carbon dioxide pollution of the atmosphere in Osaka, Chiba, Kanagawa and Okayama ended in victory for the plaintiffs. Significantly, the companies sued preferred to compromise after their conviction at first instance rather than continue to the end a fight that was tarnishing their public image. In 1995, a court recognised, for the first time, the responsibility of the state authorities in a lawsuit claiming nuisance produced by a motorway, and the Murayama government brought the dramatic Minamata case to a close: forty years after it started, after 28 years of judicial process, the state authorities – without officially admitting their responsibility – paid compensation of 2.6 million yen to each one of the 9,439 certified victims and about 5 billion yen to five representative bodies, in exchange for the dropping of all legal actions. This offer was accepted.

The anti-pollution movement is now turning away from its defensive character. Going beyond problems of damages, it seeks to become a positive-thinking force working to rebuild communities ravaged by pollution in accordance with new principles: direct control of pollution by the inhabitants themselves and redevelopment in accordance with principles of town planning aimed at encouraging neighbourhood spirit. The objective of the new lawsuits started is now no longer to repair damage but to prevent it occurring from implementation of industrial or infrastructure schemes – and local referenda are a new, powerful means of doing so.

'Going international' is something new for the Japanese protest movements, which had until then remained rather parochial. More and more organisations are establishing links with similar movements overseas, and are helping get protests organised in Asia, notably against damage to the environment caused by Japanese firms. Among many others, the anti-pollution movement in Osaka – where 19,000 certified victims of pollution live – wants to start a 'citizens' university' aimed at sharing its experience internationally, and the self-managed consumer cooperative Green Coop, to which 250,000 households in Kyûshû belong, set up a sister cooperative in Korea.

Down with the straitjacket! New social utopias

Self-managed consumer cooperatives are among the most successful examples of the 'new social movements' in contemporary

Japan. Established under the names of Life Clubs in the Tokyo-Yokohama region and Green Coop in Kyûshû, they arose from the first cases of food pollution in the late 1960s and from the 1968 students' movement. Today about 500,000 households belong to them. Their objective goes well beyond the distribution of more or less biological products. They try to spread a new social culture based on an ideal of 'small cooperative communities' (*kumiai chikki shakai*), whose inhabitants would take charge of their own daily lives, to remove them from the commercial logic of capitalism. For that purpose, for some years the Life Clubs and Green Coop developed small self-managed enterprises called 'workers' collectives' and mutual aid bodies, including insurance companies and even funeral parlours. After growing for about thirty years in relative obscurity, these cooperatives became more visible with the creation in 1979 of a political arm, the NET (short for 'network'), whose task was to get their voice heard in the local assemblies. In 1998 NET women councillors – as a matter of principle the movement puts forward only women as candidates – were sitting on the Tokyo and Kanagawa prefecture assemblies and 67 city councils including five of the dozen biggest cities (Sapporo, Chiba, Yokohama, Kawasaki and Fukuoka). The movement was brought to the front of the political stage with Naoto Kan, who had close relations with it. And it was no accident that the DP's political programme spectacularly adopted their language and their ideas on organisation of society 'in horizontal networks' and self-management (see pp. 294–5).

The general development of the value system towards rejection of constraints and of traditional social authority lay behind all these changes. The bestseller of 1996 was *Straitjacket Society* by Masao Miyamoto, an official of the Ministry of Health dismissed the preceding year, who described from the inside a childish and inefficient bureaucratic world constrained by oppressive and absurd rules of behaviour. To describe the society of the future the two fashionable words were *nettowaku* (network) and *kyôsei* (symbiosis). The former described a flexible and voluntary association of autonomous, equal actors. The latter rejected all forms of authoritarian and uniformity-imposing integration, any order based on balance of forces, and what they valued most was respect for difference and mutual enrichment through harmonious interaction. This change of mind was displayed in all sectors of social life. In family matters, the age of marriage increased constantly, reaching 27.6 for women and 30 for men in 1998. Many Japanese now avoided it for as long as possible; in 1992 20 per cent of men between 35 and 39 were still single. The number of divorces constantly increased from 20 per 100 marriages in 1990 to almost 30 in 1998 and came near the average for OECD countries (34), while the number of cases exceeded 200,000 for the first time in 1996 and reached 243,000 two years later. Increasingly women rejected the role of consenting victims in mutual-agreement separations which often left them without a house or alimony, and instead went to court. The tradition that children must care for their aged parents remained strong – in 1992 about 60 per cent of Japanese of over 65 still lived with one of their children – but apart from the fact that this figure was increased by material considerations such as the cost of housing, it was 10 points lower than in 1980. Over the same period the percentage of old people living alone rose by half, from 10 to 15 per cent (about 2,720,000 people). However, society was ageing at an ever faster rate as the number of children per woman continued to fall: 1.75 in 1985, 1.5 in 1992, and 1.34 in 1999.

In the schooling system, another bastion of the authoritarian social model, protest action has attacked the wearing of uniforms, stringent internal rules which went as far as laying down the type of haircut, and the arbitrariness of decisions on pupils' orientation made by teachers on the basis of appraisals not communicated to the families. There again families no longer hesitate to go to court. In the world of work, young salary-earners jib at following dress codes and rituals of obsequious politeness towards their superiors. The majority assert that they no longer wish to spend all their lives in the same company. As a sign of the times, while one of the older staff of the Dai-Ichi Bank involved with professional racketeers decided to commit suicide, after the Daiwa Bank's dispute with the US authorities, the young broker responsible preferred for his part to heap dirt on his superiors in a best-seller. Even in sport the success of soccer, for which a national championship was set up in 1993, expressed this new spirit; tired of the 'straitjacket' metronome of baseball teams, soccer fans were now aroused to passion over the individual exploits of the stars developing in multiracial teams (i.e. Japanese teams with foreign players).

Japan sinks! A society under stress

This general questioning of the value system, combined with the unending economic crisis and the traumas of the Kôbe earthquake and the Aum sect, caused anxiety and collective stress. A succession of grisly incidents aggravated this climate of anxiety: the murder of two small girls and then of an 11-year-old schoolboy by 'Boy A' – a teenager of 14 who placed his last victim's severed head, adorned with a rose, in front of his school (Kôbe, 1997); a series of knife fights in schools, one teacher and two pupils being killed in 1998; a mass cyanide poisoning during a town festival in Wakayama prefecture (1998); the carefully staged suicide of three small businessmen who were victims of the crisis (Tokyo, 1998); the spectacular murder of the mother of the *aidoru* (young singing star) Amie Namuro by her brother-in-law (Okinawa, 1999); the butchering, by two brothers in their early teens using baseball bats, of their mother because she was late in cooking the dinner (1999); the fatal stabbing of an old woman by a college student who just wished to see 'what it was like to kill somebody', and then the cutting of another old woman's throat by a junior high school pupil who hijacked a bus in Kyûshû (2000) – among others.

As a result public opinion expressed fears that were often out of proportion to reality. The media fanned the flames by their sensationalism. Although Japan remains one of the most secure countries in the world, a few incidents were enough for the newspapers to splash headlines about 'the revolver society' (*jûshakai*) or the 'knife society'. And while the lack of inhibition regarding sex is a traditional feature of Japanese culture, the media highlighted the behaviour of a minority of schoolgirls who practised various forms of sexual activity, from recycling their used knickers to dating middle-aged men for money – a practice known as 'mutual aid' (*enjô kosai*) and said to be practised by 5 per cent of high school girls. In this situation pessimism and self-punishment were the fashion, fed by the contrast between Japan's crisis and 'greying' and the rebounding of the US economy. Among many examples, in 1994, in her widely read article 'The Japanese Syndrome' the sociologist Mariko Sugihara wrote that 'we can only hope that Japan will have the time to light its last firework before going under', while the leading economic daily *Nihon Keizai* published forecasts that the country would enter its final recession around 2020 (see Box, p. 271).

Reacting to stress: leaders, religions, NGO and movies

Public reactions to the crisis showed contrasts. The need for leaders gave passing popularity to almost any politician with a strongman (or woman) image and outspoken tongue, such as Ozawa, Koizumi and Makiko Tanaka. The same need explained why Tokyo's voters, disappointed by the soft 'amateur' Aoshima, chose the hardened neo-nationalist veteran Shintarô Ishihara to succeed him as Governor in 1999. Escape urges brought fortunes to shops dealing in old magic on the one hand and to high-tech virtual reality – from Keiko Date, the virtual woman singer on the Internet, to the virtual chick (*tamagochi*) and Sony's Aibo robot companion dog – on the other. Disorientation could also take dangerous forms, as in the Aum Shinrikyô sect. But Aum, with its few thousand followers, was only a small group among the 'neo-new religions' that appeared in the 1980s and flourished especially among the young citizens. A few years were enough for the Ma-Hikari Kyôdan (True Light Sect), Kôfuku no Kagaku (Science of Happiness) and Agon-shû (called after a Buddhist Sutra) to have over a million followers each. They are radically different from the earlier ones like the Sôkagakkai, in their relaxed, festive and convivial aspect, very comfortable for their followers. Some offer a highly coloured and dramatic image of the cosmos, with confrontations among souls, angels and devils that resemble video games or *manga* comics. Others are involved in occultism and the bric-à-brac of magic. They no longer recruit among the people 'left behind by growth' as in the 1950s, but among students and the new categories of relatively favoured urban wage earners. Their founders also come from those same categories – the founder of Kôfuku no Kagaku even went to the élite National University of Tokyo. What these followers – young, hedonistic and not very faithful – expect from a religion that they adopt 'on trial' for shorter or longer periods is that it should teach them how to get more, and faster, from the society in which they live.

Another form of reaction against the stress is a need to participate and dedicate oneself. It was highlighted spectacularly by the rush of volunteers to Kôbe after the earthquake. In one year, according to the media, more than 1.4 million people came from all over the country to offer their help to the victims – although, admittedly, some of them went there out of curiosity. The same phenomenon recurred in 1997 for cleaning up the coasts of Ishikawa prefecture, polluted by an oil slick. The enthusiasm for the 'volunteer movement' (*boruntiâ katsudô*) was expressed in the growing multitude of non-governmental and non-profit organisations of all sorts, which went so far that the government set about regulating this proliferation. In 1999 the LDP had a law passed to establish non-profit organisations (NPOs) on a firmer basis. Ostensibly intended to favour their development, the legislation aimed – according to a strategy of winning over, a favourite one of the conservative élites throughout the post-war era – to allow the administration to 'help and advise' those spontaneous movements of civil society. Furthermore, the law did not provide any tax incentives for those willing to fund NPOs, and it retained as a principle the right for the administration to decide which NPO applying is 'of public interest'. The movements therefore greeted it with suspicion.

Cultural life also reflected the changing times. The questioning of certainties led to a revival of creativity. Japan won its second Nobel Prize for Literature – awarded to Kenzaburô Oé in 1994 – and its third Palme d'Or at Cannes, awarded to Shôhei Imamura in 1997 for *The Eel*. The work of those two prizewinners owed very little to traditional 'Japanese values'. The conservatives accused both of not loving their country, on the pretext that they gave a critical view of it, as Imamura had done in his previous Palme d'Or-winning film *The Ballad of Narayama* (1982), which painted a very grim picture of the traditional village. Furthermore, in Stockholm, Oé chose to give his speech in English, and entitled it 'The Uncertain Japan and Myself', as a deliberate contrast to the speech by Kawabata in the same circumstances in 1968 and entitled 'The Proud Japan and Myself'. Conservatives were also shocked when the Akutagawa Prize was awarded in 1997 to a young Korean woman of Japan, Yu Miri, whose *Family Cinema* described the decay of a family. Ultra-nationalist groups reacted by banning her, with threats, from holding any public lectures and autograph sessions.

Japanese cinema revived amidst the crisis and the climate of questioning. The leading studios now accounted for less than half of the films produced, since a new generation of young film makers was able to obtain funding from independent, adventurous producers and from the numerous satellite television channels through which new industrial groups entered the communications sector. The flagbearers of this new generation were Juzô Itami and an iconoclastic entertainer from television, Takeshi 'Beat' Kitano, who enjoyed complete freedom because of his immense popularity, and whose *Hanna-bi* (Fireworks) was awarded the Golden Lion at the Venice Festival in 1997. Many of their works were bitter-sweet meditations on the present time, with titles often in English. They spoke of foreigners living in Japan, like Mitsuo Yamaguchi's *About Love, Tokyo*, which portrayed Chinese students trying and failing to find their Japanese dream, or Yoichi Sai's *All Under the Moon*, about a Korean taxi driver. Many others depict in pessimistic, melancholic or ironic tone the downhill path of young people outside the social mould (Kitano's *Kids Return*), the blues of a *yakuza* who realises the emptiness of his life (Kitano's *Sonatine*), the melancholy of the *sarariman* who finds out that 'just working is not living' (Masayaki Suô's *Shall We Dance?*), or the erotic frustration of teenagers and homosexuality (Ryosuke Hashiguchi's *Grains of Sand*). Some deride institutions and customs in a *manga*-like fashion, like Masayuki Suô's *Sumô Do, Sumô Don't*, which pokes fun at the 'living gods' of sumô through the comical adventures of a university club. Others look at the crude reality of life, like Juzô Itami (*The Woman of the Supermarket*, about the distribution industry) and Naomi Kawase, the first Japanese woman to make a name for herself in the cinema, whose *Suzaku* depicts the depopulation of the countryside which destroys families. In the same vein, Fumio Yamazaki's *Dying at the Hospital* follows the progress of five cancer patients to their deaths. But the biggest box-office successes of the crisis years were *Mononoke Hime* (Princess Mononoke, 1997), an animated film by Hayao Miyazaki, whose main theme is the clash between two opposite models of civilisation, which comes to a more or less happy end through the prospect of a future 'symbiosis' of a sort; and, in a more sombre tone, the young Kiyoshi Kurosawa's *Charisma* (1992), a gory millenniarist fable set against a background of witchcraft, nature and nonsense.

'Nice new nationalism', 'Asian values' and revisionism: Nihonjinron revived

Disorientation also benefited neo-nationalism, whose following spread in different forms. The search for both lost identity and a way out of the crisis led to a 'Meiji Era Boom': academics turned to Japan's first modernisation to learn how it succeeded in adapting Western models without sacrificing its 'national soul'. Eisuke 'Mr Yen' Sakakibara himself headed a seminar on that subject and searched for a Japanese model of a 'non-capitalist market economy' (*Beyond Capitalism*, 1993). Like him, the new heralds of the 'Japan is different' ideology now commonly spoke fluent English and sometimes graduated from American universities. They were no longer afraid to express their views in the English-language media to criticise ultra-liberalism, the cult of financial profit and the model of social relationships based on the violent balance of contesting forces, which, they said, prevailed in the West. Well aware of the Japan-phobia that polemic excesses in the 1980s had set off in the West, these new-look zealots of the old *nihonjinron* frequently used the fashionable theme of 'symbiosis'. They preached a 'Nice New Nationalism' – as *The Economist* in January 1995 put it – and a new relationship between the world's cultures which should be as 'a symphony orchestra: all the instruments are different and every one plays its own score, but in the end, the whole is beautiful symphony' – according to a metaphor uttered by Prime Minister Murayama.

But Japan was also involved willy-nilly in the polemics surrounding 'Asian values' which developed in the late 1980s. This debate started in south-east Asia and was orchestrated in an aggressive way by Malaysia under Dr Mahathir Mohammad, and in a more civil manner by the leaders of Singapore. The prime objective of those semi-authoritarian regimes was to counter Washington's pressure for democracy, human rights and ultra-liberal economics in Asia by arguing that Western values and norms were by no means universal. The debate greatly embarrassed Japanese diplomats, who could not distance themselves from their US partner on this issue. But the most anti-American wing of neo-nationalism eagerly echoed the polemic in Japan. In 1995 its most high-profile spokesman, Shintarô Ishihara, co-authored with Dr Mahathir a vehemently anti-Western pamphlet whose title *No to ieru Ajia* (The Asia That Can Say No) was copied from the title of Ishihara's *No to ieru Nihon* (The Japan That Can Say No). The polemical historian Kenichi Matsumoto (author of 60 works!) kept contrasting Asians – 'farming peoples' imbued with community spirit, patient, frugal and respectful towards nature – and Westerners, individualistic 'herding tribes', bloodthirsty people whose civilisation was based on the murder of living creatures. Another historian, Heita Kawakatsu, in *Bunmei no kaiyô shikan* (Civilisation from the Viewpoint of Maritime History, 1997), contrasted the Western 'industrial revolution', based on warlike pillage of overseas resources and the destruction of nature, and the 'industrious revolution' of Japan, based on pacifism and intensive techniques for conservation of nature, and now more suited to the needs of the present world.

These theories were inseparable from the never-ending debate on the history of Japanese colonisation and the Pacific War, which was pursued with all the more virulence as the government's stance evolved towards admission of 'aggression' committed by Japan, which was intolerable to the neo-nationalists. From 1995, the Japanese Society for History Textbook Reform, led by outspoken, high-profile academics with strong support in the LDP, denounced a 'masochistic vision' of history 'fabricated by the victors' in which 'Japan was made to bear the sole responsibility for the war' and advocated 'teaching which arouses patriotism'. In 2001, it succeeded in having a 'revisionist' textbook approved by the Ministry of Education for use starting in the 2002 school year; this textbook is devoted to denying or minimising the most shocking episodes of Japan's colonisation and the war in China, notably the Nanking massacre and the case of the 'comfort women', as they were called – young Asian women forcibly used as prostitutes by the Japanese imperial army. Revisionism found a large echo among young people owing to the best-selling comics of Yoshinori Kobayashi, whose *Shin gomanisumu sengen* ('The Manifesto for a New Pride') and *Senso-ron* ('About War') echo the thesis of the Society for History Textbook Reform.

From 1997 the Asian crisis offered the nationalist hard-liners a new field for polemics. Ishihara took up Mahathir's thesis which saw in the crisis a plot by Western capitalism to get rid of a rival model whose success was too striking. In a virulent article in 1999 he compared the crisis to the Opium Wars, with capital flowing into Asia from 1990 onwards playing the same role as drugs intended to undermine Chinese society in the nineteenth century. He prophesied 'the enslavement of the Asian peoples' and gave Japan the mission of organising resistance. Similar ideas were found in academic circles also, an example being the economist Mototada Kikkawa, for whom the 'monetary war' waged by the USA using manipulation of the exchange rate was the deep-seated cause of the Japanese economic crisis which, according to him, was causing much more damage to Japan than the Second World War.

Most Japanese remained insensitive to this aggressive nationalism. However, the success of Kobayashi's *manga* and the war fantasy books of the *Deep Blue Fleet* series by Yoshio Arakami, who rewrote the Second World War to make it a Japanese victory, showed that national pride had been hurt by the crisis. In particular the relationship with the super-powerful partner America, which the Japanese had thought they had overtaken in the late 1980s but which was now displaying revived economic health, aroused frustration. Hence the sudden flare-up of anger against the American military bases in 1995 after the rape of an adolescent girl in Okinawa by three GIs. In 1999 the election of Ishihara as Governor of Tokyo aroused worry in the West -although it was probably due to his strong-willed image rather than his nationalistic sermons. Echoing both local communities' aspiration to greater autonomy and the titles of Ishihara's two bestsellers, his slogan *No to ieru Tôkyô* was aimed first of all at the central government, to which the people of the capital city were called upon to say 'No'. But his success, even so, placed the champion of hard-line nationalism in a highly visible position, which he soon began to use in a provocative manner, calling for the closure of a US military airfield near Tokyo and visiting Taiwan in great pomp to the greatest displeasure of Beijing.

While still in a minority among public opinion, this nationalism found a wider echo at the grass roots of the LDP, but also among prominent leaders like Ryûtarô Hashimoto and Ichirô Ozawa. They protested strongly in 1993 when Prime Minister Hosokawa admitted that the wars waged by Japan in Asia were indeed 'aggression'. In 1995 they prevented Murayama from settling the dispute with Asian countries by making the official apology which Tokyo had always refused on the occasion of the fiftieth anniversary of the end of the Second World War.

Throughout the period they prevented settlement of the painful matter of the 'comfort women' by thwarting every move to compensate them from public funds; and when Hashimoto sent each one of the women a personal letter of regret, his right-hand man and future successor, Keizô Obuchi, assured everyone that they had gone into prostitution of their free will (January 1997). True, the same Obuchi, after becoming Prime Minister, was to make an unprecedented gesture to Korea in presenting an official written apology to President Kim Dae-jung in October 1998; but a month later he refused to offer the same apology to the Chinese President, Jiang Zemin.

The most hard-line nationalist fringe was still backed up by the *yakuza* and the violent ultra-nationalist groups which were their political arm. The gangsters disfigured the filmmaker Juzô Itami for having 'profaned the national flag' in one of his films, and were suspected of having a hand in his unexplained suicide in 1997. In 1999 a publisher had to give up, under threats, bringing out a translation of *The Rape of Nanking*, a work by the American journalist Iris Chang on the massacres committed in 1937 by the imperial army, which the neo-nationalists deny. The ultra-nationalist groups went so far as to provoke international tension, as in the Senkaku islands in 1996 (see p. 330). Whether manipulated by some LDP elements or not, they were a threatening factor, which permanently disturbed relations between Japan and its neighbours.

JAPAN'S INTERNATIONAL POSITION

New geostrategic situation in Asia

The end of the Cold War and the rising power of China completely changed the geostrategic balance in Asia – for the worse as far as Japan was concerned. The Chinese leaders displayed increasing assertiveness and posed as natural leaders of the Asians facing the West, and won a major success in 1993 when the Bangkok conference approved their minimalist theses on human rights (see pp. 328–9). They remained completely committed to reunification of the whole 'Chinese space'; they recovered Hong Kong in 1997 and never hesitated to raise military tension to discourage any move towards independence by Taiwan. Beijing also wanted to secure key positions in the South China Sea. The Chinese had taken the Paracel Islands by force from Vietnam in 1974 and they were now disputing possession of the Spratly Islands with no less than six countries. In 1992 the People's Assembly solemnly declared both archipelagos included in China's national territory and gave the armed forces the mission of establishing effective sovereignty there; this led to incidents, especially with Filipino ships around the Mischief (1995) and Scarborough (1997) reefs.

China has several hundred nuclear warheads and full ballistic capability with short, medium and long range missiles, including sea-borne ones, surpassing Japan's defensive capacity. The Beijing leaders' stated determination to develop an ocean-going navy with missile-launching vessels and aircraft carriers means a serious threat, even if still a remote one, over Japan's sea communications routes. Since the end of the 1980s, the whole of East Asia has been the theatre of an arms race, and has bought about 35 per cent of the military supplies sold in the world, especially air and sea arma-ments. Thailand's purchase of a Spanish aircraft carrier (1996) and Indonesia's buying up of the former East German navy, even if the effectiveness of this material is doubtful, are significant in this respect. According to the armaments plans of the countries bor-dering the South China Sea, about twenty submarines were expected to be patrolling that sea around 2000. Most worrying for Japan is the fact that such an arms race has occurred while its own ability to expand armaments is still impaired by constitutional restraints.

At the same time the United States' commitment to maintain-ing its forces in Asia at great expense came into question after the Communist peril had gone. In 1991–2 the Bush administration evacuated the Subic Bay base in the Philippines and reduced American forces in Asia by 10 per cent. In 1993 the new Clinton administration defined its Asian strategy as a combination of enlargement – extending democracy – and engagement, that is, remaining involved in regional security. It promised to maintain 100,000 troops in Asia, including 48,000 in Japan. But doubt still lingered about whether Washington would risk a major confron-tation with China as long as its ambitions did not directly threaten US security. Consequently, the strategic value of the bases in Japan might have diminished somewhat in the eyes of the Ameri-can leaders. The Japanese can therefore fear a weakening of the

Security Treaty, and have to rethink the problem of security in new terms.

The numerous regional organisations were a second element of change in Asia, even though the region was not pursuing integration on the lines of Europe. Since 1989 APEC grew from 13 to 21 members. Recurrent friction occurred as the Asians resisted repeated American attempts to go beyond economic cooperation, which was supposed to be the sole object of APEC, to discuss political problems. Washington also wanted to use APEC as a Trojan Horse for its market-economy precepts, but at the Osaka summit in 1995 the Asians only agreed to a very slow and conditional transition to free trade some time between 2010 and 2020. In 1998 the Kuching summit in Malaysia, in the context of the Asian crisis, was acrimonious. US Vice-President Al Gore clashed with the host country over human rights. But despite these tensions APEC's summit of heads of state and government became of the high moments of the international diplomatic scene, where all Asia used to be in the limelight as a major area of growth until 1997 – and may well be so again in a not too distant future.

ASEAN has grown in power. It admitted Vietnam in 1995, Laos and Burma in 1998, and Cambodia in 1999. This grouping of more than 500 million people displayed a strong economic dynamism until the crisis struck and had ambitions to form its own free trade area. The ten member states' armed forces total 1.8 million men (233,000 in Japan), a thousand combat aircraft (510 in Japan), and 400,000 tons of naval vessels (326,000 for Japan); and while much of all their weaponry is obsolete, they have been rapidly modernising. Politically ASEAN, headed by Malaysia and Singapore which from the early 1990s set up as champions of 'Asian values', dared to challenge the United States over human rights. Even the economic crisis of 1997 did not make ASEAN countries give way on this point, since in 1998 they admitted the Burmese junta to the organisation in spite of all-out pressure from Washington.

ASEAN was also involved in starting two major initiatives for deeper regional integration. One was the formation of the Asian Regional Forum in 1993, the first ever regional organisation to discuss security matters. At first this was an extension of the annual ASEAN summit, but in 1996 it met in Japan – not an ASEAN member. The other initiative was the Asia-Europe

Meeting (ASEM), held for the first time in Bangkok on 1 March 1996. This new dialogue brought together the heads of state or government of the European Union, their ASEAN counterparts and those of invited countries – Japan, Korea and China. The summit adopted a schedule of meetings every two years: London 1998, Seoul 2000. There were also foreign ministers' meetings, and permanent structures were set up such as the Euro-Asia Fund for promotion of academic exchanges. Even if the agenda of these gatherings remained fairly basic, this new forum confirmed that Asia was now able to discuss matters on an equal footing with the two other poles of world power.

While Japan went through a crisis, the 1990s were 'the decade of Asia's rising power' – at least until 1997. Many countries of the region registered growth rates between 6 and 10 per cent – even more for China in some years – boosted by unprecedented net private inflows of international capital, which reached the $93 billion range in 1996. Forecasters fell over each other to proclaim Asia as 'the new pole of world power in the twenty-first century'. In 1995 the CIA *Factbook* published a table indicating that in 2020 China's GDP – on a purchasing power parity basis – would exceed that of the USA, and that six of the ten leading world economic powers would be Asian countries (China, Japan, India, Indonesia, South Korea and Thailand). The World Bank itself hailed *The East-Asian Economic Miracle* in a report that attracted all the more attention because it recognised the existence of an effective development model different from Anglo-Saxon liberalism. This rise in Asia's power was bound to have repercussions on the way in which Japan now saw its role in the world order.

'Return to Asia'? The question of regional leadership

With Asian power rising, the idea gained ground in Japan that the time had come to turn Fukuzawa Yukichi's (1835–1901) old admonition – *Datsua nyûô*, 'Leave Asia and go West' – around, and 'return to Asia' as a way for Japan to strengthen its position both politically and economically. While Japan seemed to be losing importance for the United States as a partner in the post-Cold War world, the formidable development of Asia – the region where Tokyo was able to have the most influence – seemed to offer a way to become a great power in its own right, freed from

Washington's tutelage. This was the dream of all the neo-nationalists from Hashimoto and Ozawa to Ishihara. The majority of conservative élites were more cautious and saw 'return to Asia' rather as a means of finding a new and better balance for the relationship with Washington, which would remain even so at the centre of Japan's diplomacy. The Left, which dreamed of breaking with international relations based on balance of strength and replacing them with 'symbiosis', considered that Japan should rediscover its Asian roots, to be the country through which the mutual enrichment of West and East would come; Japan could act as a bridge between them to gain a prominent role in the multicultural world of the twenty-first century. But whatever interpretation is given to it, any idea of 'return to Asia' poses the question of leadership over the emerging regional community.

Japan has considerable capacity for influence in Asia. For three decades it has been the model of economic success and political and social stability. Despite ten years of crisis, in 1999 it still accounted for 60 per cent of the region's total GDP, as against about 10 per cent for China. This economic weight, and the development aid Japan provides for Asian countries, are supplemented by 'soft power', since Japanese pop culture – *manga* comics, animation films, karaoke and *aidoru* ('idols') – has spread as successfully as that of Hollywood and Disney. The increasing number of regional fora is *a priori* favourable to Japan, because Chinese diplomacy is not fond of multilateral, open gatherings and prefers the bilateral game in which its massive strength has more chance of carrying the day.

But Tokyo also has serious handicaps to a claim to leadership. Economic friction abounds with the neighbours, fuelled by Japan's reticence over technology transfer as over opening of its market. The strategy on which Japan embarked from the 1980s to raise its international stature (see pp. 241–2) did not bear many fruit. After the adoption of the PKO law blue-helmeted Japanese troops took part in UN peace keeping missions in Cambodia, on the Golan Heights and (briefly) in Rwanda, and unarmed Japanese observers helped supervise elections in Mozambique. But some of these UN missions were not very successful, while the work of Yasushi Akashi, the Japanese UN representative in the Bosnian conflict, hardly increased his home country's prestige. And when Indonesia seemed on the brink of bloodshed and

JAPANESE OFFICIAL DEVELOPMENT AID:
A MEANS FOR INFLUENCE.

The world's top donor. In 1998 Japan disbursed bilateral aid totalling $14 billion, up 12 per cent from 1997 in dollar terms (23.5 per cent in yen terms). It ranked first among the 21 member countries of the Development Assistance Committee (DAC), ahead of the USA ($8.1 billion) and France ($5.9 billion). Its contribution amounted to 20.7 per cent of the total net disbursements by DAC members.

In 1977 Japan adopted a policy of continuously increasing its ODA, which doubled from 1977 to 1987, then again from 1987 to 1993. Owing to the worsening condition of the state budget, disbursements then levelled off, before bouncing back in 1998 on the impact of emergency financial aid to assist Asia in overcoming the economic crisis.

Not so generous. Part of the spectacular 'growth' of Japanese disbursement in dollar terms since 1977 is attributable to the yen going up from the then 270-a-dollar level to the 120-a-dollar level during the 1990s. In 1998, Japan's ODA amounted to 0.28 per cent of GNP – better than the DAC average of 0.23 and much better than the US 0.10 – for a DAC ranking of 12th out of 21.

Japan has long been criticised for disbursing a larger than average share of its assistance as loans – part of which were 'tied' (e.g. specifically designed for aid projects undertaken by Japanese companies). Although Japan raised the grant share to 86 per cent of its disbursements for the period 1996/7, it still ranks lowest out of the 21 DAC member-countries.

Human assistance is provided by the Japan International Cooperation Agency which provides technical training to engineers and skilled workers from developing countries, and by about 1,000 Japan Overseas Volunteer Corps, the Japanese counterpart of the US Peace Corps.

Regional distribution. Japan used to favour its own 'Asian backyard', which received more than 70 per cent of its ODA during 1980, but distribution has become more balanced. In 1998, Asia got only 43.3 per cent, with 29.3 per cent going to needy Africa (as against 15.5 per cent in 1990) and 10 per cent to Latin America. Still, China, Indonesia and Thailand – which are of utmost interest for Japan at both the political and the economic level – regularly rank among the top receivers.

Source: Japan's ODA, Ministry of Foreign Affairs, Tokyo.

violent disintegration, Tokyo balked at the risk involved in assuming any leadership role, and let the Western powers and Australia bear the responsibility for UN intervention in East Timor. As for environmental affairs, after grand posturing at the Earth Summit at Rio, Japan did not follow up very convincingly. It went ahead with a controversial nuclear power programme and stockpiling of large amounts of military-grade uranium. As the host country, it failed to drive the Kyoto summit on Global Warming to a successful conclusion in 1997, and in 2001 it was slapped in the face by the decision of the new Bush administration to renege on any promises made then.

In Korea and China, the two nearest and most powerful neighbours, the resentment left by the Japanese aggression still lingers. Although Japan's image is much better in south-east Asia, the ASEAN countries do not intend to be Tokyo's pawns in a diplomatic chess game with China; when Hashimoto, on an official visit to Singapore, suggested an institutional political and security dialogue, his offer was politely evaded (January 1997). The Malaysian and Singaporean leaders were disappointed to see Japan showing not much interest in their pet 'Asian values'. For Dr Mahathir the pleasure of jointly signing *'No' to ieru Ajia* with Ishihara did not make up for the disappointment of seeing Tokyo favouring APEC over his project of the EAEC (see p. 246).

Lastly, and most important, Japan still has two major handicaps inherited from its defeat: restrictions on its armed forces and divisions in public opinion and among the élites on the aims of foreign policy and ways to achieve them. In addition Japanese diplomacy has been burdened by territorial disputes with all its neighbours over territorial disputes which have never been settled since 1945 and were even rekindled by the hawkish Hashimoto's period in power in 1996–7.

Disputes: Japan vs. Russia and Korea

Regarding the Kurile islands, after the end of the Cold War Tokyo thought it could take advantage of the difficulties facing Russia to settle the dispute to its advantage, by making its financial aid conditional on the return of the four islands. But this stance antagonised Moscow and upset the Westerners as well, since they were concerned above all to consolidate the Yeltsin regime. The

Russian President twice dealt the Japanese government the snub of a sudden cancellation of an official visit (September 1992 and May 1993). He only went to Tokyo after the LDP lost power, and promised Prime Minister Hosokawa that he would seek a settlement 'along the lines of previous international agreements'. But negotiations made hardly any progress because of the ups and downs of domestic politics in both countries. In 1997 Hashimoto, longing for a big foreign policy success to his credit, restarted the process. He met Yeltsin at Krasnoyarsk and the two men promised to settle the question before the end of the century. This promise was repeated when they met again at Shizuoka the following year. Japan even offered a face-saving compromise to Moscow: it would let Russia administer the islands for an undetermined period while a 'line of demarcation' would be drawn north of them as a *de facto* recognition of Japanese sovereignty. But the talks became bogged down as soon as Hashimoto and Yeltsin lost power. The nationalist Putin is clearly unwilling to 'return' anything to Japan, and probably no offer of money or economic cooperation would suffice to change his mind.

Japanese public opinion followed these developments with detachment. In May 1997 the mass circulation weekly *Aera* even dared to write that the return of the Kuriles would be too expensive and that no Japanese wanted to live there anyway. The relationship between Tokyo and Moscow is bound to remain strained, since in opinion polls Russia always ranks second among the countries least liked by the Japanese, just after North Korea, while Moscow does not intend to let itself be kept completely out of the game in Asia, and thus loudly proclaims its rapprochement with China every time a cold spell comes in Sino-American relations and Beijing seeks a counterweight to the Washington-Tokyo axis – as in 1996 after the USA and Japan agreed on new guidelines for the Security Treaty, and again in 2000 when Moscow and Beijing expressed the same 'deep concern' about the American project for a Theatre Missile Defence system. A rapprochement between Moscow and Tokyo does not seem to be on the agenda …

The 1965 treaty between Japan and South Korea had left 'to the next generation' the question of Takeshima island, Tokdo to the Koreans. For thirty years Korea, which occupied the island, was content with this situation, and Japan confined itself to verbal protests. But in 1996 one of the Hashimoto cabinet's first acts was to declare an Exclusive Economic Zone in the Sea of Japan, to include Takeshima. Seoul responded with naval and air manoeuvres. Throughout the whole post-war period the emotional background bore heavily upon relations between the two countries. The younger generations of Koreans had not known the brutalities of the Japanese occupation, but numerous disputes kept the animosity alive – especially the trade deficit, the fight by the Koreans in Japan against discrimination, and the 'comfort women' problem. South Korean public opinion and leaders as well suspected Japan of not wanting the reunification of Korea, which would create a highly dynamic power of 68 million people on its doorstep. Consequently, in 1997, South Korea was still the Asian country where Japan had the highest rate of unfavourable opinion (67.6 per cent). Imports of some Japanese products – notably cars, large-screen television sets, VCRs and video cameras, and Japanese cultural goods such as *manga*, films, TV series and pop music – were still officially banned. On their side the Japanese ranked South Korea third in the hit-parade of the least liked countries, after North Korea and Russia.

Things changed when Kim Dae-jung was elected President of South Korea in December 1997. He was determined to establish relations with Japan on a new basis. Tokyo and Seoul were also impelled in that direction by a coming event with worlwide media coverage, the soccer World Cup of 2002, which FIFA had given them to organise jointly. In this context of goodwill the Obuchi government finally broke the supreme taboo. In November 1998, on the occasion of Kim Dae-jung's official visit to Japan, it officially expressed to South Korea, in writing, 'remorse and apology' for acts of 'aggression' committed in the past. Seoul soon began to lift the bans on imports of Japanese products. A joint commission was set up to seek a common presentation of the colonial episode in the two countries' school textbooks. There was even talk of an official visit to Korea by Emperor Akihito.

But while it seemed that the two nations were overcoming their antagonism, the approval of the 'revisionist' history textbook by Japan's Ministry of Education aroused a violent backlash in Korea. Seoul recalled its ambassador to Japan, Korean youths yelled with anger at Japanese tourists in the streets of Seoul, and a Korean member of parliament conducted a six-day hunger strike next to the Diet building in Tokyo. It may be that all the progress made over three years could be wiped out.

The third point of tension – forgotten for a long time – lay in the four tiny uninhabited islets of Senkaku, called Diaoyutai in Chinese. These reefs are located 190 km north-east of Taiwan and 150 km from the Ryûkyû archipelago (Okinawa). Both China and Taiwan claimed them as part of their continental shelf. From the seventeenth century to the nineteenth the Ryûkyû kingdom had been under the dual sovereignty of China and Japan's fief of Satsuma. Japan added it to its national territory in 1879. In 1945 the UN placed the Ryûkyûs under US administration. In 1972 Washington unilaterally returned them to Japan; on that occasion nothing was said about the Senkakus, but Japan immediately included them in its air traffic identification and prohibition zone. Beijing protested, but Tanaka was at that time about to recognise Communist China. So the problem was put off until later; so it was again in 1978, during discussion of the Treaty of Peace and Friendship. But the problem remained, and it suddenly raised its head again in a context of growing tension between the two claimants to regional leadership.

Tensions in the Japan–China–USA triangle, 1993–6

The 1990s started with the beginnings of a flirtation between China and Japan. Japan's conciliatory attitude after the Tiananmen Square episode had been followed by another powerful symbolic gesture – the first-ever visit to China by a Japanese monarch. Emperor Akihito went to Beijing in October 1992 and expressed 'his profound regrets for the unfortunate past'. These diplomatic overtures were accompanied by an upsurge in Japanese investment, which increased from $400 million in 1989 to $1.7 billion in 1993.

But by giving legitimacy again to the Beijing regime in this way, Japan's diplomacy helped it to reestablish in Asia the political influence that had been shaken by the Tiananmen Square episode. China was also able to exploit the growing tension between Washington and the south-east Asian countries over human rights. At the Asian regional preparatory meeting for the UN World Conference on Human Rights held in Bangkok (29 March–2 April 1993) the Chinese put themselves forward as leaders of a regional community determined to resist US pretensions to hegemony. The final resolution, put forward by southeast Asian countries which championed 'Asian values', declared that human rights were subordinate to the needs of economic development and denounced pressure exerted on developing countries on the subject. This text caught the Japanese in a trap. If they approved it they would be following China's lead and isolating themselves from the West. If they voted against it they would cut themselves off from the Asians. In fact they abstained – and began to reassess their policy towards China.

In any case the accommodating attitude to Beijing was arousing increasing opposition among Japanese public opinion, which had always had an ambiguous relationship with China, veering between contempt and fear. In 1992 there were strident polemics around Akihito's trip; many people, even outside the nationalist circles, feared that the monarch would be 'humiliated' by the Chinese leaders. The Japanese are increasingly worried by their giant neighbour's hegemonistic aims. While in 1994 only 17 per cent considered China as a threat, 41 per cent did so in 1996. The same unease prevailed in the business world. Although the Japanese ranked second among investors in China in the early 1990s, they scarcely contributed 7–8 per cent of foreign capital, and by 1998 they had fallen to fifth position. Japanese firms hesitated to tie up capital for the long term in large-scale facilities in an uncertain environment. They preferred trade, from which one can pull out at short notice – like the motor manufacturers who let their European competitors set up large plants in China without hurrying to imitate them.

From 1993 onwards the diplomatic flirtation seemed to be over. In 1994 China threatened to boycott the Asian Games due to be held in Hiroshima if the President of Taiwan was permitted to attend; Tokyo gave way. In 1995 Beijing deliberately carried out a nuclear test during Prime Minister Murayama's official visit, and he was also taken by his hosts to visit some sites of atrocities committed by the former imperial army. Tokyo protested against the tests with unprecedented, though relative, firmness, freezing some preferential loans it had agreed for Beijing. China responded by reviving the polemics about the past; it vehemently denounced the ambiguity of the motion adopted by the Diet on the occasion of the 50th anniversary of the end of the war and resumption of prime ministerial visits to the Yasukuni shrine by Hashimoto (July 1996).

It was in this context that the Senkaku Islands conflict suddenly flared up again. In 1991 a Japanese ultra-nationalist organisation linked to the *yakuza* had set up a lighthouse on one of the reefs, where it claimed to have leased land. In 1992 Beijing solemnly reaffirmed its sovereignty over the islets and 'unidentified ships' began to harass Japanese trawlers in the zone. A truce was agreed in 1993. But in 1996, no sooner had Hashimoto taken power when the ultra-nationalists reinstalled their lighthouse, after it had been damaged by a storm. When Beijing protested the government argued that this was a 'private matter'. There was violent reaction all over the Chinese world. Hashimoto was burned in effigy in Taiwan and Hong Kong. In September a flotilla of demonstrators from Taiwan clashed with Japanese coastguards, a Chinese demonstrator was drowned, and the flags of the two Chinas were raised on the reefs. In May 1997 Shintarô Ishihara himself landed provocatively on the islets amid big media publicity, leading to new clashes between the Japanese coastguard and Taiwanese demonstrators. One reason for the conflict was the existence, around the islets, of oil deposits of which China wanted its share. But the Senkakus also offered Beijing an excellent ground to put the Japanese-American alliance to the test, that being the major obstacle to China's regional ambitions. The four reefs were near enough to the coasts of People's China for the Chinese to operate there even without a powerful ocean-going navy. They were probably too minor an issue for Washington to back Japan at the price of a frontal confrontation with Beijing. Lastly, the conflict served Beijing's purposes in arousing pan-Chinese nationalism in Taiwan. Tension subsided in 1997. An agreement was reached on joint exploration of the oil deposits in the zone, but the dispute remains basically unresolved. Incursions by Chinese ships, including warships, in the EEZ claimed by Japan continue on a large scale (33 in the first half of 1998) and might degenerate into a confrontation again if Beijing sees that as being to its advantage.

Despite these tensions, Japanese diplomacy opposed any strategy of confrontation with or isolation of China. Throughout this period Beijing remained the leading recipient of Japanese ODA, of which it received about 13 per cent. Training programmes were still offered for promising young Chinese civil servants, and even the two countries' armed forces resumed in 1996 contacts suspended since 1987. Students from mainland China went to Japan in increasing numbers, until the Chinese community of 300,000 – to which many illegal migrants were added – became the second foreign community in Japan after the Koreans. Bilateral trade was more and more favourable to China, whose surplus on trade with Japan quadrupled between 1992 and 1999, from $5 billion to $20 billion. It was significant that Tokyo let this happen, while at the same time obstinately resisting the Clinton administration over trade disputes. The Japanese know very well that they are in immediate range of Chinese missiles and the first to be threatened if Beijing feels it is facing aggression, or if worsening of the economic and social situation in China leads to an outburst of Chinese nationalism.

Consequently Tokyo found itself in a delicate position when tension between China and the USA – the only two powers that really count in its eyes – increased after Clinton's election in 1992. The new administration's policy of 'enlargement' and 'engagement' – a push for human rights and continued military presence – had nothing to please Beijing, especially as it was accompanied by the promise of 150 up-to-date F–16 fighters to Taiwan. The Chinese leaders thus seized the first opportunity to remind Washington that no regional problem could be solved without their cooperation. In 1994 Beijing prevented passage of a US-sponsored resolution at the UN to impose sanctions to force North Korea to dismantle its nuclear programme. The USA had to accept an agreement under which Pyongyang would receive oil and two 'clean' nuclear power stations paid for by South Korea, Japan and the West via the KEDO (Korea Energy Development Organisation). Tension continued to mount. Beijing let it be clearly understood that there could be no controls over nuclear proliferation without its cooperation by delivering ballistic technology to Pakistan and carrying out nuclear tests in 1995. After Clinton authorised the Taiwan head of state, Lee Tenghui, to make a 'private visit' to the USA, Beijing recalled its ambassador in Washington and began military manoeuvres facing the Nationalist island. The crisis reached a peak in March 1996, at the time of an election to make Lee a popularly elected president. The Chinese army fired test missiles close to the coasts of Taiwan, while Washington sent two aircraft carriers very near the Taiwan Straits.

China thus proved that regional conflicts could not be resolved without its cooperation, and that it could be an obstacle to the United States' pretension to govern the world order alone. Clinton then made his choice. His administration renewed China's most favoured nation status every year and bilateral trade grew to give China a ballooning surplus with the USA ($30 billion in 1996).

Japan greeted this détente with a degree of ambiguity. The Korean crisis of 1994 – in which it had been left out in the cold except for funding the KEDO – proved that it was still a 'political dwarf' for both Washington and Beijing; as such, its interests were bound to be trampled upon by the two giants in times of crisis. Thus Tokyo welcomed détente and pleaded with Washington for new moves towards China – especially for its immediate admission to the WTO and patience over human rights. At the same time, Japanese diplomacy feared that Washington could search for a global partnership agreement with Beijing at the price of its 'special relationship' with Tokyo. To prevent this, Japan tried to reinforce that relationship while preaching further détente.

But while Japan-phobia had declined in the United States since the balance of economic power had tilted spectacularly in their favour, it was now irritation among Japanese public opinion – humiliated by the endless economic crisis, inflamed by repeated trade friction and worked on by neo-nationalism – that caused problems. In September 1995 the rape of an Okinawa schoolgirl by three GIs set off a nation-wide wave of anti-American demonstrations. Placards proclaimed in English: 'This is a place for human beings only! American beasts out!' The Security Treaty was suddenly rejected by 40 per cent of people questioned (with 46 per cent still in favour), and President Clinton decided not to attend the APEC summit in Osaka. In December there were only 23 per cent of Japanese and 28 per cent of Americans still saying bilateral relations were 'good'.

THE SELF-DEFENCE FORCES (2000)

Ground SDF. Actual strength: 148,557 – as against only 112,200 for United Kingdom. One armoured division, 12 infantry divisions, 16 brigades and 13 groups or squadrons. The number of main battle tanks – 1,070, made by Mistubishi – exceeds that of any NATO-European country except Germany.

Air SDF. Actual strength: 44,207 men and 368 combat aircraft – as against Britain's 56,700 men and women and 613 combat aircraft.

Maritime SDF. Actual strength: 42,655 (including 1,800 women), 144 major ships, 110 combat aircraft and 99 armed helicopters.

Now the fourth or fifth most powerful Navy in the world after those of the USA, Britain, France and (maybe) Russia. The three *Kongo*-class missile-launching destroyers (7,500 tons) are the most advanced battleships cruising the Asian seas, except those of the US Seventh Fleet.

American forces in Japan. 36,530 men (Marines 14,300, Air Force 14,000, Navy 6,700) and 90 combat aircraft in eight military bases, mostly in Okinawa. Most expenditure is paid for by Japanese government.

Defence budget. Contrary to those of Western powers, Japan's military spending did not diminish after the end of the Cold War, rising to 4,921 trillion yen for fiscal year 2000 (about $4.30 billion). Although this amounts to only 0.98 per cent of GDP – as against 3.4 per cent in the USA – Japan's defence expenditure is second only to that of the USA. This is especially true if one takes into account research and development expenditure, which constitutes a large part of spending in both the USA and NATO-Europe, but accounts for only 2.4 per cent in the Japanese military budget.

Most equipment is made in Japan – some under licence. The rate is 100 per cent for battle tanks, artillery and small arms, 92 per cent for ships, 75 per cent for aircraft and 55 per cent for missiles.

Towards a new posture. Since the Peace Keeping Operations Law and the new guidelines for military cooperation agreed by the US and Japan opened the way for the SDF to be used abroad, Ground SDF has improved its mobility by reducing the number of infantrymen and battle tanks while acquiring more helicopters and reinforcing its lone airborne brigade. It also created special anti-terrorist units, which some experts consider an embryo Marines corps. Air SDF will soon acquire inflight refuelling capability for combat missions as far away as over the South China Sea, while the newest *Osumi*-class transport and landing ship could eventually be modified to accommodate vertical take-off aircraft.

Personnel. Japanese armed forces – especially Ground SDF – have difficulties recruiting on a voluntary basis. While the legal limit is 265,737 men, in fact the strength is 11 per cent less. The reserve forces are only 46,700 strong, as against 246,000 for Britain. Since the beginning of the 1990s a significant number of students graduating from the Military Academy look for civilian jobs rather than joining the SDF.

Weaknesses. Article 9 of the Constitution, whose official interpretation prohibits the SDF from deploying any 'offensive' weapons, is still supported by a majority of the Japanese people.

   Although its air defence deploys a complete panoply of American-made missiles, including 120 Patriots, the archipelago remains highly vulnerable to a missile attack.

   Last but not least, the SDF has never been tested in battle.

Sources: Japan Almanac 2001, Tokyo, Asahi Shimbun, and *The Military Balance*, Oxford University Press.

Tokyo's choice: extension of the Security Treaty and outlines of a new military posture

The Straits of Taiwan crisis in March 1996 turned Japanese opinion around at a stroke. In April, when Clinton paid an official visit to Tokyo, 46 per cent of Japanese and as many Americans considered that relations were 'good' again, and listed China as the second threat to the security of Japan (after North Korea) or of the United States (after the Middle East). Clinton and Hashimoto signed a joint declaration entitled 'Alliance for the Twenty-First Century', which provided for the adoption of new guidelines for application of the Security Treaty in order to 'cooperate to preserve peace and stability in the Asia-Pacific area'. To that end the Self Defence Forces would provide backing for the US forces 'in case of a crisis' arising 'in the proximity of Japan'.

   The new guidelines were more than a mere spring-clean for the Security Treaty. They represented a fundamental change. The Treaty had until then been exclusively aimed at protecting Japan to compensate for the ban on operations by the SDF outside the archipelago and its territorial waters. In 1992 the PKO law had breached that prohibition, considering that Article 9 did not outlaw collaborating in the 'self-defence' of the community of nations embodied in the UN. But the 'Alliance for the Twenty-First Century' went one giant step further by bringing Japan on a bilateral basis into a defence system with Washington within geographical limits capable of very wide interpretation. Indeed the 'Asia-Pacific Zone' is a very vaguely defined entity, but certainly it extends further than the 1969 interpretation by Prime Minister Satô which tied the security of Japan to that of Korea and Taiwan (see p. 156), even further than the 1,000 nautical miles of which Prime Minister Suzuki had spoken in 1981. In accordance with the pacifist spirit of the Japanese Constitution, the two countries promised to cooperate for arms control and disarmament; but they were also to work together for development of military technology and equipment under an Acquisition and Cross-Servicing Agreement, and the text mentioned anti-missile defence technology in this connection. No doubt this was much more important for Washington than lip-service to disarmament, and while pointing emphatically at the 'threat' from North Korea both partners had China's missiles in mind. Beijing was well aware of this, and it issued a warning straight away that any extension of Japanese-American military cooperation would 'create extra factors of instability'. Hardly had Clinton left Tokyo than Jiang Zemin and Yeltsin signed a 'Strategic Partnership for the Twenty-First Century' – if only to show that China too had strategic options.

The change in the nature of the Security Treaty also caused controversy in Japan. Public opinion, and even the moderate wing of the LDP, remained very attached to the pacifist clause of the Constitution; 69 per cent of people questioned in 1997 on the occasion of the fiftieth anniversary of the Constitution rejected any idea of tampering with it, and 82 per cent approved the renunciation of the use of force. Besides, any attempt to amend that clause would provoke anger all around Asia. In this context technical discussions on the practical implementation of the new guidelines were difficult. They led to an agreement providing that the SDF would back US forces with logistical support 'not linked to the use of armed force': evacuation of civilians, transport of non-military material, mine sweeping in international waters, and checking of ships to enforce any embargoes (only if decreed by the

UN). But many points were left vague – among others the exact nature of the 'crisis situations' and the geographical area to which the guidelines would be applied, the sort of equipment that the Japanese would be able to transport, and the possibility for them to participate in actions without the backing of a UN resolution. As for the missile defence system, Japan committed itself only to a meagre amount of money for feasibility studies. The text was attacked by the left, but also by the nationalists led by Ozawa, who wanted to make it tougher. It took eighteen months before the new guidelines were finally approved by the Diet in March 1999.

The new guidelines were only one element in the increasingly visible change in Japan's military posture. In a more or less disguised manner the Self Defence Forces were acquiring long-distance capability. The new transport ship of the Osumi class is officially intended to transport tanks and landing craft over a long distance, but it can easily be modified to serve as a carrier for vertical take-off aircraft like the British Harrier, whose purchase is envisaged together with that of mid-air refuelling capacity and long-range transporter aircraft, ostensibly for humanitarian missions only. In 1998–9 spectacular incidents with North Korea alarmed public opinion and permitted the conservatives to go even further. In August 1998 Pyongyang tested a Taepodong–1 long-range missile, and its parts flew over Japan before crashing into the ocean. The LDP took this opportunity to cast aside the principle of 'no military use of space' and voted to launch a military observation satellite by 2002. In March 1999 intrusion into Japanese waters by two North Korean ships brought out the Navy to open fire on the intruders – the first time that had happened since 1945. Since the inability to intercept the intruders was attributed to the slowness of the decision-making process, the government had a perfect pretext to revive a bill for special measures in case of emergency, often discussed but never passed. Finally, in the wake of the terrorist attacks of 11 September 2001 against the United States, Tokyo went a step further by passing a law which authorises the SDF to intervene anywhere in the world – in a non-combat role – to support international operations against terrorism.

These initiatives inevitably led to tension with Beijing. China vainly asked Japan for an assurance that the new guidelines would not apply in the case of a crisis in the Taiwan Straits. It objected violently to any missile defence scheme which would alter the balance of forces in the region to its disadvantage. Relations between the two neighbours reached their lowest point in November 1998 when Jiang Zemin paid the first state visit by a Chinese president to Japan. Obuchi refused to offer him the written apology which he had given the previous month to the President of Korea, and on the Taiwan problem he adopted a harder line than Clinton's by refusing to agree with the so-called 'three No's' (no support for Taiwanese independence, no to two Chinas, no Taiwanese membership in international organisations of states). Jiang responded in kind by uttering the taboo word 'aggression' during a state banquet in presence of the Emperor himself.

Tokyo was gradually caught in a dilemma, since any move to reinforce its relationship with Washington alienated Beijing, while at the same time Clinton continued with the Chinese leaders a flirtation that made Japan feel insecure. In 1998 this flirtation led to a honeymoon phase when successive official visits by Jiang Zemin to the USA and by Clinton to China were both definite successes surrounded by media frenzy, while the US President did not even make a stopover in Tokyo on his way to Beijing. Although 'on the front line', Japan was also left out of the negotiations after the Taepodong incident, which America conducted face to face with the North Koreans and in close contact with the Chinese. Japan seemingly found it difficult to defend its national interest within its bilateral relationship with its super-partner, which seems to take it for granted and asks it for money rather than advice. This looks like an inescapable constraint, in which the transition from Clinton to Bush is unlikely to change anything.

The LDP's foreign policy is based today on three convictions. The first is that the United States still has a vital interest in contributing actively to security in Asia, if only because it carries on more than half of its trade there. The second is that China is a rival, even a danger, which Japan does not have the means to confront alone. Henceforth, strengthening the special relationship with the United States – even at the price of inescapable constraints and being too often taken for granted – is still the pillar of Tokyo's foreign policy, all the more so as this special relationship is also the means for Japan to increase its international stature.

Indeed the United States, by making Japan a major (if still unequal) partner for maintenance of peace, the struggle against nuclear proliferation and the promotion of democracy and economic liberalism, is giving it a political role that it cannot play on its own. So – contrary to what it seems – strengthening military cooperation with the American protector is quite compatible with the strengthening of national power cherished by the neo-nationalists and the conservative élite. Especially as strengthening the Self-Defence Forces, which is a corollary of the 'new strategic partnership' with Washington, will eventually give Japan the technical means for intervening throughout the region – if need be, because the re-balancing of forces set off by the end of the Cold War is far from over in Asia, especially in view of the economic crisis of 1997.

Japan and the Asian crisis since 1997

The crisis which hit the developing economies of Asia from the summer of 1997 onwards has contributed to Japan's slide back into recession after bouncing back in 1996–7. But politically, it has offered Japan an unprecedented opportunity to assert itself as the leader which the distressed region needs.

What was at stake in the crisis, in the view of Asian public opinion and a large portion of the élite, was the question whether the international economic regulation bodies dominated by the English-speaking world would impose their model of capitalism and force Asian countries to sell off enterprises built up by three decades of effort to foreign investors at bargain prices. Japan was seen by many as the only country which could lead resistance. This hope lay behind the plan for an Asian Monetary Fund discussed two months after the onset of the crisis, at a meeting of the region's ministers of Finance in Tokyo. Its ultimate objective was to place $100 billion at the disposal of the crisis-hit countries – without the conditions that the IMF attached to its loan packages. Japan quickly provided most of an emergency fund of $17 billion for the hardest-hit country, Thailand, where Japanese banks held 50 per cent of the country's foreign debt. The object was obviously to safeguard the funds committed by Japanese banks in Asia – $119 billion in all, compared with only $29.4 billion for American banks. But Tokyo certainly had another object also: to demonstrate leadership. However, Washington reacted to this challenge by having the plan for an Asian Monetary Fund buried at the Vancouver APEC summit in November, which gave the IMF the dominant role in bailing out the NIEs and enforcing their adherence to the market economy.

Japan did not dare to confront the USA directly. But in December 1997 the ASEAN Finance Ministers reached agreement on the Manila Framework, a mechanism for mutual supervision through which the countries of the region aimed to increase their policy making capability outside the international financial bodies, and assist each other with reform processes. Although the USA was part of the Framework, this agreement signalled the Asian countries' determination to take their monetary affairs into their own hands. Japan was naturally to play an essential role, and it measured up to its responsibilities in putting more resources than any other country to help resolve the crisis. In the second half of 1997 it extended $19 billion in emergency funding to Thailand, Indonesia and South Korea – twice as much as the USA. In 1998 its commitments of various forms totalled some $80 billion, more than the sums disbursed by the IMF. Japanese loans have been particularly valuable for Malaysia, where the President, Mahathir Mohammad, continues to challenge the West by refusing all IMF aid and adopting an anti-liberal exchange control policy. And in 1999 the Japanese Finance Minister, Kiichi Miyazawa, announced a new 'initiative' for $30 billion in the form of loans and credit guarantees.

Japan's generosity must be put in perspective. It was motivated by concern to safeguard the interests of its companies and banks all over Asia, and the loans offered by Tokyo barely compensated for the Japanese private capital fleeing the region. In addition the sharp devaluation of the yen against the dollar between 1995 and 1998 certainly played a role in the onset and continuation of the crisis by favouring Japanese exporters against their Asian competitors. Nevertheless, to the extent that public opinion in the crisis-hit countries saw the United States as being mainly responsible for the misfortune that had struck them, Japan could only score points in contrast. However, it did not succeed in asserting itself as a real leader on the diplomatic level. When Prime Minister Hashimoto, in the midst of the crisis in Indonesia which ended with the fall of Suharto, went to Jakarta to convince the dictator to accept a compromise with the IMF, he failed (March 1998), and Tokyo cautiously kept the SDF out of the UN peacekeeping mission in East Timor. Despite the fiery speeches of Ishihara and the neo-nationalists (see p. 318), the Japanese government held back from any initiative which would make it seem like the leaders of 'Asian resistance to Anglo-Saxon capitalism'. Nevertheless, over time, the crisis offers Japan the opportunity it dreamed of to advance the idea of better regional economic coordination to avoid a recurrence of the crisis. The Manila Framework is now being followed up by step-by-step moves towards monetary coordination at the regional level, not unlike the former European Monetary System. In such an arrangement the yen would naturally play the dominant role; the regional currencies would find themselves tied to it *de facto*, as much as to the dollar. And by cushioning the local economies – if only a little – against fluctuations of the dollar, this coordination would deprive the United States of a means of manipulation. In this connection the launching of the euro in January 1999 aroused a good deal of interest in Tokyo.

Europe: 'the third side of the triangle'

The end of the Cold War and the search for a new balance in the world order led Tokyo to renew political dialogue with the European Community. Until then both sides had considered this fairly unimportant. In 1984 the First EC-Japan Ministerial Meeting had been held in Brussels, but afterwards it did not convene for three years, although it was planned that it would take place annually. The prevailing climate of Japan-phobia spread to Europe. In 1982 France launched the highly-publicised 'Battle of Poitiers' against imports of Japanese video recorders, which cut imports temporarily by 90 per cent, and in 1987 Prime Minister Edith Cresson publicly called the Japanese 'ants'. Generally the Japanese found it hard to believe in a European Union whose founding concept of 'supranationality' was basically alien to them. But from 1989 onwards, in the new international context, there was suddenly plenty of talk of 'strengthening the third side' of the triangle (Asia, Europe and the United States), as Asia and Europe each feared the hegemonic pretensions of the USA as the 'sole remaining superpower'.

Dialogue resumed actively with Prime Minister Nakasone's official visit to Brussels in 1990, followed by that of the President of the European Commission, Jacques Delors, to Tokyo. It led in July 1991 to a Joint Declaration on relations between the EC and Japan (the Hague Declaration), which asserted both parties' determination to overcome economic problems and engage in political cooperation. This opened the way to establishment of a full framework of consultation and cooperation on the political, economic, cultural and scientific planes. At the same time Japan signed an agreement on EC-Japan motor trade issues; it agreed to reduce its exports to a maximum of 1.23 million units per year until 2000 – a concession that it had never until then granted willingly, except to the United States. In 1992 Japan achieved Special Member status in the Council for Security and Cooperation in Europe (CSCE). It also acquired a considerable holding in the capital of the European Bank for Recovery and Development (EBRD), although it had many reservations about the former Communist countries where Japanese companies were not committing themselves much.

On the economic plane the coming establishment of the Single Market (1993) led Japanese companies to increase their investment sharply in order to establish themselves inside 'Fortress Europe' before – as they feared – being shut out. In 1990 Japan's investment in the EU reached a peak of $9.3 billion (25 per cent of total outward direct investment), a 57 per cent increase in two years. Traditionally, the Japanese strongly favoured the countries considered the most friendly, especially Britain and the Netherlands – 59.7 per cent of their investment stock was concentrated there in 1991 – to the detriment of those considered hostile, notably France, which only received 7 per cent. But in the single market setting they started sharing investment out in a more balanced way; for example, in 1997 Toyota chose Valenciennes in France for its main European production plant. Over the same period Europe's trade deficit with Japan was cut from $45 billion in 1990 to only $8 billion in 1997, and the ratio of EU exports to Japan to EU imports from Japan increased from 50 to 78 per cent as programmes to help European businesses to export to Japan were launched with the help of the JETRO. In addition Japan in its crisis aroused less fear among European countries, which had resumed growth, and the Japanese were now less seen as a threat and more accepted as partners. Tokyo secured the Europeans' support against the unilateral pressures of the United States, especially in 1994–95 at the time of the clash over numerical targets for trade. Politically, the Euro-Japanese dialogue produced some joint action, including a joint initiative at the UN for the establishment of an arms registration system for conventional arms transfers, Euratom's membership of the KEDO, and technical assistance to Russian defence industries for conversion to civilian production.

Europe's place in Japan's international strategies still remains secondary. Japanese diplomacy has left to ASEAN the initiative for deepening of the dialogue with the launching of ASEM, and as the fear of 'Fortress Europe' has not materialised, investment there has been reduced in favour of Asia and America. Nonetheless, the EU's visibility and credibility are growing slowly but surely in Japan. Official programmes aimed at improving mutual knowledge and comprehension (such as the 'Year of Japan in France' and the 'Year of France in Japan' in 1997–9) are not without effect. European companies are taking part spectacularly in the opening of the Japanese economy, an example being the French motor manufacturers Renault, whose $5.16 billion invested in Nissan in 1997 was then the biggest stake ever acquired by a foreign company in Japan. Carlos Ghosn, the 'cost-killer' sent as Vice-Chairman of Nissan, and then as Chairman, has had immense media coverage and became one of the most celebrated figures in Japan. By succeeding in getting Nissan back to profitability, he changed the image of France – and Europe – as 'museums' trailing in economic achievement and in anything high-tech. Numerous European firms are aggressively penetrating Japan alongside American ones, creating between Europe and Japan a 'cultural revolution' which could lead to a deepening relationship, economic but also – in the long term – political.

Note: In this chapter, all currency conversions are made at the rate of 118.8 yen to 1 US dollar (the average for the ten years from 1990 to 1999).

BIBLIOGRAPHY

Chapter 1

General works, from the earliest times to the Meiji Restoration

Beasley, W.G., *The Modern History of Japan*, New York: St. Martin's Press, 1981.

Chuo Koron Collective, *Nippon no rekishi* (History of Japan), Tokyo: Chuo Koronsha, vols 1–23 (1967).

Hall, J.W., *Japan: from Prehistory to Modern Times*, Tokyo: Tuttle, 1971.

Herail, F., F. Mace, P. Souyri and J. Esmein, *Histoire du Japon*, Paris: Horvath, 1989.

Kojiki, translation by B.H. Chamberlain, Kobe: Lane, Crawford and Co., 1932.

Nihon Shoki, translation by W.G. Aston, London: Geo. Allen & Unwin, 1956.

Papinot, E., *Historical and Geographical Dictionary of Japan*, Tokyo: Tuttle, 1972.

Reischauer, E.O., *Japan, Past and Present*, New York: Knopf, 1964.

— *Japan: The Story of a Nation*, New York: McGraw-Hill, 1990.

Samson, G.B., *A History of Japan*, Tokyo: Tuttle, 1963.

Vie, M., *Histoire du Japon: des Origines à Meiji,* Paris: PUF, 1990.

The Meiji Restoration and after

General

Abbad, F., *Histoire du Japon 1868–1945*, Paris: Armand Colin, 1992.

Borton, H. *Japan's Modern Century*, New York: Ronald Press, 1955.

Haga, T., *Meiji hyakunen no jomaku*, Tokyo: Bungei Shunju-sha, 1969.

Sakata, Y., *Meiji ishinshi*, Tokyo: Miraisha, 1960.

Toriumi, Y., 'The Meiji Restoration and its Sequel', in H.A. Toynbee, *East Asia, Half the World,* London: Thames and Hudson, 1973.

Yanaga, C., *Japan since Perry*, Toronto: McGraw-Hill, 1949.

Politics

Byas, H., *Government by Assassination*, New York: Knopf, 1942.

Colbert, E.S., *The Left Wing in Japanese Politics*, New York: Institute of Pacific Relations, 1952.

343

Duus, P., *Party Rivalry and Political Change in Taisho Japan*, Cambridge, MA: Harvard University Press, 1968

Hackeitt, R.F., *Yamagata Arimoto and the Rise of Modern Japan*, Cambridge, MA: Harvard University Press, 1971.

Kurzman, D., *Kishi and Japan*, New York: Ivan Obolensky, 1960.

Mason, R.H.P., *Japan's First Election*, Cambridge University Press, 1989.

Norman, E.H., *Japan's Emergence as a Modern State: Political and Economic Problems of the Meiji Period*, query new ed. 2000.

Oka, Y., *Konoe Fumimaro, unmei no seijika*, Tokyo: Iwanami Shoten, 1972.

Scalapino, R.A., *Democracy and the Party Movement: The Failure of the First Attempt*, Berkeley: University of California Press, 1953.

Economy and development

Adams, T.F., *A Financial History of Modern Japan*, Tokyo: Research, 1964.

Allinson, G.D., *Japanese Urbanism: Industry and Politics in Kariya, 1872–1972,* Berkeley: University of California Press, 1975.

Hirschmeier, J., *The Origins of Entrepreneurship in Meiji Japan*, Cambridge, MA: Harvard University Press, 1964.

Kajinshi, M. (ed.), *Nihon keizaishi taikei*, Tokyo: Daigaku Shuppankai, 1965.

Lockwood, W., *The Economic Development of Japan: Growth and Structural Change, 1868–1938*, Princeton University Press, 1954.

Marshall, B.R., *The Ideology of the Japanese Business Elite, 1868–1941*, Stanford University Press, 1967.

Okawa, K., *Patterns of Japanese Economic Development*, New Haven: Yale University Press, 1979.

Roberts, J.G., *Mitsui: Three Centuries of Japanese Business*, Tokyo: Weatherhill, 1973.

Scalapino, R.A., *The Early Japanese Labor Movement: Labour and Politics in a Developing Society*, Berkeley: University of California Press, 1983.

Foreign policy and war

Agawa, H., *The Reluctant Admiral: Yamamoto and the Imperial Navy*, Tokyo: Kodansha, 1966.

Bergamini, D., *Japan's Imperial Conspiracy*, New York: Pantheon, 1971.

Butow, R.J., *Tojo and the Coming of War,* Princeton University Press, 1969.

Duus, P., *The Abacus and the Sword. Japanese Penetration of Korea 1895–1910*, Berkeley: University of California Press, 1995.

——, H.M. Ramon and R.P. Mark (eds), *The Japanese Informal Empire in China*, Princeton University Press, 1989.

— *The Japanese Wartime Empire*, Princeton University Press, 1996.

Feis, H., *Road to Pearl Harbour*, Princeton University Press, 1950.

Guillain, R., *J'ai vu brûler Tokyo*, Paris: Arlea, 1990.

Jones, F.C., *Japan's New Order in East Asia: Its Rise and Fall*, London: Oxford University Press, 1969.

Kirby, S.W., *The Surrender of Japan*, London: Oxford University Press, 1969.

Maki, M., *Japanese Militarism: its Causes and Cure*, New York: Knopf, 1945.

Neumann, W.L., *America Encounters Japan: from Perry to MacArthur*, Baltimore: Johns Hopkins University Press, 1963.

Rekishigaku Kenkyukai Collective, *Taiheiyo sensoshi*, Tokyo: Aoki Shoten, 1971–3.

Vie, M., *Le Japon et le monde au 20ème siècle*, Paris: Masson, 1995.

Wetzler, P., *Hirohito and War: Imperial Tradition and Military Decision Making in Prewar Japan*, Honolulu: University of Hawaii Press, 1998.

Thought, ideology, culture

Asai, K., *Literature of Modern Japan 1868-* , Tokyo: Centre for East Asian Cultural Studies, 1976.

Gluck, C., *Japan's Modern Myths: Ideology in the Late Meiji Period*, Princeton University Press, 1985.

Kato, S., *A History of Japanese Literature: from the Man'yoshu to Modern Times*, Richmond: Japan Library, 1986.

Minichiello, S. (ed.), *Japan's Competing Modernities: Issues in Culture and Democracy 1900–1930*, Honolulu: University of Hawaii Press, 1998.

Murayama, M., *Thought and Behaviour in Modern Japanese Politics*, ed. I. Morris, Oxford University Press, 1980.

Najita, T., *Japan: The Intellectual Foundations of Modern Japanese Politics*, University of Chicago Press, 1980.

Norman, E.S.., *Feudal Background of Japanese Politics*, New York: AMS Press, 1978.

Norman, H., *The Real Japan: Studies of Contemporary Japanese Manners, Morals, Administration and Politics*, London: T. Fisher Unwin, 1892.

Steinhoff, P.G., *Tenko: Ideology and Social Integration in Prewar Japan*, New York: Garland, 1991.

Chapter 2

General

Borton, H., *American Presurrender Planning for Postwar Japan*, New York: Knopf, 1967.

Cohen, T., *Remaking Japan: the American Occupation as a New Deal*, New York: Free Press, 1987.

Dower, J.W., *Embracing Defeat. Japan in the Wake of World War II*, New York: W.W. Norton 1999.
Kawai, K., *Japan's American Interlude*, University of Chicago Press, 1960.
Levingston, J. (ed.), *Postwar Japan*, New York: Pantheon, 1973.
Sebald, W.J. and R. Brines, *With MacArthur in Japan*, New York: W.W. Norton, 1965.
Tokyo Daigaku Shakaishugi Kenkyusha Collective, *Sengo haikaku*, 6 vols, Tokyo: Tokyo Daigaku Shuppankai, 1973.
Williams, J. Sr, *Japan's Revolution under MacArthur*, Tokyo University Press, 1979.

The purge and the Tokyo trial

Baerwald, H., *The Purge of the Japanese Leaders under the Occupation*, Berkeley: University of California Press, 1959.
Minear, R.H., *Victor's Justice*, Tokyo: Tuttle, 1971.
Pal, R., *International Tribunal for the Far East: Dissentient Judgment*, Calcutta: Sanyal, 1953.

Economic reforms, labour relations

Adams, T.F., *A Financial History of Modern Japan*, op.cit., p. 349.
Allen, G.C., *Japan's Economic Recovery*, London: Oxford University Press, 1958.
Bisson, T.A., *Zaibatsu Dissolution in Japan*, Berkeley: University of California Press, 1954.
Dore, R.P., *Land Reform in Japan*, London: Oxford University Press, 1950.
Fairley, M., *Aspects of Japanese Labour Problems*, New York: John Day, 1950.
Grad, H.J., *Land and Peasants in Japan*, Berkeley: University of California Press, 1958.
Hadley, E.M., *Antitrust in Japan*, Berkeley: University of California Press, 1958.
Moore, J., *Japanese Workers and the Struggle for Power, 1945–1947*, Madison: University of Wisconsin Press, 1983.
Okochi, K., *Labor in Modern Japan*, Tokyo: Science Council of Japan, 1958.
Uchino, T., *Japan's Postwar Economy*, Tokyo: Kodansha, 1978.

Politics

Cole, A.B., G.O. Totten and C. Uehara, *Socialist Parties in Postwar Japan*, New Haven: Yale University Press, 1966.

Ike, N., *The Beginnings of Political Democracy in Japan*, Baltimore: Johns Hopkins University Press, 1950.

Scalapino, R.A., *Parties and Politics in Contemporary Japan*, Berkeley: University of California Press, 1962.

Swearingen, R., and P. Langer, *Red Flag in Japan, 1919–1951*, Westport, CT: Greenwood Press, 1968.

Yoshida, S., *The Yoshida Memoirs*, Boston: Houghton Mifflin, 1962.

Culture, ideology, social life

Hirano, K., *Mr Smith Goes to Tokyo: Japanese Cinema under the American Occupation*, Washington: Smithsonian Institute, 1992.

Shea, G.T., *Leftwing Literature in Japan: a Brief History of the Proletarian Literary Movement*, Tokyo: Hosei University, 1965.

Tsurumi, S., *A Cultural History of Postwar Japan, 1945–1980*, London: Kegan Paul International, 1984.

Whiting, R., *Tokyo Underworld. The Fast Time and Hard Life of an American Gangster in Japan*, New York: Vintage Books, 1999.

Foreign policy

Johnson, S.K., *American Attitudes toward Japan, 1941–1975*, Stanford, CA: Hoover Policy Sudies, 1975.

Ridgway, M.B., *The Korean War*, New York: McGraw-Hill, 1967.

Swearingen, R., *The Soviet Union and Postwar Japan*, Stanford, CA: Hoover Institution Press, 1978.

Chapters 3–6

Politics

The '1955 system': theory and overview

Abe, S., M. Shindo and S. Kawato, *The Government and Politics of Japan*, University of Tokyo Press, 1994 (Japanese edition 1990).

Calder, K., *Crisis and Compensation. Public Policy and Political Stability in Japan, 1949–1986*, Princeton University Press, 1988.

Johnson, S., *Opposition Parties in Japan: Strategies under a One-Party Dominant Regime*, London: Routledge, 2000.

Kataoka, T., *Creating Single-Party Dominance: Japan's Postwar Political System*, Stanford, CA: Hoover Institution Press, 1992.

Kishima, T., *Political Life in Japan: Democracy in a Reversible World*, Princeton University Press, 1991.

Kohno, M., *Japan's Postwar Party Politics*, Princeton University Press, 1997.

McVeigh, B.J., *The Nature of the Japanese State: Rationality and Rituality*, London: Routledge, 1998.

Pempel, T.J., *Uncommon Democracies: the One-Party Dominant Regimes*, Ithaca, NY: Cornell University Press, 1990.

Ramseyer, M. and F. McCall-Rosenbluth, *Japan's Political Marketplace*, Cambridge, MA: Harvard University Press, 1993.

Sato, S. and T. Matsuzaki, *Jiminto Seiken*, Tokyo: Chuokoronsha, 1986.

Elections, campaigning and 'money politics'

Alletzhauser, A., *The House of Nomura: Inside the World's Most Powerful Company*, London: Bloomsbury, 1990.

Curtis, G., *Election Campaigning, Japanese Style*, New York: Columbia University Press, 1971.

Flanagan, S., *The Japanese Voter*, New Haven: Yale University Press, 1991.

Grofman, B., B. Woodall *et al.* (eds), *Elections in Japan, Korea and Taiwan under the SNTV: a Comparative Study*, Ann Arbor: University of Michigan Press, 1999.

Hayao, K., *The Japanese Prime Minister and Public Policy*, University of Pittsburgh Press, 1993.

Hunziker, S. and I. Kamimura, *Kakuei Tanaka: a Political Biography of Modern Japan*, Singapore: Times Books International, 1996.

Inoguchi, T. and T. Iwai, *Zoku giin no kenyu. Jiminto seiken o gyujin shuyakutachi*, Tokyo: Nihon Keizai Shimbunsa, 1987.

Kaplan, D. and A. Dubro, *Yakuza*, Reading, MA: Addison-Wesley, 1986.

Michidasa, H., *Seiji to kane*, Tokyo: Iwanami Shoten, 1989.

Mitchell, R., *Political Bribery in Japan*, Honolulu: University of Hawaii Press, 1996.

Pempel, T.J. (ed.), *Policymaking in Contemporary Japan*, Ithaca, NY: Cornell University Press, 1977.

Schlesinger, J.M., *Shadow Shoguns: the Rise and Fall of Japan's Postwar Political Machine*, Stanford University Press, 1997.

Schwartz, F.J., *Advice and Consent: the Politics of Consultation in Japan*, Cambridge University Press, 1998.

Woodall, B., *Japan under Construction. Corruption, Politics and Public Works*, Berkeley: University of California Press, 1996.

Periods

Curtis, G., *The Japanese Way of Politics*, New York: Columbia University Press, 1988.

Fukui, H., *Party in Power: the Japanese Liberal-Democrats and Policy Making*, Berkeley: University of California Press, 1970.

Hrebenar, R., *The Japanese Party System*, Boulder, CO: Westview Press, 1992.

Iishida, T. and E. Krauss (eds), *Democracy in Japan*, Pittsburgh University Press, 1989.

Ike, N., *Japanese Politics: an Introductory Survey*, New York: Knopf, 1957.

— *Japanese Politics: Patron-Client Democracy*, New York: Knopf, 1972.

Itoh, H. (ed.), *Japanese Politics: an Inside View*, Ithaca, NY: Cornell University Press, 1973.

Koizumi, J., *Japanese Politics in 1983 and 1984: a Fukuda Faction View*, Tokyo: Institute for Political Studies in Japan, 1983.

Kurzman, D., *Kishi and Japan*, New York: Ivan Obolensky, 1960.

Packard, G.P., *Protest in Tokyo: the Security Crisis of 1960*, Princeton University Press, 1966.

Pempel, T.J., *Policy and Politics in Japan: Creative Conservatism*, Philadelphia: Temple University Press, 1982.

Sato, S., K. Koyama and K. Shumpei, *Postwar Politician: The Life and Death of Former Prime Minister Masayoshi Ohira* (covering 1945–84), Tokyo: Kodansha, 1990.

Shiratori, R., *Prime Minister Miki and the New Stage of Japanese Politics*, Tokyo: Institute for Political Studies in Japan, 1975.

Thayer, N.B., *How the Conservatives Rule Japan*, Princeton University Press, 1962.

Watanuki, J., *Politics in Postwar Japanese Society*, University of Tokyo Press, 1977.

Opposition parties and movements

Actuel Marx No. 2: *Le marxisme au Japon*, Paris: L'Harmattan, 1988.

Cole, A.B., *et al., Socialist Parties in Postwar Japan,* New Haven: Yale University Press, 1966.

Dan, I., *Sokagakkai Komeito no kenkyu*, Tokyo: Ban Seisha, 1980.

Fujiwara, H., *I denounce Sokagakkai*, Tokyo: Nisshin hodo, 1970.

Krauss, E.S., *Japanese Radicals Revisited: Student Protest in Postwar Japan*, Berkeley: University of California Press, 1976.

Kuroyanagi, A., *Komei's Vision of Japanese Politics in 1980s*, Tokyo: Institute for Political Studies in Japan, 1980.

Langer, P.F., *Communism in Japan. A Case of Political Naturalization*, Stanford University Press, 1972.

Ouchi, K., *Analysing Japanese Politics and the New Line-Up to the Democratic Socialist Party*, Tokyo: Institute for Political Studies in Japan, 1985.

Scalapino, R.A., *The Japanese Communist Movement, 1920–1960*, Berkeley: California University Press, 1967.

Stockwin, J.A.A., *The Japan Socialist Party and Neutralism: a Study of a Political Party and its Foreign Policy*, Cambridge University Press, 1968.

White, J.W., *The Sokagakkai and Mass Society*, Stanford University Press, 1970.

Pressure groups

Mulgan, A.G., *The Politics of Agriculture in Japan*, London: Routledge, 2000.

Nihon Izokukai, *Nihon Izokukai tsushin: kikanshi shukusatsuban, 1945–1976* (digest of the *Nihon Izokukai* newsletter).

Steslicke, W.E., *Doctors in Politics: the Political Life of the Japan Medical Association*, New York: Praeger, 1973.

Yanaga, C., *Big Business in Japanese Politics*, New Haven: Yale University Press, 1968.

Political culture

Curtis, M. and B. Stronach, *Politics East and West. A Comparison of Japan and British Political Culture*, Armonk, NY: M.E. Sharpe, 1992.

Feldman, O. (ed.), *Political Psychology in Japan: Behind the Nails that Sometimes Stick Out (and Get Hammered Down)*, Commack, NY: Nova Science Publishers, 1999.

Richardson, B., *The Political Culture of Japan*, Berkeley: University of California Press, 1974.

Sautter, C. and Y. Higuchi (eds), *L'état et l'individu au Japon*, Paris: EHESS, 1990.

Yanaga, C., *Japanese People and Politics*, New York: Wiley, 1956.

What remains of the Emperor system

Seizelet, E., *Monarchie et démocratie dans le Japon d'après-guerre*, Paris: Maisonneuve et Larose, 1990.

Takeda, K., *The Dual Image of the Japanese Emperor*, Basingstoke: Macmillan, 1988.

Local government, civil society, citizens' movements

Buraku Liberation Research Institute, *The Road to a Discrimination-Free Future*, Osaka: Institute of Osaka City, 1983.

Changsoo, L. and A. De Vos, *Koreans in Japan: Ethnic Conflict and Accommodation*, Berkeley: California University Press, 1981.

De Vos, G.A. and W.O. Wetherall, *Japan's Minorities: Burakumin, Koreans, Ainu and Okinawan*, London: Minority Rights Group, 1983.

Huddle, N., M. Reich *et al.*, *Island of Dreams: Environmental Crisis in Japan*, New York: Autumn Press, 1975.

McKean, M., *Environmental Protest and Citizens' Politics in Japan*, Berkeley: University of California Press, 1981.

Pharr, S., *Political Women in Japan: a Search for a Place*, Berkeley: University of California Press, 1981.

Reed, S., *Japanese Prefectures and Policymaking*, University of Pittsburgh Press, 1988.

Steiner, K., *Local Government in Japan*, Stanford University Press, 1965.

Krauss, E. and S.C. Flanagan (eds), *Political Opposition and Local Politics in Japan*, Princeton University Press, 1980.

Ui, J., *Industrial Pollution in Japan*, Tokyo: United Nations University Press, 1992.

Yoshina, I.R. and S. Murakoshi, *The Invisible Visible Minority: Japan's Burakumin*, Osaka: Burako Kaiho Kenyusho, 1977.

(collective), *Polluted Japan: Reports by the Members of the Jishu-koza Citizens' Movement*, Tokyo: Jishu Koza, 1972.

Political economy

Fukui, H. (ed.), *The Politics of Economic Change in Postwar Japan and West Germany*, London: Macmillan, 1983.

Johnson, C., *Japan: Who Governs? The Rise of the Developmental State*, New York: W.W. Norton, 1995.

Monroe, W.F. and E. Sakakibara, *The Japanese Industrial society: Its Organizational, Cultural and Economical Underpinnings*, Austin, TX: Bureau of Business Research, University of Texas, 1977.

Preston, P., *Understanding Global Japan. A Political Economy of Development, Culture and Global Power*, London: Sage, 2000.

Stanford University Press, *The Political Economy of Japan* (1987–92), vol. 1: *The Domestic Transformation*, ed. K. Yamamura and Y. Yasuba; vol. 2: *The Changing International Context*, ed. T. Inoguchi and D. Okimoto; vol. 3: *Cultural and Social Dynamics*, ed. S. Kumon and H. Rosovsky.

Economic development, industrial and financial policy and the Japanese 'Kaisha' (chapters 3 and 4: 1952–72)

Allen, G.C., *A Short Economic History of Modern Japan*, New York: St. Martin's Press, 1980.

Abbeglen, J.C., *The Japanese Factory*, Glencoe, IL: The Free Press, 1958.

Boltho, A., *Japan: An Economic Survey, 1953–1973*, London, Oxford University Press, 1975.

Brochier, H., *Le miracle économique japonais*, Paris: Calmann-Lévy, 1965.

Clark, R., *The Japanese Company*, New Haven: Yale University Press, 1979.

Dennison, E.F. and W.K. Chung, *How Japan's Economy Grew so Fast*, Washington, DC: Brookings Institution, 1976.

Guillain, R., *Japon, troisième grand*, Paris: Seuil, 1969.

Johnson, C., *MITI and the Japanese Miracle: The Growth of Industrial Policy 1925–1975*, Stanford University Press, 1982

Kahn, H., *The Emerging Japanese Superstate: Challenge to America*, Englewood Cliffs, NJ: Prentice-Hall, 1970.

Rosovsky, H. (ed.), *Asia's New Giant. How the Japanese Economy Works*, Washington, DC: Brookings Institution, 1976.

Sautter, C., *Japon, le prix de la puissance*, Paris: Seuil, 1973.

Tanaka, K., *Building a New Japan*, Tokyo: Simul Press (translated from Japanese).

Economic development (chapters 5 and 6: 1972–92)

Abbeglen, J.C., *Kaisha, the Japanese Corporation*, New York: Basic Books, 1985.

Aoki, M., *Information, Incentive and Bargaining in the Japanese Economy*, Cambridge University Press, 1982.

— and R.P. Dore, *The Japanese Firm: the Sources of Competitive Strength*, Oxford University Press, 1994.

Burstein, D., *Yen: Japan's New Financial Empire and its Threat to America*, New York: Simon & Schuster, 1988.

Coriat, B., *Penser à l'envers. Travail et organisation dans l'entreprise japonaise*, Paris: Christian Bourgeois, 1991.

Dore, R.P., and K. Taira, *Structural Adjustment in Japan, 1970–1982*, Geneva: International Labour Office, 1986.

Emmot, B., *The Sun also Sets: the Limits to Japan's Economic Power*, New York: Random House, 1989.

Gibney, F., *Miracle by Design: the Real Reasons behind Japan's Economic Success*, New York: Times Books, 1982.

Horn, R.S., *The Rising Yen: the Impact of Japanese Financial Liberalization on World Capital Markets*, Singapore: Institute of East Asian Studies, 1987.

Hornet, J., *Japan's Financial Market: Conflict and Consensus in Policymaking*, Boston, MA: Allen & Unwin, 1985.

Kahn, H. and T. Pepper, *The Japanese Challenge: the Success and Failure of Economic Success*, New York: Crowell, 1979.

Makino, N., *Decline and Prosperity: Corporate Innovation in Japan*, Tokyo: Kodansha, 1989.

Moritani, M., *Japanese Technology, Getting the Best for the Least,* Tokyo: Simul Press, 1982.

Nakagawa, K. (ed.), *Strategy and Structure of Big Business*, University of Tokyo Press, 1977.

Okimoto, D.I., *Between MITI and the Market,* Stanford University Press, 1987.

Ozaki, R.S., *Human Capitalism: the Japanese Enterprise System as World Model*, Tokyo: Kodansha International, 1991.

Russell, D. and K. Miyashita, *Keiretsu*, New York: McGraw-Hill, 1994.
Sautter, C., *Les dents du géant. Le Japon à la conquête du monde*, Paris: Olivier Orban, 1987.
Shinohara, M., *Industrial Growth, Trade and Dynamic Patterns in the Japanese Economy*, University of Tokyo Press, 1982.
Turcq, D., *L'animal stratégique*, Paris: EHESS, 1985.
Viner, A., *The Emerging Power of Japanese Money*, Tokyo: The Japan Times, 1988.
—*Inside Japan's Financial Market*, Tokyo: The Japan Times, 1988.
Vogel, E.F., *Japan as Number One: Lessons for America*, Cambridge, MA: Harvard University Press, 1979.
Womak, J.P., D.T. Jones and D. Ross, *The Machine that Changed the World*, New York: Harper Perennial, 1991.

Labour relations, working conditions

Ballon, R.J., *Labor Relations in Postwar Japan*, Tokyo: Sophia University Press, 1966.
— *The Japanese Employee*, Tokyo: Sophia University Press, 1969.
— and H. Inohara, *Shunto: the Annual Spring Wage Offensive*, Tokyo: Sophia University Press, 1973.
Bennett, J.W. and I. Ishino, *Paternalism in the Japanese Economy*, Westport, CT: Greenwood Press, 1972.
Cole, R.E., *Japanese Blue Collar: the Changing Tradition*, Berkeley: University of California Press, 1971.
Dore, R.P., *British Factory, Japanese Factory*, Berkeley: University of California Press, 1973.
Hanami, T.A., *Labour Law and Industrial Relations in Japan*, Deventer: Kluwer, 1979.
Kamata, S., *Japan in the Passing Lane: an Insider's Account of Life in a Japanese Auto Factory*, New York: Pantheon Books, 1982 (translated from Japanese).
Kinzle, W.D., *Industrial Harmony in Modern Japan; the Invention of a Tradition*, London: Routledge, 1991.
Levine, S.B., *Industrial Relations in Postwar Japan*, Chicago: University of Illinois Press, 1958.
L'Henoret, A., *Le clou qui dépasse*, Paris: La Découverte, 1993.
Okochi, K., N. Karsh and S.B. Levine, *Workers and Employees in Japan*, Princeton University Press, 1974.
Saso, A.E., *Women in the Japanese Workplace*, Honolulu: University of Hawaii Press, 1987.
Weber, D.C., *The Labour-Union Problem of a Small Firm: the Case of Yamamoto K.K.*, Tokyo: Sophia University Press, 1971.
Woodiwiss, A., *Law, Labour and Society in Japan: from Repression to Reluctant Recognition*, London: Routledge, 1992.

Young, A.M., *The Socialist and Labour Movement in Japan*, Washington, DC: Washington University Publications, 1979.

Culture, ideology, social life

– Overview

Caillet, L., *The House of Yamazaki: the Life of a Daughter of Japan*, New York: Kodansha, 1994 (translated from French).
Fukutake, T., *The Japanese Social Structure: its Evolution in the Modern Century*, Tokyo University Press, 1982 (translated from Japanese).

– Rural tradition and change

Beardsley, R.K., J.W. Hall and R.E. Ward, *Village Japan*, Chicago University Press, 1959.
Dore, R.P., *Shinohata: a Portrait of a Japanese Village*, New York: Pantheon Books, 1978.
Ebato, A., *Postwar Japanese Agriculture*, Tokyo: International Society for Educational Information Press, 1973.
Ogura, T., *Can Japanese Agriculture Survive?* Tokyo: Agricultural Policy Research Center, 1982.
Ritchie, M., *Everyday Life in a Rural Japanese Community*, Rutland, VT: Tuttle, 1999.
Smith, R.J., *Kurusu: the Price of Progress in a Japanese Village*, Stanford, CA: Stanford University Press, 1978.

– The revival of 'Nihonjinron' and the opposing view

Ben Dasan, I., *alias* S. Yamamoto, *The Japanese and the Jews*, New York: Weatherhill, 1972 (translated from Japanese, 1970).
Dale, P., *The Myth of Japanese Uniqueness*, London: Routledge, 1988.
Doi, T., *The Anatomy of Dependence: the Individual and Society*, Tokyo: Kodansha, 1973 (translated from Japanese, 1971).
Hasegawa, N., *The Japanese Character: a Cultural Profile,* Tokyo: Kodansha, 1966.
Minami, H., *Psychology of the Japanese People*, University of Tokyo Press, 1971 (translated from Japanese, 1953).
Nakane, C., *Japanese Society*, Berkeley: University of California Press, 1970 (translated from Japanese, 1960).
Reed, S., *Making Common Sense of Japan*, Pittsburgh University Press, 1993.
Seizelet, E., *Les petits-fils du Soleil. La jeunesse japonaise et la patriotisme,* Paris: PUF, 1988.
Sugimoto, Y. and R.E. Mouer, *Images of Japanese Society: a Study in the Structure of Social Reality*, London: Kegan Paul International, 1989.

— *Constructs for Understanding Japan,* London: Kegan Paul International, 1989.

Watanabe, S., *The Peasant Soul of Japan,* Basingstoke: Macmillan, 1989 (translated from Japanese).

Basic principles of social interaction, socialization

Bouissou, J.M. (ed.), *L'envers du consensus. Les conflits et leur gestion dans le Japon contemporain,* Paris: Presses de Sciences Po, 1996.

Eisenstadt, S.N. and E. Ben Ari (eds), *Japanese Models of Conflict Resolution,* London: Kegan Paul International, 1990.

De Vos, G., *Socialization for Achievement: Essays on the Cultural Psychology of the Japanese,* Berkeley: University of California Press, 1973.

Doi, T., *The Anatomy of Self: the Individual and Society,* Tokyo: Kodansha, 1988 (translated from Japanese, 1985).

Lebra, T.S., *Japanese Patterns of Behaviour,* Honolulu: University of Hawaii Press, 1976.

Social classes and stratification, communities

Bestor, T., *Neighbourhood Tokyo,* Tokyo: Kodansha, 1989.

Henshall, K.J., *Dimensions of Japanese Society: Gender, Margins and Mainstream,* New York: St Martin's Press, 1999.

Imamura, A.E., *Urban Japanese Housewives: At Home in the Community,* Honolulu: University of Hawaii Press, 1987.

Kosaka, K., *Social Stratification in Contemporary Japan,* London: Kegan Paul International, 1994.

Pons, P., *Misère et crime au Japon. Du 17e siècle à nos jours,* Paris: Gallimard, 1999.

Steven, R., *Classes in Contemporary Japan,* Cambridge University Press, 1983.

White, J.W. and F. Munger (eds), *Social Change and Community Politics in Urban Japan,* Chapel Hill, NC: Institute for Research in Social Science, 1976.

Culture, life-style

Anderson, J.L. and D. Riche, *The Japanese Film: Art and Industry,* Princeton University Press, 1982.

Bornoff, N., *Pink Samurai: Love, Marriage and Sex in Contemporary Japan,* London: Grafton Books, 1991.

Condominas, C. (ed.), *Les loisirs au Japon,* Paris: L'Harmattan, 1993.

Jung, B.C., *The Political Character of the Japanese Press,* Seoul National University Press, 1985.

Kosakai, T., *Les Japonais sont-ils des Occidentaux?* Paris: L'Harmattan, 1991.

Powers, R. and H. Kato, *Handbook of Japanese Popular Culture*, New York: Greenwood Press, 1989.

Richie, D., *A Lateral View: Essays on Contemporary Japan*, Tokyo: Japan Times, 1987.

Schilling, M., *The Encyclopedia of Japanese Pop Culture*, London: Weatherhill, 1997.

Schodt, F.L., *Manga, manga: the World of Japanese Comics*, Tokyo: Kodansha International, 1983.

Tessier, M., *Le cinéma japonais au présent, 1959–1984*, Paris: L'Herminier, 1984.

Toyomasa, F., *Modernization and Stress in Japan*, Leiden: E.J. Brill, 1975.

Tsurumi, S., *A Cultural History of Postwar Japan, 1945–1980*, London: Kegan Paul International, 1984.

Foreign policy

– Overview

Barnett, R., *Beyond War: Japanese Concept of Comprehensive National Security*, Washington, DC: Pergamon/Brassey's, 1984.

Bouissou, J.M., G. Faure and Z. Laïdi, *L'expansion de la puissance japonaise*, Brussels: Complexe, 1992.

Drifte, R., *Japan Foreign Policy*, London: Royal Institute of International Affairs/Routledge, 1990.

Gibney, F., *Japan: The Fragile Superpower*, New York: American Library, 1983.

Nester, W.R., *The Foundation of Japanese Power: Continuities, Changes, Challenges*, Armonk, NY: M.E. Sharpe, 1990.

Rahda, S., *Japan's Options for the 1980s*, London: Croom Helm, 1982.

– US-Japan relations

Asahi Shimbun, *The Pacific Rivals: a Japanese View of Japanese-American Relations*, New York: Weatherhill, 1972 (translated from Japanese).

Clapp, P. and M.H. Halperin, *US-Japanese Relations: the 1970s*, Cambridge, MA: Harvard University Press, 1974.

Destler, M., *Managing an Alliance: the Politics of US-Japan Relations*, Washington, DC: Brookings Institution, 1976.

H. Fukui and H. Sato, *The Textile Wrangle: Conflict in Japanese-American Relations*, Ithaca, NY: Cornell University Press, 1973.

E.O. Reischauer Center for East-Asia Studies, *The US and Japan in 1987: Conciliation or Confrontation?* Baltimore: Johns Hopkins University Press, 1987.

The US and Japan in 1989: Managing Interdependence: the Challenge for Leadership, Baltimore: Johns Hopkins University Press, 1989.

Frost, E.L., *For Richer, for Poorer: the New US-Japan Relationship*, New York: Council on Foreign Relations, 1987.

Hellmann, D.C. and J.H. Makin (eds), *Sharing the World Leadership? A New Era for America and Japan*, Washington, DC: American Enterprise Institute, 1989.

Maga, T.P., *Hands Across the Sea? US-Japan Relations, 1961–1981*, Athens: University of Ohio Press, 1997.

Mochizuki, M. *et al., Japan and the US: Troubled Partners in a Changing World*, Washington, DC: Brassey's, 1991.

Mushakoji, K. and M.A. Kaplan, *Japan, America and the Changing World Order*, New York: Free Press, 1976.

Okawara, Y., *To Avoid Isolation: an Ambassador's View of US-Japanese Relations*, Columbia: University of South Carolina Press, 1989 (translated from Japanese).

Passin, H. (ed.), *The US and Japan*, Englewood Cliffs, NJ: Prentice Hall, 1966.

Rosovsky, H. (ed.), *Discord in the Pacific: Challenges to the Japanese-American Alliance*, Washington, DC: Columbia Books, 1972.

Turcy, A. and T.D. Mason, *US-Japan Trade Friction: Its Impact on Security in the Pacific Basin*, Basingstoke: Macmillan, 1991.

– *Relations with China*

Hellmann, D.C., *China and Japan: a New Balance of Power,* Lexington: Lexington Books, 1976.

Iriye, A., *The Chinese and the Japanese: Essays in Political and Cultural Interaction*, Princeton University Press, 1980.

Radtke, K., *China's Relations with Japan 1945–1983*, Manchester University Press, 1990.

Taylor, J., *The Sino-Japanese Axis: a New Force in Asia?* London: Athlone Press, 1985.

– *Relations with the Soviet Union*

Hellman, D.C., *Japan's Foreign Policy and Domestic Policy: the Peace Agreement with the Soviet Union*, Berkeley: University of California Press, 1969.

Rozman, G., *Japan's Response to the Gorbachev Era, 1985–1991: a Rising Superpower Views a Declining One*, Princeton University Press, 1992.

Swearingen, R., *The Soviet Union and Postwar Japan: Escalating Challenge and Response*, Stanford, CA: Hoover Institution Press, 1978.

– *Relations with Asia and the Asia-Pacific area*

Bartu, F., *The Ugly Japanese. Nippon's Economic Empire in Asia*, Rutland, VT: Tuttle, 1993.

Calder, L.E., *Japan's Changing Role in Asia: Emerging Co-Prosperity*, New York: Japan Society, 1991.

Chanr, M.K. and R. Hirono, *ASEAN-Japan Industrial Cooperation: An Overview*, Singapore: Institute of Southeast Asian Studies, 1984.

Manglapus, R.S., *Japan in Southeast Asia: Collision Course*, New York: Carnegie Endowment for International Peace, 1976.

Morrison, C.E., *Japan, the US and Changing Southeast Asia*, Lanham, MD: University Press of America, 1985.

Steven, R., *Japan's New Imperialism*, Basingstoke: Macmillan, 1990.

– *Relations with Europe*

Gordon, D. and R. Drifte, *Europe and Japan since 1945,* Woodchurch: P. Norbury, 1986.

Tsoulakis, L. and M. White, *Japan and Western Europe: Conflict and Cooperation*, London: Pinter, 1982.

Wilkinson, E. *Japan vs. Europe: A History of Misunderstandings*, Harmondsworth: Penguin, 1983.

– *Others*

Owoeye, J., *Japan's Policy in Africa*, Lewiston: E. Mellen Press, 1992.

– *Defence*

Chapman, W.M., R. Drifte and I.T. Gow, *Japan's Quest for Comprehensive Security: Defense, Diplomacy, Dependence*, London: Pinter, 1983.

Drifte, R., *Arms Production in Japan: the Military Application of Civilian Technology*, Boulder, CO: Westview Press, 1986.

Hoytt, E.P., *The Militarists: the Rise of Japan's Postwar Militarism since World War II*, New York: DI Fins, 1985.

Maswood, S.J., *Japanese Defence: the Search for Political Power,* Singapore: Institute of Southeast Asian Studies, 1990.

Morley, J.W. (ed.), *Forecast for Japan's Security in the 1970s*, Princeton University Press, 1972.

Chapter 7

General

Bouissou, J. M., E. Seizelet and F. Gipouloux, *Japon. Le déclin?*, Brussels: Complexe, 1996.

Ezrati, M., *Kawari: How Japan's Economic and Cultural Transformation will alter the Balance of Power among Nations*, Reading, MA: Perseus Books, 1999.

Hook, G.D., and H. Hasegawa (eds), *The Political Economy of Japanese Globalization*, London: Routledge, 2001.

Politics

Curtis, G., *The Logic of Japanese Politics: Leaders, Institutions and the Limits of Change*, New York: Columbia University Press, 1999.

Hrebenar, R., *Japan's New Party System*, Boulder, CO: Westview Press, 2000.

Otake, H. (ed.), *How Electoral Reform Boomeranged: Continuity in Japanese Campaigning Style*, Tokyo: Japan Council for International Exchanges, 1998.

— (ed.), *Power Shuffles and Policy Process: Coalition Government in Japan in the 1990s*, Tokyo: Japan Council for International Exchanges, 2000.

Purnendra, J. and T. Inoguchi (eds), *Japanese Politics Today: Beyond Karaoke Democracy?*, Melbourne: Macmillan Education Australia, 1997.

Political economy

Banno, J. (ed.), *The Political Economy of Japanese Society*, Oxford University Press, 1997.

Bouissou, J.M., 'L'économie politique de dix ans de crise au Japon', *Economies Internationales* no. 84, winter 2000, pp. 185–207.

Burks, A.W., *Japan: A Postindustrial Power*, Boulder, CO: Westview Press, 1991.

Fingleton, E., *Blindside: Why Japan is Still on Track to Overtake the US by the Year 2000*, London: Simon & Schuster, 1995.

Katz, R., *The System that Soured: the Rise and Fall of the Japanese Economic Miracle*, Armonk, NY: M.E. Sharpe, 1998.

McCormack, G., *The Emptiness of Japanese Affluence*, Armonk, NY: M.E. Sharpe, 1996.

Sakakibara, E., *Beyond Capitalism: The Japanese Model of Market Economy*, Lanham, MD: University Press of America, 1993.

From bubble to crisis

Aveline, N., *La bulle financière au Japon*, Paris: ADEF, 1995.

Boyer, R., and T. Yamada (eds), *Japanese Capitalism in Crisis: a Regulationist Interpretation*, London: Routledge, 2000.

Geoffron, P. and M. Rubinstein, *La crise financière du modèle japonais*, Paris: Economica, 1996.

Hartcher, P., *The Ministry: How Japan's Most Powerful Institution Endangers World Markets*, Cambridge, MA: Harvard Business School Press, 1998.

Meyer, P., *La puissance financière du Japon*, Paris: Economica, 1996.

Wood, C., *The Bubble Economy: Japan's Extraordinary Speculative Boom of the '80s and the Dramatic Burst of the '90s*, New York: Atlantic Monthly Press, 1992.

Administrative reform, economic deregulation

Ayama, N., *An Argument for a Wise Country*, Tokyo: PHP Institute, 1994.
Callon, S., *Divided Sun: MITI and the Breakdown of Japanese High Tech Industrial Policy 1975–1993*, Stanford University Press, 1995.
Gibney, F. (ed.), *Unlocking the Bureaucrat's Kingdom. Deregulation of the Japanese Economy*, Washington, DC: Brookings Institution Press, 1998.
Hall, M.J., *Financial Reform in Japan: Causes and Consequences*, Cheltenham: Edward Elgar, 1998.
Harner, S.M., *Japan's Financial Revolution and how American Firms are Profiting*, Armonk, NY: M.E. Sharpe, 2000.
Kaneko, J., *Sei wa kan o do shinogu ka*, Tokyo: Kodansha, 1995.
Keehn, E.B., *The Mandarins of Kasumigaseki*, London: Macmillan, 2001.
Masasuke, A., *Japanese Corporate Finance and International Competition: Japanese Capitalism vs American Capitalism*, New York: St Martin's Press, 1998.
Masujima, T., and M. Ouchi, *The Management and Reform of Japanese Government*, Tokyo: Institute of Administrative Management, 1995.
Miyamoto, M., *The Straitjacket Society*, Tokyo: Kodansha International, 1994.
Ohmae, K., *Kanri hihan*, Tokyo: Shogakkan, 1994.
Sheard, P., *Japanese Firms, Finance and Market*, Melbourne: Addison-Wesley, 1996.
Shukan Toyo Keizai Henshubu, *Kasumigaseki o kaitai-seyo*, Tokyo: Toyo Keizai Shinhosha, 1997.

Labour relations, working conditions

Gibbs, M.H., *Struggle and Purpose in Postwar Japanese Unionism*, Berkeley: Institute of East Asia Studies, 2000.
Hunter, J. (ed.), *Japanese Women Working*, London: Routledge, 1997.
Kumazama, M., *Portraits of the Japanese at the Workplace: Labor Movements, Workers and Managers*, Boulder, CO: Westview Press, 1996.
Roberts, G., *Staying on the Line: Blue-Collar Women in Contemporary Japan*, Honolulu: University of Hawaii Press, 1994.
Sako, M. and H. Sato, *Japanese Labour and Management in Transition: Diversity, Flexibility and Participation*, New York: Routledge, 1997.
Williamson, H., 1994, *Coping with the Miracle: Japan's Unions Explore New International Relations*, London: Pluto Press, 1997.

Civil society and new citizens' movements

Bouissou, J.M., 'Un nouveau Japon? Regard sur les mouvements alternatifs', Paris: CERI, 1997, partly translated as 'Ambiguous Revival. A Study of Some "Citizens' Movements" in Japan', *Pacific Review*, vol. 13 no. 3, pp. 335–66.

Lam, P.E., *Green Politics in Japan*, London: Routledge, 1999.

Le Blanc, R.M., *Bicycle Citizens. The Political World of the Japanese Housewife*, Berkeley: University of California Press, 1999.

Muramatsu, M., *Local Government in the Japanese State*, Berkeley: University of California Press, 1997 (translated from Japanese).

Smith, S.A. (ed.), *Local Voices, National Issues: The Impact of Local Initiatives in Japanese Decision-Making*, Ann Arbor, MI: University of Michigan, Center for Japanese Studies, 2000.

Steven, C.S., *On the Margin of Japanese Society: Volunteers and the Welfare of the Urban Underclass*, London: Routledge, 1997.

Yamamoto, T., *Deciding the Public Good: Governance and Civil Society in Japan*, Tokyo: Japan Center for International Exchange, 1999.

Culture, ideology, social life

– Ageing society

Campbell, J.C., *How Policies Change: the Japanese Government and the Aging Society*, Princeton University Press, 1992.

Jolivet, M., *Japan: the Childless Society? The Crisis of Motherhood*, London: Routledge, 1997 (translated from French).

– Changing gender relations

Fujimura-Fanselow, K. and A. Kameda (eds.), *Japanese Women: New Feminist Perspectives on the Past, Present and Future*, City University of New York Press, 1995.

Imamura, A. (ed.), *Re-Imaging Japanese Women*, Berkeley: University of California Press, 1996.

Iwao, S., *The Japanese Woman: Traditional Image and Changing Reality*, New York: Free Press, 1993.

Jolivet, M., *Homo Japonicus*, Paris: 1999.

Morley, P.A., *The Mountain is Moving: Japanese Women's Lives*, New York University Press, 1999.

– Popular culture

Craig, T.J. (ed.), *Japan Pop: Inside the World of Japanese Popular Culture*, Armonk, NY: M.E. Sharpe, 2000.

Kinsella, S., *Adult Manga: Culture and Power in Contemporary Japan*, London: Curzon Press, 2000.

McGregor, R., *Japan Swings: Politics, Culture and Sex in the New Japan*, Sydney: Allen & Unwin, 1996.

Raz, A.E., *Riding the Black Ship: Japan and Tokyo Disneyland*, Cambridge, MA: Harvard University Press, 1995.

Schilling, M., *Contemporary Japanese Film*, New York: Weatherhill, 1999.

– Search for a new identity, visions for a 'New Japan'

Hall, I. *Cartels of the Mind: Japan's Intellectual Closed Shop*, New York: W.W. Norton, 1998.

Hashimoto, R., *Vision of Japan*, Tokyo: KK Bestsellers, 1994.

Hosokawa, M., *The Time to Act is Now*, Tokyo: NYY Mediascope, 1993.

Ishihara, S., *The Japan that can Say 'No'*, London: Simon & Schuster, 1991 (translated from Japanese).

Itoh, M., *Globalization of Japan: Japan's Sakoku Mentality and US Efforts to Open It*, Basingstoke: Macmillan, 1998.

Ivy, M., *Discourse of the Vanishing: Modernity, Phantasm, Japan*, University of Chicago Press, 1995.

Nakasone, Y., *The Making of a New Japan*, London: Curzon Press, 1999.

Oe, K., *Japan, the Ambiguous and Myself: the Nobel Prize Speech and Other Lectures*, Tokyo: Kodansha International, 1995.

Ozawa, I., *Blueprints for a New Japan*, Tokyo: Kodansha, 1994.

Postel-Vinay, K., *La révolution silencieuse du Japon,* Paris: Calmann-Lévy, 1993.

Stronach, B., *Beyond the Rising Sun: Nationalism in Contemporary Japan*, Westport, CT: Praeger, 1995.

Yoshino, K., *Cultural Nationalism in Contemporary Japan: A Sociological Enquiry*, London: Routledge, 1992.

Media

Freeman, L.A., *Closing the Shop: Information Cartel and Japan's Mass Media*, Princeton University Press, 2000.

Pharr, S., and E.S. Krauss (eds), *Media and Politics in Japan*, Honolulu: University of Hawaii Press, 1996.

Daily life

Mak, J., *Japan – Why It Works, Why It Doesn't: Economics in Everyday Life*, Honolulu: University of Hawaii Press, 1998.

Mizuta, K., *The Structures of Everyday Life in Japan in the Last Decade of the 20th Century*, Lewiston: Mellen Press, 1993.

Foreign policy

– Looking for a new role on the world scene

Bouissou, J.M., G. Faure and Z. Laidi, *L'expansion de la puissance japonaise*, Brussels: Complexe, 1992.

Drifte, R., *Japan's Foreign Policy in 1990s: From Economic Power to What Power?*, Basingstoke: Macmillan, 1996.

Hook, G.D., H. Dobson, J. Gilson and C. Hughes, *Japan's International Relations*, London: Routledge, 2001.

Hunsberger, W.S. (ed.), *Japan's Quest: the Search for International Role, Recognition and Respect*, 1997.

L'Estrange, M., *The Internationalization of Japan's Security Policy: Challenge and Dilemmas for a Reluctant Power*, Berkeley, CA: University of California Press, 1990.

Pyle, K.B., *The Japanese Question: Power and Purpose in a New Era*, Washington, DC: AEI Press, 1992.

– Japan–US bilateral relations

Cossa, R., *Restructuring the US-Japan Alliance: Toward a More Equal Partnership*, Washington, DC: CSIS, 1997.

Council on Foreign Relations Study Group, *The Test of War and the Strain of Peace: the US-Japan Security Relationship*, New York: Council of Foreign Relations, 1998.

Curtis, G. (ed.), *The United States, Japan and Asia*, New York: W.W. Norton, 1994.

— (ed.), *New Perspectives on US-Japan Relations*, Tokyo: Japan Center for International Exchange, 2000.

Fukuyama, F., and K. Oh, *The US-Japan Security Relationship after the Cold War*, Santa Monica: Rand Corporation, 1993.

Green, M., *The US-Japan Security Alliance in the 21st Century: Prospects for Incremental Change*, New York: Council on Foreign Relations, 1998.

Sato, R., *The Chrysanthemum and the Eagle: the Future of US-Japan Relations*, New York: New York University Press, 1994 (translated from Japanese).

The Paul Nitze School of International Studies, *The US and Japan in 1991: Discord or Dialogue?*, Baltimore: Johns Hopkins University Press, 1991.

– Japan, China and Asian problems

Cha, V.D., *Alignment Despite Antagonism: The US-Korea-Japan Security Triangle*, Stanford University Press, 1999.

Cossa, R. (ed.), *US-Korea-Japan Relations: Building Towards a 'Virtual Alliance'*, Washington, DC: CSIS Press, 1999.

Cronin, R.P., *Japan, the US and Prospects for the Asia-Pacific Century: Three Scenarios for the Future*, New York: St Martin's Press, 1992.

Funabashi, Y., *Asia-Pacific Fusion: Japan's Role in APEC*, Washington, DC: Institute for International Economics, 1995.

Hatch, W. and K. Yamamura, *Asia in Japan's Embrace: Building a Regional Production Alliance*, Cambridge University Press, 1996.

Katzenstein, P. and T. Shiraishi, *Network Power: Japan and Asia*, Ithaca, NY: Cornell University Press, 1997.

Lim, H.S., *Japan's Role in Asia*, Singapore: Times Academic Press, 1999.

Mandelbaum, M. (ed.), *The Strategic Quadrangle*, New York: Council on Foreign Relations, 1995.

Postel-Vinay, K., *Le Japon at la nouvelle Asie*, Paris: Presses de Sciences Po, 1997.

Soderberg, M. and I. Reader (eds), *Japanese Influences and Presences in Asia*, London: Curzon Press, 2000.

Zhang, M. and R. Monaperto, *A Triad of Another Kind: The US, China and Japan*, New York: St Martin's Press, 1999.

– Japan and Europe

Bourke, T., *Japan and the Globalization of European Integration*, Aldershot: Dartmouth, 1996.

European Commission, *European Union-Japan Relations*, Luxembourg: Office for Official Publications of the European Communities, 1998.

Hutchings, R., *Japan's Economic Involvement in Eastern Europe and Eurasia*, Basingstoke: Macmillan, 1998.

– Japan and Africa

Ampiah, K., *The Dynamics of Japan's Relations with Africa*, London: Routledge, 1997.

Morikawa, A.J., *Japan and Africa: Big Business and Diplomacy*, London: Hurst, 1997.

– Japanese armed forces

Berger, T.U., *Cultures of Antimilitarism: National Security in Germany and Japan*, Baltimore: John Hopkins University Press, 1998.

Green, M., *Arming Japan: Defense Production, Alliance Politics and the Postwar Search for Autonomy*, Washington, DC: CSIS Press, 1995.

Harrison, S., *Japan's Nuclear Future: the Plutonium Debate and East-Asian Security*, Washington, DC: Carnegie Endowment for International Peace, 1996.

Wooley, P.J., *Japan's Navy: Politics and Paradox 1971–2000*, Boulder, CO: Lynne Rienner, 2000.

INDEX